Tahrir's Youth

Tahrir's Youth

LEADERS OF A LEADERLESS REVOLUTION

RUSHA LATIF

The American University in Cairo Press
Cairo   New York

First published in 2022 by
The American University in Cairo Press
113 Sharia Kasr el Aini, Cairo, Egypt
One Rockefeller Plaza, 10th Floor, New York, NY 10020
www.aucpress.com

Copyright © 2022 by Rusha Latif

All rights reserved. No part of this publication may be reproduced, stored in a retrieval system, or transmitted in any form or by any means, electronic, mechanical, photocopying, recording, or otherwise, without the prior written permission of the publisher.

ISBN 978 1 649 03020 7

Library of Congress Cataloging-in-Publication Data

Names: Latif, Rusha, author.
Title: Tahrir's youth : leaders of a leaderless revolution / Rusha Latif.
Identifiers: LCCN 2022009227 | ISBN 9781649030207 (hardback)
Subjects: LCSH: I'tilāf Shabāb al-Thawrah. | Youth--Political
   activity--Egypt--History--21st century. | Youth protest
   movements--Egypt--History--21st century. | Egypt--History--Protests,
   2011-2013. | Egypt--Politics and government--2011-
Classification: LCC HQ799.E3 L38 2022 | DDC
   305.2350962/0905--dc23/eng/20220304

1 2 3 4 5   26 25 24 23 22

Designed by Westchester

For my special brother, Mohammed,
and our beloved parents, Monira and Abdellatif,
with gratitude for illuminating my way to *tahrir*

Contents

List of Maps and Figures	ix
List of Acronyms	xi
Acknowledgments	xiii
Introduction	**1**
Leadership in Social Movements	10
Youth as Agents of Revolution	12
What Follows . . .	14
1. Encountering Revolution: Expectations and Reality	**17**
My Trajectory	17
Planning Research	19
Immersion in Revolutionary Cairo	21
Activist Representation	38
2. The Contract Collapses	**43**
The Third Regime and Its Antecedents	44
The Resistance Before the Revolt	51
3. Rethinking Spontaneity: Youth Political Agency Before the Uprising	**63**
The Activists	64
Family, Neighborhood, the State, and Political Consciousness	73
Activism in the University and the Street	88
The Question of the Internet	103
The Myth of Western Influence	106
Conclusion	107

4. Youth Activists and Revolutionary Praxis	**109**
The Prelude: Planning Police Day Protests	110
January 25: Managing a Popular Uprising	121
January 26–27: Planning a Revolution	127
January 28–February 1: Reoccupying the Square and Maintaining Momentum	130
February 2–3: Popular Self-Organizing in Defense of the Square	136
February 4–11: Leadership, Representation, and Voice in the Escalation of Resistance	141
Conclusion	151
5. Participation, Subjectivity, and Imagination	**153**
Sociopolitical Dynamics of Earlier Youth Movements	154
Revolutionary Subjectivity and Visions for the Future	156
Conclusion	184
6. The Making and Unmaking of Revolutionary Youth Leadership	**187**
Leadership, Spontaneity, and Youth Agency	187
Leadership and Gender	190
Leadership and Class	193
Leadership, Religiosity, and Secular Ideology	197
On Revolutionary Becoming	198
On Revolutionary Organizing and Constructing a Vanguard	201
Conclusion	208
7. The Revolution Continues?	**215**
Revolutionary Youth and Counterrevolution	217
Getting Organized	250
January 25 in the Balance	257
Appendix	263
Notes	265
Bibliography	299
Index	317

Maps and Figures

Maps
1. Map of Greater Cairo showing the major districts cited in this book.   xviii
2. Map charting the route of the January 25 protest march led by the youth who would later form the Revolutionary Youth Coalition (RYC).   122

Figures
1. Graffiti art from early 2012 memorializing revolutionary icon Shaykh Emad Effat, who was martyred during the Cabinet clashes in late 2011.   37
2a. A narrow neighborhood alley in the popular quarter of Imbaba, Cairo.   74
2b. A street scene from the popular quarter of Shubra, Cairo.   75
2c. An informal area on the edges of Shubra, Cairo.   76
3. Early banners in Tahrir Square saying "Leave" and "Step down, and have some decency."   134
4. Activists raising the first RYC banners from their stage in Tahrir Square.   143
5. Throngs of protesters enjoying the camaraderie and convivial atmosphere in what many liked to call the "Republic of Tahrir."   146
6. Tahrir protesters' demands.   147
7. A campaign banner promoting Amr Ezz's candidacy for Parliament.   158

8. A glimpse of popular-class life in Dar al-Salam, Cairo.   195
9a. RYC executive committee member Sally Tomah speaking at the coalition's final press conference in July 2012.   211
9b. Group photo of RYC leaders and key members.   212

Acronyms

IAEA	International Atomic Energy Agency
IMF	International Monetary Fund
NAC	National Association for Change
NDP	National Democratic Party
NGOs	Non-governmental organizations
NSF	National Salvation Front
NSMs	New Social Movements
RYC	Revolutionary Youth Coalition
SCAF	The Security Council of Armed Forces

Acknowledgments

I never expected to write a book, let alone one about a revolution. But I did because something unexpected happened: millions of Egyptians took to the streets, daringly and full of hope, and inspired this unlikely author. I must therefore start by thanking them—the activists, the protesters, the martyrs and their families—for their struggle and sacrifice, for giving me a story to tell, a story for the history books, a story that drew me in and forever changed me. To the ten activists profiled in this book in particular, I am especially indebted. As a long-lost Egyptian who grew up continents and an ocean apart from you, there was something I needed to learn about my life experience through yours. You have been my teachers; in sharing your personal and political trajectories with me, you have guided me on mine, and I can never thank you enough.

Studying the Egyptian Revolution was an exciting but daunting journey. Luckily, it was not one I had to go on alone. I was fortunate to have the warm companionship and unwavering support of Luis Guarnizo, professor of sociology at UC Davis, every step of the way. Not only did Luis work closely with me as my graduate advisor to conceptualize the project this book is based on, but he also stayed close while I was in the field, nurturing me as a fledgling researcher. During our regular Skype calls, he helped me gain insight into my visceral experiences in Tahrir, prompting me to experience field research not just as an intellectual exercise but also a process of self-discovery. Luis challenged me to think harder, feel more deeply, and write my heart out. With him I have enjoyed the kind of mentorship and friendship scholars dream of, and for this I am eternally grateful.

I was also privileged to work with three other distinguished scholars of Middle East, African, and Women and Gender Studies at UC Davis who guided and encouraged me as members of my committee. Suad Joseph exposed me to the rich field of Middle East youth studies and offered critical advice on how to frame and conduct my ethnographic inquiry. Amina Mama provided incisive feedback and helped me develop my gender analysis throughout the manuscript. Omnia El Shakry enriched my understanding of Egypt's complicated history as she deepened my love for it, and she helped me properly historicize my study. I admire these women tremendously, and I could not have asked for a better group of advisors.

At UC Davis, I benefited from being a part of an intimate and supportive academic community in the Community Development graduate group. I extend my wholehearted thanks to the faculty members who taught and encouraged me, as well as fellow grad students who stimulated me intellectually and made my experience there truly memorable; among them, Bernadette Tarallo, Robert Saper, Michelle Kuhns Brodesky, Galit Erez, Katie Bradley, Susan Ellsworth, and Ashley Powers deserve special mention. The UC Davis Geography Graduate Group and Women's Research Consortium provided generous grants to support me during my research and writing, and I thank them for this support. Of course, the trajectory that led me to the study of the Egyptian revolution was shaped by many professors and teachers who influenced me long before I arrived at UC Davis. Space limits me from mentioning them all here, but I sincerely thank them all for edifying me and supporting me on my journey of learning.

In Egypt, I was warmly received by scholars, journalists, and activists who supported and enriched my work as colleagues and interlocutors. Many thanks to Barbara Ibrahim-Lethem Ibrahim, Paul Amar, and Thanassis Cambanis for sharing their time, insights, and contacts as well as their good company and cheer with me while I was in the field. I also benefitted from rich conversations with Hanan Sabea, Khaled Fahmy, Dina Shehata, Ibrahim El Houdaiby, Momen el-Husseiny, Mozn Hassan, Atef Said, Ekram Yousef, Khaled Elsayed, Islam Lotfy, Moaz Abdelkareem, Khaled Tallima, Khaled Abd Elhamid, Hossam El-Hamalawy, Ahmed Ezzat, Hawary Hawary, Nourhan Hefzy, Dalia Hussein, Dalia Abd Elhamid, Mahmoud Ramzy, Mohammed Salah, Mamdouh Hamza, Esraa Abdel Fattah, Moshera Ahmad, Mohsen Kamal, Mona Shams, Lobna Afifi, Nadine Wahab, and the late Bassem Sabry.

I would not have made it through the various stages of writing and revising without the many friends who provided critical engagement and assistance along the way. Waleed Almusharaf read an early draft of my manuscript and gave me the affirmation I needed early to press on with revisions and publish. He has been a wonderful friend—indeed, a brother—and an invaluable thought partner. I am also immensely grateful for the friendship and support of the brilliant Rahma Esther Bavelaar, who took time out of her own dissertation research and writing to read a later draft of my full manuscript; her insightful comments made this a much better book. Her husband Tarek Ghanem has also been a great friend and provided wise counsel and moral support at different stages of the writing and publishing process. Hesham Sallam, Kristen Alff, and Hoda Yousef—friends and scholars of the highest caliber—reviewed drafts of individual chapters and helped me wrestle sections I struggled with into place. Their feedback and critiques were invaluable. Mohammed Abbas deserves special appreciation for providing fact checking and research support whenever I needed it. Other friends helped with tricky Arabic-English translations, copyediting, graphic design, and tech support. Among them are Munes Tomeh, Hanane Korchi, Jude Berman, Sawsan Morrar, and Omar Hashwi. I must single out Mariam El Quessny, who helped finalize the cover design with her wonderful artist's touch—thank you, Mariam.

Aside from those whose hands touched this book, many others supported me in indispensable ways. My research on the revolution was enabled by dear friends who hosted me in Cairo. I owe thanks to Darah Rateb and H. A. Hellyer for generously accommodating me when I first arrived, as well as to Sahar Eissa, who welcomed me into her home as family for most of what remained of my stay in the city thereafter. Sahar provided me with the stability and comforts I needed to endure what turned out to be a very intense fieldwork experience, and for that I am indebted to her. A special shout-out to the friends who helped me survive the often fraught experience of conducting research in revolutionary Cairo, accompanying me at protests and conferences, joining me for meals and treats, and indulging me in comic relief when I needed it most: Marwa Nasser, Irfana Hashmi, Hend Mohsen, Amr Ezz, Lolita Wagih Mansour, and Sarah Al Rifaie.

I would also like to shine a spotlight on close friends who stood by me stateside as I worked to finish the book and kept me sane. Elizabeth Hanson (aka Nabila) has long been there for me like a big sister. Whenever I was stuck in editing purgatory, she made herself available for commiseration and encouragement. Elsa Elmahdy has been a treasured friend since we ventured to Cairo to study Arabic as fresh college grads and bonded over our love of *mahalabiyya*. I survived this project—just as I did our escapades in Egypt—because I had her in my corner, grounding me with her wisdom and sustaining me with her levity. Sumaira Akhtar also helped me pull through some tough times that threatened to undermine me from completing this project; I do not know how I would have made it to the finish line without her advice, solidarity, and willingness to join me for much-needed breaks. Two friends deserve a second mention, along with their partners: Mariam El Quessny and Motaz Attalla, and Waleed Almusharaf and Rebecca Chiao—couples I met in Tahrir who followed me home from Cairo and moved to California—were my Egypt away from Egypt; their delectable *masri* humor, witty banter, and overall good vibes kept me going as I toiled on this project.

For her belief in this project and guidance through its development, I am grateful to my editor Nadia Naqib at AUC Press. Her feedback along with the comments of the press's two anonymous reviewers greatly benefitted the text. I also extend my thanks to managing editor Nadine El-Hadi for her patience and hard work in bringing this book to publication.

My utmost gratitude and deepest love goes to my family for patiently enduring this long and arduous journey with me. I begin with our devoted patriarch, my uncle Mahmoud Hadi, an accomplished writer himself whose encouragement meant so much to me. This book emanates from his selfless striving for the betterment of our larger family—thank you for your sacrifices and all you have done for us, *Khalu*. My brother Ashraf has been a pillar of support and source of assurance throughout my life. I thank him for backing my academic adventures and drive for this project, even when he would have preferred I dedicate my time to more lucrative pursuits. My sister-in-law, Amira, has also buoyed me over the years with her effervescent spirit. A special high-five to my sprightly young nephews, Zayn and Ali, for never failing to deliver when I needed a laugh. As children, they struggled to understand why their aunt was always glued to her laptop. My prayer is that the stories I found so inspiring and labored to preserve in these pages will make their way into their hearts when they read them one day and not only stir their curiosity and affection for their homeland but also move them to embrace the perennial struggle for freedom and justice that animates this book.

I am incapable of adequately thanking my parents and expressing how much their unconditional love and sacrifice have meant to me, how deeply I appreciate them for their patience, prayers, and support. I say this with deep sorrow and longing for my late father, Abdellatif Latif, a gifted engineer from whom I inherited my creative streak. He passed away unexpectedly just as this book was about to go to print, before experiencing the pride and joy he had long awaited of reading its pages and seeing his daughter thrive as a published author. My prayer now is for it to be *sadaqa jariya* for him. My heart will forever be with him and the wife he leaves behind, my mother, Monira Hadi, who carried me with so much grace over the course of this project despite my many shortcomings as her daughter. Long before I encountered Egyptian revolutionaries, she taught me by example as a special needs mom what it means to serve and fight for the most vulnerable and excluded among us. The debt I owe her is immense, but greater still is the one I owe the special young man with cerebral palsy she spends her days and nights caring for. My brother Mohammed cannot read, but I wish to address him anyway: Thank you, *habibi* Duksha, for everything you have taught me about myself, the world, and my place in it. Thank you for filling our lives with mercy and meaning and light.

    I offer my final and most heartfelt gratitude to my Creator. I thank Him for His countless blessings, the greatest being His final messenger, my beloved guide, God's peace forever be upon him.

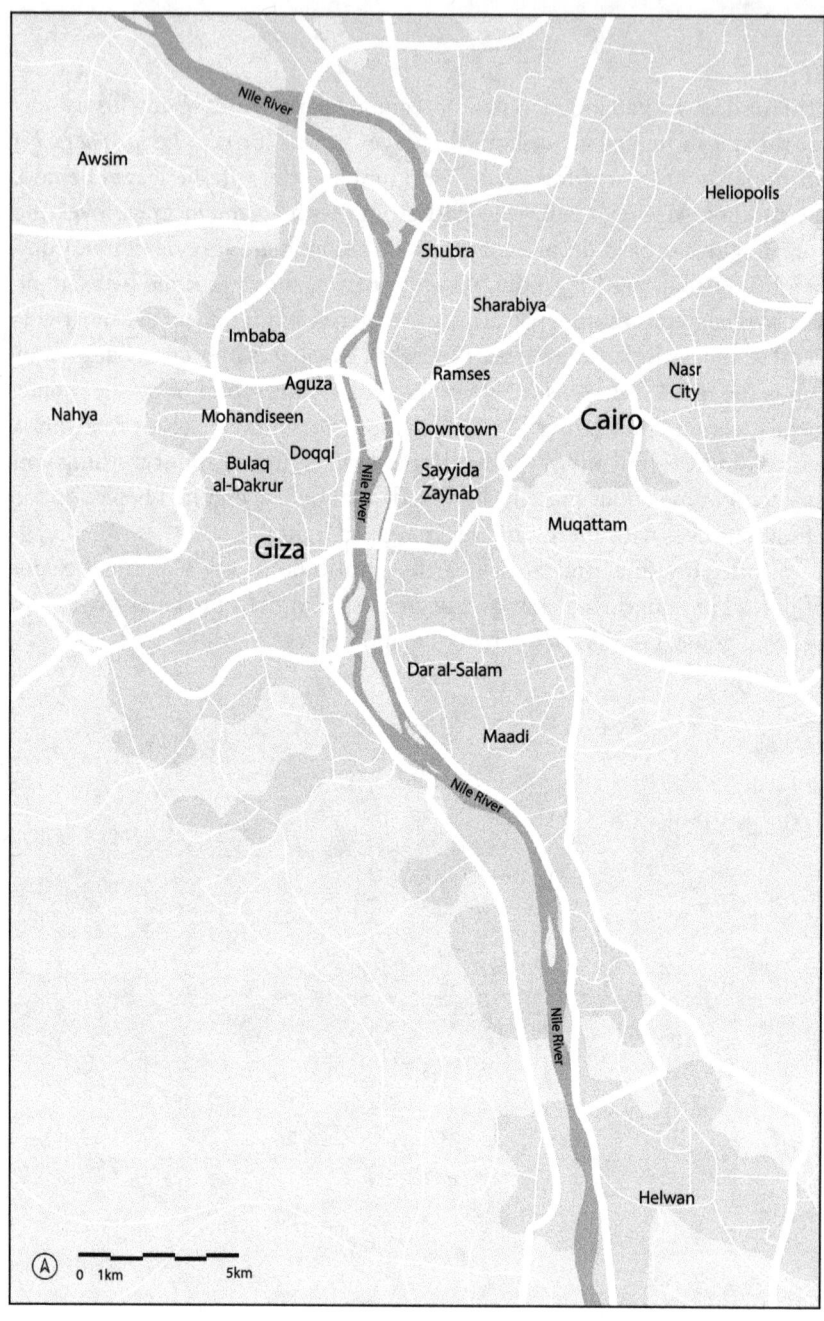

Map 1. Map of Greater Cairo showing the major districts cited in this book. Map courtesy of CLUSTER.

Introduction

Deadly clashes between protesters and police had been raging on Muhammad Mahmud Street off Tahrir Square for nearly four straight days as I made my way to the vicinity, which I had done daily since the battle first erupted. It was Tuesday, November 22, 2011, and activists had called for mass protests nationwide to force the generals of the Security Council of Armed Forces (SCAF), who had been ruling Egypt since the fall of President Hosni Mubarak, to relinquish power immediately to a civilian transitional government. Dubbed the "Second Revolution," the demonstrations were the largest Egypt had seen since the president stepped down earlier that year on February 11 and exposed SCAF's vulnerability and failures at governing. The activists hoped to press the advantage the new November uprising had given them to wrest control of the country from the generals and set it back on track toward their revolutionary goals. I was eager to return to Tahrir to find out the latest developments and learn how the revolutionaries were organizing themselves and their new sit-in to capitalize on this unexpected and hopeful political opening.

After disembarking at Sadat metro station and passing through the dimly lit underground tunnels, I emerged from the exit near Qasr al-Nil Bridge to find Tahrir basking in the glow of the last bit of sunlight before dusk. In the distance, near Hardee's and Pizza Hut, a thick cloud of tear gas and black smoke hovered over the street where mostly poor, young men hurled their righteous fury at bullet-firing police in the form of stones, Molotov cocktails, homemade bombs, and the fuming tear-gas canisters also shot at them by police. A swarm of spectators had convened to spur them on from behind. The rest of the square was jostling with the thousands of Egyptians who had turned out to show their solidarity—many of them provoked by the footage that had just surfaced of soldiers coldly dragging the dead bodies of protesters across the concrete and piling them on mounds of trash—but also to enjoy the convivial, street-fair atmosphere typical of Tahrir protests. Most incongruous was the cotton-candy man, whose enormous pink cloud of spun sugar floating over the sea of demonstrators offset the intensity of the smoke-filled scene with a bit of whimsy. Ambulances and volunteer motorcyclists transporting the scores of injured from the field clinics to the hospital rushed in and out of the precinct (a total of fifty-one killed and three thousand injured during the Muhammad Mahmud street clashes meant this was the worst incident of state violence against protesters since the revolution's start).[1] Meanwhile, wailing sirens and explosions near the protesters sporadically ripped through the murmur of conversation, battle racket, and revolutionary chants against the army—"*al-sha'b yurid i'dam al-mushir!*" (The people want the execution of the field marshal!) was just one of the refrains the more militant protesters shouted during this latest revolutionary upsurge. Near the center of the square, an effigy of Defense Minister Muhammad Husayn Tantawi dangled by the neck from a high lamppost, illustrating what they meant.

What stood out to me the most that day was not the conflicting elements of the scene—by then I had grown accustomed to Tahrir's discordant violence and ebullience. Rather, what caught my eye was a giant, white banner that was newly raised in this seemingly ever-morphing square. Unlike the usual banners that articulated the revolutionaries' demands for the state elite and greater public beyond Tahrir, this one addressed the protesters onsite. In large Arabic letters, it read,

> Rules of the Square
> 1. It is absolutely prohibited to establish any independent stage in the square.
> 2. It is absolutely prohibited to raise any slogans pertaining to any particular political party or movement.
> 3. The square has one microphone. No other is permitted.
>
> One voice . . .
>   One battle fought by us all under the slogan
>   "Sovereignty for the Egyptian people!"
>   We are all Egyptians!

The sign was oddly captivating. The voice behind the text was crisp; it spoke rightfully and authoritatively but also anonymously. It was as if its creators were trying to incite the people to take ownership of these rules as though they had written them, to stir their consciousness as a unified, revolutionary, collective actor. To me, this nondescript sign evoked the behind-the-scenes struggle of Egypt's leading revolutionaries to impose order and organization on the movement and give it direction without stepping to its forefront as leaders. In many ways, the artifact spoke to the paradoxical story of the simultaneous presence and absence of leadership in the Egyptian revolution that had fascinated me since the revolutionary movement first erupted. It might not have been clear to the average protester where this sign had come from, but I had some idea. It had all the markings of the youth activists I had been following for my fieldwork, the leaders of this leaderless revolution.

The story of how this movement first erupted is familiar to many by now. On January 25, 2011, the people of Egypt burst onto the stage of history and improvised a spectacular eighteen-day drama in revolutionary resistance that captured the imagination of audiences around the world. The rage that drove them was fueled by at least a decade's worth of crushing poverty, government neglect, political repression, police brutality, rampant corruption, and an enduring foreign policy subservient to US imperial interests and impervious to their own. Armed with nothing but their grievances and the righteousness of their cause, Egyptians of every stripe shook off their fear and joined hardened activists in the streets and city squares to challenge the people and system that oppressed them. Their resistance culminated in the spectacular fall of Mubarak, the man who ruled them for thirty years like a pharaoh, hastening what felt like an irreversible turn toward a new era of openness, accountability, opportunity, and political freedom. Excluded, demoralized, voiceless for decades, Egyptians unleashed a wave of hope with their revolutionary upheaval, which ripped across the region and evoked the faith of believers and skeptics alike in the power of the people. In so doing, they quickly became global heroes.

In the wake of this extraordinary event, one nagging question occupied observers of Middle East politics: how did this happen? How did a people berated for their apathy and stereotyped as politically backward and unready for democracy suddenly come together in one of the most astonishing revolutionary mobilizations of our time and manage to evict their deeply entrenched leader in less than three weeks?

There is no single answer to this question. Revolutions are, after all, complex processes that lend themselves to many readings, and Egypt's revolutionary movement has been no exception. Early attempts to explain the sudden outburst celebrated it as a spontaneous expression of popular frustration that was facilitated by technology such as the Internet, especially social media platforms like Facebook and Twitter. They also cited the significance of its leaderless nature, noting the remarkable absence of a single galvanizing charismatic leader—think Lenin, Mao, Castro—or a vanguard organization at its helm as has been the case in most revolutionary movements. On the other hand, the role of youth as a collective that ignited and spurred this movement has been duly noted. However, discussions about young people's role have been problematic for several reasons. First, their story has often been limited to how they used Internet tools to organize. Second, discussions about youth have mostly referenced them as a homogenous category, overlooking significant structural differences that have historically separated them, such as class, gender, and religion, in addition to other factors that might have shaped their trajectory into politics and their organizing activities during the movement. Third, they have offered little insight into how individual youth leaders—the actors in real time and space—organized for the January 25 uprising and attempted to sustain it the following eighteen days and ensuing revolutionary period.[2]

This book's reading of the revolution, then, focuses on its youthful leadership. I examine the unfolding of the revolutionary process from the perspective of the young, organized activists who were some of its main drivers. As I illustrate in this book, this process does not begin on January 25 but stretches back much further, deep into the lives of these activists and the history of their country. Specifically, I focus on those activists based in Cairo who played an instrumental role in instigating January 25 and would become the leaders of the Revolutionary Youth Coalition (RYC). The RYC was the first revolutionary entity to announce itself from Tahrir Square during the early eighteen-day uprising and functioned as one of its main nerve centers. It was comprised of the political youth groups that had been the most active before January 25 and whose collaboration had begun long before the revolt. Together, they reflected the diverse political ideologies that existed in Tahrir. In telling the story of these young protagonists, I complicate the discussion on leadership and leaderlessness in Egypt's revolutionary process. In keeping with Antonio Gramsci's contention that there is no such thing as a truly spontaneous movement,[3] I argue that the existence of the RYC and the organizing its members undertook before and during the eighteen-day uprising demonstrates that the uprising was not entirely spontaneous, leaderless, or rooted in social media, but led by young activists with a history of political engagement predating the revolution.

I have chosen to emphasize the narratives of ten RYC leaders who reflect the diverse socioeconomic backgrounds, ideological leanings, personal histories, and subjective transformations of the youth activists who participated in this movement. I trace the trajectories of these activists from when they first became politically conscious and active before the revolution up until about 2015, after they had endured nearly four years of intense revolutionary struggle against four different regimes: first Mubarak's, then SCAF's, then the Muslim Brotherhood's, then the ascendent General Abd al-Fattah al-Sisi's. In the process, I reconstruct the stories and emergent revolutionary subjectivities of these youth leaders, taking into consideration questions of gender, class, religion, and ideology. What emerges is a nuanced portrait of revolutionary youth leadership that challenges the dominant media constructs circulated in the early days of the revolt. The RYC leaders I profile in this book differ from those who appeared frequently in international news media outlets during the initial uprising. Mostly secular, upper-class cosmopolitan youth who garnered fame outside of Egypt for their English updates on Twitter, very few of these latter activists appeared to have acted in a visible leadership capacity on the ground as organizers before or during the revolution. The RYC activists differ in this respect, and in that many of them identified as members of the subaltern communities whose grievances were the main thrust behind the revolt. Through the experiences of this cohort and an understanding of their motives, hopes, visions, and struggles, we can access many of the forces that shaped the emergence of Egypt's revolutionary movement and get a sense of the people and the political ideas that will continue to compete for the country's future.

What that future will look like has always been unclear, but as of this writing, it appears far less fluid than it did during the heady days of the eighteen-day uprising. Back then, as Egypt's masses started to command more and more power and the long odds against them started to shift in their favor, the revolutionary movement's prospect for sweeping away the old order and ushering in the kind of radical social and political change the activists aspired to felt excitingly promising. But the story turned out quite differently. The unbridled optimism and creative energy that animated revolutionaries during those triumphant days would melt into bitter disillusionment, despair, and even trauma as they watched the hard-won gains they had made toward a more open, free, and fair society disappear and the dictatorship they thought they had dealt a permanent death blow prevail. Indeed, if the question analysts were asking in 2011 was how this remarkable revolutionary struggle erupted, the question that would occupy them after the coup in 2013 is how the movement was so roundly defeated by the counterrevolution. This book addresses this question too. Understanding the challenges these youth leaders faced early on in trying to direct and sustain the revolution offers one explanation for why the movement unravelled. Most notably, as we will see, their decentralized and diffuse leadership structure had its advantages in the early days of the revolt but proved a liability later, as stronger organization was needed for the movement to assert its dominance and capture the state.

Consistent with wider global trends in antisystemic movements that had moved away from rigid mass organizational structures characteristic of twentieth century struggles, activists in Egypt had adopted this fluid, horizontal, informal mode of organizing typical of New Social Movements (NSMs) in the decade before January 25 as a radical reaction to the oppressive, top-down power structure of the state and formal opposition parties.[4] At the time, this NSM approach to resistance was appropriate, given the activists' focus on developing tactics to disrupt authoritarian politics as usual and pressuring for reform. But as this study will illustrate, it had its limits when their status suddenly changed from activists to revolutionaries and they were faced with the overwhelming task of wresting power from a heavily armed state, dismantling the regime, and building the polity anew. It was one thing to challenge the regime and its institutions, they would learn, and an entirely different matter to topple and replace it. Simply put, that was never part of their plan. It was a task that required organizational capital and skills, strategic visions and transformative projects outlining a radically new social order, and schemes for taking over governance that they simply did not have and could not easily develop within the span of eighteen days. Indeed, strikingly absent from the activity of Egypt's January 25 revolutionaries during the uprising were the kind of features and radical undertakings that we have come to associate with revolutions: there was no revolutionary guard ready to seize power when it fell in the streets, no "storming of the Bastille" or takeover of other strategic institutions like state media, no attempts by revolutionaries to take up arms against the state and muscle their way into power by force. These activists had dreamt of revolution, but they had never seriously entertained the possibility and were therefore unprepared when it suddenly presented itself. Remarkably, the revolutionaries were able to push out Mubarak, but when it came time in the period that followed to compete with the mighty military establishment and the highly organized Muslim Brotherhood to take charge of Egypt's future, they were at a loss. In the end, both the revolutionary youth and the Brotherhood would lose this high-stakes political contest; far from being uprooted, the authoritarian order Egypt's masses rebelled against recovered its grip on power that had been loosened by years of political turmoil. In fact, not only does that order survive unchanged, but it appears stronger than ever under Sisi, whose regime is widely regarded as more repressive than Mubarak's.

Egyptians commonly refer to the eighteen-day uprising in early 2011 along with the turbulent cascade of events that followed as the "January 25 Revolution," and this is how I refer to it in this book. But the resilience of the neoliberal authoritarian order after the fall of Mubarak and its reassertion post July 3, 2013 under Sisi have led many to question whether the word "revolution" is appropriate, and it is for this reason that I often use the term "revolutionary movement" in its place. No doubt, Egypt had experienced the kind of massive uprisings and dramatic changes that come with revolutions—not the least of which was the politicization of broad swathes of society and a shift in the way people understood their relationship with the government—but ultimately, the upheaval failed to produce the kind of radical social and political structural change that informs classical definitions of the term. I am referring here to Theda Skocpol's conceptualization of social revolutions. Limiting her study to a handful of "great revolutions," she defines the phenomenon as "rapid, basic transformations of a society's state and class structures . . . accompanied and in part carried through by class-based revolts from below,"[5] the implication being that revolutions can only really be categorized as such on the basis of their successful outcomes. Her definition was the most widely accepted until a host of new and very different revolutions[6] from the 1970s through the 1990s defied this state- and class-based understanding of revolution, prompting the search among scholars for a new approach.[7] This study aligns with the view of scholars like Charles Tilly,[8] who suggests we are better served in our analysis of revolutions by less restrictive definitions that accommodate a wider array of cases, including those in which, as he puts it, a "revolutionary situation" occurred but did not result in a "revolutionary outcome,"[9] a description that accurately captures what transpired in Egypt. Consistent with this idea are scholarly works on Egypt's 2011 rupture that make the distinction between "revolution as process" and "revolution as change" in their analyses of the movement's trajectory.[10] The benefit of this framing, as these works demonstrate, is that it allows us to meaningfully examine the January 25 phenomenon as a revolutionary movement that was unsuccessful in the short term, without diminishing its significance as a momentous turning point in a deeper social process underway in Egypt long before the uprising, one that arguably still holds the potential to bring about revolutionary transformation. Adopting this perspective, this study sets out to understand how Egypt's revolutionary situation emerged and make sense of why it unfolded the way it did during the eighteen-day uprising and the period that followed.

In foregrounding the people behind January 25 and the micro-processes they engaged in, this book does not dismiss the many macro structural explanations for the struggle's eruption that have traditionally been the focus of theoretical literature on revolutions. Some of the most common identified by Jack Goldstone[11] and others—demographic change, shifts in international relations, uneven or dependent economic development, new patterns of exclusion against particular groups, changing urban landscapes, and the evolution of personalist regimes—all played a role in precipitating Egypt's historic rupture. But macro structural explanations alone are not enough; in privileging the vulnerability of the state over the agency of actors, their capacity to explain the causes and outcomes of Egypt's upheaval is limited. Drawing on social movement theory as it relates to leadership, I lean toward a more holistic approach for understanding the emergence of the revolution, one that accounts for the conscious agency of some of the key grassroots actors who mobilized within their structural contexts and constraints to drive it from below. After all, as Eric Selbin argues, "people's thoughts and actions—even if haphazard or spontaneous—are the mediating link between structural conditions and social outcomes. . . . Structural conditions may define the possibilities for revolutionary insurrections or the options available after political power has been seized, *but they do not explain how specific groups or individuals act, what options they pursue, or what possibilities they may realize.*"[12] This study is premised on the notion that revolutions are fundamentally "human creations—with all the messiness inherent in such a claim—rather than inevitable natural processes."[13] Following this claim, it illuminates the messy, human, relational side of Egypt's revolutionary movement through an exploration of the thoughts, feelings, and actions of the youth leaders who were some of its main creators.

Not all analysts of the revolution place as much emphasis on youth, let alone the RYC, as I do in this book. Of course, there were many other actors who played a critical role in propelling the movement. They included workers, farmers, intellectuals, student groups, professional syndicates, human rights activists and organizations,[14] Ultras football fans, cyber-activists, political parties, citizen and professional journalists, and other civil society groups, as well as the plethora of non-activist protesters representing a radically diverse cross-section of Egyptian society. Along with the RYC, they formed the constellation of actors who sustained the eighteen-day uprising and worked in varying degrees to drive the struggle forward in the months and years that followed and to advance its agenda. But the youth from the RYC deserve our attention because, as this book illustrates, they were consequential for the movement in ways the others were not. Without their organizing efforts, for example, it is difficult to imagine how January 25 would have achieved the critical mass that transformed the pre-2011 protest movement into a revolutionary one. The RYC was also one of the first and most effective initiatives of its kind in Egypt where liberals, leftists, and Islamists attempted to bridge their deep political divides and work to realize their shared vision for a more just, equitable, and democratic Egypt. In the early days of the struggle, this gave them a degree of legitimacy and clout in the eyes of the public and state actors that other groups did not enjoy. As such, it held the most promise as an organizational model for advancing the revolutionary movement toward the realization of its goals. As we try to assess the factors that led to the defeat of the revolution and identify how the cause might be salvaged, we must take into account the RYC and consider its challenges, both internal and external. Focusing on them as a pivot in the revolution is one way to bring into focus the set of changing political, social, and economic dynamics as well as the shifting alliances that precipitated and ultimately thwarted the revolution. Indeed, as an important contemporary experiment in revolutionary vanguardism, the RYC deserves our attention for the lessons it offers in revolutionary leadership and the viability of participatory democratic practice as its praxis, not just for Egyptian revolutionaries, but for social and revolutionary movements across the world.

Leadership in Social Movements

My focus on leadership in the Egyptian revolution is informed by an understanding that the agency of leaders is critical to movements, making them indispensable to our understanding of how such movements unfold. Leaders help movements and revolutions turn from prospect into reality by recognizing favorable political and economic circumstances—or the right structural opportunities—and taking appropriate action to exploit them. Defined as "strategic decision makers who inspire and organize others to participate in social movements,"[15] leaders perform a number of functions at different levels that are crucial for the mobilization, development, and outcomes of these struggles. Their roles vary: (1) there are people-oriented leaders who frame grievances and articulate the vision and aspirations of the movement, inspiring others to participate and stay hopeful, unified, and committed during the setbacks they will invariably face on the path toward change; (2) and there are task-oriented leaders who manage the practical side of the movement, devising strategies, mobilizing resources, organizing constituents, and implementing plans.[16] Indeed, a movement's success—as Egypt's recent experience with revolution confirms—rests in large part on how effectively its leaders are able to perform these functions. Leadership is vital to movements and revolutions because it is the "key mechanism by which people transform the individual resources they have"—including their backgrounds, finances, networks, knowledge, skills, and tactics—"into the collective power they need to get what they want."[17]

This study of the RYC fits in with a handful of others that have developed our understanding of the various ways leadership manifests and functions in movements, demonstrating how different leadership modes have both empowered and disempowered activists to advance and undermine their struggles.[18] As alluded to in the previous section, these leadership arrangements range from rigid, centralized structures to loose, decentralized formations that are "shifting, interactive, and fluid" in nature.[19] Also highlighted in these studies is how leadership roles within these configurations are gendered and classed. They note, for instance, how gender inequality in the societies and institutions of the challenging group usually translate into the preponderance of men in the top, formal layer of movement leadership and women in the informal, intermediary layers.[20] The literature also calls our attention to why movement leaders tend to be from middle- and upper-class backgrounds: class privilege provides them with the resources needed to lead movements—namely, money, contacts, and time. But more importantly, their class privilege provides them with educational capital. Education is critical because the tasks involved in leading social movements, such as recognizing opportunities, devising tactics and strategies, and framing grievances and demands, are seen as intellectual in nature, and the skills required to carry out these tasks effectively—reading, writing, analyzing, and public speaking—are usually developed in formal educational institutions. The significance of education is demonstrated in the fact that those from working-class backgrounds who have been able to rise to leadership in movements have generally attained a higher level of education than their peers, a trend that is reflected in the experience of the RYC leaders.[21]

My study follows the path of previous scholarship by critically examining how gender and class dynamics play out in the Egyptian revolution's leadership processes. However, the historical conditions of Egypt demand a more nuanced analysis of how these variables intersect with and are influenced by a third: religion. In Egypt, Muslim religiosity[22] is seen as an indicator of class and is associated with a well-defined gender normativity. Moreover, Islam has historically played a significant role in political movements and has been a major issue of contention between self-described secularists and Islamists. An examination of leadership in this context would therefore be incomplete without an investigation into how religion informed the participation and ideologies of youth leaders and how they might have negotiated it as they attempted to come together to realize their shared goals.

This study takes as its starting point the importance of learning more about those who come to take on leadership roles and how their different backgrounds and experiences inform their participation and leadership strategies. Understanding the process through which leaders shape movements and are shaped by them allows us insight into the movements themselves.[23] Here, the changing subjectivities of the actors involved becomes relevant as a window into this dialogic process and will therefore occupy an important part of the following analysis on youth activism in the Egyptian revolution. By subjectivity, I am referring to the "inner life process and affective states"[24] of social actors, or more specifically what Sherry Ortner describes as "the ensemble of modes of perception, affect, thought, desire, and fear that animate acting subjects ... as well as the cultural and social formations that shape, organize, and provoke those modes of affect, thought, and so on."[25] As she puts it, subjectivity matters in our analysis of political struggle because it is the "the basis of 'agency,' a necessary part of understanding how people (try to) act on the world even as they are acted upon."[26]

In keeping with this idea, my analysis of Egyptian youth leaders will emphasize in chapters 4 to 6 that movements are not just gendered, but *gendering*. Gender, after all, is "not fixed in advance of social interaction, but is constructed in interaction,"[27] and social movements are a key site where this dynamic plays out. Through their participation in movements, activists might contest the social and political meanings of gender and rework them in their own subjectivities, which in turn reflects back on their activism, reshapes the landscape of the movement, modifies its agendas, and generates new meanings of femininity and masculinity for the wider public.[28] In short, the study of activists' masculinities and femininities is critical to understanding movements, since "their making and remaking is a political process affecting the balance of interests in society and the direction of social change."[29] The same can be said of the study of activists' subjectivities in terms of class, religion, and ideology, as demonstrated in the following chapters.

Youth as Agents of Revolution

A study on youth requires a definition of the term. I understand "youth" as a socially and culturally constructed category, not a universally agreed-upon fixed age group or a natural stage in human development. "Youth" denotes the liminal phase of life between childhood (a time associated with dependence, innocence, and vulnerability), and adulthood (a time associated with independence and responsibility for oneself and one's own family). In premodern times, young people transitioned through this stage quickly, as families married off their children shortly after the onset of puberty and charged them with the responsibility of maintaining the family's agrarian livelihood. But with the onset of modernity and the forms of mass schooling that its capitalist production system required in order to thrive, marriage was delayed, and the period of youth was considerably extended and associated with new ways of being young.[30] Some observers argue that the prolongation of youth has reached new levels today in the Middle East, where economic crisis and lack of employment opportunities have made it difficult for young men to marry, extending the age of youth well into the late thirties.[31] However, while the ability to provide for a family is seen as an important marker of manhood, it is also important to note that in Arab culture, one is typically considered a youth until the age of forty, employment and marital status notwithstanding.

One of the main concerns of this study is how youth acquire their political consciousness and activist agency, the kind we saw on remarkable display in Egypt and across the Arab world in 2011. Observing Egyptian youth activists through the lens of political generation as conceptualized by Karl Mannheim in his classic thesis[32] allows for an understanding of this process. He describes generation as the dynamic interplay between the biological life-cycle and the evolving sociocultural context it is embedded in. For Mannheim, a generation is comprised of a cohort of people who share "a common location in the historical dimension of the social process, . . . predisposing them for a characteristic mode of thought and experience, and a characteristic type of historically relevant action."[33] Accordingly, what defines a generation are the pivotal events and trends its members live through in their youth—economic crises, wars, revolutions, natural disasters, and other social ruptures—and the social solidarity that arises among them as they develop a consciousness of their common circumstances and plight. In other words, much like members of a social class, members of a generation achieve "actuality" when they realize their problems are not personal but social.[34] This realization might in turn awaken them to the knowledge of their collective power and trigger their political action, as we witnessed in Egypt and other Arab countries in 2011.

The youth life stage figures centrally in Mannheim's schema as the formative moment in the life of a cohort. He saw that the young were the most likely to become agents of change, free as they are from the burden of responsibilities that come later in life with marriage, parenthood, and career. Compared to adults who have settled into their social roles, youth are more malleable, more willing to take risks, more susceptible to new ideas, and more prone to social change and historical reorientation. Mannheim also emphasized that youth are not as easily socialized into the status quo. As they grow autonomous in their engagement with the world and its challenges, the young begin to rely more on their direct experiences for meaning and less on the "appropriated memories" of older generations—the social norms, attitudes, and value systems imparted to them through schooling, family, and media.[35] Mannheim speaks of "fresh contact," a history-catalyzing process whereby the young encounter the received social and material order anew and evaluate it from the perspective of their novel context. In response, they might grow to oppose the structures they have inherited, and, to the extent that they become conscious of their shared sentiment, take collective action to change it. Whereas their elders might be more gray in their views about justice and jaded about the efficacy of action and possibility of change, youth tend to see right and wrong in black-and-white terms and are more compelled to act on the idealistic belief that the justice of their cause will prevail.[36] Fresh contacts are important because they facilitate the regeneration of society and polity through the critical participation of youth, inspiring them to steer us away from "that which is no longer useful" and toward "that which has yet to be won."[37]

While the focus of this book is not on generational agency per se, Mannheim's ideas help us understand why youth were the impetus and leading actors in the Egyptian revolt. Chapter 3 takes its cue from his ideas. It highlights the youth activists' embeddedness in the historical dynamics and sociopolitical circumstances of Egypt, noting the formative experiences—or "fresh contacts"—that provoked their political consciousness and activism. One of the main themes of this chapter is how the multiple symptoms of neoliberalism and authoritarianism—what Mannheim would characterize as "a process of dynamic destabilization"[38]—played out in their personal lives. Of course, not all members of a youth cohort will experience and react to the problems of their age in the same manner. Mannheim addresses this inconsistency with his notion of "generation units," positing that structural differences like race, gender, class, religion, ideology, and geography will separate members of a generation into subgroups that will have varied if not antagonistic responses.[39] Chapters 4 to 6 will examine the youth activists' subjectivity formation as revolutionary leaders during this pivotal historical moment along these axes of difference.

What Follows . . .

In this book, I tell the story of the revolutionary movement specifically as it relates to the youth protagonists who were so central to its unfolding. I begin in chapter 1 with a discussion of my research methodology, explaining my personal trajectory into this research, my positionality in the field, and the challenges I faced trying to collect data in Cairo's revolutionary environment. This discussion provides a clear window into the dynamics of the revolutionary process and illuminates the challenging context the youth actors found themselves in as they attempted to sustain this movement. It ends with a discussion of my interviews and interviewees. Chapter 2 provides context for the rest of the study by examining the historical processes from the 1952 revolution onward that shaped the emergence of this movement. It focuses on the erosion of the social contract that locked the people of the newly formed Egyptian republic into a relationship with the state that was based on the exchange of political quietude for social welfare, giving special attention to the political and economic developments under Mubarak that led to the final severance of that pact. It also traces the emergence of the military and the Muslim Brotherhood as two of Egypt's strongest political players and describes the decade-long resistance movement that paved the way to the January 25 uprising and forged the nation's new generation of revolutionary youth.

Chapter 3 is an attempt to look past the Facebook and Twitter tropes that have been associated with the youth who instigated this movement to tell the deeper story of their revolutionary becoming. It begins by profiling the ten activists whose stories are the focus of the study. It then goes on to highlight their trajectories into the revolution, examining the formative experiences and circumstances that shaped their early politicization and budding activism. I highlight the recurring themes in the various narratives I collected and the specific circumstances that drew this disparate group of youth actors together into a network. This chapter illustrates that the revolution was not spontaneous in the sense that it erupted from nowhere, but that it was at least ten years in the making and initiated by activists who were deeply embedded in the historical processes that gave birth to the uprising.

Chapter 4 details the eighteen-day uprising as it unfolded from the perspective of these youth activists who were deeply engaged in it, focusing specifically on their organizing efforts and challenges. This process was characterized by a series of ups and downs as well as the complex dynamics of a fluid, changing reality involving the interaction of activists, protesters, workers, the non-protesting public, the state, global powers, and international sympathizers. It unfolded in phases after critical junctures, which forced the actors involved to constantly negotiate and act around two recurring, corresponding questions: "What is happening?" and "How should we act?" It was in response to these questions that the youth activists formed the Revolutionary Youth Coalition and attempted to create other revolutionary vehicles from the square that would see the demands articulated by the people through to their realization. Why they ultimately failed in this endeavor becomes clear in this chapter and those that follow.

Chapter 5 examines the transformation in the personal and political subjectivities of the RYC leaders over the course of their engagement before and through the eighteen-day uprising. It begins with a discussion of the ways in which their sense of selves changed as a result of their participation as leaders in the movement. It also considers the ways in which gender, class, and religion shaped their participation and agency in the revolution and how their attitudes with respect to these categories changed or remained constant. It ends with an examination of the political imaginaries that drove their activism, especially their visions for the new nation-state. This chapter illustrates the kind of subjectivities this upheaval fashioned and offers insight into the development of the movement and where it might have been headed had it not been derailed.

Chapter 6 reviews the most crucial findings of this study, especially as they relate to the multiple expressions of leadership in the revolution with respect to youth as an analytical category, class, gender, and religion. It also provides theoretical insight into the organizing challenges youth activists faced and why the Egyptian revolutionary movement continued to struggle after the eighteen-day uprising.

Chapter 7 closes this book. It offers a synopsis of the major political developments since I conducted my field research in 2011 (including the eighteen months under SCAF transitional rule, President Muhammad Morsi's brief tenure, and the coup in the summer of 2013 that led to Sisi's ascent as president) and discusses what happened to the revolutionary movement and the youth who were its early leaders. It incorporates a fresh set of interviews with these activists conducted in the aftermath of the summer of 2013 crisis to illustrate the continuities and changes in their political subjectivities since our first formal set of interviews. These narratives offer insight into the predicament Egypt found itself in almost four years after the January 25 uprising and what hope might exist for the revolution's reemergence.

1

Encountering Revolution: Expectations and Reality

I was inspired to pursue this study during the revolution's early days, before fate determined that it would quickly come to a head, after two and a half weeks, and draw Mubarak's reign to a dramatic, unexpected close. In fact, the title of this book came to me when the final outcome of Egypt's turbulent uprising was still anyone's guess. When protests erupted in Egypt on January 25, something inside me was lit up. Along with observers around the world, I was captivated by the movement unfolding before us carrying the emblematic weight of history in the making. Obsessively, I followed the deluge of network news coverage, citizen journalism, and academic commentary on Facebook and Twitter. The gripping story Egyptians were telling in collectively speaking truth to power was the stuff of legends, complete with astonishing scenes of underdog heroism, cross-class camaraderie, religious coexistence, national pride, and beloved community. Taking in all of this from afar (namely, the small suburban town that was home to the University of California, Davis, where I was a student), I not only felt the stirrings of a longing, but also a beckoning. I knew I had to return to Egypt and make this movement the topic of my research. In this chapter, I explain why.

My Trajectory

I was born and raised in the United States, yet Egypt is the source I spring from. My parents were born and came of age in a small village in the Sharqiya governorate northeast of Cairo in the Nile Delta region. As adults, they studied, worked, and lived in Cairo and Alexandria before marrying and migrating to the United States in the late 1970s. Though I did not visit Egypt often growing up, nor did I know much about its history or culture, or even speak its language very well, I had an unwitting sense that home was *there*, not so much *here*. It felt inaccurate to call myself an American. This of course had something to do with the fact that though I was not there, Egypt had managed to ground and shape my experience here through the cultural expressions and everyday practices of my parents, their language, food, dress, and religious observance. It also had something to do with my large, extended family being there, not here. But even more, my sense of belonging to Egypt was reinforced by my own exclusion in the United States.

Unlike my second-generation peers from other non-Arab immigrant backgrounds, my struggle negotiating my dual American and Egyptian identities was embedded in the larger world, a highly polarized geopolitical context in which my two worlds were often in conflict. My decision to wear the hijab as a young Muslim woman not only highlighted and emphasized my difference in my Western home but made the anonymity that eases a person's integration seem like an impossible feat. Because of my hijab, I was identified as a member of that place over there whose people were angry, violent, uncivilized, women-oppressing, freedom haters. The anti-Arab, anti-Muslim climate that emerged post 9/11 only made my feelings of exclusion more acute, as comments like "go back to where you came from" and the sudden appearance of confederate flags dislocated and alienated me further.

I visited Egypt with my family a few times growing up. I even lived and went to school there for a year when I was nine years old. However, I did not come to fully appreciate my country of origin until I ventured there alone in my early twenties and took up residence in Cairo from 2003 to 2007. I had just completed my undergraduate studies and wanted to learn formal Arabic, study my faith tradition, and reconnect with my family in the countryside, whom I had not seen in seven years. But this was not the only pull. On a subtle level, my return to Egypt was driven by a desire to make amends with a country and a region that I had never quite understood and had grown to view negatively for making my life in the US difficult. I wanted to give it a chance to redeem itself. I needed to understand it on its own terms and see it differently.

And I did see it differently, and by extension the larger Middle East, and I became empathetic. I saw that Egypt was not backward, but a country with a rich civilization and culture that had become suffocated by a corrupt government and a world order that would not let it develop and flourish. More poignantly, I also learned that my other country, the United States, for its own selfish interests, was largely implicated in sustaining such an unjust world order. I understood that the anger misinterpreted as the natural, primordial disposition of Arabs actually stemmed from the intolerable socioeconomic conditions that had made their lives miserable and driven them to the brink—rising food and living costs, staggering unemployment rates, a disastrous lack of adequate public services, and the like. In reality, they had a great deal of warmth, good will, and tolerance, which, remarkably, they had managed to preserve despite their difficult circumstances.

During my stay in Egypt, my own day-to-day experiences and engagement with ordinary Egyptians led me to understand intuitively the deep socioeconomic frustrations that would later turn average Egyptians into revolutionaries. Ironically, it was this experience in Egypt that sparked my interest in positive social change and my desire to learn how I could play a role in it. This experience set me on an academic trajectory that, to my surprise, would eventually bring me back full circle, intellectually and emotionally, and in the most exhilarating and unexpected circumstances: my country's national reconstruction.

As a graduate student with a growing interest in social movements, I needed to understand how this happened. As a young person, I wanted to meet my peers who, for me, were the most compelling part of this movement. Like so many critics, I had assumed Egypt's youth were apathetic, and I wanted to know what I had missed and tell their story. As a long-lost Egyptian-American, I needed to find my story in theirs. So I set about planning my research.

Planning Research

I devised a straightforward plan for ethnographic data collection that I thought should be fairly easy to execute in the approximately three months I had allotted. My goal was to understand the role of youth in the movement.[1] In particular, I wanted to learn about their sociopolitical trajectories prior to their involvement on January 25 and over the course of the eighteen-day uprising, culminating in the momentous resignation of Hosni Mubarak on February 11. I knew I had to limit my inquiry to a clearly defined time frame because the revolutionary movement was far from over, and an attempt to research and analyze it as it was unfolding would epistemologically be a futile pursuit. Thus, with February 11 as my cutoff date, I would try to conduct in-depth interviews with at least ten activists who played an organizing role in the January 25 uprising and the ensuing revolutionary process. These activists would ideally include men and women representing the diverse youth movements that I learned from my obsessive reading of the news and media commentary had coordinated this effort as it unfolded in Cairo's Tahrir Square. I also hoped to interview key informants like local scholars, journalists, and veteran political activists who could help me understand the landscape of youth activism at the start of the movement and how it had developed in the preceding years, specifically how the political, structural climate allowed youth to emerge as transformative political actors en masse.

I was confident in my ability to conduct this research and motivated by the advantages I perceived my mixed Egyptian and American origin gave me over other foreign researchers. Like them, I thought that my upbringing abroad meant that I could maintain the objective perspective that comes with an outsider's distance and detachment. Unlike them, however, I imagined my Egyptianness meant that I could penetrate the field and access knowledge as an insider in ways they likely could not. Not only was I conversant with the culture and proficient in both formal and colloquial Egyptian Arabic, but I had also been raised Muslim, which in my mind implied that to some extent at least I shared the values and sensibilities of most Egyptians, allowing me to better understand their experiences. It occurred to me that being a veiled woman was another advantage, as it might wash out some of the otherness of my American identity and make them feel more at ease with me. Further, as a seasoned Cairo dweller, I was familiar with the research setting. In fact, I had taken many courses at the American University in Cairo, situated at the corner of Tahrir Square, and was therefore already familiar with the field site. Moreover, I was aware of the challenges that came with trying to live in this dense metropolitan city with its crumbling infrastructure. Such familiarity, I thought, would speed up my fieldwork, as I would not have to waste valuable time learning Cairo's ropes and adjusting to the research site. Additionally, I already had connections who agreed to provide me with important contacts and help me network with activists. In sum, though I was intimidated by the gravity of this project and having to approach revolutionaries for interviews to conduct it, I felt comforted knowing that my position would facilitate my entry into the field and make building rapport with my potential research participants easier—or so I had imagined. In fact, to my surprise, my experiences in the field would challenge many of these assumptions.

Immersion in Revolutionary Cairo

I arrived in Cairo in late June 2011, five months after the start of the revolutionary movement. I got settled after the initial inescapable, almost ritual hassle that had been part of my experience traveling there over the years. Thereafter, I immediately turned my attention to the field. Before my departure, I had already collected the names of young activists who appeared frequently in English-language media outlets as well as those who were independently dispatching news updates from Tahrir on Twitter during the uprising. However, I had no sense of the extent of their activism, their political leanings, or affiliations. What was clear to me was their prominence, as documented by the media and their apparent use of social media.[2] I began activating my contacts upon my arrival in the hope that they could help me better understand the network of youth activists involved and lead me to key contacts among them. A meeting with the director of the Gerhardt Center at the American University in Cairo upon my arrival and a few conversations with some of her assistants provided me with the first useful contacts that would serve as entry points into what had until then still daunted me as an elusive web of revolutionaries.

At the time of my arrival, I was also fortunate that Tahrir Square was still a bustling protest site teeming with demonstrators. The square and its Downtown vicinity had continued to be the site of political ferment since SCAF seized the reins of power earlier that year, when Mubarak stepped down. The Council's unilateral decisions, as it charged itself with the task of managing the country's transition to democratic elections, fueled rather than dampened the revolutionary flames; it was a move that activist leaders saw as the beginning of a counterrevolution, and it signaled the next stage in their battle to bring down the old power structure.

I found myself in the middle of my first Tahrir protest shortly after my arrival. Little did I know that this would be just one of many to follow. Friday, July 8, was dubbed "The Friday of Determination." Thousands of protesters gathered in Tahrir and other city squares across the country to voice their frustration with SCAF and how little had changed five months after the uprising. In a move to press SCAF to institute immediate reforms and demand that former officials from the ousted regime be prosecuted without further delay, activists staged an open-ended sit-in in Tahrir Square that would continue for three weeks. This was an unexpected development that worked to my advantage. I was able to rely on my firsthand experiences and observations at these protests in the summer of 2011 to imagine what had happened during the eighteen-day uprising at the start of that year. I was also able to meet the demonstrators and activists taking part in these current protests and learn about their wider experiences and the meanings of their participation in the movement.

Middle-class, American, female, and veiled: researcher positions in Tahrir

Tahrir Square was unlike I had ever experienced it before. The atmosphere was at once serious and carnivalesque. Men, women, and children of all ages and from all walks of life stood shoulder to shoulder under the blazing sun, cheering and chanting, waving their flags, and pumping their fists in the air to the emotionally charged speeches, chants, and nationalist songs blasting from the towering stages erected at every corner of the square. "*Eed wahda! Eed wahdah!*" (One hand! One hand!) they would shout in unison, egging each other on. Hundreds of colorful banners stretched across the streets and roundabout. Journalists and their camera crews peppered the balconies of surrounding high-rise apartment complexes. Protesters posed for photographs with their masterpiece posters, while rowdy food and souvenir vendors stubbornly forced their carts through the crowd. In the center of the square and around its periphery, hundreds of protesters took refuge from the sun in the tents pitched for the sit-in, some taking naps, others sharing meals, while others engaged in heated political debates. It was exciting, but also quite jarring, being in Tahrir participating for the first time in a revolutionary movement I had been eagerly following and cheering on from afar. It was then, during my first real engagement with the field, that I started to become aware of myself in ways I had not anticipated.

Along with the exhilaration I felt being at the center of this movement for the first time, I also felt a perplexing distance from it. I wanted to chant with my fellow Egyptians on that Friday, loudly and fervently, but I was restrained by a gnawing sense that my passionate display would be lacking in authenticity, and therefore inappropriate and disrespectful. This was because as an Egyptian whose upbringing as such was interrupted by the migration of her parents, I did not have access to the repertoire of shared experiences and frustrations that drove these protesters. Nor could I tap into the historical memory that animated my supposed compatriots for inspiration, for that, too, mostly eluded me. Though I sympathized with their cause, it was not really mine; I had not grown up with their struggle, nor would I feel the full implications should their movement fail. Ironically, when I was in the United States planning this research, I identified closely as a member of this community; now in the field, I was becoming conscious of myself apart from those I had considered my people. There, I felt that I was an American, an outsider. This transformation in my own subjectivity was a result of my lived, sensorial experience as well as the way I perceived people reacting to me.

My subjective duality began to dawn on me earlier in my fieldwork, during my first excursions into the Tahrir sit-in camp area, where I hoped to gain official entrée into the leading activist circles. I imagined this task would be easy, given that the sit-in meant all the activists I might want to recruit as research participants were stationed in the square for at least the next few days, perfectly accessible. But in fact, it was not at all this simple; gaining access, I would soon learn, entailed so much more.

I spent several days walking about the encampment area, trying to orient myself in the dense maze of tents clustered into multiple sub-communities representing the various movements, political parties, organizations—even extended families and cities outside of Cairo involved in the protest—before I worked up the nerve to introduce myself to activists and start conversations with them about my research. My hesitation stemmed in great part from my increasing sensitivity to the nuances and implications of my own position and identity in this unfamiliar, radically heterogeneous and fluid environment. I wanted to smoothly insert myself in this bubbling universe, but I could not figure out how to place myself in it. Although I had been to Cairo many times before, occupied Tahrir brought me into an almost uncomfortable proximity with very different social groups I had never previously engaged with and would have never met had it not been for my research interest in their movement. Tahrir did not just introduce me to all these radically different groups, it confronted me with them all at once, stirring anxieties in me as it kicked up and forced me to negotiate the multiple intersections of my positionalities.

When I was planning my research, I did not think much about the extent to which my own positionality could affect my data collection in Egypt. I did not imagine my gender would have any significant impact on my fieldwork; I did not expect it to limit my access to male activists, for instance, as I understood these activists to be progressive when it came to non-romantic inter-gender interactions. Nor did I expect my religion to be a hindrance, since the majority of Egyptians are Muslim, though their religiosity might vary. Similarly, I gave virtually no thought to my class position, understanding most of the activists to be members of the middle class like me. But together, all of these variables did have unexpected implications for my fieldwork, especially as they manifested in my attire, particularly my hijab, as well as my demeanor. For most people, the hijab symbolizes a Muslim woman's religious observance, which is usually associated with political conservatism. Now in the field, I started to see how the fact that I was veiled along with my socialization as an American Muslim would shape and to some extent delimit my interactions and access to knowledge.

At the Tahrir sit-in, for example, one of the groups I wanted to network with but was reluctant to approach was the "Twitterati," a group of elite and upper-middle-class, left-leaning secular youth who occupied the southeastern corner of the roundabout at the center of the square. These activists were known to international followers of the movement for their regular news updates from the square and thus seemed an appropriate entry point to start my networking. As someone who grew up in California, I related to this group's cosmopolitanism and felt comforted by the fact that they spoke fluent English. However, as a practicing veiled Muslim woman, I felt self-conscious around them. I clearly did not fit in with the women in this group who dressed less conservatively than me, smoked liberally, and slept beside their male comrades in and around shared tents. Moreover, my class position among them felt questionable. I was aware of the general aversion to the hijab among members of this class in Egypt, who associated it, in a derogatory way, with the peasant and popular classes; descriptors like *baladi* (of the country) and *bi'a* (ghetto) were common in their discourse on the subject and conveyed their disfavor. Understandably, wearing hijab around this group drew out my own sensitivities about my family's provincial origins, which I had been made painfully aware of as a child growing up among more affluent Egyptians from Cairo and Alexandria in the United States. Paradoxically, in the context of the square, my middle-class position in the United States, which had led me to become a researcher wholeheartedly interested in the Egyptian revolutionary movement, stood obscurely in the background, while my veil and its Egyptian class connotations took center stage.

When I finally found the courage to approach members of this group, I found myself feeling pressured into playing a game ironically similar to the one I was accustomed to playing in my interactions with non-Muslims in the United States: attempting to emphasize my similarity and minimize my difference. I tried to build rapport by consciously carrying myself in a manner that anticipated and preemptively challenged whatever incorrect assumptions or views they might have of me because of my hijab. Thus, I behaved in ways that highlighted my middle-class, American upbringing and tastes and relayed my cosmopolitan Egyptianness, all in an effort to position myself more as an insider and less as an outsider. For example, I made a point of speaking Arabic and mixing it with English in a way that was customary among upper-class Egyptians. This dance involved a constant and at times uncomfortable negotiation with my religious values, which I tried to avoid asserting for fear it might alienate potential interlocutors. Such negotiations were particularly trying when interacting with men, especially with Muslim men, whom I was raised to be more reserved around. With a few activists my effort appeared to work; if my hijab was at all an issue for them in the first place, my Americanness and researcher status seemed to trump their secular and class misgivings about it. I was able to enjoy some degree of camaraderie with them and rely on them for support with my research, particularly with networking. With others, I understood from our interactions that they could not see past the scarf on my head, all the more unsettling given that the ethos of the movement they were driving was one of tolerance and acceptance. In all honesty, my inability to access them was likely as much a result of some of my own discomfort with our difference and the barriers I might have erected as a result. In retrospect, I could not help but wonder how much easier it would have been to be a practicing Muslim male researcher in this setting, or an unveiled practicing Muslim woman; I imagine that playing up, playing down, or even completely camouflaging my religious identity and religiosity as the field dynamic demanded would have been much easier.

It is difficult for me to decipher the full impact my position as a practicing, veiled Muslim woman had on the quality of data I collected. Generally, those I interviewed appeared to be unfazed by my hijab and seemed to answer my questions as they would have had the same questions come from an unveiled woman or a man. However, some of my respondents might have presented a few of their answers, particularly about gender and religion, in a way that they imagined resonated with my sensibilities. While it might have diminished some of the respect secular elite activists might have felt for me as a serious researcher, my status as a practicing, veiled Muslim woman certainly did not have that effect on the Islamist activists, such as the former members of the Muslim Brotherhood. If anything, it made it easier for me to establish rapport and gain regular access to them.

I believe my hijab made it easier for them to relate to me, and I definitely felt more assured around them.

Ironically, I was also stunned to learn over the course of planning and conducting this research that I, too, had stereotypical assumptions about veiled women as a consequence of my socialization in the West. I started to become aware of this before I traveled to Egypt, when during an advisory meeting my professor pointed out that I had just judged an Egyptian woman activist as conservative based solely on my observation that she was veiled. This incident was all the more troubling considering that I myself resented such assumptions being made about me because of my veil. Somehow, I had introjected the very Western hegemonic views of Muslim women that I had experienced myself and had criticized and challenged in the United States. I confronted these same prejudiced views in the field, where I met women who, though they dressed more conservatively, demonstrated through their views and their behavior that they were anything but. Some, for example, surprised me with their left-leaning politics and their liberal attitudes about inter-gender relations. Moreover, I had also assumed that being a veiled woman would make it easier for me to build rapport with the veiled women activists I hoped to interview. Growing up as a member of the Muslim community in the United States, I felt an instant connection and solidarity with veiled women in general. Without having to verbalize it, on some level, as minority women, we understood each other and knew we were there for each other. But although it may have existed in some other way, ironically, I never sensed this kind of solidarity or sympathy from veiled women activists I met in Egypt. This may have been because Muslims in Egypt are the majority and the veil is the norm. On the flip side, I was also forced to confront my own stereotypical assumptions about non-veiled upper-class Egyptian women, whom I had imagined to be almost categorically averse to the hijab. Ola Shahba, one of my interlocutors who, I learned from our interviews, wore the veil for a number of years, is one of the women who challenged this view and helped me better understand the varied experiences and relationships Egyptian women of diverse classes had with the veil.

Class, religion, and gender, my fieldwork experience confirmed, are not fixed categories even within the same society at the same historic moment. In effect, while my hijab impeded my access to upper-middle-class and elite activists, it did not prevent me from gaining access to groups from lower social backgrounds. Gaining access to activist circles whose members came from Egypt's popular class (discussed in chapters 3, 5, and 6), such as the

April 6 Youth Movement and Youth for Justice and Freedom Movement, meant a very different set of negotiations. With these groups, my veil was not an obstacle, as it was common practice for women from this class to cover. Externally, I had many of the markings of an insider. But internally, I knew I did not fully fit. My socialization abroad as a member of the American middle class placed me a few notches above them on the social ladder. I immediately sensed our class differences in our dress and mannerisms. Their limited English was also a cue, as proficiency in English reflected the quality of education financially accessible to them. This was a group that I had, until then, never intimately engaged with in Egypt and was not sure how to relate to. However, trying to build rapport with members from this group, I found that my family's class origins in rural Egypt worked to my advantage, as I was able to connect with them by activating my rural connection and drawing on my life experiences there.[3] The more time I spent with these activists and engaged with them in interviews, however, the more I realized that class difference was not really an issue in the first place. I stopped worrying about broaching topics related to their class background in our discussions for fear of offending them, because their revolutionary activism had moved them into the intelligentsia among whom class distinctions had little place, and if anything, lower-class origins were a source of pride rather than a point of sensitivity. Though I imagined with this group I might be studying down or sideways, in this sense, I was actually studying up.

A real Egyptian?—language and culture
Before embarking on my research, I was sure that my proficiency in Arabic would give me an advantage over foreign fieldworkers and serve me well on the ground. This was true to an extent. But once I began my field research in earnest, I began to see the limitations of my Arabic as a non-native speaker and feel their effects. Though I had grown up speaking colloquial Egyptian Arabic with my family and friends in the United States, and though I had studied Modern Standard Arabic quite extensively, I had not achieved native fluency. My accent was foreign, my vocabulary limited, my collocations at times incorrect, my comprehension sometimes spotty. This had an impact on my ability to build rapport and access knowledge. Forced in some cases to introduce myself and build relationships relying solely on my Arabic because of my interlocutors' weakness in English, I became self-consciously aware of how my accent and lack of fluency not only highlighted my class difference, but also my cultural otherness. Fortunately, my

awkwardness in the language did not work entirely against me, as many found my struggle endearing.[4] Still, my limited language skills sometimes choked my expression, preventing me from engaging fully with the people I met, which meant I could only go so far in building relationships.

The more significant consequences of my language limitations became evident during interviews. I knew conducting interviews in Arabic would be challenging, but I insisted on doing it myself because I thought having a translator would interrupt the flow considerably and stifle my ability to connect with respondents. I attempted to manage this by preparing an Arabic translation of my interview guide and requesting patience from my interlocutors in the instances I might ask them to speak more slowly or provide extra clarification. This helped, and they graciously worked with me. Still, keeping up with these native speakers—let alone trying to stay ahead of them in conversation and steer the interview—at times proved an arduous task that required immense concentration and effort. That said, I believe that choosing not to use a translator was the correct decision; I do not think I would have gained as rich a data set otherwise. Fortunately, with practice, I had become a much more confident interviewer in Arabic by the end of my fieldwork.

While my indigenous status meant that I would be able to avoid the problem of culture shock, I discovered that due to my upbringing abroad, my knowledge of Egypt's norms and values was not as thorough as I had thought. I was also not immune from subculture shock. There were many instances when I found it difficult to assess what would be deemed appropriate behavior according to Egyptian standards, and so I erred on the conservative side. There were many spaces I initially avoided that were important meeting points for activists, such as Downtown open-air coffee shops (*ahawi*) that I assumed were considered to be masculine spaces and culturally inappropriate for women to frequent, but I later learned from activists that this was not entirely true. I was also not aware of certain etiquettes, such as those related to phone calls and making appointments. There were several activists whom I had tried for months to get an interview with. A friend told me that if I had been a "real" Egyptian, I would have gotten the interview a long time ago. What he meant was that my American restraint prevented me from calling repeatedly and pushing for a meeting, behavior that was customary in Egypt. Even after I had learned this, it was a very difficult practice for me to adopt. The shallowness of my cultural knowledge was especially noticeable when it came to popular and political culture. In my conversations with activists, I encountered many idioms and cultural references that eluded me, because I had not grown up watching Egyptian television or films or reading Arabic literature, for example. And I certainly was not up to speed on the latest urban slang or how to use it. This affected my ability to fully engage with Egyptian humor, the hallmark of Egyptian culture, and reciprocate it in my conversations, as I simply did not have the cultural repertoire to tap into; again, this affected my ability to build rapport. The gaps in my cultural knowledge also meant I had a steep learning curve when it came to getting caught up on all the political events and figures that were referenced during interviews and relevant to my research.

My limited cultural proficiency made me especially vulnerable in the field when I was trying to discover leading youth activists, as almost every group identified themselves as such or criticized others for making this claim. My inability as an American to figure Egyptians out quickly sometimes resulted in some very serious discomfort, confusion, and concern, as it meant I spent time with people I thought would be valuable for my research but whom I later learned to be unreliable sources. To manage this challenge, I learned to seek confirmation that what I had heard about potential research participants matched their reputation among their peers. In this way, I was able to ensure, before I interviewed someone, that there was relative consensus in the activist community that they were indeed legitimate activist leaders who fit my criteria and would benefit my study.

The revolutionary movement in Egypt attracted scholars and journalists from all over the world, most notably from the West and especially from the United States. Such attention had unforeseen implications for my research. First, there was the issue of competition for the attention of activists. Many of these researchers and journalists were, like me, on the trail of these potential informants, pleading for interviews. It was difficult enough to secure interviews with activists while they were still caught up in the revolutionary struggle; this competition certainly did not help. When I was finally able to interview them, many apologized for not giving me a meeting sooner and said they were burnt out from speaking to so many researchers and journalists.

Second, being new to field research, I was unaware of the power dynamics involved in knowledge creation across the Global North/South divide. I did not consider how the sudden influx of researchers from the West fascinated with the Arab Spring, the latest hot topic coming out of the developing world, might be perceived locally, especially among the academic community, and how this might affect my fieldwork. When planning my research, I only considered how my indigenous status would give me leverage over foreign fieldworkers. Admittedly, it had not occurred to me that there would be many more local scholars who were more qualified than I was to conduct research related to my topic of interest—and indeed, as I later learned, who already were. Though it is true that I was ethnically Egyptian and connected to the area not only through my heritage but through having lived there for some years, I was also an American who had lived most of my life in the United States and was trained by and affiliated with an American university, which meant I certainly was not local; I could not really claim to be studying my own society.

Starting to realize this upon my entry into the field, I felt myself recoil, self-conscious about my position and unclear about where I stood in the eyes of locals as a researcher across the global north/south divide. Already questioning my Egyptianness as a result of some of my disencounters in the field, I now began to question what right I had to enter this setting and announce my interest in a topic that I would discover local scholars had not only researched and written extensively about in Arabic, but had been intimately engaged with as activists.[5] I sensed from my unanswered requests for key informant interviews with local scholars, as well as some awkward moments with a few of those who agreed to meet me, that I was not the only one asking this question. I felt the need at these times to emphasize my connection to Egypt, but it did not seem to matter, given what felt like unforgivable gaps in my knowledge—a consequence of my foreign upbringing—that I sensed local informants might not have appreciated being asked to fill in. My unease was confirmed in an article by Mona Abaza, a professor at the American University in Cairo, which I came across while in Egypt. In it, she voiced her concern about the unequal relationship between so-called local experts and their colleagues in the West, who, as "tourist revolutionary academics" had "misused" them as service providers during their brief trips to Egypt, only to return home and benefit from their status as experts, while the region received no return for providing the services upon which their expertise was built.[6] I empathized with this position and resolved not to be included in this category: I committed to staying connected to the country after my research trip and producing knowledge that would benefit my research participants and their cause. Fortunately, I found that as time passed and I came into my Egyptianness more through my engagement with the activist community and revolutionary movement, my worry about being the target of these frustrations subsided, and my confidence in the unique perspectives I brought to this research topic as an insider–outsider and the contribution I could make as a result grew stronger.

Egypt in upheaval: challenges in the field

When I initially planned my research, I expected that it would be fairly easy to carry out in the three months I had allotted. And in normal circumstances, it probably would have been. But these were not normal circumstances, as it were: Egypt was in the throes of a revolution.

I was aware that the revolutionary movement was far from over before leaving the US for Egypt, but my impression (having failed to keep up with the news in the weeks before my departure because I was busy preparing for the trip) had been that despite the protesters' frustrations at the slow pace of change and the continued demonstrations they staged to voice their discontent, things were generally moving in the right direction, and a relative calm was returning to Egypt. I had no idea the climate was still so volatile. Even if I had known, I could not have fathomed what this meant, especially for my research, until I immersed myself in the field and experienced the revolution for myself.

Early on, before setting out for Cairo, I had considered how the ongoing development of this movement might affect my research. I knew that because the youth actors I hoped to recruit as research participants were probably still actively involved in the revolutionary movement, it was imperative that I stay focused on their engagement at its inception and avoid the epistemological pitfall of trying to make sense of their participation in current events. This was because, being unpredictable and having no clear end in sight, the revolutionary movement might take my research participants down unclear paths that I could not follow. Concentrating on the beginnings of the revolution would be critical, I told myself, if I wanted to complete my research in three months and avoid getting lost in the field indefinitely. But soon after I arrived, I started to realize there was much more to consider than I had anticipated.

First, there was the nature of the revolutionary movement itself. As I became more intimate with it, experiencing it up close in real time through my own participation as a protester and through my ethnographic study of the youth activists at its center, I would start to see it in all its glory: a marvelous, dizzying mess. Lacking a unified leadership steering its course, this monstrous, amorphous, living phenomenon called Egypt's revolution behaved erratically, creating an environment of immense instability, confusion, and insecurity. Its twists and turns were sudden and dramatic. At times they were even catastrophic, exposing those involved on the ground to grave danger and tragically taking lives. It was demanding, requiring its protagonists to stay alert and present, if not one step ahead in anxious anticipation of the opponents' next moves. Mechanically, it worked itself out in ebbs and flows, in fits and starts, delivering promising gains one day and defeating blows the next. It was intensely fluid and uncertain. This was the environment in which I had to carry out my fieldwork, this was my field site. Naturally, finding my footing on its shifting ground was an ongoing struggle.

This was also the turmoil my research participants were still deeply embroiled in. Their level of involvement in the struggle never changed. From the beginning, they fought on its front lines, and they continued to do so during my tenure in the field. The implications of this for my data collection process were many. The first was logistical and related to securing interviews with these activists. Being so inextricably tied to this fluid movement meant that these key interlocutors were extremely slippery and nearly impossible to obtain interviews with. As some of its main drivers, they were on call twenty-four hours a day, seven days a week, and when there was a sudden development, they were among the first to respond. Their schedules were as tentative as the revolutionary movement itself, and so were our appointments in them. As such, it was impossible to arrange meetings more than a day in advance. Moreover, it was not uncommon for me to schedule an interview with an activist only to have him or her cancel last-minute or fail to show up altogether without notice because some urgent matter related to their activism required their attention, or worse, a full-fledged crisis had suddenly arisen and snatched them away. When I was finally able to sit down with them, our meetings were often significantly delayed, frequently interrupted, terribly rushed, and/or suddenly cut short. It was always something: the sit-in in July that would last three weeks, the many Friday protests, the several violent clashes that erupted between protesters and soldiers, the Mubarak trial, the Israeli embassy protests, and of course, the month of Ramadan brought its own scheduling challenges. (Sure, some appeared to generally lack discipline in keeping their commitments, but the revolutionary environment certainly did not help.) Eventually I stopped trying to schedule interviews because the timing was never right. I waited, hoping things would let up, but they never did. The result: one week before my scheduled return to the US, I had only managed to conduct four interviews, three of which were incomplete.

I decided to stay longer and try harder to adapt. I realized there was no competing with the revolution for my research participants' attention: the revolution was the priority, and I had to learn to accept this—embrace this—and work with it as best I could. I saw that I would get nowhere trying to wait its upheavals out from a distance; I had to take the plunge and learn to negotiate with its dynamics and find openings from within. I realized I had to stop passively competing with it and instead try actively engaging with it. So I inserted myself in the movement's center, where my participants were located, joining them regularly at actions, events, and meetings, where I was able to build the rapport that facilitated my easier access to them. Now regularly in closer proximity to them, I also learned how to take advantage of their intermittent availability during the sporadic peaks and lulls of the movement. When there was a lull, I rushed to capture them for impromptu interviews. When there was a peak, such as a major disruption in Tahrir, I tracked them down in the field and accompanied them as a participant and/or observer whenever they would allow me to do so.

I did not expect to gain much from these observations for my immediate research because my focus was on a period that had long passed, but I decided it was better than nothing. And yet, this turned out to be one of my best decisions. As challenging as it was to keep up with these activists in this capacity, I was provided with amazing, unexpected opportunities to observe processes that would give me insight into my research participants and their early involvement in this movement. During the spontaneous eruptions in Tahrir Square in late November, for example, which many likened to January 25 in mood, spirit, and fragility, I was able to attend several late-night organizing meetings with youth activists which, I later learned from my interviews, resembled their meetings in the early days of the revolution. They were trying to figure out how to keep the momentum in the square and capitalize on the new explosion of popular energy across Egypt's other cities to secure gains for the revolution. I had not initially incorporated participant observation into my research methods because I was limiting my inquiry to the leadership and organizing processes activists had engaged in during the first eighteen days of this movement. I could not have anticipated that history would repeat itself and the activists would find themselves engaging in this process once again, and that I would have the chance to observe them, having missed the opportunity in January. This was perhaps the single most unexpected reward of conducting research in this environment.

Nonetheless, my adjustments and accommodations were not enough. Despite extending my stay twice so that it doubled from three to six months, I was still unable to get all the interviews I had hoped for. The harder I tried, the more the revolution seemed to quicken its pace, challenging me to keep up. The upheavals became increasingly frequent, explosive, and destabilizing.[7] I simply could not accomplish all that I had set out to do. The revolution would not let me.

Aside from the logistical challenge of trying to identify and enlist the right activists to participate in my research, this persistently turbulent movement presented me with another challenge: how to maintain my project's focus and relevance in this ever-evolving climate and how to convince potential interviewees that it was worth their time and attention. Much had happened since the eighteen-day uprising in January 2011, which was the real focus of my study, and things would continue to develop after my arrival later that June. With each of these developments, some of them extremely frustrating if not downright tragic, those early eighteen days seemed to change in significance for the activists I interviewed, taking on different constructions and meanings for them as they looked back and viewed them through the lens of recent events. This continuous reconstruction and reinterpretation of the past is something I had to contend with when I was recruiting participants and conducting interviews. Sally Tomah, for example, whom I pursued for an interview for nearly five months, agreed to meet several times, asking me to wait until things let up, but in the end, she declined to take part. Being so mired in the current political struggle and emotionally exhausted from the slow pace of change, she struggled to appreciate the significance of their work during the early eighteen days in this later moment. She said she was tired of talking about that time when "we didn't really accomplish shit." For those activists I was able to secure interviews with, although my plan had been to limit my discussion with them to the eighteen days, I realized I had to negotiate a space for recent events in my interviews, as their impact on the activists and their perception of themselves and their work was impossible to ignore. For example, I could not ignore the fact that a few days before I interviewed one activist, he had just buried his comrade, Mina Daniel, who had been killed by the army along with other Copts in what has been called the Maspero Massacre. The event confirmed for him and the other activists I interviewed that the army was not acting in the interests of the revolution, as it had claimed to be doing on February 11, but was in fact its main opponent. Events like Maspero were constantly spinning the very meaning of the eighteen days in the minds of my informants. Nor could I ignore the fact that another activist I was preparing to interview had just decided to run in the parliamentary elections, a significant step in his political trajectory and an outcome of his involvement since the eighteen-day uprising. These experiences were all connected in the present and would continuously color and shape each other and the activists' memory of them. Essentially, what I had become caught up in by virtue of the timing of my study is the dialectic between ontology and epistemology in action.

I kept trying to adapt by adjusting my interview protocol, making room for new developments as they unfolded, while tailoring my questions to each activist. Even so, the process was further complicated by the fact that I conducted most of my interviews over two or three sessions that were days if not weeks and even months apart. Between one session and the next, something could have happened to change my respondents' recollection of and feelings about the eighteen days quite significantly.

Lastly, in an environment as intense and unpredictably volatile as this one, safety was an important consideration. As an Egyptian who sympathized deeply with this movement, I wanted to be at every action, supporting the cause. As a researcher, this would also prove useful, as fuller immersion meant I might establish a new connection, learn something new, or gain a new insight. As a woman, however, I had to be particularly cautious; one of the many disturbing side effects of these chaotic times was the rise in sexual harassment and assault on women. Not only had this become an alarming, growing trend among men who took advantage of the deteriorating security situation to have a good time, but even more disturbingly, it was the method of choice used by police and regime-hired thugs to intimidate women protesters. Fortunately, I never fell victim to this kind of gender-based violence, but I regularly heard about other women's traumatic experiences and was constantly on guard as a result.

My status as a foreign, Western researcher also put me at some risk in this environment. In an attempt to discredit the revolution and turn ordinary Egyptians against it, counterrevolutionary forces manipulated Egyptians' deep, historic mistrust of foreigners and whipped up a campaign that peddled the movement as a plot by foreign agents conspiring to destabilize Egypt for their own interests. The campaign succeeded in creating an environment of suspicion and distrust of foreigners, especially those engaged in civil society and human rights work, and by extension, journalists and researchers.[8]

In fact, the introduction of the colloquial term *agendawi*—that is, someone with an agenda—into the Egyptian revolutionary lexicon reflects how conspicuous and widespread this fear was. I was initially blind to this aspect of my position in the field, thinking that my obvious appearance and identification as an Egyptian protected me from such associations. However, a few anxiety-inducing encounters during my early fieldwork with seemingly ordinary protesters in Tahrir—who could very well have been regime supporters and not opponents, as I had assumed—made me aware of my naiveté. I realized my Egyptianness did not protect me from being seen as an outsider with an agenda. The combination of my non-native sounding, less-than-fluent Arabic and, in particular, my affiliation with a foreign academic institution had betrayed me. The suspicion my affiliation seemed to raise among the protesters to whom I disclosed it left me feeling disquieted, and I became much more cautious when it came to divulging my identity and work as a researcher.

During my time in the field, I had to keep reminding myself that I was there to conduct research; my purpose was to document processes, which I could not do if I exposed myself to major risk. I had an obligation to return to my family and academic community, safe and sound, with quality data in hand. In this respect, safety presented itself as a logistical issue that I had to manage carefully in order to carry out my original objective. This was easy to do in the beginning, when I was still relatively distant and detached from the movement. But as I became increasingly immersed in it and intimate with the revolutionaries at its center, my concern for my safety and reluctance to participate alongside them in riskier protests and actions became a source of inner conflict for me. There were several moments when I felt that as an Egyptian, I should behave more like the revolutionaries who put their bodies on the line for a cause they believed to be greater than themselves, one for which many died, and yet I could not. There was more to my desire to stay safe, I realized, than trying to be a responsible researcher or an ordinary person who naturally wanted to stay out of harm's way; it was another manifestation of the detachment I still felt as an Egyptian born and raised in the United States. I admired my peers' level of devotion to our common ancestral homeland, but I did not share it. Part of me regretted that I did not know what it felt like to feel so invested and attached to this country

Figure 1. Graffiti art from early 2012 memorializing revolutionary icon Shaykh Emad Effat, who was martyred during the Cabinet clashes in late 2011. The Quranic verses read: *"And they will say, 'Our Lord! We obeyed our leaders and notables, and they led us astray. Our Lord! Give them double their share of torment and curse them a mighty curse'"* (33:67–68). Like all the other revolutionary murals in Cairo, this one has since been effaced by the state. Photograph by Rahma Esther Bavelaar.

that I would be willing to risk my life for it. And yet, I also appreciated the unique experience of solidarity my dual identity provided me. It was surreal, during the Muhammad Mahmud clashes in November, to receive an approving nod from new acquaintances in Tahrir when they learned I was a student at UC Davis, which had just made international headlines for a police pepper-spraying incident during an Occupy Movement sit-in; almost a year earlier, during the eighteen-day uprising, I had been greeted with the same gesture on campus when new acquaintances there learned of my connection to Egypt.[9]

As time passed, I began to notice that my immersion in the revolution transformed my level of investment in it, and by extension, my sense of self as an Egyptian and an American. Though I felt distant from the movement both when I first encountered it and when I later decided not to take part as a revolutionary, by the end of my fieldwork I had become very intensely connected to it. I was particularly affected by the martyrdom of the Azhari scholar Shaykh Emad Effat (see figure 1). I knew him from my previous stint in Cairo in the early 2000s; he taught a classical Arabic grammar class in Nasr City that I had the privilege of attending. I was pleasantly surprised to see him regularly in the square during protests, wearing regular clothes instead of his clerical garbs and often accompanied by his children. Had it not been for his kind smile and more particularly, his elegant gait, I might not have recognized him; he walked through Tahrir just as gracefully as I remembered him walking through the courtyards of Islamic Cairo's old mosques. His assassination on December 17 during the Cabinet clashes drew me into the movement in a new way, emotionally and spiritually. Suddenly the revolution was much more personal, and my passionate participation no longer felt performative. My subjectivity as a Muslim and a woman was also changing as a result of the dynamic and often unsettling processes I was subjected to as a researcher and analyst of contemporaneous societal changes. Through my own engagement with the revolution, I began to witness in myself the very kind of transformations I was interested in observing in my study participants, in my demeanor and my attitudes related to class, gender, and religion, for example. In many ways, I became an extension of my own research.

Activist Representation

I spent six months conducting my fieldwork, from June 24 through December 21, 2011. My primary method for data collection was face-to-face, semi-structured in-depth interviews with youth activists and key informants, recruited through convenience contacts and snowball sampling. Later, my methods evolved to include field notes, as my immersion in the revolutionary movement provided me with more and more unexpected opportunities for participant observation. I also conducted a series of follow-up interviews long-distance via Skype in late 2013 and early 2014 (see chapter 7). Interviews focused on narrative, and participants were invited to share their life stories as they related to becoming activists. They were also invited to share their personal accounts of the unfolding of the revolution from January 25 through to the time of our interviews, with special attention to the leadership processes they had engaged in as well as their personal transformations throughout this period.

I interviewed twenty-five activists, most of whom were leaders or active members of the various youth movements and youth factions of political parties that made up the RYC, which announced itself in Tahrir Square twelve days after the start of the uprising in January 2011. Briefly, the organizations included: (1) the April 6 Youth Movement, a pragmatic protest movement based on a Facebook network that emerged in 2008 in solidarity with striking laborers in Mahalla factories; (2) the Youth for Justice and Freedom Movement (Harakat Shabab min agl al-Adala wa-l-Hurriya), a dynamic, leftist youth protest movement that grew out of the April 6 Youth Movement; (3) the Popular Campaign Supporting ElBaradei (al-Hamla al-Sha'biya li Da'm al-Barad'i), henceforth referred to as the ElBaradei Campaign, a group that had gathered around Mohamed ElBaradei, former head of the International Atomic Energy Agency (IAEA) in Vienna, and attracted a number of disenfranchised youth in the years before the revolt around its general call for reform; (4) youth activists from the Muslim Brotherhood (al-Ikhwan al-Muslimin), Egypt's largest Islamist movement as well as the oldest and most organized opposition group; and (5) representatives from the various youth factions of the existing political parties—such as the Democratic Front Party (Hizb al-Gabha al-Wataniya), the Unionist Party (Hizb al-Tagammu'), and the Dignity Party (Hizb al-Karama)—as well as several politically independent youth activists. (For more on my interviews and complete data set, see the appendix.)

Although there were other groups I could have focused on or incorporated into my study, I decided to settle on the activists from the RYC for several reasons. First, I learned during my fieldwork that several of the groups under its umbrella were among the most active on the ground in the years preceding the revolution, with bases in Cairo and branches all over Egypt. Together, they strategized for January 25 and continued to help drive the revolutionary movement that ensued, especially as it unfolded in Tahrir Square and Cairo, the movement's ground zero. The effort of these youth activists before and during the uprising was significant, which made them appropriate candidates for investigating youth leadership processes in the revolution. Second, I was interested in interviewing activists who reflected the diversity of youth leadership in the square in terms of class, gender, religion, and political ideologies. I was especially keen on securing interviews with female and Christian activists, who appeared to be a minority in these circles. The leading activists in the RYC were diverse in terms of these variables and as such were a fitting group to focus on.

Lastly, it must be said that I decided to focus on activists from the RYC for the sake of convenience. I made many attempts early on to obtain interviews with activists from other important groups that took part in organizing January 25, like the Revolutionary Socialists and the administrators of the We Are All Khaled Said Facebook page, but my requests went unanswered.[10] Moreover, I was not fixed on seeking a representative sample of youth activists for my study, as my purpose was never to generalize as one would with a statistically representative quantitative study, but to analyze and gain qualitative insight into the dynamics, determinants, and effects of youth leadership in the revolutionary movement. I wanted to learn how this experience could be explained in light of existing theories. As such, I felt that seeing these processes through the eyes of the activists from the RYC was sufficient for my project; and given how difficult it was to find the right activists to interview and secure their participation in my project in this environment, I decided not to expand my sample, as gaining entrée into a wider set of organizations in the network of revolutionaries would have required additional time and logistical effort that I could not afford.

As robust as my data set is, it is important to note what is missing. There is little representation of leading women activists in this study and no representation of Christians. This is simply because there were very few that fit my sampling criteria in terms of playing an active leadership role in organizing for January 25, and those who did, like Sally Tomah (who happened to be both a woman and a Christian), were very difficult to access for interviews.[11] Most of the formal leaders of the movements who made up the RYC's executive committee, for example, were Muslim or secular males. Even outside of the RYC, the Christian and women youth activists I was introduced to did not act in a visible leadership capacity as organizers, and few of them appeared to have a history of organized activism before the revolution. Nonetheless, I was able to secure extensive interviews with Ola Shahba, another important female activist, along with several interviews with other women activists from the movements under the RYC umbrella, all of whom provided me with interesting insights into the gender dynamics among the formal leadership. Their perspective complements that of male activists who shared with me their views on gender relations in the movement.

Something must also be said about the age of my respondents and my reason for including older activists like the forty-two-year-old Basem Kamel as youth leaders. I decided to include Basem in my sample because he was a key member of the RYC and because I was repeatedly advised by other youth activists in Tahrir to speak to him. Since his younger peers clearly viewed him as a youth like themselves (albeit more of a senior, mentor figure at times) and he largely identified as such, especially in the context of the revolution, it was necessary for me to reflect this in my study. Stated differently, because my goal was to capture what it meant to be a politically active youth leader in Egypt in this moment of revolution and upheaval, I had to account for the broad understanding of what it meant to be a youth leader in the minds of my research participants during this period. After all, youth, as suggested in the previous chapter, is not simply a chronological status but rather a social construct similar to other constructs used to represent social classification or stratification, like race, class, and gender, in that it is based on the consensual understanding between actors within a given cultural context. Failing to take it as such would make my study unsound by imposing a Western understanding of youth and missing a fundamental structural dimension of the movement. In any case, in Arab culture, as mentioned earlier, one is typically considered a youth up until the age of forty. I believe the fact that Basem was close to this age in January 2011 is sufficient justification for including his narrative. The same is true of Mohammed Al-Qassas, one of my other respondents, who was thirty-seven when the January 25 protests erupted.

For the sake of efficiency, I have organized this book around the narratives of ten of the twenty-five activists I interviewed, whose real names are used with their permission and encouragement.[40] Not only are these some of my strongest interviews, but they are also some of the most illustrative in terms of the diversity of activist backgrounds and experiences before and during the revolution. But before introducing these activists and their stories, it is important first to understand the larger historical context that shaped them and gave rise to their movement.

2
The Contract Collapses

The youth-led protests that ignited Egypt's streets in 2011 were not fueled just by bitterness toward an unyielding dictator and his rapacious cronies, but by a rejection of the entire political and socioeconomic order forged through three successive regimes over six decades. Ironically, this oppressive arrangement had emerged from a moment of national hope and renewal in the early 1950s, when Egypt freed itself from the control of a corrupt monarchy, shook off the grip of British subjugation, and began to reinvent itself as a modern republic. Energizing this leap forward was a tacit social contract between the new republic's founding military elite, led by the charismatic Gamal Abdel Nasser, and the civilian masses they would soon rule over. The terms of the agreement were simple: in exchange for the people's obedience and forfeiture of their political rights, the regime would provide them with a strong state, social welfare, and a shot at prosperity for them and their children. But as time passed, the state reneged on its end of the deal. By 2011 Egyptians found themselves in the grasp of a highly militarized, neoliberal, authoritarian police state that left them with neither social protections nor democratic inroads into the political process whereby they could effect change. The contract was void. As government incompetence and corruption grew along with its neglect and abuses, so too did the people's anger and resentment until they collectively erupted onto the streets in a sudden and stunning display of defiance.

Focusing on the country's recent history, this chapter traces the breakdown of the unspoken pact between the Egyptian state and its citizens, highlighting the key political, economic, and social developments and lightning-rod issues that finally drove the masses to rebel. It describes the ten years of resistance that gave way to the popular revolt and the factors that shaped the emergence of youth as leaders at its forefront. This context is key to understanding the revolutionary uprising and its aftermath, discussed later in this book.

The Third Regime and Its Antecedents

When Egypt's youth took to the streets in 2011, they were revolting against the only leader most of them had ever known. Hosni Mubarak, Egypt's longest-serving president, was catapulted to power thirty years earlier—not by the people's choice, but by a bullet. Appointed vice president by Anwar Sadat in 1975, he became head of state in 1981 after Sadat's assassination and would continue his controversial legacy. Indeed, the story behind the historic 2011 revolution begins not with Mubarak, but with his predecessor, whose domestic and foreign policies broke radically from Nasser's and set the agenda for the republic's third regime under the leader who would be deposed by his people.

Though Nasser's state-guided development project, initiated in the 1950s, improved the lives of millions of Egyptians by providing them with education, state employment, health care, and subsidized goods and services, it ultimately failed to deliver on the promise of economic prosperity.[1] By the time Sadat came to power in 1970, the welfare state—with its large and inefficient public sector, vast and inert bureaucracy, and extensive system of subsidies—had proven unsustainable.[2] Moreover, the pressures of a growing population combined with excessive military spending and the heavy financial costs of war with Israel following the bitter 1967 defeat had mired Egypt in an intractable economic crisis that challenged the new president.[3] As Sadat saw it, the state-dominated economy was incapable of mobilizing the resources Egypt desperately needed for an economic recovery. His success in recovering the lost Sinai territories from Israel in the battle on October 6, 1973 known as "The Crossing" emboldened him to make his dramatic break from Nasser on domestic and foreign policy and launch his own socioeconomic program for Egypt. In 1974, he launched the policy known as *al-infitah* (the opening), which opened up the country to domestic and foreign investment and set Egypt's economic liberalization—and the circumstances that led to the 2011 revolution—in full motion.

Sadat's move to integrate Egypt's economy through the *infitah* into the Western capitalist system was part of his effort to align Egypt geopolitically with the United States instead of Russia, which had since the Suez crisis of 1956 been Egypt's superpower patron and guarantor of regime stability.[4] It was carried out alongside a limited political opening to bring Egypt into closer alignment with American democratic sensibilities in an attempt to secure US backing.[5] Sadat calculated that an alignment with the United States would pay dividends for Egypt in the form of economic aid and investment and the recovery of the Sinai territory lost to Israel in the 1967 war.[6] The United States obliged, but made aid contingent on peace with Israel. The deal was sealed with the controversial Camp David Accords in 1979, to the outrage of Arabs across the region, who saw it as a betrayal of the Palestinian and Arab Nationalist causes championed by Nasser. Henceforth, aid would flow into Egypt and subordinate the country to American foreign policy and economic objectives, with deleterious consequences for the Egyptian masses.[7]

Following Sadat's lead, Mubarak took Egypt's economic dependency on the United States to new levels, straying radically from the promise of a strong, sovereign nation that was core to Nasser's pact with the public. Mubarak maintained Sadat's peace agreement with Israel and developed the strategic relationship the late president had forged with the United States into a full-fledged military alliance. In exchange for Egypt's critical help in maintaining US interests in the region, Washington gave its client state $1.3 billion in military aid and hundreds of millions more in economic aid through its USAID program every year for the rest of Mubarak's tenure.[8] Those interests included facilitating the uninterrupted flow of oil from the Middle East to the United States, protecting Israel's security, and generally ensuring that US hegemony in the region went unrivaled.

Over the years, Egyptians would grow increasingly hostile to this arrangement.[9] In practice, it prevented the country from living up to its historic self-conception as the avowed defender of Palestinian and Arab interests. By forfeiting Egypt's geostrategic power and military leverage to the United States, the regime was seen as not only sacrificing defenseless Palestinians, but becoming complicit in their subjugation and the region's increasing vulnerability to Israel.[10] Mubarak's alignment with the United States on foreign policy issues undermined his legitimacy in the eyes of the Egyptian public; indeed, the view that he was a tool for US imperialism played a significant role in his 2011 ouster. But as problematic as Mubarak's foreign policies were for many Egyptians, it was the intolerable economic and political circumstances at home, shaped in large part by the conditions and constraints that came with US sponsorship and private investment, that were the main drivers of the January 25 revolt.

Continuing the economic trends set in motion by Sadat's *infitah*, Mubarak accelerated Egypt's neoliberal transformation and presided over the final obliteration of the Nasserite social contract. As alluded to earlier, the goal behind the *infitah* was to open up the country to foreign investment and build up a vibrant private sector as a means of ushering Egypt into a new period of prosperity. It was touted as the solution to Egypt's economic woes, but in reality it only exacerbated them as it widened social disparities. The *infitah* created a crony capitalist class out of those who exploited their proximity to power to cash in on the rewards of the rapid and unregulated economic transformation. At the same time, it eroded the socioeconomic standing of the millions of Egyptians who had risen into the middle class under Nasser's populist policies, with many falling back into poverty as safety nets were scaled back, government jobs were reduced, welfare services were increasingly privatized, and soaring inflation depressed wages and living standards.[11] To the public, the government appeared to be reneging on its vow to establish equality and social justice—the vow that had formed the basis of the people's original consent to be ruled and had underpinned the regime's legitimacy.[12] Egyptians grew increasingly bitter toward the country's leadership for renouncing its solidarity with the poor to become allied with the rich, and they made their discontent known. The simmering anger produced by the *infitah* boiled over in January 1977, when Sadat dramatically slashed food subsidies under International Monetary Fund (IMF) prescriptions to reduce mounting external debt. The initiative was met with explosive bread riots across Egypt that forced him to quickly abandon course. But Egyptians continued to struggle under Sadat, and anger against him continued to mount. The culmination of this was his assassination four years after the riots following another unpopular move: his decision to sign the peace deal with Israel. The economic challenges he left his successor to deal with were daunting.

Indeed, Egypt's financial troubles persisted and grew into a full-blown crisis under Mubarak. In 1991, crippling national debt forced the president, under intense US pressure, to concede to a series of structural adjustment reforms to secure debt relief and the flow of credit from the IMF and World Bank. Under these new terms, the government was required to further cut spending on social services and subsidies, privatize and deregulate public sector enterprises, relax price controls, and liberalize foreign trade.[13] To be sure, the changes led to significant economic growth, but the impact on the masses was devastating. Between the mid-1990s and mid-2000s, these policies translated into a dramatic increase in inflation and cost of living, insufficient wages, a steep rise in unemployment, and burdensome education and health-care costs.¹⁴ State employment opportunities dried up; between 1994 and 2001, the number of public sector employees dropped by half.¹⁵ The rate of poverty skyrocketed, with the number of Egyptians living on less than $2 a day estimated to be as high as 40 percent on the eve of the 2011 revolution.¹⁶

Meanwhile, the same changes that impoverished wide segments of the population further enriched the elite at their expense. Over the years, the people witnessed their nation's resources being systematically pillaged by regime allies, business tycoons, and families intimate with the regime while they were left to suffer. This exploitation was epitomized in the regime's aggressive privatization efforts in the mid-2000s, when public services, like health care and education, started to fall under the control of the business class and major state assets, like steel factories and energy plants, increasingly passed into the ownership of the well-connected for a shockingly small fraction of their true value. The staggering inequality generated by neoliberalism under Mubarak was especially visible in the contrast between the luxury residences and glittering gated neighborhoods that were home to Cairo's fabulously rich and the ramshackle dwellings and overcrowded quarters of the city's desperately poor. This widening class divide brewed palpable resentment among Egypt's disenfranchised and underprivileged. There was a growing sense under Mubarak that the relationship between the state and its citizens was being permanently restructured to the violent exclusion of the latter. With government indifference to their plight and no social protections to secure their loyalty, middle- and lower-class Egyptians felt increasingly less beholden to the state and were being primed for revolt.

Exacerbating the socioeconomic grievances of Egyptians under Mubarak was the fact that they were denied recourse to formal political avenues through which to seek redress. Indeed, as the economic situation turned alarmingly bleak, so too did the political conditions. Mubarak built on his predecessors' legacy of authoritarianism, despite auspicious signs early in his presidency which suggested that he might expand on Sadat's limited democratic reforms and move the country toward liberal politics. When he became president, Mubarak relaxed government restrictions on activism, released political prisoners, permitted the press more freedom to criticize government officials (though he remained off-limits), and presided over the expansion of civil society. Non-governmental organizations (NGOs) multiplied and professional syndicates found the space to call for political change. Mubarak maintained the multiparty system introduced by Sadat and allowed it some room to thrive, if only for a short period. Combined with changes made to election laws, this gave rise to an active opposition whose persistent calls for democratic reform resulted in small policy changes that enabled it to achieve increasing representation in Parliament.[17] But it soon became clear that genuine democratization was not on the Mubarak agenda. This is because these political openings—as unprecedented and promising as they were—were simultaneously limited and undermined by authoritarian strictures that Mubarak carried over from previous regimes and developed further.[18]

Mubarak continued to hold the extensive executive powers he had inherited from Nasser and Sadat and proceeded to expand them in his quest to consolidate one-man rule. Immediately after ascending to power, he reinstated the draconian Emergency Law that Sadat had lifted shortly before his assassination—a law that would remain in effect through 2011 and ultimately provoke the youth-led uprising—and used it to suspend the constitutional rights of citizens in his battle against militant Islamists. This law allowed the state to apply restrictions on the freedoms of expression and assembly, which not only undermined Islamists, but other opposition forces seeking to engage in legitimate political activity.[19] It also permitted the detention of civilians indefinitely without charge and their trial before military courts. He also expanded police powers, developing the security apparatus created by Nasser and extended by Sadat into a brutally effective security system that targeted civilians. By the late 1980s, Mubarak felt threatened by the power and influence—however limited—his opponents had succeeded in gaining as a result of his earlier liberalizing reforms; it was time to contain them. He did this through legislative means, such as devising constitutional amendments that guaranteed election victories to the ruling National Democratic Party (NDP), as well as coercion, brutally cracking down on opponents across the spectrum and the Islamists in particular.[20]

Islamists emerged as the biggest challenge to the Mubarak regime in the late 1980s and 1990s and were the main target of his repressive efforts. One such target was al-Gama'a al-Islamiya, a militant Islamist group that was a radical offshoot of the moderate Muslim Brotherhood, the organization founded in 1928 in the Suez Canal town of Ismailiya by schoolteacher Hassan al-Banna. The Gama'a launched a furious insurgency against the regime and counted government officials, police, foreign tourists, and Egyptian bystanders among its 1,200 victims. Its violent campaign climaxed in 1997 with a grisly attack on tourists at the Temple of Hatshepsut in Luxor that took the lives of seventy-one people.[21] The regime's response was ruthless and fierce, marking a turning point in the evolution of the police state. Indiscriminate mass arrests and widespread use of torture, much more pervasive and extreme than under Nasser or Sadat, became a defining feature of Mubarak's security policy and would later constitute one of the many grievances that drove the 2011 revolt.[22]

The other Islamist threat to the regime came from the Muslim Brotherhood itself, which by the late 1980s had become the most powerful opposition in the country. This was partly a result of the latitude the regime gave the organization in the hope that it might offset the influence of radical Islamists, and it was partly a result of the organization's decision to participate in democratic politics. Even though the Brotherhood remained officially outlawed—a status it had held since the time of Nasser—it was allowed to run candidates in parliamentary elections starting in 1984 under other party tickets, and it managed to win significant representation as the largest opposition. The movement made major inroads into civic organizations too—namely, university student unions and professional associations, where they repeatedly swept the elections. Their influence was felt in the lawyers', journalists', doctors', and engineers' syndicates, for instance, which they dominated for much of the 1990s.[23] Mubarak had intentionally allowed the Brotherhood to seep into Parliament and gain control of these academic and professional bodies, believing this would facilitate their integration into his authoritarian system. But the extent of their victories alarmed him because it implied that the Brotherhood was positioning itself to challenge the regime as legitimate representative of the middle class.[24] It did not help that, emboldened by their increasing power, they used these forums to criticize the regime.[25]

But perhaps the greater challenge the Brotherhood posed to the state came in the form of its extensive social services network, which gave targeted support to the poor in neglected neighborhoods and villages across Egypt. Charitable work was not new to the Brotherhood; it had been central to its outreach and activism since its founding "and served as a way to demonstrate its communitarianism and ideological commitment to alleviating poverty and lessening inequality."[26] The Brotherhood ran schools; food distribution centers; transportation services; orphanages; programs for widows; and hospitals, where they offered more affordable and higher quality health care than the state. At a time when the government's public services were receding as a result of the economic crisis prompted by the *infitah*, these Brotherhood services were regarded as critical to public welfare.

This was problematic for the state insofar as it highlighted the government's failure to deliver its obligations under the social contract and attend to the needs of its citizens. Meanwhile, the Brotherhood's largesse strengthened its claim to legitimacy, allowing it to nurture a massive grassroots support base of those who relied on its services. Combined with its parliamentary gains and sway over civic institutions, the Brotherhood's social positioning as the public's alternative provider amounted to a direct challenge to the authority of the state that by the mid-1990s Mubarak could no longer tolerate.[27] The president reacted by extending his mighty crackdown on the Gama'a insurgents to the Brothers, even though the group had long renounced and disengaged from violence.[28] Several of the youth leaders featured in this study were among those who experienced this crackdown, either directly or indirectly through the experience of family and friends.

Most Egyptians initially embraced the state's war against militant Islamists like the Gama'a, seeing them as a destructive, perilous force with no basis in religion.[29] Their violent rampage did not just challenge state authority, but threatened Egypt's stability and the security of its citizens.[30] With a mandate from the people to eradicate the militants, Mubarak grew his security apparatus and surveillance operation exponentially during this time to become a pervasive and domineering force in society. The massive policing was not so much about keeping Egyptians safe, which was the official justification, but about preserving the neoliberal state and keeping the regime and its capitalist elite in power.[31] Authoritarian repression was a necessary function of the neoliberal order, designed to keep opponents of this system at bay and its victims suppressed.[32] The victims of this heavy securitization were not just radical Islamists, but anyone who dared to oppose the regime. Tens of thousands of dissidents across the political spectrum were jailed and tortured. Chilling stories began to circulate of prisoners being electrocuted and sodomized during interrogations. Phones were tapped, and anyone who was remotely suspect was monitored. Public protests were forbidden; those that did occur were met with harsh force. Strikers were confronted with live ammunition. Trade unions were neutered, NGOs and mosques were raided, and security forces became a growing presence on university campuses and Egypt's streets. By 1998, Mubarak had successfully stamped out the extremist insurgency to the people's applause, but at a steep cost to the public; in the words of journalist Hossam El-Hamalawy, "Mubarak's iron-fist rule and the outbreak of the dirty war between the regime and Islamist militants . . . meant the death of street dissent."[33]

The Resistance Before the Revolt

The regime's war against militant Islamists had all but silenced the street until regional conflicts in the early 2000s stirred the public again, giving rise to several waves of resistance that continued to grow in strength and momentum. The sight of protest became normalized for the public as activists developed new tactics and mobilizing frames to challenge the regime and draw larger segments of the population into street politics.[34] With each act of resistance, opposition forces chipped away at Mubarak's domestic power base as they focused public attention on the broken social contract and intensified their call for change.

The Palestinian uprising of 2000, known as the Second Intifada, brought Egyptians in the tens of thousands out in peaceful protest, the largest public outcry since the Bread Riots of 1977. In expressing solidarity with Palestinians, Egyptian demonstrators began to speak out publicly against the regime as they criticized Mubarak's relations with Israel and his unwillingness to intervene on their fellow Arabs' behalf. The Intifada demonstrations were followed by even larger protests in 2003 in reaction to the US invasion of Iraq. The regime had actually permitted the historic anti-war protests on March 20, reasoning that allowing Egyptians some room to vent their anger at the United States would help contain popular outrage and even win the president public approval. But this was a major miscalculation. The protesters did rail against the United States as expected, but they also openly criticized the regime for enabling US aggression. It made no difference to the protesters that Mubarak had advised the Bush administration against going to war; in their eyes, he was implicated in the crime by virtue of allowing American warships to pass through the Suez Canal and refusing to leverage Egypt's power and influence to stop US imperial exploits. What began as demonstrations against US and Israeli policies developed into protests against the Egyptian regime that challenged its legitimacy. The other unintended effect was subtle but critical: the astonishing turnout showed Egyptians that they had the capacity to generate the kind of people power needed for a potential revolutionary challenge to the state. These watershed demonstrations revived street dissent and initiated ten years of resistance through which Egyptians gradually overcame their fear and gained the confidence to take on the regime directly.[35] Crucially, the Palestinian Intifada and the invasion of Iraq were responsible for politicizing and radicalizing a new generation of Egyptian youth, including the architects of the January 25 uprising who are the focus of this book.

A slew of protest movements was born of these events, resuscitating the country's culture of political resistance. Veteran activists who had cut their teeth on the student movement in the 1960s and 1970s formed the Popular Committees Supporting the Intifada, which introduced scores of newly politicized youth to activism. The horizontal, loosely structured movement worked across Egypt to raise awareness and support for the Palestinian cause, organizing protests, collecting donations, arranging aid convoys, and calling for the boycott of American and Israeli goods.[36] Building on this effort was the annual Cairo Anti-war Conference first held in 2002. The event was remarkable for convening hundreds of intellectuals, human rights workers, journalists, unionists, artists, and activists of all ideological stripes, including secular and Islamist groups locked in long-standing political feuds. Connections and alliances were forged around common grievances as participants discussed platforms and strategies for resisting predatory US policies in the region.

Out of this common ground and creative energy grew Kefaya (Enough!), a game-changing movement that emerged in 2004 and set a new precedent for collective action and political dissent. Whereas the previous initiatives organized around regional developments outside of Egypt, Kefaya turned inward to demand democratic reform and a new social contract based on political freedoms. The coalition that coalesced under the Kefaya banner included communists, socialists, Islamists, liberals, Nasserists, and independents who put aside their political differences to work for shared goals. These figures had been actively calling for political reform since the 1970s, but they had been largely ineffective because they worked separately.[37] They had also been constrained by the domestic fight against militant Islamists, which the regime and its US backers prioritized over local democratic reforms.

But things changed with the Al-Qaeda attacks of September 11, 2001, when the United States started to realize that turning a blind eye to authoritarianism in Egypt (home to one of the leading hijackers), which had previously served US security interests, was no longer a tenable policy; it was time to press Cairo to implement democratic reforms.[38] Kefaya exploited the political space pried open by Washington's pressure to launch a sharp and brave critique of Mubarak, his family, and the authoritarian status quo. It advocated for constitutional and democratic reform, shattering all kinds of taboos as its proponents cried out against corruption and repression, the merger of power and wealth, the utter disregard for human rights, and the regime's cooperation with the United States and Israel. But the movement's most immediate concern and the impetus behind its crystallization was that it became increasingly clear that the aging Mubarak intended to hand off the presidency to his second son Gamal in the upcoming presidential election. It was ironic, in light of the country's recent political history: under Mubarak, the republic seemed to be regressing toward a monarchy, the abolition of which had constituted the very basis of the social contract.

By 2002, Gamal Mubarak, the investment banker-turned-politician, had risen, with his father's help, within the ruling NDP to become one of its most powerful figures. As the leading force behind Egypt's economic neoliberalization, Gamal and his shady business associates—many of whom would ascend to ministerial posts responsible for portfolios linked to their own private interests—enriched themselves at the public's expense, selling off state land and public entities as part of their aggressive and thoroughly corrupt privatization scheme that treated Egypt's assets as their personal holdings. Apart from the beneficiaries of Gamal's plunder, no one supported the idea of him in power—not the opposition demanding free and fair democratic elections; not the public, who resented the privileged scion and his cronies for abusing their power to appropriate the country's wealth; and certainly not the military elite, who rejected Gamal on the grounds of his lack of military credentials and his determination to privatize state assets that were under military control.

It is important to underscore the threat that Gamal Mubarak posed to the military, Egypt's most powerful institution. After Nasser installed the first military regime in 1952, the army acquired an outsized role in the country's affairs, extending its reach beyond the barracks into the domestic sphere, where it established its dominance over Egypt's politics, economy, and society. Through successive regimes, it was able to weather and capitalize on key moments of change to increase its autonomy, secure its political authority, and develop a vast business empire through its control of the public sector.[39] The military benefitted under Mubarak in particular. After budget cuts were introduced in a package of liberalizing reforms, the president tried to secure the loyalty of officers by giving them vast business privileges that facilitated the dramatic expansion of their profitable enterprises. He also increased the number of appointments of generals to high-ranking government posts, especially governorships, turning Egypt into an officer's republic. Along with the political leverage the army developed through its tight-knit relationship with Washington and the

American military establishment, these advancements endowed the institution with considerable power and influence, none of which it was prepared to give up.[40] The fact that the military opposed Gamal's succession due to its entrenched interests is key to understanding why the generals aligned with the protesters during the eighteen-day uprising to remove Mubarak, and why the revolutionary struggle declined thereafter (see chapter 7).

In 2005, Mubarak bowed to US pressure and agreed to hold the country's first multi-candidate presidential election, a definitive shift from the last three referendums in which he had featured as the sole choice on the ballot. But far from captivating the public, the president's promise was received with deep skepticism. The president's new election laws placed severe restrictions on independent candidates while privileging the NDP. Kefaya activists were therefore convinced that Mubarak had no intention of facilitating a free and fair election that might actually allow an opponent to win. Instead of appeasing his critics, the clearly disingenuous gesture emboldened them to double down on their critique.

The announcement about the upcoming election also galvanized Egypt's judges into action. They took advantage of the occasion to demand the independence of Egypt's courts from executive control and interference, vowing to stymie the election by refusing their duty under the law to supervise and validate the voting process unless they were allowed full autonomy in their work. The boycott's tacit criticism of the electoral system dovetailed perfectly with Kefaya's demands for reform and prompted its activists to claim the judges' struggle as their own as they rallied around them in solidarity.[41]

Their joint demonstrations were peaceful, but this did not deter the regime from responding with its typical heavy-handedness. Rows of black-clad riot police immediately encircled the demonstrators in a chokehold. Protesters were beaten with truncheons. And in one particularly disturbing episode on May 25, 2005, which would foreshadow things to come during the revolutionary period after the 2011 uprising, several women were forcibly isolated from their fellow demonstrators and stripped and sexually assaulted by police-hired thugs. The incident was unprecedented and stirred vehement public outcry. Police crimes of this nature against women were not new, but they had mostly been confined to police stations and distant locations, such as villages in Upper Egypt where the female relatives of militant Islamists had been the victims of these tactics in the 1990s.[42] However, this was the first time they were committed publicly in broad daylight—in bustling downtown Cairo with ample media presence, no less—with the clear purpose of humiliating women (and the men powerless to protect them) and intimidating them from protesting. But the incident had the opposite effect; women grew louder in asserting their right to public space with a campaign called The Street Is Ours (al-Shari' Lina), also known as the Women for Democracy Movement.[43]

In the end, the presidential election proceeded, monitored by co-opted judicial personnel, and predictably, it was rigged. In a race between ten candidates, Mubarak came out the winner with a preposterous 88 percent of the vote. Meanwhile, his main challenger, Ayman Nour, the respected lawyer and leading member of Egypt's liberal opposition who might have been the people's preferred choice, was hauled off to prison on trumped-up charges of fraud. Nour's true crime, however, was his audacity to challenge the president for his seat, a move that further contributed to the buildup of the resistance movement against Mubarak.

As for the subsequent parliamentary elections, they unfolded rather differently. Weak and unorganized, secular parties fared poorly, but astonishingly, the officially banned yet tolerated Muslim Brotherhood won a historic eighty-eight seats running its candidates as independents, forming the largest opposition in Parliament against the ruling NDP between 2005 and 2010. With just a fifth of the seats they were still a minority, but their success was enough to raise red flags about the possibility of an Islamist takeover if Egyptians were really allowed to choose who led them. The outcome served Mubarak's agenda well. By allowing the Muslim Brotherhood just enough room to demonstrate their popularity and ability to perform well in elections, the president was able to play on Washington's fear of Islamists. The message it seems he wanted to convey to US leaders was clear: keep pushing for democratization in Egypt and expect the Muslim Brotherhood, which was diametrically opposed to US and Israeli interests, to seize power. Sufficiently alarmed, the United States began to tone down its support for Egyptian democracy and human rights in 2006 and 2007, dialing back its pressure on Mubarak to respect the right to free speech and public protest.[44] With the United States off his back, Mubarak had the political cover he needed to hunt down dissenters. The judges' movement and Kefaya were stamped out as scores of activists from the anti-regime, pro-democracy movement were brutally attacked, jailed, and tortured.[45] Still, however short-lived US pressure for reforms had been, for these activists it opened a door to the possibility of a democratic future that could not be shut again.

The state crackdown occurred just as Kefaya was losing steam due to internal conflict and frustration with the movement's inability to make progress towards its goals. Its main shortcoming—and the cause of its waning influence—was its elitism and its failure to make its cause accessible to ordinary Egyptians. Instead of reaching out to the masses and drawing them in to create a stronger and larger movement, Kefaya's activists and intellectuals mostly preached to the choir. This was a major point of contention between Kefaya and Youth for Change, a movement that formed under its umbrella and would later give rise to the youth movements behind the 2011 Tahrir uprising. The youth activists were much more invested in raising the political awareness of average citizens and relating the abstract discourse on democracy and human rights to their particular needs, struggles, and concerns. They produced their literature in Egyptian colloquial rather than formal Arabic, started discussions with common Egyptians in the streets, and distributed leaflets and held flash protests in poor, densely populated areas.[46] Nonetheless, Kefaya still takes the credit for being the first movement to organize protests explicitly demanding an Egyptian president step aside, the first to make creative use of culture in its actions, and the first to use the Internet to subvert the regime and engage supporters, specifically through a mass online petition drive.[47] Kefaya spawned a host of other associated groups—Workers for Change, Journalists for Change, Doctors for Change, Teachers for Change, among others—that drew all kinds of professionals into mass politics. Even if Kefaya's members failed to offer solutions to the problems that plagued Egyptians or unite over a concrete political vision beyond the end of Mubarak's reign, Kefaya took protest tactics and cross-partisan cooperation to a new level, innovating a non-hierarchical, cross-ideological model of resistance for subsequent movements to draw from and build on in the lead-up to the revolution.

Just as the Kefaya movement was fading and the street was retreating from calls for political change, the heat was rising among Egypt's working class. Increasingly burdensome economic pressures resulting from neoliberal policies were taking their toll on the population as the cost of food skyrocketed and wages remained abysmally low, prompting outcry from struggling workers. Their plight took center stage in 2006, when the 27,000-strong workforce of the enormous state-owned textile mill in the Nile Delta town Mahalla, the largest in the region, staged an impressive three-day strike over the government's refusal to pay promised bonuses.[48] Despite security intimidation, the workers stood their ground and won. The strike unleashed a wave of labor unrest that spilled over into other sectors. Inspired by Mahalla, cement plant workers, train operators, tax collectors, doctors, and university professors held their own subsequent strikes.[49]

But the biggest labor shake-up occurred two years later, when as many as forty thousand Mahalla workers, now much more militant and audacious in their demands, announced plans for another strike on April 6, 2008, in demand of a higher national minimum wage and better working conditions.[50] The news prompted young opposition activists to circulate calls on Facebook for a nationwide strike, beckoning the public to skip work and stay home in solidarity with Mahalla's workers on the day of their action. Their Facebook event attracted a hundred thousand members. This was an important development because "for the first time, massive numbers of youth engaged in public life and actively expressed their opinions outside the traditional triangle of power in Egypt—the government's ruling party, weak but legitimate secular opposition parties, and the effective but illegitimate Muslim Brotherhood."[51] Alarmed by the developments, thousands of police were dispatched to occupy the town of Mahalla to preempt the strike. Public sympathy for the workers soared as YouTube footage emerged of the violence wielded against demonstrators, complete with tear gas, rubber bullets, and live ammunition.[52]

The labor unrest between 2006 and 2008[53] captured the imagination of youth activists who participated in the Kefaya movement and shifted their attention toward socioeconomic reforms and raising awareness about the working-class struggle.[54] New youth movements, which for the first time operated independent of the older generation, began to pop up. The leftist Tadamun (Solidarity) movement focused on providing the labor cause with legal support and media coverage. The April 6 Youth Movement grew out of the calls the young activists made for a nationwide strike in support of the Mahalla workers. Inspired by the strike's success, they continued to agitate in the street around a host of issues affecting the public in coordination with other youth movement organizations, like the left-leaning Youth for Justice and Freedom Movement, which grew out of April 6. Like Kefaya, these groups were organizationally fluid and decentralized, but they set themselves apart with even more innovative actions and street tactics as well as their focus on establishing a support base among common Egyptians in the hopes of engendering a popular struggle.[55] They were also innovative in their use of social networking tools like Facebook and Twitter, which allowed them to circumvent State Security as they organized actions and mobilized protesters. Equally important, these movements were pivotal in tying the demands for political change to demands for socioeconomic reform. The emergence of these movements and the new trends in resistance they introduced were all key developments on the path toward the January 25 revolution.

Momentum against Mubarak continued to develop with ElBaradei's entry into the political fray upon his return to Egypt in February 2010. The former head of the IAEA and 2005 Nobel laureate had made a name for himself challenging the basis for the US invasion of Iraq—namely, the claim that the country's leadership was in possession of nuclear weapons. Now he was beginning to take on the despotic power-wielders of his native Egypt, injecting new hope and zeal into the opposition. His bold campaign targeted the entire Mubarak regime, calling for an end to the three-decade state of emergency, legal and constitutional reforms to allow free and fair elections, and Egypt's deliverance from the chokehold of the Mubarak family and their corrupt associates. ElBaradei enjoyed wide appeal as a refreshing newcomer to the political scene, a high-minded politician unlike the many others in the opposition, who were seen as co-opted by the regime.[56]

With his global stature and daring politics, ElBaradei rallied supporters from different backgrounds, generations, and political ideologies. Two groups in particular organized around him. One was the ElBaradei Campaign founded by a group of youth activists in 2010 in anticipation of ElBaradei's return. Members of this group included young men and women from all walks of life—Muslim and Coptic, students and professionals, poor and rich, seasoned activists and the newly anointed—who campaigned for his candidacy in the 2011 presidential election as a way of advocating for change and building up grassroots resistance to the possibility of Gamal Mubarak's succession. The other was the National Association for Change (NAC), a broad alliance of intellectuals, civil society leaders, and ideologically diverse politicians rallying behind ElBaradei as their leader. They launched a door-to-door petition drive around what they called the seven demands for change,[57] which youth groups like April 6 were heavily involved in. The Muslim Brotherhood also threw its weight behind the effort, collecting thousands of the near one million signatures. The success of the campaign confirmed that something was shifting in Egypt. In readily signing the petition despite the grave security risk it entailed, Egyptians demonstrated they were fed up with the status quo and ready for dramatic—perhaps even revolutionary—change.

Popular anger reached new heights in the summer of 2010, when a young, middle-class man named Khaled Said was dragged out of an Internet cafe and viciously beaten to death in public by police in the coastal city of Alexandria. Why the police lynched Khaled was never clear, but his family and friends believed it was because of a video he intercepted and shared online showing the police divvying up the spoils of a drug bust.[58] The state tried to smear him as a drug addict and pin the cause of his death on suffocation from allegedly swallowing a bag of narcotics, but the leaked morgue photos of his bloodied and disfigured face exposed their lie. The gruesome photo of Khaled after the attack instantly went viral and sparked deep outrage across Egypt. It was a shocking image, especially when juxtaposed against the air-brushed portrait of the handsome young man Khaled had been. This kind of police violence was not new in Egypt, but its usual victims had mostly been from the lower classes. According to Rabab El-Mahdi, the abuse that Egyptians of lesser means experienced at the hands of police was related to the neoliberal state's failure to appease the masses through economic relief and its fear that they might erupt as a result. This forced the regime "to shift toward the use of coercion to keep the 'losers' in check" and guarantee its stability.[59] Poor Egyptians were routinely dragged into police stations, where they were subject to all sorts of human rights abuses. In fact, an active bloggers' movement in the mid-2000s heightened awareness of police violence by circulating disturbing amateur cell phone videos that revealed the systemic use of torture and sexual violence by security officers to extract confessions or intimidate citizens into staying in line. But the effect of Khaled Said's killing was different precisely because he was not poor; the tragedy awakened the middle class to the imminent threat of the dark police state in ways that it had not felt before.

Young people in particular immediately identified with the ordinary, seemingly kind lad wearing a gray sweatshirt and a half-smile for the camera. Khaled Said was neither a political activist nor an Islamist radical, just your average middle-class twenty-something-year-old who was said to like computers and music. Many felt it could have just as easily been them in those before-and-after photos, if not their son or their brother or their friend. It was a rude awakening that made one thing blatantly clear: no Egyptian was safe from the state's wrath, no matter how diligently they observed their end of the authoritarian bargain and avoided the police and politics. The senseless murder gave rise to the We Are All Khaled Said Facebook page, a digital rallying point for Egyptians fed up with police brutality, corruption, and Emergency Law. The anonymously administered page was an instant hit, quickly registering three hundred thousand followers within a few months, making it one of the country's most popular dissident platforms and powerful grassroots catalysts for change.[60] Crucially, it would also serve as one of the main mobilizing platforms for the youth activists profiled in this book, who launched the protests that precipitated Mubarak's fall. Khaled Said's death marked a surge in protest that persisted until the January 25 revolt; to be sure, his iconic image served as one of its main catalysts.

Egypt seemed to have reached its breaking point by late 2010, when the results poured in from the first round of the latest parliamentary elections. Most of the secular parties boycotted the elections expecting widespread fraud, but the Brotherhood decided to give it their best shot and see what gains might come of it. To no one's surprise, Mubarak's ruling party emerged victorious; voter intimidation, low turnout, and election rigging proceeded as usual to facilitate this outcome. What did stun the public, however, was the number of seats the Muslim Brotherhood won: zero. Hardly anyone believed that the Muslim Brotherhood, the most organized opposition in the country with the largest support base, could have failed so miserably in the elections on their own, especially after they had won eighty-eight seats in the previous contest. So dismissive were Mubarak and his associates of public opinion and so confident were they in their undying lordship over the country that they had not even bothered to try to hide their election rigging. The regime's gall had reached new heights and presaged the kind of manipulation Egyptians could expect from the ruling elite to secure Gamal's win in the upcoming presidential election.

Even though Mubarak preserved a veneer of democracy by holding elections, it was mostly for show. Real power remained in his office and the shadowy people and institutions that comprised what Egyptians called the "deep state"—the military officers, security services, intelligence agencies, and bureaucrats that collectively ruled Egypt. By early 2011, it was glaringly clear that the system was corrupt beyond repair, that challenging the regime through elections and trying to change the system from within was a lost cause. Egyptian patience was worn thin by the incompetence, apathy, arrogance, and shameless corruption of the country's leaders. A pervasive sense of hopelessness gripped lower- and middle-class Egyptians as they experienced the damaging effect of the government's contempt for them and felt helpless to do anything about it.[61] There was a dangerous breakdown in the neoliberal state's capacity and willingness to carry out its functions, whether economically, socially, or politically. The symptoms were everywhere one turned: the everyday tyranny of the police, the widespread culture of bribery, the crumbling infrastructure, the endemic sexual harassment women experienced daily on Egypt's streets, Cairo's infamous traffic and pollution, the wretched condition of public transportation, the Hepatitis C epidemic that was ravaging the Delta, the rise in sectarian anti-Christian violence, the growing population of street children, the desperation of legions of unemployed young men unable to step into adulthood or start families or even move out of their parents' homes. This feeling of being cheated by the state out of a dignified life and a promising future was especially acute among Egypt's youth, who constituted more than half of the country's population and made up 90 percent of its unemployed.[62] They saw themselves as the biggest victims of the order forged in the 1950s with the consent of their parents and grandparents. They also understood they had the most to gain from its overthrow.

And while the valorous resistance of the Egyptian opposition over the previous decade had not achieved the hoped-for results, the effort, it was soon to be revealed, had not been a waste. Through that process they had developed a valuable cross-partisan network and links among movements. They had also created a common language around shared grievances and demands for freedoms, social justice, and the rule of law and devised new tactics for protest and resistance. Soon, however, Egyptians would collectively realize that if they wanted to see change, they would have to adopt a much more creative, radical course of action. This lesson was driven home by Tunisians, whose unexpected revolt in December 2010 demonstrated what was possible for Egyptians if they tapped into their people power. If Tunisians could rise up in the streets and take down their dogged dictator and his regime in a matter of weeks, what was to stop Egyptians—whose numbers were after all far greater—from doing the same? This was a question a handful of diverse, hardened youth activists grappled with as they plotted their own day of mass action set for January 25, 2011—activists who emerged from Egypt's complex and stormy history and would soon become some of its most important agents.

3
Rethinking Spontaneity: Youth Political Agency Before the Uprising

The explosive uprising that seized the Egyptian street on January 25, 2011, caught Western observers, pundits, and politicians off guard. Initial attempts to explain the eruption described it as a spontaneous expression of popular frustration that was facilitated by Internet technology, especially social media platforms like Facebook and Twitter. In fact, a new expression was minted to refer to the movement, "the first Facebook revolution."[1] As for the youth who were highlighted as the instigators and leaders of this uprising, their story was generally limited to how they used these Internet tools to organize.

The problem with the "spontaneity" and "Facebook" tropes is their a-historicity, as they isolate the eruption of the movement from precedents. They almost suggest that the consciousness and resistance of these activists was born instantly and online. Even more problematic, insisting on the significance of Western-owned Internet companies like Facebook implies that this genuinely local movement was indebted to the West—specifically the Silicon Valley—diminishing Egyptian ownership of it. These kinds of interpretations neglect the painful and patient history that led to this momentous social explosion, rendering invisible critical factors that shaped the youth's politicization and the revolt they instigated. A closer look at the trajectories of these vanguard activists tells a different story of revolutionary becoming, one that reveals the embeddedness of these young protagonists in the very historical processes that gave birth to the uprising. These processes brought together a highly diverse group of individual actors, political and civic groups, communities, and state policies and institutions at a particular historical moment shaped by specific geopolitical circumstances.

In this chapter, I tease out some of the factors that shaped this movement and the youth at its center. Here, I explore the formative experiences of several of the youth activists who would go on to form the RYC in light of the historical context presented in the previous chapter. I highlight the recurring themes in the youth narratives I collected and the specific circumstances that brought these disparate youth and their groups together in the political arena. Close examination reveals how these actors' personal histories are embedded in the complex, multilayered history of the country. The development of their political consciousness and activist commitment grew within the context of three distinct but interrelated scales of social interaction: the micro scale, where they interacted with and were shaped by their personal histories, the circumstances and experiences of their immediate families, and the characteristics of the neighborhoods in which they grew up; the meso scale, where they interacted with social and political institutions, including those responding to state policies; and the macro scale, where they interacted with regional and global processes that had shaped and been shaped by Egypt. The experiences of these activists within these domains illuminates the kind of "fresh contacts" Karl Mannheim argues are responsible for forging new political generations. In the case of the cohort of young people in Egypt who would become known as *shabab al-thawra*, or "the revolutionary youth," contacts with the various elements of the social and political order they inherited—such as abject urban poverty, endemic police abuse, authoritarian repression, widespread corruption, and rapid technological change—would spark in them a consciousness of their shared plight, politicizing them and eventually catalyzing them to fight for radical change.

The following are the brief profiles of ten of the activists I interviewed for this study, nine men and one woman, followed by a more detailed discussion of their experiences. Here it is important to note that while the main focus of this chapter is on class dimensions, religious affiliation, and political histories, gender is an equally crucial dimension that is more fully addressed in the following chapters.

The Activists
Amr Ezz
Amr Ezz was twenty-eight years old at the outbreak of the revolution. The second of seven siblings—three boys and four girls—he was born and raised in a small apartment in Imbaba, a densely populated working-class district in the city of Giza,[2] which borders Cairo proper. Amr's father was uneducated and worked as a cab driver when he was younger, but had since been managing his own dry cleaning business. His mother had earned a

high school diploma and was a homemaker. Religiously, his parents leaned toward Salafi Muslim conservatism, and they looked the part: his father wore a hanging beard and his mother dressed in black from head to toe and wore the face veil when out in public. Amr and his brothers, however, opted for the less religious, clean-shaven look, and his sisters preferred to wear Western outfits and colorful hijabs. Amr was exposed to politics at a young age through his father's early involvement with the non-militant segments of al-Gama'a al-Islamiya (the Islamic Group), the Salafi Islamist movement. Eager to effect political change, he studied law at Cairo University, Egypt's oldest public university, where he received his bachelor's degree in 2006.[3] He participated in a number of political initiatives and movements before he decided to join the April 6 Movement, becoming one of its most active members and one of the officers responsible for mass action. Soon after I met him in 2011, he was elected the president of the mass action committee for the April 6 Youth Movement Democratic Front, a breakaway from the original April 6 movement.[4] Ideologically, he identified with the liberal current.

Tarek El-Khouly
Tarek El-Khouly was twenty-six years old when he and his peers helped make Egyptian history. An animated young man of short stature, he was one of the more articulate activists I met, quick with his words and impassioned in his speech. The third of four brothers, he was born and raised in Sharabiya, another densely inhabited quarter in Cairo that began as an informal settlement in the historic Shubra district. His grandparents had migrated to Cairo from villages in the governorates of Munufiya and Qalyubiya northwest of Cairo, where he still had relatives whom he visited. His father operated a small hardware shop and his mother was a homemaker, and neither of them went to school beyond the secondary level. Tarek, like his older siblings, went to college. He graduated with a degree in law from Alexandria University, Egypt's second oldest public university. He did not come from a family with a history of political engagement; rather, he discovered politics on his own as a university student. He dabbled in a number of political initiatives before settling with the April 6 Movement in which he collaborated with Amr. When we met in 2011 he was the official spokesperson of the April 6 Youth Movement Democratic Front and one of its most active, leading members. Ideologically, he leaned toward liberalism, though he cited Islam as one of his political reference points (*marga'iya islamiya*).

Mahmoud Samy
Mahmoud Samy was twenty-one years old at the start of the revolution and the youngest of the activists I interviewed. Also a member of the April 6 Movement and one of the officers responsible for mass action, he was respected as one of the movement's most creative and effective street action strategists. The second of four siblings, one girl and three boys, Mahmoud was born and raised in Awsim, an informal, peri-urban neighborhood on the edge of Imbaba, Cairo, that was developed on agricultural land. The area maintains some rural characteristics and is inhabited by many farmers. The particular neighborhood Mahmoud grew up in was more working class than rural, however, and featured many small trade workshops. His father was born and raised in Gamaliya, a historic working-class district near the Mohammed Ali Citadel. He earned a high school diploma and worked as a car mechanic, a trade Mahmoud picked up from him at the age of fifteen in order to work and help provide for the family. His mother, however, had called Awsim home since she was born. Her family was poor and unable to put her through school, but she managed to teach herself to read and write. Mahmoud did not let his family's difficult circumstances limit his life chances, either. He managed to get a high school and college education while continuing to work as a mechanic to help his parents, eventually earning his bachelor's degree in business from Ain Shams University, another one of Egypt's oldest public universities, right before the start of the revolution. His worldview was shaped by the peasant and working-class environment in which he grew up. As he became more politicized, he experimented with several different political currents, but never committed to a single one.

Mostafa Shawky
Mostafa Shawky stood out with his fiery personality and hurried speech; he seemed to speak a mile a minute. This street activist was also twenty-six when the revolution first erupted and was valued by his peers for his shrewd political analysis and commitment to the working-class struggle. The sixth of seven children—four boys and three girls—Mostafa was born in Jordan, where his father had migrated to work as a carpenter, but he was raised in Dar al-Salam, a popular working-class neighborhood in Cairo, mostly by his mother after his father passed away. His mother and father came from the impoverished Sayyida Zaynab area, one of Cairo's oldest—indeed, historic—popular quarters. Neither of them was educated. He described his family as having lower-class beginnings, but said that his mother helped them move

into the bottom rung of the middle class by improving their financial circumstances through the careful management of their father's social security payments, which they began to receive after his death. Thanks to her frugality, she was able to afford the private tutoring[5] that helped Mostafa score high enough to get into the engineering program in college. He earned a bachelor's degree in electrical engineering in 2007 from Helwan University, a public university established during the Nasser era. He would have preferred to study political science or journalism, but he put his own wish aside to please his mother, who aspired for the prestige of a son in engineering. Coming from a family with no background in politics, Mostafa discovered and developed a passion for politics on his own. He identified as a socialist, specifically subscribing to Trotskyist Revolutionary Socialism. His leftist persuasions seemed fitting, given his slight resemblance to Antonio Gramsci and Leon Trotsky in their youth, with his popping eyes and round spectacles, his darker complexion and African-textured hair notwithstanding. He was one of the founding and leading members of the Socialist Renewal Current (Tayyar al-Tagdid al-Ishitraki) and the Youth for Justice and Freedom Movement. After Mubarak's resignation, he was also involved in founding a larger socialist party called the Popular Socialist Alliance (al-Tahaluf al-Sha'bi al-Ishtiraki).

Ola Shahba

Ola Shahba was thirty-two years old when she found herself in the throes of revolution. The eldest of three siblings, she was born and raised in Mohandiseen, an upscale district of Giza. Ola grew up in an affluent family and mentioned that her less privileged comrades teased her for being a member of the bourgeoisie. She considered herself a practicing Muslim, and at one point even chose to wear the hijab for a few years before deciding it was not for her. This was during the Islamist revival that swept through Egypt in the mid-2000s, which had particular resonance with Egypt's elite youth. The move surprised her family, for it was not customary for her class standing nor did they think it suited her carefree personality. But it was precisely Ola's rebellious spirit—her desire to defy class expectations and live to her own tune—that drove her to cover. Her mother was brought up in a wealthy, educated family that had been in Cairo for generations, but her father hailed from Zagazig, a city in the more rural Sharqiya governorate, where he spent a portion of his childhood before migrating with his family to Cairo. Ola's mother worked as a journalist and hosted a radio news program. Her parents were not affiliated with any political parties or groups, but she described them both as being politically conscious. Ola could have gone to the American University in Cairo along with most of Cairo's elite youth, but wanting to be a little closer to the average Egyptian and naturally averse to class segregation and social inequality, she instead opted to enroll in Ain Shams University's prestigious, newly established English School of Commerce. There, she could still receive an education befitting her social standing but be around students who were from poorer and less privileged families, allowing her to have a less sanitized, more typical Egyptian education experience. She worked in Egypt for a number of years and spent time in the United States working as a fellow at Columbia University, before going to Europe to pursue her master's degree in anthropology of development from the School of Oriental and African Studies (SOAS), University of London. A socialist, she joined Mostafa in the Socialist Renewal Current, and later, the Youth for Justice and Freedom Movement. Ola was valued by her peers in both groups as one of their most dedicated and reliable leaders.

Basem Kamel

Basem Kamel defied the image that typically comes to mind when one thinks "youth activist." He was forty-two years old when I first came to know him in 2011 and, as mentioned in chapter 1, was the oldest of the activists I interviewed. Detecting my surprise when he told me his age, he decided to humor me: "I still see myself as a young man, or do you see otherwise?" This was followed by a jovial admission that he was pushing the boundaries of the "youth" category. A slightly balding gentleman who kept his hair and beard trimmed a shade thicker than stubble, he carried himself with the maturity of a grounded and respectable husband, father, and seasoned professional. Basem and his wife had three children, the oldest being fourteen when we met. He described himself as an observant Muslim, noting that both his mother and wife were veiled, but stressed that by no means was he a fundamentalist. He had continued to live in the family apartment complex his father had built for them when he was a child in Helwan, a popular working-class, industrial area, though he described the particular neighborhood he lived in as more middle class. Basem grew up with three siblings and lived in Saudi Arabia during his primary school years, after his father migrated there to work as a social worker, a field in which he continued to work upon their return to Cairo. His father received a bachelor's degree in social work, whereas his mother was uneducated. Before Basem was born, his father had been a member of the Muslim Brotherhood, but withdrew from the group shortly before marrying. Basem obtained his bachelor's degree in architectural engineering from Cairo University and a professional certification in project management from the American University in Cairo. He had been politically aware from a young age but never committed to a particular ideology or group. This changed in 2010 when he became an active member in the ElBaradei Campaign, which would be his gateway into revolutionary activity. After the eighteen-day uprising, Basem became a founding member of the Egyptian Social Democratic Party (al-Hizb al-Masri al-Dimuqrati al-Igtima'i), identifying himself as a social democrat. He would also become one of the few youth revolutionaries to win a seat in the first post-Mubarak Parliament, before it was dissolved by the military six months later.

Zyad Eleleimy

Zyad Eleleimy was thirty-one years old when the revolution erupted and by then had already established a name for himself as a successful, left-wing attorney. He received his bachelor's degree in law from Cairo University and had since run his own practice. Zyad stood out in our personal interactions with his slow pace and soft-spokenness, which stood in stark contrast to his burly frame and radical politics. But this was Zyad in personal interactions; in rallies and protests, this revolutionary knew how to roar. When we met, Zyad was recently divorced with a young son, whom he spoke of fondly. He and his younger brother were raised in Aguza, an upper-middle-class area in Giza, by their mother, after their father died when Zyad was still a young boy. Later as an adult, he moved to his own flat in a more affluent area in the Muqattam district of Cairo. Both his parents were politically active as university students and later became members in leftist political parties. His mother continued her activism as a journalist through her widely read columns. Zyad had identified with communism when he was in his teens and early twenties, but later felt that it was not a practical solution to Egypt's problems and embraced social democracy instead. Like Basem, he was a leading member in the ElBaradei Campaign before the revolution and later became a founding member of the Egyptian Social Democratic Party. Also like Basem, he went on to win a seat in the short-lived 2011 Parliament.

Mohammed Al-Qassas

Mohammed Al-Qassas was thirty-seven years old when I interviewed him in 2011. A prominent Islamist activist, he was respected as a mentor by his younger peers across the ideological spectrum. There was nothing overtly Islamist about this activist's appearance, other than the *zabiba*, the brown forehead mark commonly borne by religious Muslim men who regularly press their face against the ground in prostration during the five daily prayers. Otherwise, he was an average stout Egyptian, clean-shaven rather than bearded, with an affable personality. Qassas, as family and friends commonly referred to him (and how I will refer to him henceforth), grew up the eldest of four siblings, two boys and two girls. He was born and raised in a middle-class neighborhood called Manshiyat al-Bakri originally home to many educated, government employees, located in the generally more upper-class Heliopolis district of Cairo. His parents came from the countryside in the governorate of Kafr al-Shaykh, an area where they still had relatives whom they visited regularly. His mother completed high school and his father was trained at al-Azhar University, Egypt's premier Islamic seminary. His father worked as a government employee during the day and volunteered as a *da'ee* (preacher) in the local community during his off-hours. As such, religion was a big part of Qassas's family life growing up. Qassas went to Cairo University's historic Dar al-Ulum College, an institution that specializes in Arabic, literature, and Islamic Studies. On his first day as a student, he joined the Muslim Brotherhood, and shortly thereafter became politically active. He continued with the organization after graduating and moved up in its ranks and came to be respected as one of the association's youngest, most dedicated leaders. Before the revolution, he had been the director of the Brotherhood's Central Student Bureau's Mass Action Committee, which was responsible for the organization's student activities across Egypt's universities. Qassas remained affiliated with the Brotherhood until he was dismissed several months into the revolution for his differences with the senior members over the direction of the Islamist movement. Later, he joined others in founding the Egyptian Current Party (Hizb al-Tayyar al-Masri) in which he would revise his Islamist ideology (discussed in chapters 5 and 6). Qassas worked in media and managed his own small production company. He married shortly before the revolution and had recently become a father to an infant boy when we met.

Mohammed Abbas

Mohammed Abbas, who was known among his friends simply as Abbas (which is how I will refer to him in this book), was twenty-five years old and still a college student when Egypt's youth grabbed headlines around the world on January 25. Throughout the Tahrir protests of 2011, this good-humored, impassioned young revolutionary could often be found on the stages leading chants and riling up the crowd. He walked with a bow-legged gait in measured steps and frequently wore short-sleeved, button-down plaid shirts that were slightly fitted to his thickset arms and torso. In conversation, he was quick with his jokes and generous with his boisterous laugh. Abbas was born and raised in Imbaba as the third of four children, the rest of whom were girls. His mother, an uneducated woman, had migrated to Cairo from the Gharbiya governorate with her family when she was twelve, and his father, a high school graduate, had migrated from Mansura as an adult in search of work. In Imbaba, Abbas's father was able to secure a job as a post office manager from which he earned 1,500 LE per month, a meager salary that would have guaranteed his family's poverty had it not been for his ten-year stint in the Gulf as a migrant worker and the land he inherited in his village, both of which afforded them a middle-class standard of living. Abbas came from a family with many members in the Muslim Brotherhood, so for him, joining the group was a given. He graduated from Cairo University in 2011 with a bachelor's degree in business administration. Until 2012, he ran his own small advertising agency. Abbas was a member of the student circle under Qassas in college, and like him, he was also banished from the Brotherhood a few months after the start of the revolution for his objection to the leadership's decisions. Upon his dismissal, he joined Qassas and the former young Brothers in founding the Egyptian Current Party.

Abdelrahman Faris

Abdelrahman Faris was thirty years old and recently engaged when I met him. Physically on the smaller side, he was fervent in his revolutionary opposition but mild in his temperament. Abdelrahman grew up in a polygamous family, his mother being the second of his father's four wives, each of whom lived in their own homes with their children. He was the oldest of seven full siblings, five brothers and two sisters. He also had nine half siblings, several of whom are older, from his father's other wives. He lived between Cairo and Fayoum, the capital of a governorate by the same name southwest of Cairo, where his mother's family is from and immediate family resides. His father, however, is from the city of Mansura in the Daqahliya governorate northeast of Cairo. His mother received a bachelor's degree in social work, and his father a certificate from a teaching institute. Abdelrahman spent several of his formative years in the United Arab Emirates, where his father was employed by the Ministry of Religious Endowments as an imam at a mosque and a Friday sermonizer. He was raised in a large Muslim Brotherhood family, but he grew disenchanted with the organization as a young adult and decided to part ways. However, he remained interested in politics. To his parents' frustration, he decided not to go to college after completing high school, instead choosing to dedicate himself to politics and street activism, taking on odd jobs to support himself. He jumped between movements and political parties, eventually becoming an independent activist. His political engagement before January 25 made him a good candidate for one of the RYC's executive committee seats reserved for independent activists. After the revolution, he joined the Egyptian Current Party as a founding member. He also returned to Cairo University to pursue a degree in journalism. Staying true to his independent streak, he described his ideology as a mix of liberalism, socialism, and Islamism. Like so many other young Egyptians who found love during the uprising, he met his fiancée, Hend, on January 25 during the protests.

The profiles above reflect the diverse backgrounds of this heterogeneous group of young Egyptian revolutionaries. Several of them, like Amr, Mostafa, Mahmoud, and Tarek, grew up in one of Cairo's many dense popular and working-class neighborhoods. This group also included those like Basem and Abdelrahman, who grew up with more comforts and spent a portion of their childhood in Gulf countries, where their fathers had migrated for work during the early years of the oil boom. With the exception of Qassas, whose father is an al-Azhar graduate, their parents generally received a modest education, earning credentials not usually exceeding a high school diploma or an institute certificate. As such, these activists were the first generation in their families to earn university degrees. Their mothers tended to be homemakers, while their fathers worked as government employees, laborers, and small business owners in the informal economy. Then there were activists like Zyad and Ola, who came from more comfortable backgrounds and grew up in more upscale areas. Both their parents had received higher education, earning undergraduate and graduate degrees, and enjoyed prestigious careers in professions like journalism, medicine, and teaching in higher education. Their class difference is also apparent in their English proficiency, a product of the opportunities they were able to afford. Interestingly, despite the variation in their socioeconomic backgrounds, all of the activists traced their origins to the countryside, going back two or three generations from one or both parents, and several still maintained those rural ties when we spoke. Additionally, all of them identified as Muslims, though they differed in their interpretation and degrees of practice.

The details of this diversity are significant because they show the historical embeddedness of these actors. They reveal, for example, the impact of socioeconomic policies on their families' trajectories and search for upward mobility, which in turn shaped them and their own personal histories. This is evident in the rural–urban migration of their grandparents and the transnational migration of their parents to Gulf countries as a result of the opportunities and constraints that emerged with the changing national and global political economies under Nasser and Sadat.[6] It is also illustrated in the structural educational opportunities and constraints they encountered as a result of Nasser's educational reform. Implicit in their stories is the history of a post-independence, modern developmentalist state undergoing a radical neoliberal transformation and the political, social, economic, and religious factors that played into its evolution and the transformation of Egyptian society. Their stories, in turn, have woven themselves back into the fabric of forces that continue to shape Egypt's emergent present and distant future. In the following section, I take a closer look at the individual experiences of these activists from the micro, meso, and macro perspectives to better understand the factors that engendered their consciousness and led to their active participation as drivers of the January 25 revolution.

Family, Neighborhood, the State, and Political Consciousness

In many ways, the emergence of the January 25 revolutionary movement and its youth protagonists are rooted in Cairo's complex urban history and its physical transformation as a global city. Cairo's development is the consequence of rapid urbanization, decades of inadequate housing and urban planning policies, Egypt's shifting position in the changing global economy, and the active participation of denizens in shaping the city from below. The interaction of these dynamics configured the physical and sociopolitical environments these youth inhabited.

For several of the activists I interviewed, their family and neighborhood experiences shaped the emergence of their political consciousness.

This was particularly the case for those who were less privileged and grew up in *manatiq sha'biya* (popular quarters), including informal settlements and slums known as *ashwa'iyat* (from an Arabic word meaning "random" or "disorderly"), which are home to more than 65 percent of Cairo's eighteen million inhabitants.[7] Unlike *manatiq raqiya* (upscale areas) built according to formal central planning, many *sha'bi* (popular) quarters originated as planned working-class neighborhoods surrounding major industrial poles that later grew with the development of informal settlements along their periphery, radically expanding the city through sprawl. Built illegally on agricultural

Figure 2a. A narrow neighborhood alley in the popular quarter of Imbaba, Cairo. Photograph by Mark Hanna.

Figure 2b. A street scene from the popular quarter of Shubra, Cairo. Photograph by Mohammed Fayad El Abd Fayad.

land and in contravention of zoning laws and construction regulations, informal housing has long been Cairenes' solution to the absence of affordable housing and adequate housing and urban development policies. Because the government has failed to guide this development, *shaʻbi* areas have suffered from high population density, unsafe and haphazard construction, few open-air spaces, poor infrastructure, and a dire lack of public services. In these intimate and bustling quarters, alleyways are narrow, roads are often unpaved, and mounds of garbage sit uncollected in the streets (see figures 2a–c). Compare this to *raqi* (upscale) areas, with their wider and greener thoroughfares, public squares and gardens, and posh cafes, boutiques, and restaurants.[8]

Figure 2c. Informal area on the edges of Shubra, Cairo. Photograph by Mohammed Fayad El Abd Fayad.

Informal urbanization first appeared in the decade following the Second World War, when Nasser's aggressive industrialization program attracted a surge of migrants from Upper Egypt and the Delta seeking better opportunity.[9] Soon, the rural–urban influx and natural demographic growth surpassed the government's ability to meet the demand for affordable public housing, giving way to the first major expansion of informal settlements. New informal districts were born, while others connected to areas like Imbaba continued to grow. Under Sadat, the mid-1970s saw the beginning of a new phase in informal development much larger than the previous one. Henceforth, informal settlements would not only become home to the urban poor, but also to "the young, the middle class, educated families, university students, and public sector employees"—even professionals like professors, lawyers, doctors, and engineers—"in search of accommodation at a reasonable price."[10] Driving this dramatic expansion of informal development was a combination of government housing policies and private sector dynamics unleashed by the *infitah* that closed this segment of the population off from the formal market.[11] During Mubarak's reign, informal settlements continued to develop as a result of more inadequate housing policies owing to neoliberal structural adjustment, monetary devaluation, and cuts in public expenditures. According to estimates, from the 1970s to the 1990s, 80 percent of new residential units in Cairo were built informally.[12] Increasingly, the neoliberal order under Mubarak had ghettoized urban life, polarizing Cairo between struggling popular quarters and affluent, gated communities.

Home to Amr, Abbas, and Tarek, Imbaba and Sharabiya are among the largest and most populous of these quarters. This is how Amr described his specific neighborhood in Imbaba and what it meant to live in these parts of Cairo:

> I live in a very poor area. I mean, not a really poor area in the sense of an *ashwa'iya* (slum), but a really *sha'bi* area. With the *sha'bi* areas, the idea is that the culture and environment are not conducive for someone to think about something like this [that is, politics], or that one is even cultured, that he reads, that he interacts with and stays connected to political groups.... I might be the only one in our street who works in politics in a very big area with thousands of youth.... People are more concerned with making ends meet and raising children. The majority of them are not in a position to think about things other than work, food, school, and so on.

Abbas, who also lived in Imbaba his whole life, emphasized the deteriorating socioeconomic state of the area:

> Imbaba is one of the most neglected areas in Egypt, despite the fact that it's one of the largest and most heavily populated. I mean, there are three million people in central Imbaba alone. That's a state within a state! So it's been really neglected, even though it's at the center of Cairo ... within close reach of the country's central district. Nonetheless, the area is seriously neglected—I'm talking major neglect in the provision of services and in education. And the number of people living in the area is frightening!

Sharabiya, the district where Tarek lived, is not any different from Imbaba:

> I live in a neighborhood that is considered to a large extent—it's a neighborhood called Sharabiya, and this neighborhood has all the manifestations of poverty and corruption.... I'm referring to financial corruption around construction violations and day-to-day living. There's even a severe lack in simple services and infrastructure. All of this for sure affected me in a big way.... Sharabiya is in Cairo, a little after Ramses[13] ... not quite an *ashwa'iya* (slum), but a *sha'bi* area. There are services in it, but they are seriously inadequate. And *baltaga* (thuggery) is widespread in it, especially during the times of elections. So my upbringing was in this kind of a neighborhood. This of course shaped my existence in a profound way. I was angry about the living conditions people were subjected to, which I felt they didn't deserve, and the cultural degeneration that Mubarak's regime gave birth to among the people, that all they ever thought about was eating and drinking and that's it. The people became, from generation to generation, occupied with nothing but working, eating, and drinking until they die. This was the condition of people around me, and I refused to live like this. I wanted change for this country.

Several other activists made similar comments about their neighborhoods and the areas where they grew up, suggesting that living the day-to-day reality of the state's neglect, as manifested in the pressure of exponential demographic growth, the lack of adequate municipal services and crumbling infrastructure, and the cultural decay among its inhabitants informed their budding consciousness and activism as adults. Poverty was undoubtedly one of the main factors affecting their lives, surrounded as they were by people whose existence was limited by their everyday struggle to survive, eking out a life at the margins of the economy and society, forsaken by their own government.

Equally significant was the state's abuse in the form of repression and endemic corruption. Tarek's reference to *baltagiya*, thugs or gangsters, speaks to the domestic weight of Mubarak's police state, felt especially in popular quarters and slums. There, security forces entrenched themselves and encroached on citizen life. According to Salwa Ismail,[14] police presence in these parts began to take root in the 1980s and 1990s, when police were deployed to squelch Islamist opposition. The expansion of security politics in these areas was also a response to the growth of the informal economy and housing development as a result of the state's withdrawal from welfare provisions and its adoption of neoliberal economic policies. Informality was problematic for the state insofar as it translated into the autonomy of citizens and their spaces. No longer the beneficiaries of the neoliberal patriarchal authoritarian state, vast swaths of the population were now untethered from the unspoken social contract that had demanded their political complacency in exchange for the state's provision of social goods. The fear was that this independence would find expression in a political challenge to the state. To contain this threat, local police stations were set up to carry out surveillance and *baltagiya* were recruited as informants and coercive muscle to control popular quarters through the intimidation of their residents. As an arm of the increasingly corrupt police, these hired thugs supported police drug operations, colluded with them in protection and extortion rackets, intimidated voters at the polls and helped rig elections, violently snuffed out local dissent, and generally preyed upon community members.[15] With the support of *baltagiya*, the police and the rest of the state's security apparatus were able to dominate daily life in these quarters and create a pervasive feeling of *haybat al-dawla* (awe of the state) among Egyptians.[16] This securitized atmosphere had a chilling effect on residents and engendered in them a timid deference to state authority.

It is this paradoxical mix of the state's absence and omnipresence—in the form of utter neglect on the one hand and corrupt, intrusive policing of the social on the other—that marked the environment many of these youth grew up in. Tarek and his peers shared several experiences that demonstrate how this reality affected them personally. Though Tarek never had any serious confrontations himself with police or *baltagiya*, he told me that his father was among many shopkeepers in his neighborhood whom police and gangs regularly harassed and extorted payments from in exchange for protection from break-ins. They were also forced to pay illegally imposed levies and bribes to avoid the threat of fines for false violations. These fees were costly and immensely taxing on his father and family. The irony here is that the state's inattentiveness to their need for adequate employment and other social safety nets left struggling families like Tarek's, who had no choice but to earn a living through the informal economy, vulnerable to exploitation from its own agents. Tarek zoomed out from his particular family experience to comment on the widespread culture of fear of police among residents in his area. It was not rare, he said, to witness

> an officer get into a confrontation with a citizen in the street and then assault him while bystanders watched helplessly, too afraid to intervene. The residents would often act oblivious, as if they didn't see anything, because of how fearful they were. People in Sharabiya were even afraid to drive in front of the local police station, fearing they might get randomly stopped by an officer and arbitrarily detained. So repression had reached endemic levels.

Tarek's remarks speak to the typical citizen–police encounters that are a regular feature of daily life in these quarters. They illustrate the unbridled power and authority the police have enjoyed over society. These were not benevolent forces concerned with the protection of citizens and maintaining law and order. On the contrary, they were invested in subjugating the populace and establishing state dominance. It is important to note that police aggression did not just inspire a rampant fear of physical harm among ordinary Egyptians, but perhaps more potently, the fear of public humiliation that frequently accompanied it.[17] The literature on police conduct in these informal areas is replete with stories of citizens complaining about police brutality, disrespect, and insult. Indeed, the public nature of police discipline Tarek alludes to and the indignity felt by those who experienced it played an important role in producing the docility and acquiescence in ordinary Egyptians that frustrated Tarek and planted in him the seeds of contempt and resistance.

Tarek shared another tale illuminating how state corruption played out in his life. Soon after he left for college in Alexandria, his younger brother was killed on his way to school in the type of car accident that had become all too common in Egypt. According to Tarek:

> This car accident happened for a number of reasons. It was because of the negligence of the driver, who had dramatically exceeded the speed limit. Because he was driving a government car, he knew that if he injured someone or made a mistake, he wouldn't really be punished, and that's what happened. . . . Ten years have passed since his death, and until now a court ruling has not been issued. I mean, this is also a sign of collapse—the delaying of justice, that is, and the degeneration of the state of the judiciary . . . this is peak oppression. So all of this gave birth to this feeling inside me, that I came to reject the current situation and reject becoming an individual among those—those who are "normal"—who work and eat and get married and die. . . . I refused this.

Tarek's experience does not just reflect the social costs engendered by an inefficient justice system, but also the problems with law enforcement and the abuse of power by those holding government positions. Like many Egyptians, Tarek's family, with their modest means and lack of connections, had been unable to obtain justice or redress the wrongs perpetrated against them by those affiliated with the state. Even the more privileged, like Ola, were subject to the corruption of the justice system, where inside connections prevailed over law and order. She described an incident that took place when she was twenty years old, in which she got into a dispute with a drunk driver who had blocked her at an intersection, yanked her out of her car, and physically assaulted her, believing she had tried to run him off the road:

> I took his license plate number and I went to the police station and I filed a complaint and did everything [I was supposed to do], and then suddenly, three months later, I found out that I was being accused of beating him and breaking his eye glasses. And we discovered that he was a professor—a medical doctor and a professor in the school of medicine—and that he had the *wasta* (connections) to do all the stuff, paperwork and everything, so I wouldn't be notified when my complaint was going to court and his complaint was going to court, so I was sentenced for my absence. And then I just had to kind of just let go of my complaint in return for him letting go of his.

In effect, abusive situations and terrible injustices like those experienced by Tarek and Ola are evidence of a failed system that put the state beyond the reach of the average citizen by placing its agents and their hangers-on above the law.

Amr shared two experiences that played an important role in awakening him to politics. The first is a small incident he recalled from his early days as a schoolboy in one of Egypt's countless overcrowded classrooms:

> As far as the neglect of the regime and how it affected me... When I was in school, I started to think, "I shouldn't be sitting with all these kids in this classroom. The teacher should be paying attention to me." I started to look at everything around me from this newfound perspective. I remember that when I was young... I stirred up a huge problem and argued with the teacher. The issue was that we were three students sitting at one desk, and more kids came, so then we were four at the desk, even though we had barely fit as three. The kids began to argue that we should only have three at the desk. And I began to argue that we should actually each be sitting in our own desks. They didn't know what to do with me! They understood the logic behind the other kids' argument, considering they just wanted a return to the norm, but I drove them nuts.

Beneath Amr's humorous anecdote is a serious criticism of government policies and the crisis of the underfunded and overcrowded education system. It reflects the pervasiveness of the state's neglect and the extent to which it was normalized among the poor. His experience also shows how far the current system has diverged from the Nasserist ideals of official education as the main institution forming the new, modern Egyptian citizen. Nasser's education reforms, including the elimination of school fees, were meant to upend what was then an elitist education system and provide fair opportunities to the poor. Since then, state schools have largely failed to live up to their egalitarian promise as a result of decades of inadequate funding and education policies. In fact, class distinctions would become even more pronounced with the development of private education after Sadat's *infitah* and Mubarak's neoliberalization, which provided its beneficiaries a quality of education far superior to that of their peers in state schools and privileged them in the labor market as a result.

In addition to the lamentable condition of their neighborhoods and schooling, the early political formation of these activists was critically influenced by their families' direct experience with politics and the state. In the next account, Amr describes the second experience he credits for sparking his political awareness:

> My father was a member of al-Gama'a al-Islamiya, and he was arrested several times. This might be the thing that made me tune in. This was when I was a child. Its effect on me was that . . . I couldn't let the things I saw pass without understanding them. I had to understand what was going on, and why they [that is, *amn al-dawla*, or State Security] were coming in such large numbers and in such a menacing way to arrest him, and then he disappeared for several months, and after that he came back and was left alone. . . . This was in 1992 or 1993, and I was ten years old at the time. I would always wonder why my father continued down this path despite the fact that it was wrecking our lives. My father was part of the non-militant wing of the Gama'a. . . . There were a lot of members like him who were against militancy. But the Security was stupid and didn't distinguish between the two. So this experience is what drew me into politics and made me want to understand what *balad* (country) meant, what *nizam* (regime) meant.

He went on to say,

> My entry into politics, or the start of my thinking about politics and the country and administration and the government and the police . . . it was this environment that I lived in that made me think about these things. It made me leave the sphere of the family, the street, the house, and the area . . . to what is bigger than this. I started to read and watch and follow the news. I started to understand that this country that I live in, it's mine, it doesn't belong to them. These people should represent me [but they don't. . . .]

Amr's story is significant. Neglected by the regime and left to fend for themselves, residents of informal settlements established an autonomous way of life independent of the government. Operating outside the framework of the state, these areas, marked by density and a lack of clear spatial design and order, lent themselves as oppositional spaces for radical, militant Islamists. This was the case for Imbaba, where the Gamaʻa had entrenched itself in the 1990s and gained support from the local community by "appropriating existing governing institutions and practices," including the provision of social welfare services such as health care, neighborhood safety watch groups, and dispute resolution.[18] Emboldened by their increasing power, the Gamaʻa declared Imbaba "a state within a state," provoking the infamous police siege of December 1992 that Amr is referring to. In this drama, more than fourteen thousand paramilitary troops descended upon the area in an Islamist crackdown that gave way to a six-week occupation and saw the arrest of six hundred alleged militants.[19] Amr's personal experience in the crossfire between Islamist militants and the state reflects his multilayered embeddedness. The informal life of Imbaba, where he grew up, and the Islamist insurgency it gave way to, showed the trickle-down effect of a global capitalist economic order filtered through a disastrous state neoliberalization project.

Amr's narrative shows how his father's political engagement informed his own consciousness and shaped his outlook. It appears that other activists who came from families with a history in politics were similarly influenced. Indeed, several other activists I interviewed came from families with an Islamist political background, particularly an affiliation with the Muslim Brotherhood, an experience that greatly affected their own political perspective. A thorough discussion of the history of the Brotherhood is beyond the scope of this study, but suffice it to say that since its beginnings in 1928, the organization's relationship with Egypt's successive regimes has been a highly complicated one, especially after the founding of the republic. Nasser began his heavy crackdown on the Brotherhood in 1954, seeing the organization and its vision for an Islamic state as a threat to his socialist, Arab Nationalist project. After being forced underground for several years, the Brotherhood then found the opportunity to reconstitute itself under Sadat, who allowed its members a fair amount of freedom in the hope that they might form his support base and serve as a bulwark against the leftists, who opposed his de-Nasserization project. Like Sadat, Mubarak was motivated by expediency, and he alternated between cracking down and tolerating the organization based on what was in the best interests of his regime in light of local circumstances and international pressure. But even when given some room to operate, the organization remained officially outlawed. This arc of the Brotherhood's experience left an indelible mark on many family histories in Egypt, including that of Basem, who shared the following about how it affected his consciousness.

> My father was a member of the Brotherhood a long time ago, when he was young. After he got married, he retreated from political activism. But of course, the background was still present and the culture was still present. He talks regularly about the Brotherhood and he talks about Abdel Nasser. In our house, we heard talk of politics from the time we were kids. When we grew up, we stayed informed and became engaged. . . . It was a regular habit of ours to watch the news—we had to watch the news every day. And as we got older, we started to read, we started to think for ourselves. I was raised to believe Sadat was good because he eased up on the Islamists, and he was against Abdel Nasser, and that sort of thing. But after I started to think for myself, I realized no . . . each had strengths and weaknesses.

Like Amr, Basem indicates that merely being around a parent with an affinity for a sociopolitical group was responsible for his initial political awareness and prompted him later to think and form opinions about matters for himself. That is, neither Amr nor Basem joined the same groups as their fathers, but instead drew on the political awareness they gained from their direct exposure to politics at home to chart a different path for themselves. This was also the case for Abdelrahman, whose family had been members of the Muslim Brotherhood for generations:

> I belong to a family that belongs to the Brotherhood. A historic family that has been with the Brotherhood since the 1950s. But I'm the only one who isn't in it, since a long time ago, from when I was young. My mother's grandfather and after that my grandfather were members of the Brotherhood, then my mom and my maternal uncles and my father and my paternal uncles. I was the first from the family to leave. . . . Anyone born into a Brotherhood family, it's like being Christian or Muslim: you're born into it. . . . Even during the period during which I was taking part, I wasn't really considered Brotherhood. They had something called *ashbal* (scouts). It was for the young kids. In the Brotherhood, you're not a full member until you pledge allegiance. When I left the organization, I wasn't fully

aware politically. But the idea of being shackled, or that I had to follow something specific, for me it was difficult.

Despite his decision not to follow the family tradition and formally enlist with the Brotherhood, Abdelrahman's family history in the organization and experience of repression contributed to his growing political awareness, and later, his activism:

> My mother's grandfather was imprisoned for ten years during the era of Gamal Abdel-Nasser. . . . My maternal uncles were also imprisoned—even though I differed from them politically, it still affected me. My father was imprisoned also. So all of this played a role in my life. Besides that, in our family we had two candidates who were Members of Parliament representing the Muslim Brotherhood: my maternal uncle and my maternal aunt's husband. They were in Parliament in 2005. I saw how violently they were treated by State Security. Also, my maternal uncle was imprisoned when he thought about running [for Parliament] in 2000. . . . His district was the one that also belonged to Yusuf Waaly, who was the minister of Agriculture, and he had considerable influence there in the countryside [that is, Fayoum]. So I stood by my uncle during the elections [by campaigning]—in fact I stood with all the candidates even though I might have fundamentally differed from them [politically], because in the end this was someone who was standing against nothing but a depraved regime.

Zyad's inclination toward resistance was also genetic. His political engagement was in great part shaped by the political engagement of his own left-leaning family since the time of Nasser. He joked, "Abdel Nasser arrested my grandfather, Sadat arrested my mother and father, and Mubarak arrested me several times." His grandfather was a member of the Democratic Movement for National Freedom (known in Arabic by the acronym HADITU for al-Haraka al-Dimuqratiya li Taharrur al-Watan), which had been the largest communist party in Egypt before the Free Officers declared the dissolution of all political parties in 1953. His parents were active in the student movement in the 1970s and became members of the communist Conference Party. In fact, his mother was tried under Sadat in 1977 for her alleged involvement in instigating the Bread Riots and spent six months in prison. His father, a veterinarian by profession, passed away when Zyad was young, while his mother continued to influence his outlook as a journalist, an intellectual, and an outspoken critic of the regime. But Zyad's family was not entirely left-wing. On the contrary, he referred to his grandmother and his uncles as *felool*, sympathizers with the ousted Mubarak regime. Nevertheless, it must be emphasized that Zyad and his leftist family were not an anomaly; several other Egyptian activists whose life stories are not included here also came from privileged and working-class families with a history in socialist politics and labor resistance.

For many of the activists who did not come from a family tied to the Muslim Brotherhood, the organization nonetheless played a crucial role in the formation of their political lives, often as the first organization they turned to seeking opportunities for social and political engagement. This path made sense, given their Muslim backgrounds and how pervasive the organization was in their local communities as a provider of social and religious services (for example, as children and young adults, several of them attended Islamic study circles organized by the Brotherhood in their local mosques, many of which had likely been built by the organization). This was the case for Mahmoud, who joined the Brotherhood chapter in his neighborhood, Awsim, for three years when he was a young teen, staying in the organization until he was about fifteen, before leaving it at the end of his second year in high school. Mahmoud would eventually leave the organization, not so much for ideological reasons, though their ideology was something he came to criticize later, but because he felt he could not adhere to its strict religious codes or live up to its expectations when it came to devotion and practice. Nonetheless, his engagement in the Brotherhood's political activities, particularly the constraints the older guard placed on the younger generation when it came to the degree of political autonomy they could exercise during protests, prompted him to ask questions about social change and resistance and eventually drove him to seek answers elsewhere (see chapter 5 for more on Mahmoud's experience with the Muslim Brotherhood).

Others, including Amr, Tarek, and Qassas from my group of interviewees, had their first dalliance with the Muslim Brotherhood in college. As young men who had been raised Muslim, had grown up in popular quarters where the Brotherhood was active, and were now seeking an outlet through which they could engage in campus and sociopolitical life as new university students, the organization was their natural first choice. Again, this was not surprising, given the familiarity of the Brotherhood to them, and especially considering that it was the most active organization on campus and very easily accessible. While Amr and Tarek never became fully incorporated members into the organization, Qassas did and later became known as one of its most active, exemplary young members.

What these histories demonstrate is the crucial role this organization played, either directly or indirectly, in the political formation of Egypt's January 25 activists. Indeed, most of these young activists had had direct experience of the Brotherhood in one form or another at some point in their lives, whether through their family, their neighborhood chapters, or their university chapters. In other words, the Brotherhood had a significant impact on their worldview and engagement; being the largest, most organized and established Islamist opposition group in Egypt, it was integral to the experience of living, growing up, and resisting in Egypt. (Chapters 5 and 7 discuss in detail activist attitudes toward the Muslim Brotherhood in the aftermath of the eighteen-day uprising.)

Activism in the University and the Street

The university and the street appear as central and often overlapping themes in the narratives of these activists. They serve as primary sites for their initial political activation and arenas for their engagement. Second in their narratives to these public spaces of political action is the sphere of formal opposition politics. The following sections take a closer look at their growing consciousness and activism within these three arenas, which, once again, reflect their embeddedness in the local, national, and international scales of politics.

The university and the police state

Egypt's universities have long served as incubators of political activism for youth across the ideological spectrum, spawning student dissidents ranging from the secular left to the far Islamist right. Their history as such dates back to the independence movement in the early twentieth century, when students and faculty from diverse political persuasions joined workers and labor unions in the struggle against the British and the corrupt Egyptian monarchy. Student activism was choked after Nasser came to power in 1954, when his regime banned all political parties and introduced repressive university reforms to silence students and faculty opposed to military rule. This changed, however, with Egypt's humiliating defeat in the 1967

Arab–Israeli War. Students once again became actively engaged in national politics and were at the forefront of mobilizations against domestic and foreign policies. Led primarily by leftists, students staged several uprisings that were key to shaping the country's political trajectory. In 1968, they rose up to demand heavier penalties for those responsible for the 1967 defeat, the protection of political freedoms inside and outside the university, and the liberalization of the country's political system.[20]

The student movement reached its peak between 1972 and 1973, when students rose up again to demand that Nasser's successor, Sadat, take decisive action to recover Israeli-occupied Sinai through military force. They also called for the democratization of the political system and socioeconomic reforms. In fact, students like Zyad's mother played a leading role in the Bread Riots that shook Egypt in 1977. Eager to extinguish the movement, Sadat fought the influence of his leftist student opponents by shoring up Islamist groups on campuses. The strategy worked, and Islamists would sweep the student elections of 1978–1979. But then Sadat signed the 1979 Camp David Accords, and the plan unraveled as Islamist students joined leftists in their vehement criticism of his foreign policies. Sadat eventually cracked down on student activism with the Student Law of 1979, banning political organizing on campus. The measure restored power to the campus police units, known as the University Guard, which had been established under Nasser. It also gave the university administration authority over student unions, including the right to vet election candidates and to interfere in the unions' decision-making.[21]

For most of his tenure, Mubarak would more or less continue in the vein of his predecessors; the state repression on campus and the violations of academic freedom that had marked their university policies would characterize his as well and shape the budding political consciousness of a new generation of youth leaders.

The story of Qassas is a case in point. As one of the two older activists I interviewed, his student activism as a young Islamist dated back to the early 1990s during a time of renewed campus repression. Qassas emphasized that his enrollment at Dar al-Ulum college at Cairo University was key to shaping the person he is today. When he became a student, he immediately decided to join the Muslim Brotherhood group that was active on campus, which by then had grown to outnumber the leftists and dominate student life. Despite the restrictions imposed by the 1979 Bill, the Brotherhood was permitted to develop their campus presence through much of the 1980s by avoiding nonviolent political activity. Instead, their activism focused mostly on cultural issues and foreign affairs, which the Mubarak regime tolerated. But this dynamic had started to change by the time Qassas joined as a first-year student. The regime had begun by then to increase the policing of campuses and tighten its control over the university administration, professors' clubs, and student unions as part of its larger crackdown on militant Islamists and its wider offensive against the Muslim Brothers, who were becoming too powerful through their domination of civic associations for its liking.[22]

Initially, Qassas's political awareness and activism, along with that of his fellow student Muslim Brothers, was sparked by the troubles of the Muslim world, specifically the Palestinian–Israeli conflict, the Gulf War, the Bosnian War, and later the Kosovo War. They continued to organize around these events until the government's interference in university administration drew the attention of the student body toward the regime, leading to an inevitable confrontation. According to Qassas, this standoff was triggered by the government's appointment of academics loyal to the ruling NDP to important administrative posts, as well as its interference in student union activities, especially its efforts to bar Islamist and other opposition students from contesting elections:

> In 1995, there began a greater interest in political work, by which I mean speaking about the regime. There were some events before 1995 in 1993, 1994, and 1995—these events were related to the deans and presidents of the university, who obtained their positions through appointment instead of elections. For us this was a dangerous development. And at the time, the first person the university hired was Mofeed Shehab . . . he was one of the most important men of the old regime. And he was a minister of state in the ousted regime and one of the most important people who provided a legal framework for the regime—we resisted him fiercely. So, then, the deans started to be appointed—and actually before that they began appointing leaders in the syndicates instead of allowing the free elections upon which they are built. . . . So this appointing frenzy was spilling over into civil society in Egypt in general, including the university. They began to interfere in the university's student unions, dividing the students and harassing them. This was an escalation. In 1995, they arrested a group of members from the Brotherhood's *shura* council and subjected them to military trials—this was the first time this

had happened in many years, for a civil society organization to be subject to military trials—so [my friend] Waleed, for example, in one of the [campus] protests, he was leading the chants, and he called out, "Everyone shout after me three times: 'Hey Mubarak! You're a tyrant!'" (Of course after that he was arrested and tortured. . . .) So, I see that this was the beginning of my face-off with the regime, in this time period, the year 1995.

From Qassas's view, the appointment of administrative leaders based on political loyalty to the ruling party and the manipulation of student union elections were serious affronts to university independence: they violated the academic freedoms the institution stood for. These measures awakened and even radicalized many students against the regime. Equally significant, Qassas's remarks highlight the continuity between university and national politics and the fluidity of youth resistance between these spheres, as had historically been the case in Egypt; once again, this reflects the embeddedness of young people in these multiple scales of sociopolitical interaction and struggle. It is also important to note that these events marked a critical shift in relations between Muslim Brothers like Qassas and the leftists on campus, who began to view the regime as their common enemy and started to collaborate in their activism.[23] As the following sections will illustrate, this cross-ideological alliance would eventually spill out of the university onto the street and play a key role in shaping the resistance that would precipitate the revolution.

The university experience was also a turning point for activists like Amr, Tarek, and Mostafa who saw the corruption and callousness of the state firsthand through the institution and for the first time entered into a space in which the exchange of ideas represented a new, exciting, and transformative world. For Amr, Cairo University was a novel experience. He described his first year as being a transition from the "world of harshness to the world of the intellect." In his second year, he began to search for opportunities to engage in campus life, joining an *usra tulabiya* (student club), an official student organization permitted by the university administration through which he could lawfully organize and participate in student activities. On one occasion, he petitioned an administrator for funds for an initiative his student club hoped to launch, and he was shocked by his response:

The professor rudely shouted, "We have no money for you, and whatever we want you to do you'll do!" And it was as if someone was talking to me like I was begging them. Do you know this mannerism I'm talking about? At the time I said to him, "You're not giving us anything from your pocket. These people are doing work out of their own good will, they have nothing to gain from it, and the manner in which you're speaking to us is unacceptable."

The demeaning treatment Amr experienced at the hands of a school administrator was a common part of the student experience in Egypt's universities. This lack of civility was a symptom of the eroding culture and respectability of the institution, in part a result of the government policies that had subordinated the university to the regime, sidelining student and faculty interests.

Tarek and Mostafa cited their direct confrontations with the police state on campus as a major factor in their radicalization. In each case, they had asserted their rights to free speech, and in each case, they were punished for it. Tarek spoke about the time he had publicly criticized a school administrator who was a member of the ruling National Democratic Party at an off-campus event:

In the first year of college, during the second term, there was someone named Mohammed Abdallah. He was the most prominent figure in the ruling National Democratic Party in Alexandria, and he was the president of my university. So during this time, there was a really big symposium being held in the biggest theater in Alexandria. I entered into a direct confrontation with him at the event, and I said to him, "You're corrupt, and you're a member of a failed party." So he decided that I should be prohibited from taking my end-of-the-year exams. As a result, I was forced to stay in college for eight years! And the State Security officers used to say to me, "Come on now, we're making you stay in the university all these years, so get it together already, learn your lesson!" . . . *Eight years!* This made me determined to get my revenge on this regime. . . . So yeah, corruption, it had touched us from every angle.

Mostafa's life-changing experience was similar to Tarek's in that he, too, was asserting his legitimate right to free speech and was reprimanded for it. His story reflects how entrenched the police state really was in the day-to-day life of university students, who were under constant surveillance on campus. Shortly after Mostafa began his studies at Helwan University, he decided to engage in campus life by taking part in student cultural activities. He helped organize and host seminars on a variety of subjects, which inevitably became political and critical of the regime in tone because "whatever subject you talked about, in some way you would be forced to discuss the general affairs of the country, which were corrupt in every way possible—economically and socially and everything else!" This inability to escape mention of the regime's shortcomings and failures became problematic for Mostafa: after organizing one particular event that featured a prominent economist from the opposition, he was prohibited by the university from participating in any other official cultural activities on campus. According to Mostafa, this ban was a result of pressure from State Security, which disapproved of the kinds of seminars and activities he was organizing.

> This came as a huge shock because I was working within a very official framework and had the permission of the college president . . . . The first hurdle we faced was that before holding any cultural seminar or festivity at our college or in the university, we had to get permission from State Security. They would interrogate us about who was coming and what they were going to say, and then bombard us with ridiculous questions about things, like what kind of questions and comments would come from the audience and who would ask them. Then they would amend and change your plan. You would sit with the officers of State Security and they wouldn't know anything, they would have no clue about anything [about the topic of the planned event], and they were sticking their noses in something that you were specialized in and understood well. So we had to deal with brazen interference from a group of idiots who didn't understand a thing in this field, and it was immensely aggravating. The situation then became—it was exasperating, actually, being prevented from engaging in a cultural activity that was official because of a State Security decision. This was a major turning point for me. So as soon as Students for Change [a branch of the Kefaya movement] appeared on my campus, I joined right away.

Mostafa's story illustrates the depth and extent of the state's policing of university life and its corrosive effects. His experience was all the more troubling, as he emphasized, because he was operating within the official boundaries the university and the police had set on campus. In the end, the repressive restrictions on free speech and academic freedoms were too much to bear for students like Tarek and Mostafa. Instead of quieting students, these policies had a radicalizing effect, as a growing number decided it was time to take on the regime directly. This is captured in the declaration of Students for Change, which advocated for the achievement of "political democracy both within society and within the university and against corruption and for the realization of equality of opportunity,"[24] connecting the plight of university students to the wider struggle for change beyond the university.

Regional and global conflicts and the birth of new social movements, 2000-2003

The eruption of regional and global conflicts around the time when Amr, Mostafa, Tarek and others like Ola, Zyad, and Abbas were college students played an even more crucial role in their politicization and radicalization than university repression. All of these activists cited the outbreak of the Palestinian Intifada in 2000—and the thunderous local solidarity protests it gave way to—as the event that officially transformed them into activists, their divergent ideological leanings notwithstanding. This momentous conflict opened the door to ten years of struggle in which all these activists would become entrenched political actors, while their political networks rapidly extended beyond their local milieu. The US invasion of Iraq in 2003 and the global anti-war movement gave rise to equally seismic demonstrations that further consolidated their political commitment and identity as dissidents (see chapter 2). Not only did they participate in the wave of protest that stormed onto the Egyptian streets, they also participated in and helped organize protests and other acts of civil disobedience on their university campuses. Amr recalled his participation in the boisterous anti-Iraq war protests of March 20, 2003, which ended in the one-day occupation of Tahrir Square, as a personal turning point:

> I used to participate in protests at Cairo University, but not passionately.... In 2003 a big event took place, which was the war in Iraq, and I participated in a protest from 12 p.m. to 1 a.m., for more than thirteen hours. It was at the university, and we were beaten mercilessly. Central Security Forces and tear gas and tons of arrests. After experiencing this climate, I said I must continue to be active.

Zyad, who began his political activism around the age of sixteen, also around the Palestinian cause, was one of the active student leaders of the Students for Supporting the Intifada at Cairo University. "They arrested me after the demonstrations, and they broke my leg. And they broke my arm for supporting Iraq [against the US invasion], and arrested me then also," he said. Qassas too was active around the Palestinian issue. Along with twenty-one other Muslim Brothers, he was arrested for protesting in solidarity with Palestinians and detained for nine months, while several of his other colleagues were handed three- and five-year prison sentences. Brotherhood runaway Abdelrahman, who did not come to activism through the university, was also brought into the political arena by events around Palestine and Iraq, where he connected and engaged with other youth activists for the first time through street activism—in fact, he decided to move to Cairo from Fayoum so he could participate regularly in actions related to these events.

An important development during this period was the Cairo Anti-war Conference, launched in December of 2002 ahead of the anticipated invasion of Iraq by the United States. Secular and Islamist activists, including Abdelrahman, Qassas, and Zyad, convened with intellectuals to discuss plans for anti-war protests and develop joint positions against the occupation of Palestine and US imperialism. It was during the Palestinian solidarity and anti-war conference and demonstrations that many of these youth became acquainted with each other and began to network and later coordinate their resistance efforts.

The rise of the anti-regime struggle, 2004-2006

This period saw the increasingly important role organized political institutions came to play at a crucial juncture in the political maturation of the January 25 youth leaders, responding to their urge to belong to formal collective institutions that represented their political ideals. The 2004 Kefaya Movement is one such example, figuring—along with the Youth for Change Movement that operated under its umbrella—as a common stepping stone in the trajectories of these activists (see chapter 2). Each of my interlocutors said they participated in Kefaya's historic protests and mass actions, and those like Amr, Tarek, Ola, and Mostafa who were new to street politics cited them as crucial to raising their awareness, igniting their passion, and shaping their activist becoming. Moreover, as they later began to establish and organize within their own independent youth movements, they borrowed from the tactics innovated by these groups—such as flash protests in popular quarters—and improved upon them.

Equally important was the 2005 independent judges' movement, which was launched to protest the executive authority's direct interference in judicial affairs. The "Judges' Intifada," as it was also known, was an energizing development for reform activists because it marked the entry of a powerful, official institutional force into their movement. The judges' resistance mobilized the streets in a game-changing way, and each of my interlocutors was among those who protested alongside them in solidarity. In fact, Qassas's third arrest under Mubarak's reign was for his participation in the May protest discussed in the previous chapter. Amr and Abdelrahman both talked about the traumatic and humiliating experience of being beaten during the protests and unable to help esteemed judges being assaulted and women activists who were beaten, stripped, and sexually violated by police-hired thugs in front of them. Abdelrahman said:

> When you see the judge, who is supposed to be a symbol of the state that inspires awe as well as a symbol of justice and equality, getting beaten by a police officer and slapped across his face or his ID card is torn up or he is arrested . . . when you see a member of Parliament getting beaten and he has parliamentary immunity, and his clothes are torn . . . it shows there's no dignity for the human being, even for the person who of all people should get it—the judge or the woman or the Member of Parliament. . . . All of this constantly affected us.

Having become politically charged by the street, several of these youth sought out more formal outlets for political engagement. While in college, a friend of Amr's who was a member of the ruling NDP's youth faction suggested he join them, but Amr decided against it after learning what it meant to be a young member of this party:

> So he told me about their activities and what they do. And I said if this is politics, then I'm not going to work in politics. It would be better if I went to a recreation club. They were organizing recreation trips for them, soccer games. . . . The youth who were good would get to go on Safari trips, they would have dinner parties, that kind of thing. Basically, they were keeping them in the dark.

It was around this time when Amr learned from a college professor about the rich history of the liberal Wafd Party. Wafd is Egypt's oldest political party, dating back to the days of the monarchy. It was founded by the celebrated nationalist leader Saad Zaghloul as part of the 1919 independence movement against British colonial occupation. Amr was enamored with the party's story and decided to go down to the headquarters and see if the opportunities for engagement with this group were more promising than those with the NDP youth faction, but he was discouraged by what he found. Though it had once been at the forefront of progressive national politics, the Wafd Party had since fallen from grace, having been largely co-opted by the ruling establishment, as evinced in stances it had frequently adopted supporting Mubarak's NDP and its alleged backdoor dealings in exchange for positions of power.[25] Amr reflected on his experience with the party, comparing it to his encounters with the NDP:

> I went and found the same programs. . . . I went once, twice, three times, ten. I found that the youth had no role, that the leaders were working for their own benefit. The youth did nothing. It's likely that the majority of the youth who were involved were youth who entered so that they could get close to politicians who would help them get ahead. But in the end, I was looking for something that I could do. Something to make me feel—to make this country mine again. . . . I wanted to work in politics because, personally, I used to feel that my country was occupied, that I didn't have a role in it. I didn't go down and vote in elections. And even if I had, the election would be fraudulent. . . . The management of the country, when something went wrong, I wasn't able to hold the people running it to account. . . . So I had this deep sense that the country didn't belong to me. . . . I was looking for political work that would make me feel like this country was mine, but I found nothing.

But things changed for Amr in March of 2004, as they did for his peer Abdelrahman. Ayman Nour, a member of Parliament and a former member of the Wafd Party, had just established the liberal-centrist Ghad Party (Hizb al-Ghad, the "Tomorrow Party"). Amr had first been exposed to Nour at a lecture he gave at Cairo University. He continued to follow Nour after the lecture, intrigued after learning about his initiatives in Parliament and his struggle to reform the Wafd Party from within. But then Nour split to form his new party. Amr, who had by then lost interest in the Wafd, found this exciting and hoped that with Nour he would find the opportunity for real political engagement he had been searching for. He was encouraged by the diversity of the party's founding members, which included ordinary Egyptians like housewives and workers as well as reputable politicians:

> The idea appealed to me.... He might do something new [I thought to myself]. Let's see, I have nothing to lose.... At this time, it wasn't yet a party, it was still the Ghad movement. When I arrived I found that there was a serious interest in the youth.... I found the thing that I had been looking for. I found that youth who arrived knowing nothing could slowly climb through the ranks and end up in positions of leadership.

Abdelrahman, who was also seeking real opportunities to become politically engaged, expressed the same sentiment about Ayman Nour and Ghad, which he joined after experimenting with a number of other parties like the socialist Tagammu' Party:

> The thing that attracted me the most, that resonated with me most about the Ghad Party at the time that it was founded.... We saw that the party was somewhat revolutionary.... The party represented something youthful for us. It responded to youth aspirations. We saw that Ayman Nour wasn't much older than us. He spoke to the youth in their language, he'd meet them without arrogance.... It was encouraging.... Nour is one of the people I'm indebted to politically. He helped me develop my political awareness.

Even Qassas, who was a member of the Muslim Brotherhood at the time, said he had felt encouraged by the promise of Ayman Nour, and in a chance meeting with him near the party headquarters in downtown Cairo, had personally expressed his support for Nour's efforts.

Both Amr and Abdelrahman benefitted from the extensive training, mentorship, and opportunities for engagement provided to them in the Ghad Party, and they cite their work on Nour's 2005 presidential campaign as one of their most exciting and edifying experiences. In fact, Abdelrahman was charged with managing Nour's election campaign in Fayoum. But in 2006, following the fraudulent election and Ayman Nour's imprisonment, several internal problems came to light within the Ghad Party leadership, and the youth became increasingly marginalized. Frustrated, Amr and Abdelrahman began to transition to street youth movement work.

While Amr and Abdelrahman were immersed in the work of Ghad, other activists, including Mostafa, Ola, and Mahmoud, explored leftist political parties and groups. They joined the Trotskyist Revolutionary Socialists for a time before also leaving to join and/or establish new groups.

Youth movements, labor, and the socioeconomic struggle, 2006–2009

As the Kefaya movement began to die down and its political demands became less strident—a consequence of subsiding external pressure for reforms after the 2005 election and increasing political repression—a new kind of resistance focused on socioeconomic reform was quickly escalating in Egypt's streets. As noted in the previous chapter, the labor unrest that had begun in Mahalla in late 2006 and the wave of protest it sparked across a range of economic sectors over the next few years captured the imagination of the newly politicized youth, inspiring them to break away from the older generation and establish new youth movements like April 6 and Tadamun in solidarity with the workers. What we begin to see, then, is how the global and national political economy—particularly as it relates to neoliberalism—also began to shape the consciousness and activist orientations of these evolving activists.

Several of the activists I interviewed were active in, if not among the founders and key leaders of, these groups. Amr, Tarek, Mahmoud, and Abdelrahman played important roles in April 6's leading efforts in public relations and in organizing the group's mass actions in and outside of Cairo. They were among the innovators behind a host of new street protest tactics, such as thirty-minute flash protests and leafletting campaigns in popular neighborhoods, which they used to raise awareness among the struggling working and lower classes about a range of issues that were critical to them. These included the frequent power blackouts in Shubra, which were the result of state neglect and a diminishing supply of natural gas to run power plants—this, while Egypt supplied Israel with 40 percent of the natural gas the latter used to generate its electricity, selling it to them at six times below the international market rate in defiance of Egyptian public opinion about the privatization and export of natural gas and the normalization of relations with a longtime foe.[26] Other issues they took up included rising food prices, youth unemployment, and persistent garbage collection problems. These protests were well received, and for the first time even managed to draw the participation of apolitical local citizens. Activists organized such protests in working-class areas like Shubra to help people make the connection between their local, socioeconomic struggles and national and international politics—without mentioning Mubarak or the regime so as not to frighten them away. Their activities once again illustrate their embeddedness in the multilayered and intersecting social and political arenas as well as their creativity in adapting to both limited resources and repressive conditions. Abdelrahman was active in Cairo's April 6 branch and was also the activist responsible for the group's activities in the Fayoum governorate southwest of Cairo.

Here it is important to highlight the fluid, flexible membership characterizing this emerging political vanguard, in contrast to the traditionally rigid, singular militancy that once predominated in Egypt among political organizations across the ideological spectrum. Activists enjoyed membership in multiple groups, which strengthened the resistance network. For example, although the young Muslim Brothers Abbas and Qassas were not formally members of April 6, they participated in its street actions. Mostafa was an active member of April 6 but later quit to start two left-leaning youth movements, the Youth for Justice and Freedom Movement and the Socialist Renewal Current, which played an equally important role in street agitation and continued to work and organize actions with April 6. As for Zyad and Ola, they became active members of the leftist Tadamun workers' solidarity movement.

Meanwhile, Mahmoud was intimately getting to know the labor struggle from the inside as a worker for the leading petroleum company Petrojet, a position he took up to support himself through college. There, he came to experience the desperation of workers under neoliberalism—the low wages, long hours, and miserable working conditions. He also understood the limitations and ineffectiveness of striking as a mechanism for change in an Egyptian context, where thousands in urgent need of work made laborers all too expendable. Mahmoud shared that he had made several attempts to convince his coworkers to go on strike in order to force their supervisors to give them their rights, but their response was always the same: "They would simply say, 'he [the manager] could not do any of that and just fire us and get other people.' They would tell me, 'You know how it is. For each one of us, there are a thousand workers ready to work. They're desperate for it.'" These conversations led Mahmoud to an epiphany: "In the end, I thought to myself, 'This whole order has to change.'" Through his dialectical engagement with the working-class struggle, Mahmoud began to recognize the problems with trade-union activism in a neoliberal context and the need for a radically new, socially just system that abolished their vulnerability as workers altogether.

Youth movements and social revolution, 2010-2011

In 2010, the year before the revolution, the fear resurfaced that Mubarak's son Gamal would take his father's position in the 2011 election. The opposition movement reacted by renewing its demands for political reform, but this time combined them with demands for socioeconomic reform. This effort was led by activists from April 6 and the newly formed ElBaradei Campaign, which Basem and Zyad had helped found.

Zyad by this point was a seasoned activist. The young leftist attorney had participated in all the major resistance efforts to date: the pro-Palestinian movement, the anti-war movement, Kefaya, and the workers' solidarity movement. And like the courageous others who dared to take to the streets in defiance of the state, he had endured vicious police beatings and multiple arrests. Basem, on the other hand, had steered clear of the political activist scene and all the danger that came with it, after some cautious involvement in college. For most of his adult life, he had abided by the old Egyptian adage, "walk by the wall," which basically means mind your own business, work hard, focus on your family, and above all, know your place and stay out of politics and away from the police if you want to live and prosper. And that is precisely what he did. He became an architect, built a profitable firm that employed his brothers, married in his twenties, raised three children, afforded his family a decent middle-class lifestyle according to Egypt's modest standards, and avoided confrontation with authorities.

But even so, Basem was not thriving. He was not immune to the intolerable realities that afflicted every middle-class Egyptian, and he voiced his protest against the status quo in the safe company of family and friends. He took note of the Kefaya movement and admired the effort but was skeptical about its ability to effect any meaningful change. The way he saw it, Mubarak and his system were unassailable. But something changed for Basem with news of ElBaradei's return to his native Egypt following his retirement as the UN nuclear weapons chief. Like many other Egyptians, Basem was captivated by the idea of the internationally renowned statesman and Nobel laureate who was a staunch and vocal critic of the US invasion of Iraq and a fearless advocate for democratic change in his home country. ElBaradei was a man of ideas and vision, the complete antithesis of Mubarak and a welcome alternative to Gamal as his successor.

Basem was inspired by what ElBaradei represented: an alternative for political leadership in Egypt and hope for the nation's deliverance from suffocating authoritarianism. He followed the Facebook page set up by the movement that was rallying around ElBaradei's return, contemplating whether he should get involved. Abdul Rahman Yusuf, the activist poet who was the page's administrator, put out a call inviting followers to join an organizing meeting to help build a movement of real people operating on the ground. Never one to make rash decisions or take on commitments he could not see through to their end, Basem considered the risks: he could get arrested and tortured or even killed, which would leave his family without a provider. He worried about his aging parents in particular and the anguish he might cause them. In the end, his moral conviction and newfound idealism trumped his fears, and he resolved to do his part to make the country better. "I liked the guy," Basem admitted. "And the idea that he could be the president? I thought, yes, he could, and at the time I will stand by him." Basem showed up at the meeting downtown, where he met Zyad and a handful of other seasoned and novice organizers. Together, they planned the politically charged event in 2010 in which a thousand well-wishers showed up at Cairo International Airport to welcome ElBaradei. It was the first event in Egypt organized around the high-profile dissident. Soon, Basem and Zyad would become his closest aides.

According to Basem, the ElBaradei Campaign was not so much about trying to get the man elected president; ElBaradei served more as a symbol to show that, contrary to what the ruling class would have people believe, there were options besides the Mubarak clan, that change was possible. Basem and Zyad helped develop the organization's branches across Egypt and coordinated a massive canvassing campaign with other opposition groups, including the Muslim Brotherhood, that managed to secure one million signatures for the seven demands for change.[27] Meanwhile, the April 6 Youth Movement also continued to expand into the governorates, where it played a significant role in raising awareness.

With the tragedy of Khaled Said's death and the emergence of the We Are All Khaled Said Facebook movement, the seven demands for change were joined by heavy criticism of the security apparatus and a denunciation of its egregious abuses and human rights violations to form a comprehensive set of grievances that these groups believed were beyond any redress through mere reform of the existing system. Along with Youth for Justice and Freedom, the Muslim Brotherhood youth, and youth from other political factions, as well as independent activists, these groups combined their organizing and mobilizing skills to coordinate a string of joint mass actions in the year preceding the January 25 uprising, featuring new and creative tactics. In one such protest, on the day Khaled Said's murderers were to be put on trial, two hundred activists—an impressive turnout at the time—descended upon Imbaba to "make some noise" in protest of police brutality. Before they began chanting, they marched through the street sounding whistles and striking pot covers together like cymbals, in a demonstration that was well received by locals. These resistance efforts were stepped up following the fraudulent parliamentary elections of 2010 and the Alexandria church bombing on January 1, 2011. The youth movement's response to the latter development was critical; activists established interfaith solidarity between Muslims and Coptic Christians by staging protests to resist sectarianism and call out the government's failure to protect the religious minority from sectarian violence, presaging the show of Muslim–Christian unity that was a hallmark of the Tahrir uprising weeks later. The last joint effort around which the activists organized before January 25 was the Parallel Parliament initiative, in which they attempted to negotiate a space for their participation and radical politics in the formal opposition (discussed more in chapter 4).

According to Qassas, this joint work was the culmination of sustained cross-ideological coordination, collaboration, and friendship-building over ten years of continuous struggle. Its roots extended back to the mid-1990s, when opposing political camps at Cairo University first decided to transcend their long-standing conflicts and ideological differences to coordinate resistance against the state, their common foe. These initial efforts convened student activists like Qassas, an Islamist, and Zyad, a leftist, who in turn influenced a younger generation of activists such as Abbas and Mostafa of similarly divergent political currents. Through conferences, solidarity demonstrations, door-to-door awareness-raising campaigns, and even time spent together in prison, this diverse and persevering cadre was brought together by and became intimate through their embeddedness in the same multilevel struggle, shaping and being shaped by an emergent collective consciousness.

The Question of the Internet

The question of the Internet and the role it played in politicizing activists is an important one, given all the social media tropes through which the revolution has been framed. This includes those perpetuated by figures like Wael Ghonim, the Google executive and anonymous founder and administrator of the We Are All Khaled Said Facebook page, who told CNN, "This revolution started on Facebook" and remarked that he wanted to "meet Mark Zuckerburg some day and thank him personally."[28] The Internet figured in different ways in the narratives I gathered, but it was certainly not central. As demonstrated in the activist trajectories sketched in this chapter, the political awareness of these activists was shaped by their personal experiences and interaction with the ten-year resistance movement in historically determined places. The Internet was a space they went to, having already developed their political consciousness, to express their views—a space that was highly valued, given their exclusion from mainstream politics, print media, and social and political talk shows[29]—and connect with other like-minded people. In other words, these youth might have been wired, but their consciousness was not born instantly nor was it born online. This was the case for Mahmoud, who, after engaging in resistance through the Muslim Brotherhood, began for a time to use the social networking site Hi5 to share frustrations about the status quo that he could not express freely among the Brothers (see chapter 5 for more about Mahmoud's experience). Similarly, several activists, including Amr, Qassas, Abbas, and Abdelrahman, took part in the blogging trend that emerged in the mid-2000s to share their thoughts on contentious issues with their peers and voice their discontent, but again, their engagement through this medium was very transient.[30]

Of course, this is not to downplay the role of cyberspace in the birth and evolution of this struggle. Movements like April 6 and We Are All Khaled Said developed through Facebook and other social networking sites, which they relied on as tools for mobilizing, connecting, networking, and raising awareness; these digital tools were especially valued in the police state for allowing activists to organize and engage in contentious politics while escaping the notice and surveillance of the watchful State Security, which was digitally unsophisticated and still largely unfamiliar with these technologies.[31] But the point here is that these organizations would have been nothing without the already-politicized youth who were leading them, activists who were not politicized by the Internet but by their experiences offline. In many ways, they were Gramscian-like "organic intellectuals" who came into their consciousness by way of their immersion in the same political, social, and economic struggles of the classes whose cause they would champion.³² In other words, although these virtual sites played an important role in awakening and politicizing a new generation of youth in the lead-up to January 25 by allowing them to witness injustices like police brutality more directly (through visceral images and videos of torture gone viral, for example), they were not responsible for the politicization of the young leaders I interviewed, who had engaged in resistance before the revolution. This is reflected in Mahmoud's comments about how he decided whether or not he should join April 6:

> I thought they were an Internet group, so they weren't going to be able to do anything concrete. But as soon as I felt that we could get together—notice I say we, not the Internet—then I joined. The Internet is just a tool for people to get together, like any other tool. It's when you get together that something happens. Succeed, fail, it doesn't matter really. All you can do is what you can do after all.

Mahmoud's remarks are consistent with the tendency of the activists I interviewed to think of themselves loosely as street activists rather than Internet activists. Ola said:

> I'm definitely more of a street activist. I'm there online, but I wouldn't say I'm an online activist. I'm not even that much on Twitter. I'm on Twitter on a daily basis, like I have two-thousand-something people I mostly know follow me. I follow only 150 people. I tweet, but I don't tweet while doing things. I'm not in a protest and then I tweet. It doesn't happen this way. So I'm not that much of an online activist. If I had to choose, being a street activist is more fulfilling. You can sense things, you don't get disconnected. . . . You can correct yourself because people are correcting you, you get to see things happening, you get into discussions, you know more and you do more and you affect more.

Qassas agreed and had a different take on the role of the Internet within the context of the history of communication:

> This matter is connected quite a bit with the awareness of the street and its feeling. These means helped a great deal. . . . It's not that [without the Internet] this revolution wasn't going to happen. . . . If

the Internet hadn't been there, for sure some other means would have emerged. For sure. This is what I want to say—that the Internet helped, yes, but this is a consequence of our time. . . . In earlier times, poetry was the means. Shaykh Imam's songs in 1977 and 1978—that was the means. . . .[33] So of course the Internet helped a great deal; I can't deny this. But it was a tool. It's a tool in the end for expressing the situation in which people find themselves.

In other words, Qassas suggests that the Internet functioned like any other communication tool throughout the history of social movements, albeit more efficiently. Just as the pamphlets circulated in colonial America cannot be credited for the American Revolution, neither can the Internet, and more specifically platforms like Facebook and Twitter, be credited for the Egyptian revolution. Even if they were necessary, they certainly were not sufficient. In sum, analyses that focus on the importance of these tools miss the more crucial story: the tremendous effort and sacrifice of the many actors who resisted the regime and worked tirelessly for years, determined to bring this movement for political and social transformation to fruition.

The Myth of Western Influence

Among the other tropes associated with the consciousness of politicized youth and the eruption and success of the initial uprising was the connection to Western movements like Otpor, the Serbian democratic youth movement that kickstarted the Color Revolutions across Eastern Europe in the early 2000s, and the influence of works like Gene Sharp's handbook in resistance, *From Dictatorship to Democracy*, published in 1993.[34] When I questioned my research participants about the role these two played in their trajectories as activists and the eruption of the revolution, they were generally dismissive. Mostafa, of the Youth for Justice and Freedom Movement, mentioned that a few activists from April 6 went to a training in peaceful change and nonviolent resistance by Otpor in Serbia, but that its impact on the activists and revolution as a whole was terribly exaggerated. Amr cited the Otpor Movement as one of a number of experiments in change that some of the youth activists from April 6 had learned about through film screenings, which also included documentaries on the 1999 Seattle World Trade Organization protests and the feature film *V for Vendetta*, but emphasized that they were not at all critical to their consciousness and that their reach among youth was very limited.

Gene Sharp's book did not figure prominently in the narratives I gathered either. Mostafa stated squarely that although some activists had read the book, it was by no means the inspiration behind their activism or the Egyptian revolution:

> Gene Sharpe had no connection, either near or far, to the development of Egyptian youth's awareness in the revolution. There was something called nonviolent tactics of war, and it was somewhat of a trend for a time for the youth to read up on it, but it was read very little by just a few.... There were some groups among the youth who thought, "Wow this is neat," and others who saw it as a joke, that it had nothing to do with—that it didn't relate to the collective consciousness of the Egyptian public. These were just nonviolent peaceful tactics. They were beneficial on the level of, you know, like when you read something to exercise your brain, warm it up.... It might have sparked the creativity of some Egyptian youth. But it had nothing to do with the Egyptian revolution. What had a connection and a real, practical impact on the youth and their revolution was what happened in Tunisia, down to the details. That's what was being transferred, copy and paste, to Egypt.

These remarks are consistent with the other findings presented in this chapter, which demonstrate that this sweeping movement and the activists driving it emerged out of the utterly local.

Conclusion

So was the January 25 revolution spontaneous? Not in the sense that it erupted in a vacuum. This chapter illuminates the deeper, more nuanced and grounded history that fed into the revolution as it manifested in the lives of the young actors who were at its forefront. Their radicalization was not instant; on the contrary, it occurred through a long and gradual process in which they first became aware and critical of their personal and family circumstances, then engaged in an effort to influence change, then mobilized against those in power as they agitated others to do the same. The backgrounds and individual experiences of these activists might have differed, but together, they speak to the mountain of social, economic, and political grievances that nullified the social contract binding Egyptians' submission to the state in exchange for the state's provision of welfare.

Their embeddedness in the country's political and socioeconomic trajectory and the experiences it generated for them transformed them into full-fledged oppositional subjects who would become ripe for an even more confrontational role as adversaries of the state and its institutions, one for which, as we will see, they were organizationally unprepared. On the eve of January 25, little did they know they were about to be made into revolutionaries. How they became such and how their revolutionary subjectivities evolved is the topic of the following chapters.

4

Youth Activists and Revolutionary Praxis

It was just after sundown on February 11, 2011, when the end finally came, and rather swiftly. In a breaking televised address that lasted an entire thirty-two seconds, an ashen and grim-faced Vice President Omar Suleiman unceremoniously announced the resignation of President Hosni Mubarak, jolting Tahrir Square and Egypt's streets into wild jubilation. What just less than a month earlier had been a distant, almost absurd dream for many of Egypt's young activists was now real: a popular revolutionary struggle had erupted—in part at their instigation—and forced the exit of the deeply entrenched dictator, effectively ending his suffocating thirty-year reign. How did this happen? How did what was expected to be a modest day of protest on January 25, 2011, turn into a millions-strong popular revolt that ousted the seemingly indomitable leader in a mere eighteen days?

Focusing on the period stretching from the weeks immediately preceding January 25 through February 11, this chapter examines the revolutionary movement process as it evolved from the perspective of the youth activists profiled in the previous chapter, who were deeply engaged in it as organizers. This process was characterized by a series of ups and downs determined by a fluid, changing reality that emerged with activist agitation, state reactions, the people's shifting perceptions and responses, and global solidarity and sympathy for their cause. This complex process unfolded in phases after critical junctures, which forced the actors involved to constantly negotiate and act around two recurring, corresponding questions: "What is happening?" and "How should we act?" The *what* question captures their evolving understanding of the emerging, transforming sociopolitical resistance phenomenon on the one hand, and their constant assessment of its revolutionary potential on the other. The *how* question refers to their attempts to figure out how they should respond and carry the resistance forward to affect the change they desired. The question of *how* in turn required them to consider *who* should be involved and in what configuration to ensure their project's legitimacy and ultimate success. Also critical to this process was the question of *where*—the geographical spaces in which they should act to maximize their effectiveness.

Ultimately, what the activists were trying to figure out is what role they should play, if any, as leaders in this nascent revolutionary struggle. In this sense, the implicit questions they engaged with were no different from those that occupied celebrated revolutionary strategists from the Marxist tradition. These questions were specifically concerned with the extent to which leaders should mediate the people's processes of spontaneity and consciousness[1] to direct their action and secure their sustained participation in the resistance—the latter, of course, being crucial to the success of the revolutionary struggle.[2] Wary of the ephemeral nature of spontaneous uprisings, Vladimir Lenin,[3] perhaps the first to elaborately conceptualize what leadership should look like in revolutionary movements, argued that the masses needed guidance and leadership from professional revolutionaries tied to a highly disciplined and bureaucratically centralized vanguard organization. He insisted that without an organized intervention infusing them with revolutionary consciousness and orienting their activity toward overturning the system, the masses would remain short-sighted in their demands for change and fall short of abolishing the status quo.[4] Lenin's contemporary Rosa Luxemburg,[5] on the other hand, had much more faith in the revolutionary will of the masses; she believed they were capable of achieving a radical revolutionary class consciousness on their own and becoming their own leaders through their engagement with the struggle.

How did these ideas play out among Egypt's youth activists and shape their agency during the eighteen-day uprising? To what extent were the masses who participated in the 2011 protests able to self-organize and maintain their revolutionary consciousness without the help of an organized body leading them? Were the people capable of evolving from their spontaneous action into a revolutionary class on their own? Was it possible for the activists to lead without stifling the spontaneity, radicalism, and creative energy of the masses?

The Prelude: Planning Police Day Protests

The year 2011 was not the first time activists would take to the streets on January 25. This tradition began in 2009, when Hosni Mubarak first declared January 25 a national holiday to commemorate the fifty police officers killed by the British in Suez in 1952, after they refused to evacuate the Ismailiya Police Station and surrender their weapons. The holiday was also instituted to celebrate the continued service of the police in maintaining Egypt's security. The youth's appropriation of the national holiday was symbolic: rather than a celebration of the police, it was a chance to call attention to and raise voices in unified condemnation of the ruthless police state. The repression and corruption of the previous year—demonstrated in the brutal police murder of the young Khaled Said, the blatantly fraudulent parliamentary elections, and the interior minister's suspected complicity in the Alexandria Church bombing that claimed twenty-three lives[6]—had enflamed public opinion and set up the upcoming holiday as the perfect occasion for the expression of their discontent. It was a given, according to my informants, that January 25 would be a day of protest, as demonstrated in the wide calls to protest, on and offline.

As illustrated in the previous chapter, independent and organized youth activists had become tightly networked and intimate by early 2011 as a result of their shared experiences in the arena of political resistance and coordinated street action in the decade prior. So when calls for the 2011 Police Day protests began circulating, carried largely by Egypt's young through social media sites like Facebook and Twitter, it was only natural for these activists to build on their past efforts and harness each other's organizational capital to ensure a successful day of protest. In fact, members of the April 6 Youth Movement, Youth for Justice and Freedom Movement, and the ElBaradei Campaign cited that their joint preparations for Police Day were a spin-off of their collaboration on another important resistance effort already underway when calls for January 25 protests were renewed—namely, the Parallel Parliament initiative, which opposition parties and figures attempted to organize to undermine the recently fraudulently elected Parliament. These activists took issue with the old guard, who dominated the initiative. They disputed with them over the number of seats that should be reserved for youth representatives. They also clashed over their different visions for the initiative. The youth aspired for a more radical project whereby the public would elect the members rather than having them appointed by their respective political parties and movements, as the senior politicians insisted. During this time, the young organizers met regularly among themselves to discuss their demands and plans for a youth boycott of the initiative should the opposition figures continue to refuse them, confident that their withdrawal would undermine the initiative's legitimacy. According to Basem, the architect from Helwan and leader in the ElBaradei Campaign, "The official link between our groups started from this point."

Distrustful of the old guard figures who had marginalized them in the Parallel Parliament, and frustrated with their patriarchy and reluctance to consider more radical forms of resistance, these activists were explicit about wanting to keep their January 25 coordinating efforts for young people alone. According to Tarek, the April 6 leader from Sharabiya:

> We decided we'd coordinate with all the youth forces . . . and the youth factions in the national forces, so we said, "We'll coordinate with the youth of the Gabha Party, for example, but not the Gabha Party itself. . . ." We wanted to concentrate on the youth because we found the elders would distract us, the elders were always making their own calculations. They might be willing to negotiate with the regime. They might be willing to accept a compromise on demands we wouldn't accept. We were more mobile. None of us had homes to worry about, we didn't have our own families. . . . If we're talking about our mothers or fathers, they had grown tired of us a long time ago and left us alone. So all of us were like this. . . . And most of us were even poor, so none of us possessed anything that we'd lose. Just our lives.

From the very beginning, Tarek and his peers very consciously intended theirs to be a youth effort. They understood that in order to shake up the state and precipitate real change in the country, they had to split from the unimaginative traditional politicians and do things in their own daring way.

Meanwhile, young Muslim Brothers like Qassas and Abbas were also eager to see a massive demonstration that day. They hoped to enlist the official participation of their organization, the one opposition group capable of turning out the most demonstrators, but the Brotherhood's Guidance Bureau refused. The position the young Brothers agreed on with the leadership instead was that those Brotherhood members who wished to participate could do so as independents, not in the organization's name. "They didn't want to participate in an official manner because they saw that the invitation was unclear, and they didn't know who was behind it," said Qassas. "And they said we couldn't participate as 'youth of the Brotherhood' or 'students of the Brotherhood.' So we said, 'Ok, fine, we'll figure it out. We'll mobilize with our friends, and we'll figure it out.'" Shortly thereafter, they joined their peers from the other youth movements and political parties after learning about their joint organizing efforts for January 25. The latter were thrilled to have the young Brothers on board and admired them for having the nerve to split from their leaders. Other groups that collaborated with this cohort of young actors were the administrators of the Rassd News Network, an alternative media outlet, and the We Are All Khaled Said Facebook page, specifically its administrators Wael Ghonim and AbdelRahman Mansour.[7]

According to Ola, the thirty-two year-old socialist from the Youth for Justice and Freedom Movement, by mid-January, the core of the informal alliance that would later become the RYC was already in place and had begun to plan, "not having the revolution in mind." So what did they originally have in mind for January 25 and how did this plan evolve?

The original demands around which these activists organized differed little from those of previous years. They included the resignation of the hated Interior Minister Habib al-Adli, the cancellation of the Emergency Law, the pardon of political prisoners, instituting a two-term limit for the presidency, and, given the recent, brazenly rigged elections, the dissolution of both Houses of Parliament—the People's Assembly and the Shura Council—followed by new elections. They also had socioeconomic demands: raise the minimum wage to 1,200 LE per month and institute unemployment benefits. As the young Brother Abbas put it, the idea of revolution at this point was far from their minds: "The departure of al-Adli was the height of our demands." Ola agreed: "The expectation was to bring down al-Adli, the interior minister. That was the demand of January 25. A huge thing. And that was like the aspiration—that yes, we'll be able to bring him down, most probably. Nothing about Mubarak. Nothing about the regime."

But then came a tremendous development. On January 14, just eleven days before the planned protests in Egypt, Tunisians made history by chasing out the brutal and corrupt tyrant who had ruled over them for twenty-four years. Like other Arab nations, Egypt had been transfixed by the country's growing rebellion, sparked by the public self-immolation of twenty-six-year-old fruit-seller Mohamed Bouazizi, who had been driven to despair by police abuse and humiliation, an experience all too familiar to Egyptians. Many had expected the police state to violently suppress the struggle and restore the status quo. Then they woke up to the electrifying news that Zine El Abidine Ben Ali had fled the country. It was the first time protesters had brought down an Arab dictator, and they did so in a mere four weeks. Tunisians—led valiantly and creatively by their youth, as documented by scholars like Alcinda Honwana[8]—had liberated themselves from authoritarian rule through a sustained, widespread, peaceful movement, accomplishing what many in the region had thought to be impossible. Egyptians in particular watched with excitement and envy. Witnessing their neighbors break loose from their fear and successfully topple their dictator completely transformed their outlook. Average Egyptians who had long resigned themselves to a life of economic hardship and repressive state rule under the pretext that this was the regional norm now had to reconsider their political apathy and passivity. Understandably, they also expressed wounded pride. Egyptians were supposed to be the cultural and political leaders of the Arab world, but here they were being historically outstripped by Tunisians, the citizens of a much smaller, less consequential Arab nation. Their competitive instincts had been stirred. Many engaged in national self-shaming: "The Tunisians have become better than us," admitted a young Egyptian man to a reporter. "They're real men."[9] This gender reference, it should be noted, is not incidental; as this chapter will illustrate, Egyptians' notions of masculinity and femininity informed their reactions to ongoing developments, which in turn shaped the particular way the revolutionary movement unfolded.

The success of the month-long Tunisian popular uprising sparked the imagination of Egyptians and presented the possibility of a different outcome for their upcoming day of protest. But was it an intentional revolutionary uprising? There is no categorical, clear-cut answer to this question.

For Egyptian activists eager to convince the people of their power to make a difference, the Tunisian triumph offered an alternative, more radical framing to inspire their participation on January 25. Debates thereafter centered around how to take advantage of this development in their planning, specifically as it related to whether or not to reframe the upcoming day of protest as a day of revolution in order to secure a larger, more passionate turnout. The majority advocated for a more cautious framing approach. According to Basem, the architect:

> There were people who were saying, "We're going to start a revolution," and we kept telling them, "No, not a revolution, we're just holding protests." We knew that it could be a revolution, but if I tell you we're going to have a revolution and it ends up being a few

protests with a pathetic turnout, we'll frustrate you, we'll frustrate the people. Whereas if I tell you I'm going to have protests and it turns out to be a revolution, then the people will be elated and optimistic.

Ola's view differed: "We called it a revolution in the announcement, but we were joking about that. [At the time we were thinking,] 'We know it's not a revolution, but we have to give it the maximum.' And we knew if not that many people joined, we would all get arrested." Other activists made light of the call to revolution as well, which demonstrates that they did not see themselves to be planning a revolution, nor did they anticipate this development. Qassas said, "We were saying 'revolution' and joking about it. . . . People were saying things like, 'Hurry up, we're going to be late for the revolution!' and 'Dude, you're going to make me late for the revolution!'"

According to Mahmoud, the April 6 activist from Awsim, the goal was simply and generally to "create or participate in a big event in Egypt to show and convince people that change is possible." The significance of Tunisia for these activists was that it indicated that positive, radical change in Egypt—whatever that meant and however ill-defined or unclear the route to it might be—was possible and something they were capable of initiating. "The miracle happened," Abbas said. "Tunis was the hope. We can do it. We're capable." This confirmation from Tunisia energized them. "Tunisia fired us up!" Tarek of April 6 exclaimed. Mostafa from the Youth for Justice and Freedom Movement agreed: "Tunisia's experience made us imagine anything, and to be fearless when we're doing this. And it drove us to do this and to insist on it in a very strong manner." Mostafa's vague reference to "this" is telling, reflecting the possible directions their protest could take which they could not yet foresee. According to Abdelrahman, the independent activist with familial ties to the Muslim Brotherhood, while Tunisia sparked their imagination,

> still, the connotations of "revolution" hadn't occured to us, despite the fact that the demands that we were going out with on these days, if they were realized, it would mean a complete change of the regime. When I go out and demand the cancellation of Emergency Law, and the pardon of political prisoners, and the dissolution of Parliament and the Shura Council, and that I demand the resignation of the interior minister, and his prosecution, and that I demand

minimum wage—these are demands in and of themselves for complete change in the regime. But the idea of an actual revolution wasn't something we were really considering.

Abdelrahman's remarks are significant. They confirm that January 25 represented a continuity in the decade-long opposition movement brewing in Egypt. Still, despite their recognition of their likely limited impact, activists continued to be ambitious in terms of their demands and impassioned in their call for change.

The coordination of the youth cadre at this stage was geared toward drawing a critical mass of protesters out onto Egypt's streets; in this respect, their efforts were not limited to Cairo, but were national. "Our idea at this point was that we would mobilize people, and they would be the ones to do the work," said Tarek of April 6. As such, they focused on extending and amplifying the call to protest as well as the strategic planning of Cairo's demonstrations to ensure mass participation. In terms of outreach, this group worked with the We Are All Khaled Said Facebook page administrators and the Rassd News Network to promote the call, inspire participation through various mobilization frames, and circulate plans for January 25, including protest locations, times, and tips for weathering the cold, resisting police, and countering the effects of tear gas (Tunisian activists coached them on how to use onions, vinegar, and Pepsi via Twitter). It was on these websites that they announced twenty protest locations around Cairo, intended to decoy the police from a secret twenty-first location where they planned to concentrate their efforts and amass a sizable crowd.

Organizers also successfully enlisted a wide range of organizations both in Cairo and across the country. In Cairo, they secured the participation of the young and zealous soccer fan clubs, known as the Ultras, belonging to the city's two main teams, Ahly and Zamalek. This was crucial for the movement's success, as the Ultras were extremely organized and enjoyed a vast membership of young men who were experienced in physical confrontations with security forces.[10] Members of the different youth movements also engaged in a massive, covert leafleting campaign in Cairo's popular quarters. In the days preceding January 25, April 6 handed out half a million fliers.[11] Through a closed Facebook page, young Brothers mobilized five hundred protesters from their network, including many young Sisters. Moreover, movement leaders worked intensively to ensure that coordination, outreach, and planning of local protests were not just happening in Cairo, but also among their branches in the governorates. April 6 and the ElBaradei Campaign worked extensively in the governorates to raise awareness about and incite participation in the January 25 mobilization.

Drawing on the best of the tried and tested street tactics from their repertoire of contention, movement leaders in Cairo devised a meticulous, secret strategy that included flash mobs and mobilizations in blighted popular areas, hoping to provoke a massive show of resistance. The consensus among these organizers was that the true success of the day would rest upon the participation of the average, non-politicized masses—*al-shaʿb*, or "the people," as it were, especially those from the working and lower-middle classes, without whose endorsement change in the country would never occur. Consistent with the mobilizing logic of relative deprivation, the method was to take the protest to the people and tailor it to their concerns with chants that spoke to their socioeconomic frustrations, such as rising food prices, the lack of adequate social services, and the growing gap between the rich and poor. Such chants included the now famous *"Aysh! Hurriya! Adala igtimaʿiya!"* (Bread! Freedom! Social Justice!), or the alternate *"Aysh! Hurriya! Karama insaniya!"* (Bread! Freedom! Human Dignity!), and *"Inzilu min buyutkum! Gayeen nigib huqukum!"* (Come out of your homes! We're going to get your rights!). There were also quirkier ones that resonated with Egyptian humor, like: "*Ghallu al-sukkar! Ghallu al-zayt! Bukra nibiʿ afsh al-bayt!*" (They raised the price of sugar and the price of oil! Tomorrow they'll make us sell our furniture!), which rhymes in Arabic. This was a conscious departure from the contentious politics of the long-standing opposition groups, which staged most of their demonstrations in front of downtown government buildings, like the attorney general's office. By early 2011, the youth activists had become critical of this approach, describing it as elitist; they blamed the slow pace of change on the opposition's failure to make politics and protests relevant to the concerns of struggling Egyptians. The youth approach, on the contrary, focused on creating a real language of politics that appealed to the average Egyptian, one that abandoned empty declamations and distant political principles and instead spoke to their immediate needs and concerns.

The activists I interviewed confirmed that the secret strategy for this particular protest was the brainchild of April 6 activist Mahmoud Samy, a dapper and astute young man recognized for his clever innovations in street-protest tactics. A son of Cairo's popular quarters himself, he was well versed in the spaces, mobility, and vulnerabilities of its subaltern inhabitants and understood how to negotiate them in his planning to the advantage of January 25's day of protest. This class capital informed his selection of Nahya Street in the impoverished, informal quarter of Bulaq al-Dakrur, near his neighborhood Awsim, as the site of their twenty-first secret location and the start of their march. The goal was to figure out how to get Egyptians to overcome their fear of the police who patrolled their neighborhoods and join their protest. "When I thought about it," Mahmoud said,

> I recalled that one of the things we often encountered before this during protests is that the people watching were afraid to join us. Why were they afraid to join us? Because our numbers were small. So you have two choices: you make it so that there are no police, or you make sure that your number is large. How do you make yourselves many? There was the idea of the snowball, that the more headway your march makes, the larger it swells.

The idea was to start with a secret rally in a low-profile, confined space situated in one of Cairo's many crowded popular neighborhoods. There they would concentrate a few hundred of their fellow activists to impart the illusion of a large crowd to spectators needing the assurance of safety in numbers before deciding to join in. What attracted Mahmoud the most to Nahya Street in Bulaq, of all the popular areas he surveyed, was the bridge at the end that connected it to Arab League Street, a major, bustling thoroughfare peppered with high-rise apartment buildings, retail shops, and restaurants. The overpass perfectly tied this informal area to the upscale district of Mohandiseen, where they could potentially draw in even more demonstrators, showcasing in their march a diverse cross-section of society. If they planned it right, they would surprise police and observers with a dazzling show of resistance hitherto unseen in these parts. With the support of fellow April 6 organizer Amr from Imbaba and another peer from the Youth for Justice and Freedom Movement, Mahmoud designed a route and plotted the details of a march that would take them from their meeting point near a small, nondescript bakery at the far end of Nahya Street down Arab League Street, allowing their numbers to snowball before they would link up with the demonstration at Mustafa Mahmud Square. There, they planned to lead a standing demonstration for a few hours before dispersing (see map 2, p. 122). To ensure the successful execution of this protest, they visited the area regularly in the two weeks leading up to Police Day to carry out practice runs, timing how long it would take to walk, jog, and run to see how much time they would need to synchronize with the marches coming from Shubra and Giza that were being planned by other groups like the Revolutionary Socialists. They also developed strategies for possible police ambushes.

There was no firm intention to protest in Tahrir Square at this stage, although Mahmoud and his peers had long dreamed of descending upon and conquering the square with thousands of protesters. Located in Cairo's Downtown, Tahrir—which appropriately means "Liberation"—was the largest public space in the city, and it derived its symbolic weight as the flash point for political resistance from the surrounding institutions of state power. Mahmoud shared that there was some talk of the conditions under which they might consider heading to Tahrir. He said that the agreement was to continue to Tahrir if luck was on their side and their numbers reached one thousand, a target which they felt at the time was quite ambitious. This reflects how unlikely they felt it was that they would be able to rally a large enough group of protesters to make such a dramatic and daring move.

Movement leaders also understood that their unity and nationalism were equally critical if they were going to secure potential protesters' recognition of its legitimacy and gain their confidence and buy-in. As such, they were conscious of framing the mobilization in a way that demonstrated their unity, concealed their ideological divisions, and appealed to every Egyptian. Their decision to march together under the unified banner of "The Free Youth of Egypt" and the flag of Egypt, while suppressing the movements' individual banners, reflected their strategic unitary approach. Tarek from April 6 explained their logic:

> We agreed that we would go out for the first time—it's been years since this happened in protests—under the flag of Egypt. We used to all go out with our [movement] flags. So, say the scene included April 6 and next to it, the Youth for Justice and Freedom, etc. If I said to someone, "Come close, come join us," he would be reluctant because he's not from April 6, so why would he join? But if we all carried Egypt's flag, and I said come, he would come. This was January 25. None of us carried anything other than the flag of Egypt.

Similarly, they chose chants intended to arouse Egyptian nationalism and patriotism, rather than specific political slogans. They shouted, "Who are we? Who are we? We are all of the Egyptian people!" and "Egypt, our mother! Your children are here!"[12] Equally important, the activists agreed that the protest would be nonviolent in order to strengthen its legitimacy and maximize popular participation.

As youth movement leaders coordinated with one another to prepare for what they hoped would be a tide-shifting day, many others—some with a history of activism, others new to contentious action who were inspired by the solidarity building up online and planning to protest for the first time—acted of their own accord to help mobilize a greater turnout. Among these activists was twenty-six-year-old Asmaa Mahfouz of April 6. On January 18, she recorded and shared a YouTube video of herself on Facebook that instantly went viral. Speaking fervently into the camera in language free of political jargon hoping to tap into the affect of common Egyptians, the petite veiled woman urged fellow Egyptians to join her in the street on January 25. Asmaa's fiery appeal stood out for several reasons. First, in making her identity known, especially as a young woman, Asmaa and her video represented a bold departure from the anonymity of recent forms of youth cyber activism. Second—and the reason her message is said to have resonated so widely with viewers—she activated normative understandings of what it meant to be a *ragil*, a "real man," as her mobilizing frame. She called on male viewers to embody courage, honor, and selflessness by confronting oppression and corruption, standing up for the weak, and coming to the support and protection of honorable women protesters. "If you think yourself a man," she challenged,

> then come with me on January 25. Whoever says women shouldn't go to protests because they will get beaten, let him have some honor (*nakhwa*) and manhood (*rugula*) and come with me on January 25. Whoever says it is not worth it because there will only be a handful of people, I want to tell him, "You are the reason behind this, and you are a traitor, just like the president or any security cop who beats us in the streets." ... Sitting at home and just following us on the news or Facebook leads to our humiliation—it leads to *my humiliation*! If you have honor and dignity as a man, come. Come and protect me and other girls in the protest. If you stay at home, then you deserve all that is being done, and you will be guilty before your nation and your people. And you'll be responsible for what happens to us on the streets while you sit at home.[13]

Asmaa's method was to shame men into action. She cleverly appropriated the language of patriarchy in her call to men by framing it as an invitation to them to reclaim their masculinity and assert their position in the gender hierarchy that placed men as protectors of women—ironic considering that Egyptians, in many ways, were revolting against patriarchy. As journalist and astute observer of the Egyptian revolution Jack Shenker succinctly put it, "When it came to gender, resistance and reinforcement were often bound together."[14] Lastly, Asmaa's vlog was significant for challenging normative beliefs regarding appropriate behavior for women. Speaking out as an articulate, principled, and veiled (think: pious, proper) young woman, Asmaa helped legitimize street protest in the eyes of the public as a respectable and noble practice for other young women. Her call is just one of several examples of how gender norms and dynamics fed into the unfolding of the uprising.

January 25: Managing a Popular Uprising

On the morning of January 25, Mahmoud, Amr, and the rest of their cohort anxiously prepared to execute their plan. To ensure top secrecy, the plotters only informed ten activists of the Nahya location. Each was told ahead of time to have their cells meet them at a second location somewhere in Cairo of their choosing, and from there they were to lead them clueless to Nahya. Everything went according to plan. At 12 p.m., approximately 250 activists managed to evade the notice of police and meet in the small plaza in front of a local bakery known as Al-Hayyis nestled in this dense and crowded impoverished area. Zyad the attorney, who spoke softly unless he was in revolutionary mode and railing against the establishment, delivered a rousing address directed at local residents peering over from their balconies. "Today is January 25, Police Day!" he roared into the megaphone. "We decided to come here today to tell the Egyptian government that we will no longer be silent!" He beckoned the crowds to join them: "Today we either stand side by side and take our rights together, or we lose the chance! It's now or never!"[15]

Zyad had their ears. The rally quickly began to swell and flow over into the neighboring alleyways. Activists began marching, calling on the multitudes watching from their balconies to join them: *"Ya ahalina! Indammu ilayna!"* (Our people! Join us!), they chanted, *"Inzil! Inzil!"* (Come out! Come out!). The numbers that heeded the activists' call dramatically exceeded their expectations. Expecting to rally a thousand residents at best

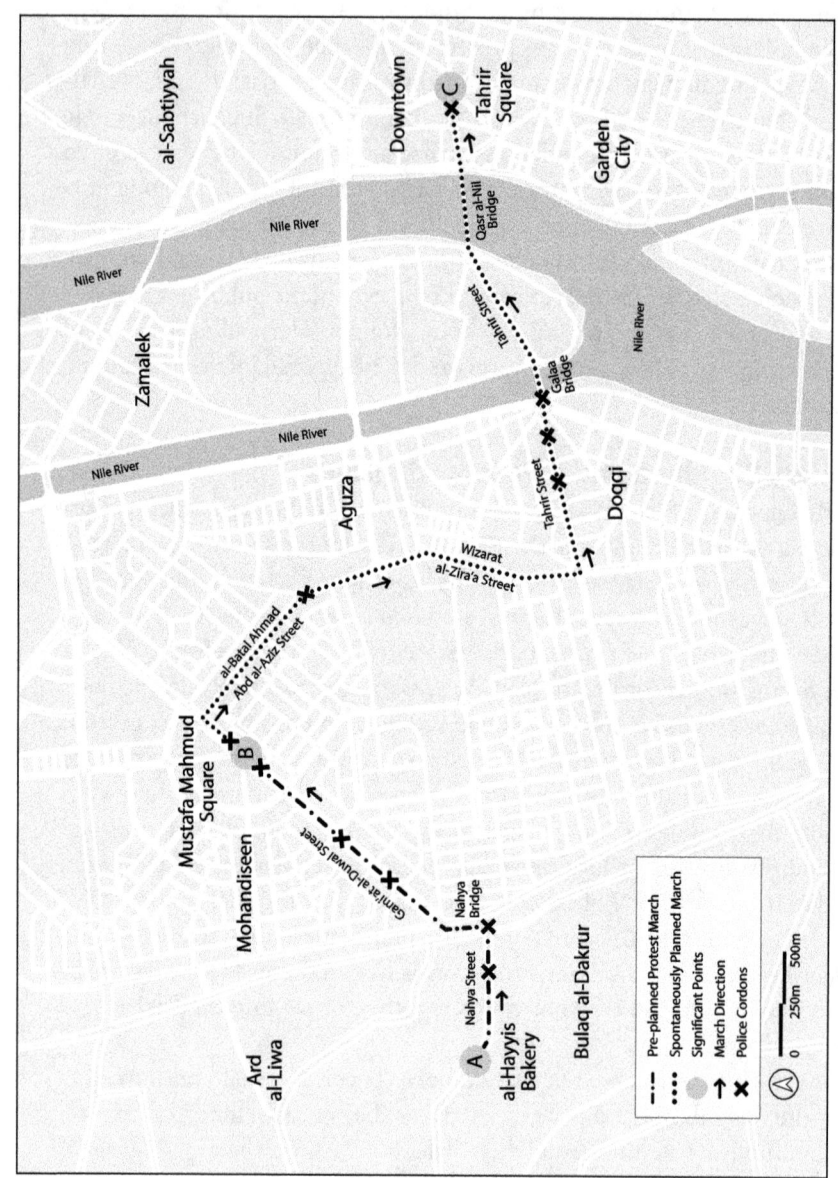

Map 2. This map charts the route of the January 25 protest march led by the youth who would later form the Revolutionary Youth Coalition (RYC).

from Nahya Street, instead they left it with a stunning march at least five thousand protesters strong, which only continued to snowball as it made its way down Arab League Street (see map 2).[16] Their numbers were so large that when the nearby Central Security Forces caught wind of their march and rushed to the pedestrian walkway on Nahya Bridge to block them, the protesters were able to forego that route altogether and take over the traffic lanes instead, making a mockery of the officers who were hopelessly outnumbered and could do nothing to stop them. It was a triumphant moment for the activists who, for the first time, had managed to overwhelm and disorient security forces. They were deliriously happy. Abdelrahman described their utter shock and euphoria as they poured over Nahya Bridge and splashed onto Arab League Street:

> I'll never forget the scene when we got onto Arab League. It was as if the people were gushing from beneath the ground. This was one of the most moving scenes . . . and we began crying and hugging each other, and we kept shouting, "*Intasarna!*" (We won!) What had we won exactly? Who knew?! What was coming, nobody knew!

Mostafa also recalled the moment excitedly:

> Just the fact that we were able to participate in a march like this, that we were able to witness a march this big, was a sheer victory. We started embracing each other and kissing each other, and the people were looking at us like, "Who are these crazy people?!" . . . Before this we'd organize a march and at times we'd be only twenty or thirty people. When there were five hundred in our protests we were over the moon. . . . Now, we couldn't see the beginning of the march from its end! We were so beside ourselves you would have thought we were drunk. I'm talking borderline hysteria. . . . And then there was this feeling at this moment, that if this many people had mobilized, that meant something major had shifted in the country. A leap had happened in the people's political consciousness—a radical change, a deep desire for freedom.

As the Nahya marchers approached Mustafa Mahmud Square at 2 p.m., they were met with thousands more protesters. Their numbers were also so large that they were easily able to break through the cordons of the security forces that tried to contain them. At Mustafa Mahmud Square, it became clear to those leading the march that the enthusiastic response of the people was unprecedented, qualitatively and quantitatively different from anything they had ever experienced before and from what they had expected. At this point, they agreed it required a different course of action. Realizing they had a potential uprising on their hands, activists from this point onward started making on-the-spot decisions, which were informed by the rich political experience gained through their active participation in multiple, albeit much smaller, street demonstrations. This gave way to a very present organizing process in a fluid dialectic between the unfolding street events and their political skills. Tarek's reflection captures this best:

> My feeling at this moment was that the street had mobilized, finally! . . . The explosion that we wanted had actually happened! All of us were thrown into a state of shock because we didn't. . . . I mean, we had thought a lot about how we would get the people to come out, but we had never thought about what we would do with the people if they did come out. We were all dazed and like, "What are we going to do with all these people?!" Because we hadn't expected that they would come out. So when they actually did, it was like, "Ok, so what are we going to do now?" That's when we started to say, "To Tahrir Square!"

Their first extemporaneous decision, then, was to direct the march to Tahrir. A few of the young men leading the march, including Zyad and Abbas, quickly sketched the route they would follow, while other activists, including Amr and Ola, worked to tighten the ranks of demonstrators and rile them up with their chants. This was just one of many marches headed to Tahrir that day, but it was the largest and most innovative in terms of organization and tactics. By the time they reached Tahrir in the late afternoon, after successfully breaking through several police cordons, they estimated their number was as high as eighty thousand,[17] providing the critical mass that helped facilitate the people's game-changing siege of the square. Upon their arrival, they were elated to find it was already swarming with demonstrators and others were still coursing in from various streets. The mood was festive. Something new was happening, and they could all sense it. The police state's vulnerability had been exposed by the diffusion of their street action. Security forces were unable to suppress their demonstrations. The people were no longer afraid, but emboldened by their numbers and the Tunisian example. Their spirits soared.[18]

The cohort that had led the march from Nahya Street continued to improvise once they reached the square. There, they met hourly with other activists, intellectuals, and politicians, gauging the mood on the street and government reaction in between their meetings as they attempted to reach a consensus regarding what to do next. Meetings centered on trying to evaluate the phenomenon at hand and determining the appropriate unified response.

Meanwhile, Qassas, Abbas, and a few other young Brothers who had participated in the day's events darted off to the Muslim Brotherhood's Guidance Bureau to inform them of developments in the square. They intended to convince the leaders that what was taking place was a genuine and legitimate grassroots people's uprising that required their notice and organizational support, aware that any future effort to sustain this resistance needed the organization's official buy-in and participation if it was going to continue and be successful.

It was in Tahrir Square later that day when the Tunisian chant *"al-Sha'b yurid isqat al-nizam!"* (The people want the fall of the regime!) spontaneously made its Egyptian debut. To the surprise of the activists, the thunderous chant was initiated by protesters, not by one of their own, officially turning the movement's tone into a revolutionary one. For the activists, this development meant that there was no turning back, that the phenomenon on their hands had to be supported, developed, and pushed to its end, whatever that may be. Ola's face lit up as she relived the spine-tingling moment:

> The people surprised us and started chanting, "The people want the fall of the regime!" And it was like, "Oh my God!" And none of those activists or politicians or whatever started this. It was purely the people. "What is happening?!" [we asked ourselves and each other]. We couldn't go back. We just decided [in that moment] we're not going back.

Together with activists, intellectuals, and representatives from other opposition groups they met with regularly in Tahrir, these youth leaders drafted and dispatched their first communiqué from the square on behalf of the protesters stating their intention to continue their resistance. After they received news that security forces planned to evacuate the square around midnight, debates centered around whether they should continue their occupation or disperse while protesters were strong and their morale was high and plan for a bigger return to the square on Friday, January 28. They decided against emptying the square voluntarily; the way they saw it, a police attack on them would only lend legitimacy to their cause, harden the resolve of protesters to return, and perhaps even win them new recruits. They remained in the square until around 1 a.m., when ten thousand riot police accompanied by three thousand special forces troopers descended upon them violently, scattering their congregation and arresting protesters.[19]

The medley of youth activists who had coordinated the Nahya protest agreed that they would continue to work as a group, building on their past efforts. The resolve to carry on was driven by an understanding of how much was suddenly at stake. A sense of urgency took over as it became clear that a unique historical opportunity was at hand and that missing it would be too costly, existentially and politically. First, as the activists who had helped instigate this uprising, they would be the first to be pursued by State Security should the movement fail. Amr, the April 6 activist from Imbaba who helped plan the protest from Nahya, put it to me squarely:

> There were people who had the option to negotiate, and there were people who didn't. We would either continue and win, or we would die. The situation for us differed from everyone else's, those who came and participated and then returned to their homes. . . . Our only option was victory. Defeat meant we would either have to escape to avoid being imprisoned, or we would have to seek asylum.

The second cost was the fear of losing this once-in-a-lifetime opportunity to effect dramatic change in the country. Tarek of April 6 recalled having a discussion with his friends about what happened the last time so many Egyptians gathered for a protest:

> So one of us spoke up—I can't remember who, but he said something very important. He said that this same thing happened at a protest in 2005, there were around ten or twenty thousand people who arrived at Tahrir Square, and by the evening, each of them had gone home. These few words were extremely frightening for us. That we would come and sit for a little, and then at night we'd go

home, and that would be it.... We were practically in tears thinking our protests would soon be over.... The experience of 2005 had us scared to death, that twenty thousand people had been in Tahrir and they had gone home. So we were afraid that the situation would end this way. We weren't going to be able to do this again. This was it.[20]

Lastly, they feared that their failure to take this movement to the end would cause their generation to lose hope in the country and refuse to challenge the system again. Amr of April 6 said:

When I tell you that we didn't have another opportunity.... This situation for us had turned into a big dream, and this dream was suddenly being realized, and losing this dream was going to lose us this entire generation. This entire generation had no—it wouldn't have a voice after this. This generation was going to get frustrated and leave political work forever. The situation for us was dire.

By the end of January 25, it was clear that the movement had reached a national scale, with protests similar to Cairo's in other cities across the country, including Alexandria, Mansura, Zagazig, and Suez. As mentioned earlier, many of these protests were planned and coordinated by youth affiliated with the movements that organized Cairo's protests.

January 26–27: Planning a Revolution

The continued unrest and pockets of demonstrations in the streets the following day indicated to these activists that a revolutionary movement was indeed underway. The unexpected uprising in the port city of Suez was particularly compelling, in part because of the city's illustrious history of popular resistance against the 1956 Tripartite Aggression by the British, French, and Israelis, and against the Israeli raids in the October War of 1973. The confrontations between police and protesters here quickly became more violent than elsewhere, with police firing live rounds on protesters and the latter setting fire to police stations and other government buildings.[21] Many of my interlocutors cited the martyrdom of four protesters in Suez on January 26 as a turning point in the movement's radicalization and revolutionary becoming. According to Tarek of April 6: "The situation would have been over if it hadn't been for Suez.... On the 26 and 27, what made the revolution continue were the events in Suez. . . . Four martyrs fell and ignited the fuse of the revolution. If it hadn't been for them, the revolution would not have continued."

Mostafa shared how the bloodshed in Suez secured his commitment and that of his peers to revolution. Again, what is worth underscoring here is that Mostafa, even as someone who identified as a socialist and was already theoretically disposed to the idea of revolution, was still acquiring his consciousness as a revolutionary who sought to upend the state as the movement unfolded:

> On January 26, we understood that we had become a group of revolutionaries (*thuwwar*) and that there were people in the street and the masses were with us. That we were not just an uprising that would end, but in a real revolution and in a revolutionary battle. . . . And as a result, we were transformed into revolutionaries . . . and we were obliged to continue our journey and what we had started. This was a moment of transformation for sure. . . . You reach a stage in which you can't give in to despair or turn back, no matter how much fear you have, because now there's blood. . . . I think that one of the critical moments in any revolution in the world is the spilling of blood. But also, it's one thing when an activist is tortured and killed in prison, it's something else entirely when ordinary people go out into the street and die. This was a turning point, for sure.

Abbas agreed. For him and many others, continuing after the killings in Suez was a matter of moral obligation. The outrage he felt back then animated his recollection:

> This martyrdom, it made us say, "No more of this." . . . January 26, yes, it was an important moment. That people have died and we're sitting doing what? We're sitting comfortably and they're dying?! It was like, "What are you doing at home?!" It became a matter of principle [to participate and continue the struggle]. Truthfully, everyone felt it.

Mostafa's and Abbas's reflections confirm Mohammed Bamyeh's firsthand observations of the unfolding phenomenon: "The collective perception that a revolution was happening at the margins, where it was least expected, gave everyone the confidence necessary to realize that it could happen everywhere."[22]

In light of the Suez killings, Mostafa, Abbas, and the others mobilized quickly to prepare for what they hoped would be a massive show of dissent on Friday after Muslim congregational prayers, what they called "The Friday of Rage." They convened secretly several times in the following days to strategize for the 28th. It is worth mentioning that primarily in attendance at these crucial meetings were male activists; this is because young men tended to dominate the leadership of these particular movements, and also because they held most of their meetings late at night, making it difficult for active women to attend due to familial constraints and safety concerns. During their meetings, the organizers identified the main mosques all over Egypt that would serve as starting points for protests. They also called on all citizens to depart from every mosque and church after Friday prayers and head to their cities' main squares. For Cairo, they drew up blueprints for marches that sketched their convergences and routes to Tahrir, which they spread widely through Facebook, Twitter, email, and text messaging. They even manipulated the news coverage of the unrest to promote the day's actions and circulate information about locations. Initially they concentrated their secret mobilization efforts on Faysal Mosque in Giza. But after learning that ElBaradei would be praying there, they switched to Istiqama Mosque in the working-class neighborhood Imbaba to avoid the security onslaught a march including ElBaradei would inevitably invite. Imbaba was ideal because Amr and Abbas, as residents of the area, knew its labyrinth of streets and alleyways well and could plot a march route that would allow them to pick up the largest number of protesters. During their briefings, they also discussed plans for navigating the Internet and mobile phone communications blackout they had learned the government would begin enforcing that Thursday evening. They would reorient themselves with landlines, and Zyad from the ElBaradei Campaign would stay behind and run a call center from his home to field reports and centralize communication among the organizers.

Also broached at these meetings was the uncomfortable topic of violence. On January 25, activists and protesters had insisted on the peaceful nature of their protest; in fact, *"Silmiya!"* (We are peaceful!) was one of their hallmark cries. But January 28 was different. Combined with the increasing police violence against demonstrators on Wednesday and Thursday, the imminent communications blackout generated a sense of foreboding among activists that the state was about to lash out against them in a manner inappropriate for global viewing. Expecting the police to use excessive force against protesters, activists were forced to seriously consider the use of self-defense measures and offensive tactics to force the police to retreat. Although the idea made them nervous, they decided to bring some makeshift weaponry and protective preparations that they made to use for self-defense as needed.

By this point, the Muslim Brotherhood and other political parties had announced their decision to participate formally in Friday's protests, along with other smaller groups who had boycotted January 25, like the Nasserists and Tagammu' leftists. The Brotherhood's participation in particular was a huge game-changer, given the number of supporters they could easily mobilize. The youth had no doubt that the Brothers were motivated by opportunism, but they were nonetheless happy to have their organizational support and manpower. For them, it was clear that in order for the Friday of Rage to be successful, Egyptians of all ages and from all backgrounds would have to join forces, and it was beginning to look like this would be the case.[23] They were at once nervous and elated.

January 28–February 1: Reoccupying the Square and Maintaining Momentum

The turnout on January 28 was spectacular. In cities across the country, hundreds of thousands flooded the streets in open revolt. The state's shocking suspension of Internet and cell phone communications, meant to frighten citizens into not demonstrating and impede communication about protests, had the reverse effect: the state's audacity provoked ordinary Egyptians otherwise disinclined to protest to take to the streets, some out of curiosity, others in defiance. Rousing Friday sermons in Egypt's countless mosques denounced dictatorship and generated torrents of angry protesters demanding freedom and the end of Mubarak's rule. In Cairo, ordinary Egyptians swept up in the euphoric experience of their people power were determined to overrun the security forces and march to Tahrir. This was it. If the fear barrier had been broken on the 25th, whatever remained of it was ground to dust under the trampling feet of demonstrators on the 28th.

For the youth activists, this triumphant show of people power represented a qualitative change in the role they would play moving forward. They shifted from being in a leadership role on January 25—drawing out protesters, leading them in chants, keeping their march together, and directing them to Tahrir—to becoming just a handful among hundreds of thousands participating in what had become a volcanic popular revolutionary movement embraced across the country. This change, albeit a positive development in one sense, would soon become the movement's Achilles heel.

"The people were the ones who were now leading," said Abbas, giddily recalling the thousands-strong march he tried to direct from Istiqama Mosque with Amr, Mostafa, and other youth leaders. They kicked off the protest inside the mosque immediately after the prayer, leaping to their feet with a rush of adrenaline to bellow the first cries for bread, freedom, and human dignity. To their joy, the congregants quickly followed suit. As the organizers guided the procession through the district's web of streets, absorbing more and more bodies as they moved along, protesters in the swelling crowd acted on their own initiative. "That was it!" Abbas exclaimed.

> I mean, how could you possibly direct all these people? . . . You're not even the ones leading the chants. The people are now chanting among themselves in different clusters in the march. . . . That's it, you no longer have a differentiated role. Your role is that you march among the people.

Ola was in the same march. She described it as "being out of control," which, in the spirit of Rosa Luxemburg's deference to the masses, she celebrated as a positive development:

> In the Imbaba march on the 28th, one of my tasks was to make sure that the chants were unified within the march. On the 28th, those of us who had this task, we were congratulating ourselves that it's out of control. This meant success, real success, because we couldn't control it. Something else took over—thousands of people took over! It was a happy moment for us.

The numbers represented the vast diversity of Egyptians—men, women, young, old, urban poor, middle-class professionals, Muslims, Christians, secularists, Islamists—and surpassed the activists' capacity to lead them. Together with their rebellious countrymen, Ola and her fellow organizers endured a violent day of police assault, replete with baton-beatings, copious amounts of tear gas, high-pressure water cannons, buckshot, live ammunition, sniper fire, and the murderous mowing down of protesters with paddy wagons and armored riot vehicles. But the insurgents were not to be deterred. The onslaught only steeled their resolve to hold their ground and fight back. Many of them risked their lives in front-line clashes with the police. Hundreds were killed and thousands more injured. Ola was regularly cited by her peers for her impressive leadership and valor that day in what famously became known as the Battle of the Bridge. In this epic standoff, thousands of protesters engaged in a four-hour tug-of-war over the Qasr al-Nil Bridge with riot police who were blocking their entry to Tahrir Square. As the only woman on the front line, Ola worked tirelessly to manage and rotate the front ranks, transport the wounded and killed away from the front, and fish for fuming tear gas canisters to throw back at the police or into the Nile. Her performance stunned many of her peers and earned her the honorific recognition of being *bi mit ragil* (worth a hundred men). Not all of the activists could match her stamina though. Her comrade Mostafa from the Youth for Justice and Freedom Movement, for example, collapsed from exhaustion before they came upon the bridge and was shipped home in a taxi by his friends.

Similar pitched battles, acts of heroism, and scenes of chaos played out across the country. On this angry Friday, the protesters-turned-revolutionaries made it their goal to cripple the Central Security Forces and force the collapse of the police state. "People were dying and not caring," Amr of April 6 told me, describing the incredible display of fearlessness and grit that day. He himself sustained an almost fatal blow to the head. "Everyone felt like they were doing something larger than themselves. . . . The collective feeling was that we had to do whatever it took to rid ourselves of these wretches."[24] This time, they were willing to engage in more violent acts of resistance to achieve their goal: they rushed the ranks of riot police; lunged bottles, chunks of broken-up pavement, and Molotov cocktails to break their will and force their retreat; and torched riot vehicles and police stations. In Downtown Cairo, they burned down the headquarters of the ruling NDP, the symbol of political corruption. In Alexandria, protesters furiously tore down giant posters of Mubarak in a similar act of defiance.

The day's violence and chaos subsided in the early evening as the Interior Ministry withdrew the police from Egypt's streets and Mubarak deployed the military. Four days of relentless clashes in Cairo, Alexandria, Suez, and other cities, with little food, drink, or rest, had left the riot police completely battered, drained, and ultimately incapable of suppressing the hell-bent masses. Here it is worth highlighting a remarkable development:

the spontaneous formation of popular committees (*ligan sha'biya*) in urban centers across Egypt that assumed responsibility for protecting their neighborhoods in the wake of the security vacuum created by the police retreat. With news circulating of prisons left unattended and escaped convicts roaming the streets, citizens organized themselves into grassroots neighborhood watch groups to guard their families and homes.[25] As for the army, it was unclear at this point what position they would take with respect to the protesters. For their part, the protesters received the soldiers who were taking up stations across Egypt under commands to restore order with a mix of celebration and caution. Many earnestly began to chant, "The army and the people are one hand!" in an attempt to neutralize their threat and secure their solidarity. This chant drew from the historically constructed image of the army as protector of the people—a trope that had endured since the Free Officers overthrew the monarchy and expelled the British in the 1950s—as well as the belief that the young conscripts, who were themselves of the people, would never turn on them. It was one of several tactics improvised by activists and protesters that Neil Ketchley collectively refers to as fraternization, "a repertoire of contentious performances that made immediate, situational claims on the loyalty of regime forces."[26] The chant speaks to the intense uncertainty, confusion, fluidity, and anxiety that characterized the early days of the uprising.

In Cairo, as the day's violence began to settle and after protesters successfully reoccupied Tahrir, youth movement activists directed their efforts to supporting the developing sit-in, sustaining the momentum of resistance, strengthening the square internally, and guiding the demands of protesters. In addition to bringing blankets, food, and tents along with other protesters and opposition forces, the young men and women helped organize clinics to nurse those injured in the clashes and security checkpoints into the square. The logistical demands of supporting this mushrooming movement also encouraged the activists' creativity. Their innovations began with a rudimentary internal radio broadcast system to communicate with the masses and later evolved to include the erection of a stage with loudspeakers in a prime location in front of the Mugamma' government building, on the southern edge of Tahrir Square, from which they continued to agitate and raise the morale of the protesters with speeches and musical performances.[27] Mixing political discourse with the arts and broadcasting technology was a significant turn, as was the unprecedented creative expression through political graffiti, music, poetry, and installation

Figure 3. Early banners in Tahrir Square saying "Leave" and "Step down, and have some decency." Photograph by Hossam El-Hamalawy.

art unleashed by the popular outburst. Activists from this cadre also distributed bulletins, dispatched press statements, and raised enormous banners around the square to keep protesters focused on the same objectives and the public outside Tahrir aware of their agenda. The latter focused on Mubarak's downfall but also reflected new demands, such as constitutional amendments ensuring free elections and the formation of a transitional government, which started to emerge from the protesters following the recent escalation in violence (see figure 3). These were a prelude to a much larger banner enumerating seven demands, which appeared in the square on February 4, as discussed later in this chapter.

Overall, the messaging was unified and consistent. Other tactics included vigils and funeral processions through Tahrir for killed protesters along with their elevation as martyrs for the cause. Activists also encouraged the embrace-the-soldier fraternizing strategy to win over the army, which they still perceived to be neutral at this point and likely to play a decisive role.[28] In the days following the Friday of Rage, the state's response had gone from exceedingly fierce to much more restrained. This was partly owing to the global response in support of the revolutionary movement, facilitated by the presence of scores of journalists and scholars from around the world. Their actions were also influenced by pressure from allies like the United States to exercise caution.[29]

Meanwhile, movement leaders and others in the square continued to strategize for the escalation of resistance. This was especially important as Mubarak had begun to make cosmetic changes in his cabinet, which activists feared the people might interpret as a victory and therefore withdraw support and abandon the square. They were particularly angered by Mubarak's decision to appoint the hated intelligence officer Omar Suleiman as vice president. Suleiman managed the American extraordinary renditions program and had presided over the unspeakable torture of Egyptian detainees. The youth discussed plans for civil disobedience and called for the first *milyuniya* (march of millions)—they were the first to mainstream this Arabic term that quickly became a staple in revolutionary resistance—to take place on Tuesday, February 1 from Cairo's Tahrir Square to the Presidential Palace in Heliopolis. According to Al Jazeera English,[30] over one million protesters gathered in downtown Cairo that Tuesday afternoon, a number which in the activists' estimates had grown to two million later in the day, and was supplemented by the millions demonstrating in other parts of Egypt. It was the largest mobilization Egypt had seen yet, thanks in part to the military statement that had come out the evening before acknowledging the legitimacy of the people's demands and assuring them that the military would not use force against them.

But these numbers began to dwindle significantly later that Tuesday evening, after Mubarak delivered his *khitab atifi* (sentimental speech). Protesters watching the speech on giant makeshift screens in Tahrir felt growing frustration and despair as Mubarak dug in his heels and made it clear he had no intention of leaving power except on his terms. The president vowed to complete the duration of his term and promised not to run for another one. He expressed his attachment to Egypt and desire to be buried there after a life spent in its service. He also managed to patronize the youth: "The homeland is undergoing critical events and difficult tests which have started with honest young people and citizens," he said. "They have the right to demonstrate peacefully to express their worries, but they were exploited very soon by those who wanted to exploit the situation to create chaos and destroy the constitution."[31]

The performance pulled at the heartstrings of the masses. They began to express sympathy for the old patriarch, who appeared bruised by their treatment. As much as they wanted to see Mubarak gone, many began to express their desire to give him a chance to finish his term and allow him a dignified departure. By this point, mobile phone services had returned, and protesters in the square were receiving nonstop phone calls from parents, family members, and friends discouraging them from continuing. After a week of immense violence and instability, Egyptians outside the square were eager for a return to normalcy.

Activists and committed protesters were demoralized by the public's reaction. The effect of Mubarak's speech revealed to them just how fragile their nascent movement was, how impressionable and susceptible the leaderless masses were to counterrevolutionary messaging. They took to the stages and petitioned the people not to be deceived by the president, not to forget all their innocent countrymen who had been killed and injured by his security forces the last few days for demanding their rights (at least 840 people would be killed and six thousand injured by the end of the eighteen-day uprising).[32] Although a strong contingent remained steadfast in demanding Mubarak's immediate departure, it was clear that much of the public had already lowered the bar of their demands. The proof was in the diminished numbers that spent that night in the square, the lowest count since the sit-in began. Adding to activists' despair was the news they received after the speech of pro-Mubarak protests and marches scheduled for the next day, signaling the first divisions among Egyptians after the powerful unity they had enjoyed the previous week. At this point, it was clear to them and the steady protesters trying to sustain the momentum of resistance that their struggle was losing traction in the street and would face an imminent end if something did not happen to shift popular support back in their favor. But they were at a loss for ideas. The situation, as Amr put it, required a divine intervention.

February 2–3: Popular Self-Organizing in Defense of the Square

The infamous attack on protesters in the square known as the Battle of the Camel was the development they needed. On the afternoon of Tuesday, February 2, Mubarak loyalists, who turned out to be mostly paid civilians and criminals, made their way Downtown from their first organized pro-Mubarak rally in Mohandiseen and attacked the people of Tahrir. At one point, men on horses and camels brandishing whips, clubs, and other crude weapons charged into the square in a move meant to disperse the sit-in. Tahrir occupiers rushed to defend their territory against the ambush. Instinctively, they assumed whatever roles they saw were needed and felt they could fulfill, and a massive, self-organizing defense operation was forged in the throes of a violent showdown that lasted well into the next morning.

The protesters' first concern was to secure the eight entrances to this sprawling square after the alarming withdrawal of the soldiers who had assumed this duty since the 28th. Immediate efforts also focused on breaking up sidewalks for stones and delivering them to the fighters at the three main fronts for use as ammunition. The roles continued to develop from there. A medical corps was born, with volunteers rescuing the injured from the combat zone and transferring them to makeshift hospitals where doctors and volunteers tended to them. Foragers ran back and forth replenishing the fighters' food and water supplies. Spotters stood watch at different entrances to the square, banging ferociously on the green metal rails with rods and stones to warn their comrades of impending attacks from different directions. Activists took turns manning the intercoms, receiving reports from the various fronts and keeping the demonstrators abreast of developments and where more help was needed. Makeshift barracks sourced from sheet metal found at nearby construction sites were erected, and Molotov cocktails and hails of stones soared back and forth through the night sky as Tahrir devolved into an urban war zone. The army, to everyone's frustration and confusion, stood by and watched. Apparently, their promise not to use force against the protesters did not imply a promise to protect them. In hindsight, it would become clear that the army was attempting to play its own political cards right.[33]

The cadre of activists behind the January 25 march from Nahya Street participated along with the other protesters under siege in these various roles as they emerged; according to them, everyone in the square that day was a leader and played a vital role in ensuring the collective survival of the group. My interlocutors emphasized the invaluable effort of women during the battle, both secularists and Islamists, and specifically women from the Muslim Brotherhood. They noted that although their numbers were fewer relative to men, women were found alongside them in all the same roles. Indeed, this was a juncture in which, for all practical purposes, traditional gender divisions of labor were cast aside and a level, inter-gender synergy took over. Ola, for example, alternated between fighting alongside her male comrades at the front and receiving and sharing news on stage to help manage the resistance. Tarek described how her ferocity and steadfastness in the clashes shamed some of the young men, including himself, who did not have the same level of fight in them. Along with the other zealous young women, Ola motivated the young men to "man up" and spurred them to action. "May God forgive her," he joked. "We were hurt so badly that day because of her!" In these intense moments and spaces of revolution, where men and women were interacting in new, visceral ways to ensure their mutual survival, masculinities and femininities were being refashioned in ways that were not based on unequal power relations. After telling me how blown away he was to see the grit of women protesters, Amr recounted an amusing incident during the fighting in the square, when a man in Tahrir, feeling the need to assert his manhood by acting upon his duty to protect women, had the nerve to shout that the women should stay out of harm's way and retreat to the *saniya*, the circular grassy area in the center of the roundabout in the square:

> The guy got torn up. I mean TORN UP. He was torn to shreds! They shouted back "Why?! You go home! What do you mean the girls get in the *saniya*?! If you guys die, do you think they're going to come and tell us to get up and go home?! We're in this with you, either we die together or we survive together!"

In Tahrir, women asserted their equal membership in the collective. They also asserted their right to fight for that collective and rejected the imposition of patriarchal norms that treated them as weak, vulnerable, and in need of protection (this, even as some like Asmaa Mahfouz had, early on, used these same conventional notions of masculinity and femininity to mobilize male participants and subvert the state, reflecting the paradoxical ways in which women variously appropriated and resisted gender norms as they tried to drive the revolution).[34] In the trenches alongside their male counterparts, women were actively remaking the gendered social order as they were revolting against the patriarchal, authoritarian political order. In the process, they seemed to be shaping new masculine orientations toward women. In the following chapter, for example, Ola talks about how her male comrades changed their attitudes about women and their approach to inter-gender activism after fighting shoulder to shoulder with her and other women in Tahrir.

In addition to the contribution of women, my interlocutors underscored the indispensable role of young men from Egypt's popular quarters and slums in the battle. According to Salwa Ismail,[35] this subaltern class of youth had a long-standing vendetta against the police, who had a heavy presence in their neighborhoods and frequently subjected them to discipline and humiliation. At the forefront of this group were Salafi Jihadis and underprivileged members of the Ultras. The Ultras, unionized soccer fans known for their militant, hyper-masculine culture and theatrics at football matches, had a history of violent encounters with police.[36] These young men drew on their organizational and technical skills as well as their sheer contempt for the police to hold down the fort at the fiercest battlefront on Abd al-Mun'im Riyad Street, the road leading into the square from the Egyptian Museum. The consensus among activists appears to be consistent with what I heard from leftist activist Khaled Tallima, himself a son of one of Cairo's popular quarters, namely Awsim. "Let's be real," he said matter-of-factly.

> The ones who protected the square during this time were the youth from *sha'bi* areas. I mean places like Shubra and Imbaba and Matariya and Sabtiya. And anyone who claims otherwise is delusional, an opportunist, and a liar. The Muslim Brotherhood claims that it is the one that protected the square during the Battle of the Camel, and this is not true. It's just not true. It was one of many groups that participated, just like the others. But the ones who protected the square are the young men from the *sha'bi* areas. And the proof is in the fact that the majority of the martyrs that day were from the *sha'bi* areas. . . . Why them? They just had more fire and, to put it simply, they were *rigala* (real men).

Khaled might not have given enough credit to the Brotherhood; many other activists and protesters I spoke to recognized that they had in fact played an indispensable role in the square's defense, especially in organizing the ranks of the rock-throwing brigades at the fronts. Nonetheless, the point here is to highlight the vital role of marginalized, lower-class, non-politicized young men in sustaining the collective struggle. For Mostafa, watching these young men practically "leaping to take bullets with their bare chests" was a humbling experience: "We discovered that we were *welad sis* (sissies)."

Clearly orchestrated by an embattled regime trying to cow the protesters and quell the uprising, the February 2 attack on the Tahrir sit-in actually had the opposite effect. Activists credit it for solidifying public commitment to the revolutionary cause and ensuring its continuation. Significant here is how local moral codes related to gender mediated the public's evolving interpretation of developments and their shifting feelings toward the protesters. Anthropologist Farha Ghannam[37] illustrates this through her study on gender dynamics in the popular working-class neighborhood al-Zawiya. Residents of the area went from being distrustful of the protesters in the early days of the uprising to being supportive. At first they resented the demonstrators for obstructing their access to work, threatening their livelihoods, and undermining their safety. State censorship of the media meant their access to news was limited to official propaganda, which convinced them the Tahrir dissidents were responsible for destabilizing the country. They even repeated preposterous claims that protesters were being manipulated by outside forces who were bribing them with free meals from the KFC in Tahrir. They were moved by Mubarak's speech and felt it was reasonable to allow him to finish his term. But the attack his so-called supporters launched against the peaceful protesters changed all that. Egyptians immediately recognized the assailants as *baltagiya*, the same thugs who preyed on their communities and were routinely employed by the state to terrorize protesters and voters during elections. Their excessive and unjust violence and self-interested behavior distinguished them from *gid'an*, honorable and decent men who acted with restraint and only resorted to violence out of necessity. The protesters succeeded in winning back the public during the battle because they enacted some of the key virtues associated with *gad'ana*, or decency, that defined manhood, and by extension, womanhood. These included courage, toughness, resilience, protecting and standing up for the weak, a sense of partnership between men and women for their mutual good, and the appropriate use of violence. According to Ghannam, "whereas the rebels had proven themselves to be *gid'an*, brave and decent men and women willing to sacrifice their lives for the dignity and good of the whole nation, Mubarak's government and its supporters were seen as *baltagiya*, thugs who protected their own interests."[38] In short, gender and class dynamics operated in subtle but powerful ways to orient the conduct and reactions of the various players in this struggle and shape the movement's twists and turns.

Against all odds, the people of Tahrir won the battle. Following their victory, they were even more determined to hold onto the square and press forward until their demands were met.

February 4–11: Leadership, Representation, and Voice in the Escalation of Resistance

The Battle of the Camel set the stage for the youth leaders' repositioning and later maneuvering in the square. Up to this point, the young organizers behind January 25 had avoided the limelight, opting instead to try to direct and support the movement as it unfolded, seemingly organically, from behind the scenes. Apart from the fact that they were not convinced it was their place, they did this because they wanted to preserve the popular ownership of the revolution, which prided itself on being leaderless. Stepping to the forefront as leaders, they believed, would make it easier to discredit and delegitimize the movement and diminish from the people's sense of agency and ownership. When I asked whether they felt like they could have taken a stronger, more visible lead, Zyad from the ElBaradei Campaign told me:

> Look, it was a very difficult question. At the time we felt that if we announced ourselves as the leaders, this might make it easier to attack the square, because they'd say, "They're just doing this because they want to be the leaders. They're not doing this so things will be better." So this might have weakened the situation in the square. The most important thing for us was that the square remained unified, so it was more important to play the role of leadership, directing them without saying you were the leaders, so you wouldn't be attacked, so they wouldn't discredit you politically.

This was an attitude youth activists maintained throughout the eighteen-day uprising. Promoting the idea of leaderlessness and keeping quiet about their own role was not just an ideological decision based on a rejection of the country's political culture of the male, charismatic leader, but also a strategic decision to protect themselves against repression and to prevent the regime from mischaracterizing and delegitimizing the movement as orchestrated by a tiny subversive group.

But the lack of an official leading revolutionary body soon became problematic; the Battle of the Camel prompted a group of opposition figures and other prominent Egyptians to enter into negotiations with state officials over a settlement to end the political crisis. They called themselves "The Council of Wise Men"—note the conspicuous absence of women and youth—and positioned themselves as a collective that could rise above the fray and mediate between protesters and the government. They leaned toward a compromise in which Mubarak would immediately hand over his powers to his newly appointed Vice President Omar Suleiman for the duration of Mubarak's term. For the youth activists who planned January 25, these developments showed that it was necessary to form a revolutionary organization that spoke to the public with legitimacy from the square and expressed its radical position to protect it from being sold out by the traditional politicians, many of whom had joined the movement late. As Mostafa of the Youth for Justice and Freedom Movement put it:

> After the victory of January 28 and the start of the sit-in, it [a discussion] started that we must have an entity that could win the confidence and trust of the people.... There had to be a transformation from [ad hoc] coordination to a coordinating entity, from just coordination among different groups to a body that expressed itself from behind a name.

What unfolded thereafter among the various opposition actors was a process of figuring out how to carry this movement forward in the absence of a unified leadership. Essentially, the questions they engaged with in this process were these: As we attempt to delegitimize and oust the current regime, how should we compensate for the absence of a leading revolutionary body in order to see this process through? What configuration of opposition actors might the people accept as the carrier of their collective will and support as the representatives speaking and working legitimately on their behalf to complete the revolution? How can we secure the sustained commitment of the masses to this revolutionary resistance?

The Revolutionary Youth Coalition (RYC), known in Arabic as I'tilaf Shabab al-Thawra, formally announced itself in a press conference on February 6 (see figure 4). The first revolutionary organization to emerge from the square, it was essentially the institutionalization of the informal network of ideologically diverse youth factions that had been coordinating the popular mobilization long before January 25, which included the liberal-leaning April 6 Youth Movement, the left-leaning Youth for Justice and Freedom Movement, the liberal-leaning ElBaradei Campaign,

Figure 4. Activists raise the first RYC banners from their stage in Tahrir Square shortly before announcing the formation of the coalition. Photograph by Hossam El-Hamalawy.

young members of the Muslim Brotherhood, the liberal Democratic Front Party, the leftist Nasserist pan-Arab Dignity Party, as well as several independent activists.[39] The RYC was launched with the express purpose of making it clear to the public and government that those who were meeting with Omar Suleiman and other government officials did not represent the square—incidentally, the famous declamation "*la tafawud qabl al-rahil*" (no negotiations before the departure) was their innovation—and to declare that despite the deadly assault, they would continue to occupy the square until their demands were met. According to Zyad, "The people started to leave, so someone had to say, so that the square would continue, someone had to say that we were going to carry on. In the middle of the attacks, we said no, we are going to complete this [so that the people keep on going]."

The RYC announced thirteen executive committee members, twelve men and one woman, Sally Tomah, who also happened to be the only Coptic Christian in the RYC's leadership (incidentally, according to my interlocutors, she played an important role in reaching out to the Coptic Church and securing its support for the movement). They met daily among themselves and with other activists, protesters, intellectuals, and political figures in a large, green operations tent in Tahrir to discuss next steps and plot strategies for escalating resistance. There, they also received local and international journalists interested in learning about their reactions to developments and next moves. In addition to continued calls for million-man protests on Sundays, Tuesdays, and Fridays, they coordinated with other groups like the Revolutionary Socialists to push for nationwide strikes and other acts of civil disobedience. Mostafa suggested that the leadership of these activists was demonstrated in two primary skill areas. The first was visionary leadership, which involved analyzing events, conceiving larger operational strategies for the movement, deciding when to negotiate with the elite, and defining the political position of the RYC. The second area was field leadership, which involved logistical planning at the street level, organizing protesters, and leading chants. Mostafa noted, "there was no hierarchy in the RYC's leadership, only [to a certain extent] in the groups that comprised it. But there was specialization." Operating horizontally as a leadership team and guided by the principles of participatory democracy, they arrived at collective decisions through voting mechanisms.

The RYC was careful to avoid laying claim to leadership and representation of the popular struggle, insisting that *al-sha'b* (the people) were its rightful and only legitimate leaders. Instead, members of the RYC continued to assert in press releases and media appearances that they were only speaking on behalf of those organized groups they were affiliated with, which my interlocutors admitted made up a relatively small percentage of the square, perhaps no more than 10 percent.

Their reluctance to step into the limelight had a lot to do with their unwillingness to disrupt the remarkable synergy born among protesters in Tahrir in the wake of the battle. Liberating the square had inspired people's collective ownership of it. Following their victory, the potent energy and self-organizing that went into the defense of the square naturally turned inward to support the renewed occupation, giving way to a radical collaborative project in popular self-governance. Driven by a sense of solidarity and mutual responsibility toward the collective, protesters from all walks of life cooperated to meet the emerging needs of their new community. There was no shortage of skills, talents, or resources in this self-reliant society: doctors ran field clinics and pharmacists managed dispensaries; Ultras football fans helped organize checkpoints into the square; engineers and IT experts developed the technical infrastructure of the encampment; teachers organized pop-up kindergartens; barbers provided free haircuts; volunteers collected garbage and swept the streets; musicians gave performances to energize the protesters; and restaurant owners donated food, along with daily visitors who made a habit of bringing enough to share with at least ten others.[40] Students, factory workers, farmers, middle-class professionals, scholars, the illiterate, families, street children, religious clerics, performers, women without hijabs and others in black face veils—everyone had a place and a voice in this magical, intimate commune. Mubarak had warned that the demonstrators would sow chaos. Instead, Tahrir's citizens showed incredible self-discipline and creativity as they enacted the inclusive, participatory democracy they aspired to and were repeatedly told they were incapable of. What they achieved in the space of their protest through their inspired horizontal practice was nothing short of a utopian polis, where a spirit of unity, fraternity, and mutual aid prevailed and the very ideals of dignity, freedom, and social justice they demanded were brought to life. Together, they created what many described as the freest, happiest, safest place in Egypt, a model representing a radical alternative for their future. In this sense, the "Republic of Tahrir," as many liked to call it, was a "leaderful" movement,[41] the culmination of the efforts of many individuals and groups, not just the RYC leadership and the movements they represented (see figure 5).

Nonetheless, as the entity representing the youth who had instigated this uprising, the RYC appears to have enjoyed recognition from the state, media, opposition figures, and protesters as a legitimate voice on behalf of the square and a force to be reckoned with. Its demands, after all, were the same as those of the people. They were articulated clearly for the world to see—as an act of escalation following the Battle of the Camel—in a massive banner several hundred feet long, signed by "Egypt's sit-in youth," that was unfurled down the front of an apartment building in Tahrir Square (see figure 6).[42] But even more, what added to the credibility of the RYC was the prominence of the organizations taking part and its cross-ideological makeup, making it one of the first experiments of its kind in Egypt, a country whose political opposition had historically been polarized by conflict and mutual sabotage. Tarek of April 6 argued that for the Egyptian people who were tired of the self-interested behavior of the political old guard, this united youth front was a refreshing and very encouraging development. Nonetheless, it is difficult to fully assess the kind of reception they enjoyed among protesters in the square.

Figure 5. Throngs of protesters enjoying the camaraderie and convivial atmosphere in what many liked to call the "Republic of Tahrir." Photograph by Hossam El-Hamalawy.

My interviews with these activists as well as with other non-organized but active protesters during the eighteen-day uprising indicate that while large segments of the protesters saw the RYC (as a brand, not the individual activists themselves, whose faces were largely unknown in the square) as leaders, others regarded them more as media spokespeople targeting the audience outside of the square, if they were even aware of their presence at all.[43]

Many of my interlocutors also highlighted that one of the most significant things about the experiment was the participation of the young Muslim Brothers, who were widely respected for taking part in the protests despite the initial refusal of the older Brotherhood cadres to endorse the movement. Their presence anchored the RYC with the weight and support of Egypt's largest organized opposition.[44] After the success of January 25, the Brotherhood began taking cues from its youth who were participating in the RYC. According to Amr and Basem, the Brotherhood's Guidance Bureau had semi-officially authorized their youth to coordinate with the RYC on their behalf and began to follow their lead.

Figure 6. Tahrir protesters' demands: the president's overthrow; the dissolution of both houses of parliament; an end to the state of emergency; the formation of a transitional national unity government; a new parliament elected to create constitutional amendments for presidential elections; and prompt trials for those responsible for killing the revolution's martyrs as well as for all corrupt officials and "thieves of the nation's wealth." Photograph by Hossam El-Hamalawy.

Although the RYC made no claims to leadership, it was the closest thing to a revolutionary vanguard organization in the square. Yet, given that this was an ideologically plural movement that lacked a single political doctrine driving it, there remained the need to institute a wider consensus on how to move forward through the establishment of a more fully representative body. Given the attention the RYC already enjoyed, several groups sought entry into it or pressured it to revise its format in order to be more inclusive and representative of the multiple currents and opposition groups in the square, which included other youth groups as well as intellectuals and old opposition figures. The RYC declined their bids for entry and restructuring for several reasons. First, there was the concern that opening up membership into the RYC—especially to groups they knew to be conflict-prone or others they had no previous experience with—would disrupt the chemistry they had achieved that made them effective as a group. Through years of working together on the street, they had become confident in their mutual commitment to the principles and policies that guided their coordination—namely, trust, compromise, and a commitment to upholding decisions voted on by the group. They could not be sure that new additions would abide by their standards. Second, there was the logistical problem that came with expansion. As a group that was committed to decision-making through horizontal rather than vertical, hierarchical processes, it was difficult enough to arrive at collective decisions, given their ideological differences. Deliberations were already time-consuming enough as they were. Inviting more voices to the table would only compound these problems and slow down the decision-making process significantly, if not make it impossible altogether. Third, there was the concern that adding new voices, especially those that tended toward reformism, would dilute the youth's radical position.

According to my interlocutors, however, the group's decision to preserve its structure and close off membership to most of the other groups was no less problematic. First, it provoked those to whom the RYC refused entry to coalesce into different bodies. The most notable of these was the Revolutionary Youth Union (Ittihad Shabab al-Thawra). To some extent, the RYC accepted this development; they believed that the emergence of new groups from the square was inevitable as the numbers of protesters exceeded the organizational capacity of any one group. But generally they saw it as problematic, because the scene became crowded with many coalitions and unions that ultimately detracted from each other's strength. The RYC activists suggested that this was especially true after the eighteen-day uprising, which saw an exponential rise in the number of bodies claiming to represent the revolution's youth; it became very confusing for the public.[45] Second, refusing new membership subjected them to the criticism of the oppositional old guard. Although these political figures took the youth more seriously and some were gladly willing to follow their lead, many of the older activists resented the fact that the youth were calling the shots and taking the limelight. Qassas, who at the time was still a member of the Brotherhood, insists this frustration was the subtext behind their vehement objection to the label *thawrat shabab* (youth revolution) and their insistence on calling it a *thawrat sha'b* (people's revolution). They also argued that the youth were not experienced enough to handle this leadership role. While activists felt patronized by such insinuations, they agreed that any leadership to emerge from the square had to be comprised of known leaders from opposition groups as well as their own.

These tensions illustrate the increasing complexity of the organizing process and the structural limitations inherent in the horizontal, leaderless model adopted and promoted by the RYC and other revolutionary actors. Rather than disbanding, the RYC instead decided it would work with other opposition groups to establish a larger revolutionary coalition organization and participate in it as a unified member. This became all the more urgent as it was clear to them that Mubarak would eventually be forced to step down and the resistance movement still had not managed to come up with a viable leadership alternative to take over. The RYC activists participated in many such initiatives, including attempts to create a salvation government headed by ElBaradei, and later, on the eve of Mubarak's resignation, the Revolutionary Salvation Front (Gabhat Inqadh al-Thawra), which was made up of the thirteen RYC executive members and thirty prominent opposition figures.[46] Most of these failed for reasons similar to those the activists cited as reasons not to expand the RYC. Logistically, it was nearly impossible to create a horizontally structured, democratic body that included representation from all the political currents, parties, and opposition forces. This was especially true, given the long-standing tensions among many of the actors and the severe time pressure on them to act, lest they be outmaneuvered by the state elite. Qassas referred to one such initiative in which the number of representatives exceeded seven hundred and included figures from all over Egypt. When that number was finally reduced to seventy specific people in a series of votes, those involved objected and the effort collapsed. Zyad of the ElBaradei Campaign lamented that when the participants in this initiative had finally agreed on the structure of the group they would call the Revolutionary Salvation Front, and they were ready to hold a press conference to announce themselves, the senior opposition figures involved in it argued with the youth about who would read the press statement. It was one example of the kind of pettiness and political struggle that rendered the opposition ineffective.

This intergenerational power struggle had historical roots and played a significant role in the decision of the youth to maintain their own organization. They felt frustration with the political old guard for marginalizing and excluding the youth in the political arena, especially during the Parallel Parliament initiative that began taking shape in late 2010. Now in the revolutionary spotlight, the youth were eager to assert their right to play a prominent political role. The RYC's decision to preserve its structure was also driven by its founders' frustration with the opposition's historic inability to overcome ideological differences, which they felt they had transcended to become more effective and advantageously positioned to spark and direct the revolution. These frustrations spilled over into revolutionary organizing during the uprising. Despite many attempts to create these larger revolutionary vanguard organizations, the opposition became divided over petty quarrels and many of their efforts failed. According to Basem of the ElBaradei Campaign, the opposition's failure to agree on a leadership structure was due to the senior opposition figures' refusal to set aside their differences, personal ambitions, and egos to rally around a single leader selected from among them. "Truth be told," he said,

> I had serious issues with all of these figures. . . . There was this idea among them that, "Yeah, I won't accept anyone else as a leader, I'd rather see the whole thing go to hell." Each one was like, "Yes, it's true that I might not be able to play the role of leader, but certainly leadership shouldn't go to anyone else." They were the cause of all our woes—before, during, and after the revolution!

The failure of these groups to advance a spokesman or create a leading body had become especially problematic by February 11. While the rest of Egypt erupted with euphoria upon news of Mubarak's resignation, a handful of activists—particularly the hard-core leftists—were unsettled by what they believed was in fact a military coup. The opposition, which had failed to come up with its own unified leadership, was partly responsible for this result and for not being there to direct the movement. In the absence of this direction, the revolutionary masses had focused their demands on Mubarak stepping down. When against all odds they succeeded, the bewildered and overjoyed protesters lost sight of their other demands and emptied the square. Had a clear opposition leadership been in place before then, it might have convinced the people that their revolution was not yet complete and that they needed to remain steadfast in Egypt's squares until power had been handed over to a civilian body that would manage the transition to democracy. Instead, the people entrusted this task to the Supreme Council of Armed Forces (SCAF), which would soon reveal itself to be the revolution's staunchest adversary.

Conclusion

The eighteen-day revolutionary mobilization was neither a spontaneous popular uprising, nor a carefully planned revolution driven by actors bent on seizing state power. It began as a mass protest carefully choreographed and coordinated by a heterogeneous group of highly networked young activists, which later grew rapidly and, unexpectedly, spread through Egypt like wildfire. The movement had been able to gain momentum quickly because at this particular historical juncture, popular sentiments against entrenched inequities had been exacerbated by events in Tunisia, where another despot had just been ousted from office by sustained mass demonstrations. As it unfolded, the Egyptian movement continuously recalibrated and shifted direction, adapting to various ups and downs. Also notable about this process are the strengths and inherent limitations of the politically plural, informal networks of actors using the leaderless trope as a strategy to protect themselves and the movement (discussed more in chapter 6).

The RYC was the most prominent revolutionary organization to emerge from the square during the eighteen-day uprising. However, it was not a revolutionary organization in the traditional sense of the word: it did not position itself as the leader of the movement or the alternative to the current governing body. The closest it came to acting in this capacity was through its efforts to build a revolutionary coalition or interim government comprised of figures from the opposition and youth movements, efforts which ultimately failed. In the end, it is unclear what effect the RYC actually had on the outcome of the eighteen days. Several groups argue that its impact was limited. Some assert that the people were the real leaders of this organic movement, operating on their own as a collective driven by a sense of historical mission and an emergent street logic; this group argues that the RYC had no influence over the people's process. Others argue that the real grassroots pressure came from striking workers and professional syndicates.[47] Their nationwide strike began on February 9 and was seen as a major turning point in the uprising and the factor that forced the military to take action. A third group claims that the uprising would not have maintained its strength and momentum had the Muslim Brotherhood not thrown its weight into the movement. Lastly, the structuralists assert that the military, which used the uprising to stage a coup to protect its own power and economic interests, was the decisive factor. According to the latter, the insurgent masses and their revolutionary aspirations had merely provided the generals with the perfect cover to preempt Gamal's succession and regain power in the ruling alliance, having long been marginalized under Mubarak.[48]

Notwithstanding these different views, the RYC was an important pressure group, especially during the initial uprising. Although its influence might have diminished after Mubarak's resignation, it remained active. It struggled along with the many other revolutionary actors to keep the revolution on course during the transitional period, enduring many setbacks and challenges to its internal cohesion along the way, until it ultimately decided to dissolve in 2012, after the democratic election of Egypt's first post-uprising president, Muhammad Morsi. According to my interlocutors, a revolutionary government might not have emerged from the square during those momentous eighteen days, but there was leadership. This leadership came from both organized youth activists, who helped ignite the movement and worked tirelessly to support it from behind the scenes, and from the people, who sustained the movement with their creative, horizontal improvisation and refused to let their struggle be co-opted.

The eighteen-day uprising represented a dramatic rupture in Egypt's trajectory and in the lives of those who took part in it. This was certainly the case for the organized youth, whose persistent but much smaller-scale street activism in the preceding years suddenly catapulted them to the forefront of the revolution as leaders, a development they could never have imagined. The experience transformed them each in different ways. The following chapter looks at their subjectivities coming out of this experience. It explores the multiple motivations, views, and visions of the youth actors at the center of this movement to open a rich window onto Egypt's changing social and political landscape at the peak of the struggle.

5
Participation, Subjectivity, and Imagination

One of the central arguments of this book is that the Egyptian mass revolutionary mobilization that blindsided the regime and toppled Mubarak was neither thoroughly planned, nor completely spontaneous. Rather, it unfolded as part of a dialectical process in which purposeful actors and a historically determined contextual reality shaped one another through a series of rapidly evolving political actions and events that continuously transformed political actors and reconfigured their actions and subjectivities. As actors instigated events, those events, having developed in ways no one could control, shaped the actors' emerging outlook and influenced their imagination of what was possible. This chapter examines the transformation in the personal and political subjectivities of the RYC leaders over the course of their engagement before and through the eighteen-day uprising. How did sociocultural dimensions such as gender, class, and religion shape their participation and agency in the revolutionary movement? And how did their participation as leaders in the movement shape their subjectivities? Understanding the activists at the core of this movement, the changes and continuities in their attitudes with respect to gender, class, religion, and ideology, and their emerging visions for the new nation-state offers us valuable insight into the development of the movement and its shifting direction, while also providing us with a sense of what they were trying to achieve. But before discussing the subjectivities of these youth leaders, it helps first to take a brief look at the youth movements these activists participated in before the revolution and their coming together as the RYC for a better understanding of the sociopolitical contexts that shaped their changing selves.

Sociopolitical Dynamics of Earlier Youth Movements

The following is a sketch of the four main RYC movement organizations with which my interlocutors were affiliated through the early days of the revolution. The profiles focus on their ideological orientation and sociodemographic composition.

The April 6 Movement

The April 6 Movement in which Amr, Tarek, and Mahmoud were involved was a pragmatic movement originally founded in solidarity with workers. Although the movement did not subscribe to a rigid ideology, most of its members identified as liberal in the sense that they espoused rights and freedoms, pluralism, a civilian state, and the rule of law.[1] Before the revolution, its membership exceeded two thousand activists working in all of Egypt's governorates, the majority roughly between the ages of twenty and twenty-five. Most of those members were young men, outnumbering women roughly five to one, but women are said to have played an active role in the organization. Among them were Coptic Christian activists, although most of them were Muslim (not a surprising fact, given that Christians are a minority in Egypt). In terms of class composition, Amr said that they were educated, that most of them would generally be considered middle or lower-middle class in terms of family income, and that the majority came from Cairo's popular quarters or cities in Egypt's governorates.

The Youth for Justice and Freedom Movement

The Youth for Justice and Freedom Movement, with which Mostafa and Ola were affiliated, was also a pragmatic movement, embracing many Islamist-leaning as well as secular activists; however, its general political orientation was leftist. Again, most of its members identified as Muslims, while a few identified as Coptic Christians. Before the revolution, it had around five hundred active members across the governorates of Cairo, Alexandria, Gharbiya, and Kafr al-Shaykh. According to Ola, most of them were younger, in their early to mid-twenties, and came from working-class and lower-middle-class families living in poor popular neighborhoods, including informal areas (she was perhaps the exception, having been in her early thirties and from an affluent area). Again, like April 6, the majority of the members were young men, outnumbering women by roughly five to one; nonetheless, Mostafa described the women as having been much more committed, active members of the organization than the men.

The ElBaradei Campaign

The ElBaradei Campaign, to which Zyad and Basem belonged, transcended ideologies, although the majority of its members seem to have leaned toward liberalism or social democracy. It was larger and considered much more organized than the aforementioned movements, with members active in all of the governorates across Egypt. According to Zyad, their membership also cut across the three tiers of Egypt's middle class, coming from affluent as well as popular quarters. The male-to-female ratio was approximately three to one, and Zyad emphasized that women were very active in the organization and played a strong leadership role in the movement and its chapters across Egypt. He also claimed that there was a strong Christian presence in the organization, although they might not have been the majority. The movement's ability, compared to the others, to achieve more diversity in terms of the background and ages of its members (many, like Basem, were closer to middle age) had a lot to do with the wide appeal of ElBaradei himself and the real prospect for change he represented.

The Muslim Brotherhood

The Muslim Brotherhood, with which Qassas and Abbas were affiliated, is Egypt's oldest and largest Islamist movement (a status it arguably maintains, despite being outlawed in 2013;[2] see chapter 7 for a discussion of the turn of events that drove them underground). Its members have been heterogeneous in terms of their religious interpretation and ideology, some leaning toward right-wing Salafism and Wahabbism, and others inclining toward the classical Sunni tradition long preserved and developed by scholars in the renowned al-Azhar University in Cairo, which informed the organization's founding. (This diversity was true of the organization before the revolution; however, due to the many disruptions and fractures it experienced after 2011, the current ideological makeup of its members is unclear.) Membership of the Brotherhood is also diverse in terms of socioeconomic status, with members in the most affluent social strata and among the lower-middle class and poor. They live in urban working-class neighborhoods and suburban gated communities as well as rural areas. In terms of gender, the name of the organization is very telling. Although women have played an important role in the organization, this has mostly been in the area of providing social services rather than politics; they have not occupied leadership positions in the larger movement, neither before nor after the revolution.[3] Likewise, they are not officially organized within the movement in the same way as men, who must go through certain stages before they can pledge allegiance and become full members; rather, women gain affiliation through their male family members (see chapter 6 for more about women in the Muslim Brotherhood).

These were the immediate sociodemographic contexts that, before the revolution, shaped the activism of the youth leaders who would become leaders of the RYC. These, along with the personal experiences outlined in chapter 3, help us to understand the transformation in the personal and political subjectivities of these actors throughout their activist careers and especially through the revolution. The following sections take a closer look at the continuities and changes in their sense of selves, in their attitudes and understanding of gender and class relations, and in their religious and political ideologies.

Revolutionary Subjectivity and Visions for the Future
Sense of self

In moments of rapid social change, social distances are often reduced, and very different people change by virtue of their close contact with one another and their immersion in the same transformative circumstances. The activists I interviewed were altered by their experience of the revolution in different ways. I asked the RYC leaders how, if at all, their participation at the forefront of the revolution changed their sense of themselves. The four who were most affirmative in their response—Amr and Tarek of April 6, Mostafa and Ola from the Youth for Justice and Freedom Movement—shared some characteristics in common. None of them came from families with a history in politics; they had discovered politics on their own with little family support for their work. They also experienced some degree of social marginalization—Amr, Tarek, and Mostafa as young men from the less-privileged popular class, and Ola as a woman, marginalized because of her gender despite her upper-class standing. Frantz Fanon[4] spoke of the transformative power of liberation wars in empowering the colonized with a sense of agency, self-confidence, and dignity. Engaging in revolutionary activity seemed to have a similar impact on those among my research participants who had experienced marginalization and exclusion. Amr, Tarek, and Mostafa were instilled with a sense of pride in having proved the importance and worth of their activism, despite the criticism they had received for engaging in it. Mostafa's remarks capture this kind of shift in the attitude of family and friends toward their activism well.

My family completely and categorically rejected my activism [before the revolution]. This was connected to this idea that, "You're going to send yourself to hell, and you're going to take us all with you. This isn't your domain, this is the arena of the people who have the privilege of leisure and time in their lives"—the types who have a "Poppy and Mommy,"[5] if you will—"those are the ones who work in politics, not the ones like you." And these problems only got worse when State Security started coming to my home. I started getting arrested—once, twice, three times. These problems grew so bad that they began to lose hope in me, they thought I was losing my mind. But after the revolution and its success, their attitude transformed 100 percent. That these kids did it! These kids that we used to make fun of did what they said they would do. But still, my mother is anxious. . . . Of course, she's very happy about our accomplishment, and that her son was able to participate. . . . My siblings, all of them rejected this [my activism] except one sister. . . . After the revolution, there's been absolute support from all of my siblings and some worry from my mother of course. . . . Yeah, so I found support, pride, and appreciation. "Everything that you're doing is right, may God give you strength, we're happy for you and proud of you"—that kind of thing. And infinite support.

Following Mubarak's ouster, Mostafa and other RYC leaders made regular appearances as the honored *shabab al-thawra* (revolutionary youth) on Egyptian talk shows to comment on political developments and discuss their positions. Mostafa went on to talk about what it was like for his family to see him on TV and how their new perception of him and support for him and his work motivated him to continue his activism following the uprising:

The idea that—the first time your family and friends see you on TV, this is a scene that has a great impact on them. . . . This appreciation and new treatment made me feel a heavier responsibility, and also support to continue my journey . . . [I learned that] as long as you're confident that you'll succeed, you'll find support in the future. You trust that once you succeed you'll find support, so then you learn to put up with a lot of criticism. . . . Even though they don't agree with you, they now understand that you do see what's right and that you see more than they do.

Figure 7. A street banner promoting Amr Ezz's candidacy for Parliament, with the RYC logo. It says, "Egypt will change with its youth." Photograph by the author.

Reflected in Mostafa's remarks is the self-feeding process that the activists' role creates: expectation and praise begets more action, expectation, and praise, resulting in the social reproduction of their leadership roles.

The changing attitude of the activists' families and friends toward their engagement and the affirmations they offered them after February 11 dramatically impacted the way the activists perceived themselves and their futures. I noticed this in Amr who, along with Tarek and other RYC peers, was running for Parliament on his merit as a member of *shabab al-thawra* when I was in Cairo during the 2011 election season, carrying out my fieldwork (see figure 7). These were the first parliamentary elections after Mubarak's overthrow, and they were the first serious youth foray into formal electoral politics. I spent a lot of time shadowing him on his campaign trail, particularly in Imbaba, where he grew up. Amr had clearly become a bit of a local celebrity—just one of the social rewards his revolutionary activism generated for him. He admitted to me at the time that this newfound attention and support was tremendously validating and life-transforming:

> I myself changed a lot. In my immediate community, in the streets, people criticized what I was doing. They thought it was a waste of time and effort—my friends in the streets, my relatives, my family to a certain extent. Right now, those same people see me as a hero. Of course, this had an impact on me. You know, when the climate

around you is frustrating and people are discouraging, it only adds to your frustration. But when there is optimism in the air—like right after the revolution [i.e. Mubarak's resignation], for example—and the community also begins to understand and know the value of what you've been doing, the importance of the role you're playing, for sure this had a positive impact on me. It affected my dreams and aspirations. It affected my whole life. There's a chance I'll be a candidate for Parliament. I had never even dreamed of any of this at all.

Tarek echoed Amr's and Mostafa's sentiments. Like them, his parents had completely rejected his work, particularly his father, who believed it was a waste of time and even threatened to kick him out of their home if he did not stop. After the success of the uprising, however, they began to appreciate his activism and sacrifice. In fact, he went from being a marginal member of his family to one of its most important heads, regularly deferred to in family decisions.

Their participation at the forefront of the revolution helped Amr, Mostafa, and Tarek step out of their marginalized masculinities. In risking their lives to take a stand against the tyrannical state despite their underprivileged position, these young men proved themselves to be "real men" according to the moral universe of Egyptians in which manhood is equated with courage, nobility, and an orientation toward justice. The public recognition and family affirmation they received for this in turn built up their confidence and sense of themselves as men and drove them to assert their political agency even further, for example by running for parliamentary seats in the first post-Mubarak elections. Moreover, through their activism and persistence, they also overcame the belief that young men of their social standing could not have an impact in the public political sphere. In doing so, they helped normalize and restore the respectability of activism and political engagement for young men and women from similar backgrounds. In fact, it appears that Mostafa, Amr, and Tarek prompted their families and communities to adjust their definitions of what it meant to be a man to accommodate the activism they had once perceived as recklessness. All of this speaks to the idea that notions of masculinity and femininity are fluid and dialectically shaped.

Ola, who as a woman experienced similar social marginalization, also saw a radical transformation in her sense of self. She became conscious of this change on the street, during her confrontations with the police, when she stepped up to help organize the ranks of protesters on the front lines during the celebrated Battle of the Bridge on January 28—the only woman to do so:

> Yes, many discovered, including me, that I can be a street activist, not just a field activist, but like a battle activist, like someone who can be depended on when we're planning an action on the ground. That was a discovery even to me.... Especially on the 28th and the Battle of the Camel afterward, it was obvious to my comrades and colleagues that I became a battle organizer.... The 28th was a major thing for me. It affected me psychologically, it affected how I realized things, it affected how I discovered things about myself, it affected how my comrades would deal with me. I proved to others that as a woman they could trust me ... even if they didn't turn into believing in women in general, I think they believed in my ability to do such things. It affected my confidence in being in such confrontations. It also gave me confidence because I discovered that ... most of the time, and especially also in the Battle of the Camel, I'm sober and conscious and can kind of think of tactics and strategize while being in such a confrontation.... So I discovered myself.

Similar to Mostafa, Amr, and Tarek, Ola's experience speaks to the gendering effect of the movement on its protagonists and society. Her discovery of her own strength and power made her that much more aware of her marginalized position as a woman in Egyptian society, and she grew much more intolerant of such marginality and male chauvinism as a result:

> Of course I got so annoyed and became so tense during the sit-in [during the eighteen days] with anyone who would treat me in a masculine, macho way. So angry. I was more diplomatic before that, but I totally lost my patience afterward.... It was like enough is enough! Any man who would say, like, "Stand aside because we're doing this," or "Let the men talk," or "Let me on the stage," ... or "Who are you to tell me, you're just a woman." This was from outside our group. Within our group someone would just say, like, "Give me this, I can do it better." I was going crazy, screaming at everyone. I was very calm when it came to discussions and meetings and political discussions, and when it came to that [the way men marginalize women], I would have a fight every day.

The subjectivity of these actors was also transformed by the responsibilities they came to shoulder as movement leaders and the opportunities they were afforded during and after the eighteen-day uprising, opportunities that would not have come their way had they not been at the center of the revolutionary movement. This of course contributed to their political maturity and influenced the ways in which they tried to help steer the revolution. Tarek said:

> The transitional period [following Mubarak's ouster] transformed our personalities entirely, from talented individuals to professionals. I believe that many of us became professionals in how we managed our organizations. We took specific expertise from our seven months' engagement—continuous contact with the army, the government, and veteran politicians and economists. . . . We continued to come up with tactics for dealing with the army, to come up with tactics for the government, and to benefit from the expertise of the elders [older and respected intellectuals]. None of us ever thought we would one day witness the start of a revolution, nor did any of us think that we might someday be the people strategizing for a grassroots uprising, and then become parliamentary candidates, and meet with ministers, and the prime minister, and engage with the military council, and sit with the states' most powerful men and the presidents of foreign states. . . . We never imagined any of this.

Tarek's remarks illustrate perfectly how actors evolve and transform with political developments as they continue to shape one another.

Gender positions and attitudes

The issue of gender is deeply embedded in revolutionary movements. Given the patriarchal contexts in which they usually unfold, where men dominate formal politics, these social-transformation-seeking movements tend to have a gender component to their agenda and enjoy the extensive participation of women, which is often seen as crucial to their legitimacy. And yet, the wide participation of women is rarely reflected in the highest formal leadership positions.[6] In those few instances in which women acquired top visionary leadership positions in revolutionary movements, it was something they inherited from martyred husbands or other male relatives who were leaders.[7] Nor do the revolutions usually fully realize the sweeping transformations in gender relations they initially promise or set out to achieve.[8] History is replete with examples. In the Algerian War, for example, women fought alongside men as equals for their collective liberation from French colonial rule, taking up combatant as well as non-combatant roles. In spite of their indispensable contribution, however, they were excluded from public political life after independence and forced to keep struggling for their emancipation as women.[9] Similar scenarios have played out in revolutions and liberation struggles in countries like France,[10] Mexico,[11] Mozambique,[12] Zimbabwe,[13] Iran,[14] and Vietnam,[15] just to name a few. The same is true of Egypt's own anti-colonial struggle, in which women and feminists like Huda Sha'rawi played a prominent role, only to be sidelined by the Wafd Party after independence.[16] To what extent was this reality—the limited representation of women in revolutionary leadership despite their critical role in the struggle—reflected in the Egyptian revolution, particularly in the organizing activities of the RYC? How did the youth's attitudes and perceptions about gender roles change with the revolution, if at all?

I was interested in understanding why women did not have a stronger presence in the RYC's leadership—the executive committee was officially made up of twelve men and one woman (who was also the only Coptic Christian), along with Ola, who was considered an unofficial leader. My questions invited a range of responses.

With the exception of one, all of my male interlocutors generally claimed a liberal, progressive attitude toward women's rights, roles, and participation in society and its institutions before the eighteen-day uprising and after; that is, they claimed their attitude had never changed because it was the same before and after. This was the case for the leftist activists, the liberals, and the independents. It was also the case for Islamists like Abbas and Qassas, the activists from the Brotherhood, despite the fact that women in their organization generally did not, according to them, play much of a political role, and if at all, operated separately from men—something Qassas and Abbas said they were critical of. Qassas said:

> When I was in the student union, there were some female students with us, but ... the interaction was usually through an intermediary ... one or two, for example, that I would talk to. ... There was joint work in some activities, and they had their own activities. After that, the situation was a little worse. There was a

complete separation between the male and female students of the Brotherhood....

He went on to talk about how this changed with the revolutionary uprising, how the gender barriers erected by strict religious interpretation began to dissolve—a watershed moment for women in Islamist groups:

> The girls and the women, even the ones from the Brotherhood and the girls that wore the face veil... they all came down, and they threw rocks, and they stood by us.... All the comments like, "How can I go out by myself?" and "How can I take part in a general protest?" and "How can I raise my voice in chants?" These were a huge problem for us in the university, this question of whether a girl could go to a protest and chant out loud. "Was it alright for her to chant?" We'd ignore the protest and let the country go up in flames while we debated the issue.... It took years for me to convince the girls to get up and speak on stage. But during the time of Tahrir, all of that was forgotten. The girls came out. And they carried rocks. And they chanted.... This was new for Egyptian society. And new for the political groups, especially from the Islamist currents. This female participation [especially from Islamist women] was present and strong.... And it signaled that a change was happening in society, that there would be more reception for the presence of girls and women [in public life]—supposedly.

Such narratives might very well underestimate the role of Islamist women before the revolution and exaggerate the changes it brought about for them, as discussed in the following chapter. But the point here is to illustrate the ways activists experienced gender dynamics in their movements and the consistency in their view of themselves before and after the uprising, with regards to their progressive attitudes toward gender and politics.

That said, Qassas and Abbas seemed to have changed in how they personally interacted socially with women. Their peers observed that being in this dynamic, unsegregated, intimate yet open setting where they fought side by side with women had changed their behavior, most obviously in their willingness to shake hands with women, which they had previously avoided as a measure of religious conservatism and piety. This shift in behavior coincided with Qassas's wider understanding of the intent of Islamic law, its implementation, and its accommodating nature. This change in his thinking, he said, began to develop before the revolution and was later accelerated by it.

Tarek of April 6, the one activist who felt that his gender outlook had significantly changed, had this to say about his transformation:

> The view of men toward women is, he sees her as though she's an object and that he's the one who should care for her, that she's a being that is weaker than him, that she ... needs the protection of men.... And [during the movement] we found that the girls were the ones who were protecting men in the protests! ... So my view of girls changed. And I started to deal with women as if they were fellows, equals.... I started to deal with intellects, and a person, and not a man or woman. Like during meetings. Before, I might not have valued the opinion of girls in the same way I valued the opinion of guys, that sort of thing. Earlier, that is. Right now, for me, I hear a girl and it's as if I hear a guy—I hear an intellect and I hear a human, whether she's right and he's wrong or she's wrong and he's right.... In other words, the sex of the person in front of me doesn't make a difference to me. So yes, my view changed of course. And that there are girls who are even better than guys! There are girls who have abilities greater than guys.

Tarek's pre-January 25 understanding of women as lesser than men and in need of male protection was consistent with the wider patriarchal culture that reinforced this gender dynamic and that was particularly strong in the popular class in which he was embedded. What is poignant about his remarks is how the experience of organizing and fighting alongside women like Ola during and after the eighteen days, relying on them for aid and support, and even being outperformed by them, provoked in him a clear shift toward a more egalitarian masculinity.

As for the issue of women's leadership in the RYC, its executive committee was comprised of the leaders of its individual member organizations, all of whom happened to be men, though women were active—to varying degrees—in the organizations as well. Answers to the question of why there were not more female leaders in these organizations revolved around the patriarchal nature of Egyptian society and women's self-limiting ideas about the role they could play in public life, having internalized this patriarchy.

Moreover, questions as to whether or not they thought it was necessary to have more female leadership, given that this was a democratic movement that espoused the participation of the marginalized, gave way to discussions about quotas, which they felt to be undemocratic. Basem, Amr, and Qassas in particular seemed unconvinced by the idea of quotas.[17] When I asked Qassas, for example, whether he thought there should be more women leaders in the executive committee, he said:

> No. Why? From the beginning, we refused the idea of the quota. As a democratic form, it seems to me that the idea of a quota, that women should have a quota in society, a quota in Parliament, a quota in the Coalition, this is not democracy. And likewise, for the Christians to have a quota, this is not democracy. In the end, this results in division, not unity. I want it to come naturally. So what does this mean [for us as the RYC]? . . . There's a group, and this group is a collective of other groups. April 6 delegated two people—whether they bring two guys, two girls, two Christians, it's not important to me. They came on behalf of their movements. That's it.

Mostafa's following comments echo Qassas's sentiments and seem to dismiss the possibility that there might have been structural constraints in the organization that prevented women's advancement to leadership positions.

> I have a general criticism of this view. . . . This view takes into account form over substance. In the beginning and the end, we're all the same, and the ones who, with their competence and experience, impose themselves on the scene are the ones who have the right to be leaders.

And yet, despite their hesitation around the idea of quotas, this appears to be the mechanism through which they had invited Sally Tomah, the only woman who was an official RYC leader, to be part of the leadership. This was reflected in comments made by other male activists, as well as by Ola, who played an unofficial leadership role. Amr and Zyad said that they had invited Sally to join them on the executive committee, after the members agreed that the absence of female and Christian representation was a problem; Sally, who was both of these, solved that problem. Ola, who had been present in early meetings when Sally was proposed as a candidate, suggested that she was also a strategic choice for the members of the ElBaradei Campaign who nominated her: they could convince the others to allow her in as an independent because she was a woman and a Christian, but since she was really a member of their organization, she could act as a third representative. This last point is important, Ola underscored, because Sally's insistence on taking her own positions, which at times differed from that of her colleagues in the Campaign, created problems. She had to insist on her own voice and fight to be heard. According to Ola, Sally had to work harder to be respected because she was a woman. The two also resisted the gendering of leadership roles within the movement. One clear example of this was attempts to relegate them to be moderators in the first few press conferences after the uprising, while the men in the group read statements and answered questions. Ola also noted that as secular-leaning women activists, she and Sally endured gender-specific attacks on their character and reputation from outside their circles in the months following the eighteen-day uprising, being labeled promiscuous because of their outspoken participation, for example. Of course, she stressed, men in their groups did not face the same consequences for their participation as a result of their gender.

It is worth noting that though the RYC activists claimed progressive attitudes in terms of women's rights and role in public life, none of them self-identified as feminists. This was not just true of men, but also of women, including Ola. For example, while the RYC helped organize and participated in many of the protests in the months after Mubarak's ouster, they avoided taking part in the March 8 International Women's Day protest, dubbed the Million Women March organized by Egyptian feminist groups, which ended with women protesters getting sexually harassed and chased out of Tahrir Square by men. Some made the argument that the political timing of the protest was inappropriate, a refrain commonly heard in the aftermath of liberation struggles, when women started to advocate for their rights. The concern was that their demands for rights during this fragile transitional moment would "fracture an edifice that is still under construction."[18] Ola's frustration with the protest had more to do with the feminist groups organizing it, which she saw as being out of touch with the street and disconnected from the struggle of ordinary, working-class Egyptian women. Ola's disinclination toward feminism in Egypt was common among politically active women and had a lot to do with the feminist movement straying from its radical, rebellious roots as a force against local and colonial patriarchy. Under Mubarak, the movement had been co-opted by the state with the help of First Lady Suzanne, whose sponsorship of women's rights and development initiatives associated feminist discourse with elitism and the authoritarian regime. There was little faith among critically conscious women that the state feminism known in Egypt, in which autocratic male leaders dispensed limited rights to women while ruling the rest of society through violent repression, could ever bring about genuine equality and emancipation for women. For Ola, that kind of gender equality and improvement in women's quality of life could only come through a radical challenge to the state and the institution of socialism, and she criticized these groups for "not taking positions related to changing and uprooting society." That said, whether or not Ola and her peers identified with the contemporary feminist movement in Egypt, the spirit of feminism, with its rejection of patriarchy and insistence on freedom, equality, and dignity for all, infused their outlook and animated their activism.

Class positions and attitudes

While leaders shape structures, structures also determine who leads and how. Social movement leaders tend to not be fully representative of the aggrieved on whose behalf they work, whether this is with respect to their gender, as alluded to in the previous section, or with respect to their class. Revolutionary theory posits that the top leaders of social and revolutionary movements are usually upper-middle-class men, or men of working- and lower-class backgrounds who moved up the social ladder through education (see chapter 6). This has historically been the case not only for the leadership of movements in Western nations, but also for movements and revolutions in the developing world.[19] How did this theory fare among the young leaders in the Egyptian revolution?

According to Amr, most of the RYC members and its leaders came from the popular class, especially those in charge of strategizing for the January 25 protest; their class capital meant they understood the human and spatial geographies of these neglected urban areas better and knew how to make the sociopolitical struggle relevant to their people, which enabled them to perform well as leaders. Of course, most of these youth leaders enjoyed educational capital in the form of university degrees, as is typically the case for movement leaders, but not necessarily in the liberal arts or social sciences, as tends to be the case according to theories of social movements. Amr also argued that what made the uprising successful in ousting

Mubarak were the young, non-politicized, male protesters who came out from these areas, many of whom were accustomed to confrontations with the police. Many of the Ultras who were at the forefront of the fighting, for example, came from these subaltern communities. This is important to note, given the media constructs that labeled the youth driving this movement as middle class and elite, as discussed in chapter 6.

I asked my respondents whether being in such close proximity and interacting with people from social classes different from their own during the revolution affected them in any way or changed their perspective about different class groups or class relations. Most said that they had not experienced this type of transformation, because their activism during college and before the revolution had already facilitated their close engagement with different segments of society, and because they tended not to view people according to such distinctions. However, two of them appeared to be somewhat affected. Mostafa and Tarek, both of whom identified as members of the popular class, were impressed by the turnout and the effort of middle- and upper-middle-class youth in the revolution. Tarek's reflection is especially poignant. He speaks to how encounters and close interaction with other ways of being, though jarring at first, eventually became normal and affected his own subjectivity:

> We had people from upper classes in the Coalition's leadership and even in the movements that make up the Coalition.... We even joked with them about being from the bourgeoisie. You'd find that they lived very simply, and that some of them, especially those with socialist ideas, some of them, you'd find that they lived as ascetics. They could probably have eaten at swanky restaurants every day if they had wanted to, but they would go and eat at the simplest restaurants instead, because that was their thinking, their ideology.... You'd find that inside political life, there were things that were confusing like this, they weren't really understandable.... Myself, personally, in the beginning when I first became immersed in the political scene ... I was shocked by many things.... You'd find someone who was bourgeois and he lived like a socialist. I mean, you became shocked by the different types of people you saw.... Perhaps one had decided to grow his hair out and never to cut it again, strange stuff like that.... The girl who'd leave her family and go down and get beaten in the street, you'd sit and think, "Ok,

what is this?! This is a girl, why would she put herself through this madness?"... These are things that surprise and puzzle you. And in the beginning, you're shocked by what you encounter—[you think] these people are not normal. But then you get used to them, and then you become like them and not normal.

Tarek's comments illustrate perfectly how intimate interaction with difference can slowly transform one's outlook and inform one's process of selving,[20] as was the case for the other activists I interviewed, who were changed in different ways through their activism in the revolution.

Religion and politics

Religion played a central role in the Egyptian political sphere long before January 25 and continued to do so through the revolutionary period. This was especially true after Mubarak was overthrown, during the eighteen-month transition period and the Morsi presidency, a time in which the Islamist elite manipulated religion in their identity politics to ascend to power and used it as a mechanism to discredit the opposition, regularly dismissing those opposed to them as secularists, Copts, atheists, and misguided Muslims. In this context, understanding how leading youth revolutionaries characterized themselves in terms of religion and secularism, and how they thought about the relationship between religion and politics, provides crucial insight into the kinds of emergent subjectivities that drove this movement early on. It also gives us a sense of where the revolutionary struggle might have been heading before it was derailed by more powerful, established forces.

I asked my research participants how they looked at religion and members of other faiths differently, if at all, as a result of their interactions with them during the revolution, as well as why there were not more Christians in the RYC's executive committee. I also asked them what they thought the relationship between religion and politics or the state should look like. My questions yielded interesting responses regarding the place of religion in society, especially Islam, and how, if at all, this should be treated in the new political discourse and accommodated in the reconstruction of the state.

My research participants (who were all Muslim, for reasons discussed in chapter 1) expressed open-mindedness when it came to other faiths, saying that religious tolerance was never a question in their minds. In fact, they had built relationships and friendships with Copts and atheists through their activism well before the revolution (certainly, there were members of their movements who identified as both), so they sensed little change in themselves in this regard. The question of why there were not more Christian leaders from the RYC yielded similar explanations as to why there were so few women: leadership in the organizations was a reflection of wider participation in public life. Christians' presence in the leadership was proportionate to their representation in society; they were a minority. Besides, as many of them argued with respect to gender, quotas were not appropriate means for addressing any kind of underrepresentation.

Discussions around the relationship between religion, ideological leaning, and politics yielded some interesting findings that reflected a wider trend in Egypt's early revolutionary political scene, in which actors and constituents tried to figure out where they stood politically as they negotiated the relationship between their respective faiths and politics. This negotiation centered around their common recognition of Egyptians' sociohistorically rooted disposition toward religion—"The Egyptian people are religious by nature" (*al-sha'b al-masri mutadayyin bi tab'u*) was a common refrain—and the central role religion played in their culture and history.

Each of my respondents identified as Muslim, but they differed in their views on the role religion should play in politics. There were left-leaning activists like Ola and Zyad who saw no place for religion in politics, arguing that religion is a sacred relationship between God and people and should not be mired in the temporal political sphere. Zyad did not believe in the idea of using Islam as a source for legislation (*marga'iya islamiya*), maintaining that the vastly different interpretations and versions of Islam that existed in Egypt made such a venture impossible.

In contrast, Mostafa identified strongly as a Muslim as well as a Marxist, claiming that there was no conflict between the two:

> I'm a Muslim and a believer. Even after I became occupied with political work. . . . I became a Revolutionary Socialist and a Marxist like they say—I'm a Marxist, and to the extreme left, a Trotskyist Marxist. Even after I became a Trotskyist . . . we're a group of youth that came out of college together and we still work together in general political work even now. And we created around us a current among the Marxist groups in Egypt that is considered strange, they weren't used to it at all: a current that is made of believing, conservative Muslims. . . . We fast—we're the only Marxist group that fasts in all of Egypt—and we pray. So the distinction is that we were

able to recruit a generation of youth who were convinced by Marxism and socialism and believed in the rights of the downtrodden around the world. . . . This generation is Muslim, and they don't see any contradiction between Marxism and religion.

What Mostafa means by "conservative Muslim" is subject to interpretation, but the point is that his group was attempting to pioneer a new way of being leftist that accommodated the religiosity of Egyptian society. This type of adjustment occurred in other ideological circles as well. Several were engaged in revising their ideology and forging new currents to accommodate Egypt's local reality as it spoke to their revolutionary goals. This was the case for Amr and Tarek, who identified as ideologically liberal; they became more progressive when it came to advocating for women's rights, for example, but remained conservative when it came to the idea of supporting homosexual rights, which offends mainstream religious sensibilities in Egypt, both Muslim and Christian. But it was even more so for the young activists from the Muslim Brotherhood who split from the organization in the months following the initial uprising to start their own political party.

Here I will briefly return to the Muslim Brotherhood and RYC members' experiences of it before the revolution to help us understand their relationship with the organization and their view of it afterward. As discussed in chapter 3, most of the male activists I interviewed had some experience of the Brotherhood, whether it was through their family connection to the organization, like Abdelrahman; through their community chapters, like Mahmoud; at university, like Amr and Tarek; or as organized members within the movement, like Qassas and Abbas. Only Qassas and Abbas would remain with the organization for the long term, until even they officially parted ways a few months after Mubarak's resignation. Understanding why these activists chose not to commit to the organization or why they left gives us insight into their evolving political subjectivities at the height of the revolution.

Although Abdelrahman cited his independent streak as the original reason for his decision to break from family tradition and disaffiliate himself from the Brotherhood, he also cited the organization's reformist rather than revolutionary orientation as the more crucial reason, believing that Egypt's situation needed a more radical change. This sentiment was shared by Qassas and Abbas, who in the years leading up to the revolution came to realize that reform was not enough to remedy the problems of Egyptian society and that revolution was necessary. Indeed, generational differences in the Brotherhood started to appear around this specific issue.

Mahmoud and Amr originally tried to participate in the Muslim Brotherhood because it was the most organized opposition movement with a presence in the streets, and yet each ended up leaving for nearly the same reasons. Amr shared his experience:

> I tried to participate with the Muslim Brotherhood, but they didn't have answers to my questions. Their youth were like, "It's not your business." I'm not able to do something without knowing what it's about. When we were planning an action, I would ask them what the goal was, what the reason was. They would say, "What business is it of yours? You work and that's it!" It's not that they were closed-minded, but that they themselves didn't understand. They just worked and that's it. They understood that what they are engaging in is part of a struggle for the sake of God, so it's none of their business. I didn't like this.

Amr's frustration with the lack of transparency, critical thinking, and resistance to debate, discussion, and questioning among the youth in the Brotherhood was shared by Mahmoud, who had a similar experience with the organization. He talked about going down to a protest along with other young Brothers at the behest of the leadership, and then being ordered to leave once the confrontation with the police escalated, a decision he could not understand:

> I found that we were told to stand there a bit, and then to yell a bit ... and that's it. Time to go home. So I said to the people gathered there: "Umm ... why are we going home?" "Well," came the answer, "because they [Central Security] are bringing more people, and things could escalate." Ok, well why the hell did you bring us then? Did we not come so they could escalate and we could have the chance to refuse to back down, because an injustice has been perpetrated? Wasn't there an injustice perpetrated? It made no sense. And at the time I thought to myself, are we not Muslims? Should we not, as Muslims, not permit injustice to continue? No matter what? So I said that. [And their response was:] Orders ... There was even one guy who didn't leave.... And the security

forces grabbed him and began to beat him. The Brotherhood guy standing next to me, I remember as we watched this, said: "Good! He deserves it! We had an order and he didn't obey it." . . . That was a somewhat decisive day. I thought, what does this mean? It's now good that the Central Security Forces are beating us? What kind of orders are these? You are ordered to cry out against injustice, and then when different orders are given, one more injustice is good? I had only one thing to say: Fuck that.

This was an important moment for Mahmoud's developing consciousness and activist becoming, as a young, average, Egyptian Muslim man who wanted to affect change. The questions this incident and others like it stirred up for Mahmoud were important ones that reflected a deeper questioning about and objection to the way religion, power, and politics were operating to inform the conduct of the Brotherhood, which was clearly authoritarian in nature. The incident also made him realize that the Brotherhood's authoritarian structure and patriarchy stifled his own agency and his ability to play a role in affecting the change he wanted to see in society. He explained:

> You know when there are adults talking, and there are kids around and they send them to play in their room? It's like that. The Guidance Bureau is having these conversations with folks upstairs, and they send us to play in our rooms. They send us to play a bit, and it's a way of sending a message to the regime. Simple. . . .

He went on to say,

> There was a need to do something, and at the same time, a total understanding that we have no tools with which to do anything . . . the Brotherhood would limit our thinking. I don't mean that they made us feel stupid, or treated us as though we were or anything. It's not something related to intelligence. But it was something related to imagination. There was no space for the search for methods through which we could originate mechanisms through which we could reach our goal, if that makes any sense. We were always waiting for them to tell us how to proceed. I guess that's what I mean.

Shortly thereafter, Mahmoud left the organization, not so much for ideological reasons, initially, but because he had no interest in adhering to the standards of religious discipline the organization expected. Later, he experimented with the Revolutionary Socialists, from whom he heard what he thought were fair criticisms of the Brotherhood that also shaped his view toward the organization: the Revolutionary Socialists did not question the organization's sincerity but did criticize its classism, its general tendency to side with capital and power, and its divergence from its original revolutionary nature as presented by its founder Hassan al-Banna in his writings. That said, he would not commit himself to socialism either, because the idea of a "Third International" was just as far-fetched and improbable to him as the Muslim Brotherhood's "caliphate."

Qassas and Abbas both said they initially joined the Brotherhood for the opportunity it gave them to serve their faith and their country, both of which they loved dearly. Like Mahmoud, however, they would come to struggle with several of the Brotherhood's ideological positions and organizational decisions. Nonetheless, they remained loyal members, even through the eighteen-day uprising, although they began to take political stands that the leadership did not endorse. Qassas said their decision to bear these differences and continue with the Brothers was related to the regime's repression of the organization, which fostered group cohesion as it focused the members' attention on resistance against the regime, a struggle he believed in. Moreover, he did not want to abandon his longtime friends in their struggle. When Mubarak stepped down and state repression seemed no longer to be an issue, these schisms came to the fore and resulted in deep rifts, especially along generational lines. Along with many of their other young Brotherhood peers, Qassas and Abbas could no longer follow leadership decisions that did not resonate with them or chime with their revolutionary aspirations. This ultimately led to their expulsion from the organization, which came in two stages. The first was when they defied the Brotherhood leadership's decision to boycott the mass demonstrations on May 27, 2011, known as the "Second Revolution of Rage," and support the RYC's decision to participate. The Brotherhood at this point announced that it had no representatives in the RYC. Their formal expulsion came less than two months later, after Qassas, Abbas, and their peers established the Egyptian Current Party, defying an edict forbidding members from joining any political party other than the Brotherhood's newly established Freedom and Justice Party (FJP). The young Brothers believed that the Brotherhood should remain a religious movement and adamantly opposed its formation of a political party. They believed that the pursuit of power would precipitate the destruction of the organization and eighty-year-old movement.

The young Brothers' decision to found their own political party was an important one and is pertinent to our discussion of emergent political subjectivities in revolutionary Egypt. It reflected a wider post-uprising trend among political actors to insist on a new discourse regarding the relationship between religion and politics. The Egyptian Current Party was an attempt to forge a new way of doing politics that was local to Egypt. It was premised on an acknowledgement and celebration of Egypt's predominant Muslim and less dominant Coptic identities, its Arab and African identities, and the general culture of its people, speaking to what the founders described as the *basata* (simplicity) of the average Egyptian, as well as the revolutionary intellectual. Guided by the revolution's aspirations for social, economic, and political justice, the Egyptian Current adopted only those concepts from the liberal, leftist, and Islamist currents that it thought would be agreeable to the average Egyptian's sensibility in the service of these objectives. At the same time, the party sought to transcend these ideologies to accommodate and unify a wider array of Egyptians.

Though Qassas, Abbas, and their co-founders believed in a *marga'iya islamiya*—that sharia should be a source for legislation—they subscribed to the position that Islamic law is "not a monolithic rigid body of law but rather a highly diverse and flexible set of objectives, legislation and legislative guidelines."[21] As such, they believed the focus should be on challenging the right-wing Islamists' literalist interpretation of Islamic law (and avoiding those matters in which there are differences of opinion among Muslim jurists) rather than arguing for the divorce of religion and politics, which they saw as impossible in the Egyptian context. Not only would the latter only strengthen the more conservative Islamists, such as the Salafis, who positioned themselves as defenders of Egypt's Muslim identity against the threat of secularism, it would also allow them to avoid developing a sophisticated political project suitable for a diverse, democratic Egypt. In brief, the Egyptian Current Party attempted to position itself in the center of the political spectrum as a viable alternative to left-wing secularism and right-wing conservatism.

Understanding the transformation in the political subjectivities of these actors gives us insight into their revolutionary struggle and the directions in which they hoped to drive it, as well as those factors that acted against it. These ideologies were fashioned over the long term, in the street, and through a dialectical interaction with local events and developments.

The next sections take a closer look at how the activists understood concepts like democracy, citizenship, and participation, which were frequently invoked to describe the objectives of their revolution. Understanding the political subjectivities of activists—including their feelings about the role Egypt should play regionally and globally—sheds light on the nature of the revolutionary movement and how activists wanted to see it unfold.

Envisioning democracy

The 2011 Egyptian revolution has been called a "democratic revolutionary movement." The qualifier raises important questions: How did these activists understand democracy? What does the democracy they envisioned for Egypt look like?

Responses to these questions were diverse. Basem described democracy as a tool for people to choose their leadership. For him, it was not so much about a particular system as it was about the means for the people to have a voice:

> Look, the principle of democracy that we want to adopt is that the people have a voice, very simply. That the ones who rule these people, the people are the ones to have chosen them. Whether it's in the form of a prime minister or a president, whether it is under a parliamentary or a presidential state . . . whether the governor [of the provinces] is hired by a president I voted for or is someone I voted for myself . . . the point is that in the end, there has to be a mechanism for the people to choose. . . . In the end, I have a voice. Each person should have a voice that must be counted and know that he is going to make a difference. This is democracy, simply put.

Qassas's position expanded on this. He argued that since the time of Sadat, Egypt has had a democracy in appearance but that it was essentially hollow. He wanted to see a democracy with true participation of the public and representation of and accountability to their interests.

For Zyad, democracy was about something much deeper than elections; it was that "each one feels the law that is written expresses him and that the law is being implemented . . . that despite our differences, we feel that it speaks for us—that I find myself in this law, and even if I don't . . . I see that it's fair." His democracy was one that is transparent and speaks to the diversity, needs, and historic experience of Egyptians.

Zyad's concept of democracy was not just about political life; it was about social rights as well, as expressed in the resounding revolutionary demands for bread, freedom, and social justice. Mostafa and Ola agreed, emphasizing the importance of social justice in the equation and their frustration with the Western "bourgeois" connotations around the term "democracy" as it was used to describe Egypt's revolution. For them, the ballot box was an illusion; their democratic revolution was about completely overhauling the system and transforming state–society relations by turning power over to the people, something much more far-reaching. In fact, revolutionaries would later coin the term *sanduqratiya* (ballotocracy), during their resistance against the SCAF and Muslim Brotherhood regimes to criticize the kind of minimalist, procedural democracy reactionaries were trying to force them to accept in place of the radical one they aspired to. Incidentally, this deep desire to dismantle the system completely and avoid settling for cosmetic changes and reforms at all costs translated into the reluctance of many of them to "play politics" during the transitional period by participating in the 2011 parliamentary elections, for example, in favor of continuing to protest in the street. (This had negative repercussions for the movement, which are discussed more in the following chapter.) Ola said:

> Don't let people convince you that with a parliament and with a prime minister and I don't know what, that we're going to realize these things. These things aren't realized in this way. These things will be realized when the revolution continues and becomes victorious and we bring another system that brings us into social justice—a radical, totally different system, a system that brings people into power. . . . Because no revolution is really victorious until the people who made it are in power. And by "people," I don't just mean young people. The young people everyone talks about weren't the only ones who made this revolution happen in the first place, so even if they were to gain power, that doesn't mean this revolution is victorious. All the people have to be in power: they really get to say which government, which parliament, how they should run—all these things. A direct practice of decision-making. That's it.

Mostafa developed Ola's position further. His vision of a democracy inserts and entrenches the average Egyptian citizen in the state power structure. In his vision, there is almost no need to hold the leaders accountable, because the people themselves have sovereignty and are the ones leading, from the bottom up:

> As for the democracy of the election box, I accept it as a transitional measure. But real democracy is when there is the highest level of the people's participation at all levels of decision-making. So instead of a system of local management, I'll have a form of local government. Like in Scandinavia, where decisions are made from the bottom up and not vice versa. I create institutions from the bottom, and as a result I've established a form of popular participation. This participation of the people is the true reflection of democracy, that there is people's participation in all the decisions made in the country. This is the form of democracy I believe in. It might be different from that of a liberal. I differ with him regarding the type of democracy that I aspire to. The ceiling of his ambitions stops at what I call a "bourgeois democracy." I strive toward something more like a popular democracy.

He went on to talk about the issue of social justice and how that fits in with notions of democracy:

> The second thing is that I don't see it as just a democratic revolution and that's it. I see that the people went out from the first moments and said what? Two slogans: "Bread, freedom, and human dignity," and "Bread, freedom, and social justice." So this revolution was a revolution for democracy and freedom, and it was also for social justice. That there is a society in which there truly exists social justice: justice in the distribution of wealth, justice in the tax system, justice in the rent system and the system of social security.... Social justice is one of the most important rallying points of the revolution. There are people who tell you that the Egyptian people didn't go out because they are hungry, but for dignity and freedom. And it's as if a revolution against hunger is a slur, when it's the complete opposite.

For Mostafa, in order for this social justice to be realized, the people who suffer the most from its absence should be at the center of the decision-making process; only this way can they ensure the social contract between them and the state is upheld, protect their rights from violation, and achieve the dignity and respect they demanded. It is important to note that the vision for democracy espoused by these activists does not reference the experiments of Western superpowers like the United States and Britain as a model. In fact, Ola argued that the United States itself was in dire need of a democratic revolution along the same lines as Egypt's; as she saw it, the entrenchment of neoliberalism and lack of social justice proved American democracy was failing because it did not represent the people's interests, particularly the downtrodden. Here, Abbas's perspective is important. Consistent with his "Egyptian Current" ideology, Abbas argued that whatever democratic form takes root in Egypt, it cannot be imported from outside, but must be constructed around Egypt's multi-faceted identity and local experience.

Reimagining modern Egypt

If revolution is about social and political transformation, then what sort of transformation did these activists imagine for Egypt? How did they relate to Egypt differently or view it differently after this process? What role did they want to see Egypt play in the region and in the world? My findings consistently showed that the future these activists dreamed of for Egypt and pursued through revolt was driven by their memory of its past and the way they related to it. In other words, their imagination sprang from their embeddedness in Egypt's historical trajectory. Amr's discussion on why he became politically active is one of many that reflect this:

> One of the things that would often bother me is that when I read history, I would be distressed because our generation wasn't going to have a place in it.... I felt that I didn't want to exist during this time, I didn't want to be present with these people... I wished, for example, that I was present in the year 1919,[22] or earlier or later or during a specific historical event, and that I had a role in it.... I used to often look for anything [to engage in] that history would talk about later—you know, that history would one day say, "You know what, the people who lived in the period before this, they did something.... These people persevered in something, and they finished what they set out to do."

Amr's comments relay the pre-January 25 frustration and disenchantment of the members of his generation who felt handicapped by their moment in history and damned to obscurity, unable to improve their own lives, let alone aspire to leave a mark on the pages of their nation's long and rich history. My interlocutors expressed this feeling repeatedly, especially young men like Amr and Tarek. Indeed, their longing for historical agency was one of the ways in which they expressed their masculine anxieties, particularly as they related to their desires for dignity, recognition, and relevance.

Tarek's reflection echoes Amr's sentiments, contextualizing his generation's misery in the legacies of Egypt's previous generations and the sociocultural highs they experienced. These include the liberal age in the early 20th century; Arab Nationalism under Nasser; the vibrant student movement of the 1960s and 1970s; and the glory days of the October 6 War under Sadat, when Egypt redeemed itself after its loss in the Six Day War and recaptured Sinai from Israel:

> I believe we were the most miserable generation in the history of Egypt, or what we can call contemporary or recent history. I believe that the generation of King Farouq—Egypt during the time of Farouq was different. Egypt was a beautiful country. They used to call it the Paris of the East and stuff like that. So that was a great generation. The generation of the 1960s, this was also a giant generation. The generation of the 1970s was also—they caught some of Abdel Nasser and Arab Nationalism . . . even when Egypt still had some dignity under Sadat, which was the generation of my father. This was the generation that lived the nationalist state and lived through the speeches of Abdel Nasser and the politics of Sadat and all of that. . . . They lived the love of Egypt, they lived the dignity of Egyptians. We didn't experience any of this, nor did we know anything about it. . . . We were a generation that came and was born during the time of Mubarak, a time in which Egyptians were humiliated both inside and outside the country, a time of cultural degeneration and widespread illiteracy.

Tarek's comparison of bygone Cairo to Paris is significant; it gives us insight into how he and other young Egyptians in a globalized world related to and envisioned the future of modern Egypt. After sharing his dream that "Egypt will be three words: free, advanced, and democratic," Tarek went on to reminisce about the glory days of Egypt's modern, Western, liberal experiment:

> A long time ago Egypt was special... In the 1960s and 1970s there was opera, it had state theaters in which the greatest novels were acted out on Egyptian stages. It had a lot of cultural and social activity.... Egypt was something else! I mean, Egypt was the second country in the world where a train line was put in. The second country in the world! The second country after England.... The latest fashions used to appear in Egypt before they appeared in Paris. It had an opera house just like Paris's, the one that got burned. So Egypt is a country that was beautiful, and until around the 1970s, before economic liberalization and before Mubarak... Egypt was something else completely.

Tarek's nostalgic recounting of Egypt's modern past and the paradoxes that came to characterize it—European influence as well as Arab Nationalism—is telling, especially in the context of a discussion about the nation's future. It reflects a desire to preserve Egypt's Western cosmopolitanism and to return to its regional role as leader of the Arab world—a dream that is a hybrid formulation of the most celebrated aspects of its past. What is perhaps equally significant is what is missing from Tarek's recollection of Egypt's past when considering its future: its premodern Islamic history. I do not mean to infer that Tarek did not appreciate this part of the past, but merely that it did not appear to be a model for his or other young revolutionaries' vision of Egypt's future, at least not exclusively. There seems to have been no desire on their part, for example, to establish an Islamic state, a fear that some Western media outlets expressed in the wake of the revolution. In other words, their imagined future Egypt was not a reinvention of their Islamic medieval past, nor was it anti-Western.

Mostafa's reflection is also informative, revealing a very global perspective. It shows his generation's frustration with Egypt's global status as a developing nation—a departure from its historical position as the birthplace of civilization and a far cry from its centuries-old national self-image as *Umm al-Dunya*, the "Mother of the World."[23]

> There was a moment when you felt that if you truly became free, if things went according to what you desired, and the country really

became free ... you would be able to stand in the line of all the strong and developed countries and be able to help any downtrodden person in the world. That I might be able some day to direct my country in a way that helps those who are dying of hunger in Somalia and those who are being exposed to massacres in Latin America, and so on. That you could be a help to the oppressed around the world.

Like Tarek, Mostafa wanted to see Egypt become advanced, along with other Arab countries also going through revolutions. The future Egypt he imagined was a developed industrial nation that had moved out of its third-world status to become a first-world nation. As such, Egypt would go from a country receiving aid to one dispensing it, and in that process, reclaim its dignity as a nation globally.

The revolution was an important event for the activists in that it gave them the opportunity to correct the image of Egypt regionally and Arabs globally, proving Egypt's civilizational legacy was still alive and allowing them once again to command the respect they felt they had lost as a nation. Zyad's comments reflect this development in the revolutionary subject. Citing the utopian days of the Republic of Tahrir and the continued resistance in 2011 following Mubarak's ouster, he said:

We're telling the people that the civilization that you've been hearing about for seven thousand years, it's still present. Its appearance has changed, but it's still present. The despotic regimes made it so that it didn't show, but it comes out during certain moments.... Something really big happened ... that showed the whole world the civilizational things, the small ones that we see. We have our own problems, of course, and they're related to a degree of backwardness, to the lack of education, and so on, but there is a civilizational tradition inside each one of us.

Egypt and the anti-imperial struggle

While Egypt's youth revolutionaries may not have been culturally anti-Western, they were certainly anti-imperial. This is perhaps best reflected in the RYC's rejection of Hillary Clinton's request to meet with them after the eighteen-day uprising. According to their press statement, this was because "the US administration took Egypt's revolution lightly and supported the old regime while Egyptian blood was being spilled." Moreover, they did not welcome Clinton's visit "because the US administration long supported Mubarak's corrupt, dictatorial regime financially, politically, and morally." The activists were under no illusion about how the United States felt about genuine democracy in Egypt, given how much was at stake for the former as a global power that relied on their nation to preserve its geostrategic interests in the region. After condemning past American policies toward Egypt, they ended with a poignant assertion summing up the shift in the relationship between the two countries that they intended to ensure moving forward: "The Egyptian people are the masters of their own land and destiny and will only accept equal relations of friendship and respect between the people of Egypt and the people of America."[24]

Activists' anti-imperialism was even more apparent in their comments about the leadership role they wanted to see Egypt play in the region once again, and particularly around the issue of Palestine. In fact, the Palestinian struggle figured strongly in the narratives of these activists; not only was it a trigger for their activist becoming, as illustrated in chapter 3, but it also continued to inform their resistance during the eighteen-day uprising and in the months afterward. As Tarek put it, quite squarely:

> The Americans [the US government] are hated.... They're hated in the Egyptian streets and they're hated by the activists, whose first issue of concern is Egypt, and their bigger issue, Palestine.... We went to Tahrir in Cairo so that we could get freedom for Palestine. So this is our larger goal. We are getting freedom for Cairo as a step toward securing freedom for Palestine.[25]

Identification with the Palestinian struggle in the revolution was so strong in the narratives of activists that some even talked about how, when they were in the square, defending themselves with stones against the police and Mubarak supporters, they felt a lot like Palestinians during the second Intifada.

The revolution confirmed the belief of these young Egyptian activists in their nation's ability to stand up to imperial powers and their regional interests and reformulate geopolitical relations and the balance of power in the region. Qassas said:

> Mubarak always made us feel that we're some poor people who are unable to find food to eat, that we don't have any international value, that we're not able to fight America, that we're not able to face Israel. After the revolution, I discovered, no! We're a big deal, and we're capable of doing a lot of things if we have the political determination. No, we're capable. And we can make changes right now through strong political will.... The idea itself felt achievable, that we're able to change the map of the world right now.

Understanding that "what we do [in Egypt] changes everything," as Qassas put it, these young activists were fighting for a foreign policy that reflected public opinion with respect to developments in the Middle East, especially the Israeli–Palestinian conflict, as much as they were fighting for systemic political and socioeconomic justice at home. Mostafa saw the revolution as a turning point in the way Egypt would engage with the Palestinian struggle: "This role is going to be central and pivotal and it will change dramatically. We won't be complicit in the siege of Gaza, no: we will be supporting them in their resistance and their project." Speaking to this same sentiment, Abbas remarked:

> We were certain that the work we were doing inside the square wasn't just for Egypt. What we're doing isn't work just for Egypt. For this reason, we're waging this immense resistance effort against the military council. We're doing this not because the council is bad, but because it's going to return us to the same old politics. And we don't want the same politics. We want Egypt to be the country that we know it is, a state whose history is known: Egypt, the axis of the Arab, Muslim world.

In short, not only did Abbas and his peers want to transform Egypt, they also wanted to challenge and unsettle the international geopolitical order that kept their region and its people at the mercy of US and Israeli imperial interests. In many ways, they were keeping alive the nationalist mission of the political generations that had preceded them.

Conclusion

Each of the youth activists I interviewed was changed in some way through their participation in the revolution according to their multiple and intersectional positionalities in it. None of them was the same person they had been in early 2011, before the start of the revolution. The narratives discussed in this chapter illustrate the dialectics of their subjective transformations and how such transformations affected their political goals and visions for the future. Curiously, their vision and imagination embraced the paradoxes of Egypt's present and past, reflecting a hybrid mindset—part anti-imperialist (pan-Arabist, pro-Palestinian), part Western-oriented. Indeed, they might have voiced a desire to build a radically different democratic system, yet they expressed no qualms about drawing from Western political philosophy for inspiration (recall Mostafa's reference to the Scandinavia example). In the process, they sought to forge a new and creative discourse about the role of religion in politics that was particular to Egypt's experience, one that would transcend the rigid notions of secularism (understood as the absolute separation between religion and state) and religious governance based on Islamic law. Like their own personal histories before the revolution, their political subjectivities during it were embedded in multiple scales of social and political interaction—local, regional, and global. That is, they saw their revolutionary struggle as not just an attempt to vindicate the rights of local people and the nation by correcting the wrongs perpetrated against them by an unjust neoliberal authoritarian order, but also as connected to the construction and development of the larger Arab region and world beyond.

6
The Making and Unmaking of Revolutionary Youth Leadership

Egypt's experiment in revolution was a profoundly complex affair, produced through countless intersecting and colliding processes involving a range of actors, institutions, and structures. This study contributes to our understanding of this revolutionary struggle by tracing the story of the youth who were so central to its unfolding. There are many facets to this story: the individual and relational experiences that shaped their political consciousness and maturing activism in the lead-up to January 25, the sudden eighteen-day rupture that signaled a defining moment in their trajectories and a unique chance to lead the country toward sweeping change, and the myriad transformations they endured as participants in and leaders of this movement. All of these fed into the evolution of this struggle. The preceding chapters illuminate this story by focusing on the factors that shaped the engagement and subjective development of the activists. They also shed light on the micro dimensions of youth organizing and leadership in the revolution. This chapter examines the different ways youth leadership was expressed and made manifest during the revolution and how they influenced the development of the revolutionary movement. What can we learn from this historic process? What does it tell us about existing theories of revolutions and the people who carry them out and lead them?

Leadership, Spontaneity, and Youth Agency

It should be clear by now that while the January 25 uprising might have been unexpected, it was not leaderless, spontaneous, or rooted in social media; it was spearheaded by young activists who had been engaged in sociopolitical action long before the uprising. Many of these activists had participated in the key movements that revived the political street years before the eruption of January 25 and were the founders and leaders of the youth movements responsible for taking the culture of resistance to new levels. A heterogeneous group, they were socialized through different streams of the same micro, meso, and macro sociopolitical processes, which ultimately shaped their activism and led to their almost synchronic convergence in the street. There, they became highly networked and coordinated even as their organizations remained loosely structured and decentralized.

The mass mobilization was launched in the streets and through well-established networks of resistance, not on the Internet, which the activists only employed as a tool. In the throes of their confrontation with the oppressive structures and institutions of the state and between repeated rebuffs from the political old guard, their dream for sweeping transformative change was born and their will to see it through was fixed. Thus, when the January 25 Police Day mobilization became—thanks to their organizing efforts—one of the largest mass protests in recent Egyptian history, they seized the opportunity and drove it forward while the old guard opposition leaders trailed behind. The activists had not anticipated the record-breaking turnout when they took to the streets that day, but they ran with it and did their best to capitalize on the moment's revolutionary potential. In this sense, these young activists were leaders of the revolutionary movement—at least during its initial stages. This movement was born out of their dreams for a better future; indeed, it came into being and grew thanks to their daring initiative, organizing skills, personal sacrifice, and early refusal to allow it to be co-opted, hijacked, or quashed.

The ten years of resistance leading up to the eruption of the revolutionary movement and the active participation of these youth in that struggle shows the revolution had precedent. To call the uprising "leaderless" and "spontaneous" given this genealogy, then, is problematic, as it detracts from the agency of the youth activists and other grassroots actors who worked toward it. At the same time, however, the revolution was in fact leaderless in the Leninist sense, lacking a charismatic leader or even a centralized, cohesive vanguard body at its helm. It could also be described as spontaneous according to the Marxist understanding of that term in the unplanned manner that it unfolded in the eighteen days after the initial youth-sparked protest. But based on the discussion in chapter 4, I contend that it is more suitable to describe the revolution as a manifestation of the active and conscious dialectical engagement of actors with the rapidly evolving realities their efforts engendered. This characterization captures the dynamic political process that it actually was.

This brings me to the next issue: the "youth" label itself. Many, including the youth activists, have criticized the portrayal of the revolution as primarily a youth undertaking. They argue that the youth construct is hollow and misleading, that youth vanguardism has been typical of all revolutions in history and as such does not warrant special attention. After all, it is new generations with their imagination, convictions, energy, and fresh outlook that usually impel the turn toward radical change. Moreover, they caution, the focus on youth eclipses the crucial role of other actors, like workers, unions, and professional syndicates, as well as the people at large. But these objections only capture part of the story; there is another part that needs to be taken into account.

The role of youth is significant and deserves our attention. The explosion in Egypt was ignited in part by many structural problems, one of the most prominent being the demographic youth bulge: half of Egypt's population of eighty-five million is under the age of twenty-five.[1] In this cohort were droves of educated, ambitious youth who found zero economic opportunity and suffered indignity as a result. In revolting, they were very much "claiming youthfulness," as sociologist Asef Bayat puts it, or "extending and defending the youth habitus," which he describes as "a series of dispositions and ways of being, feeling, and carrying oneself (e.g. a greater tendency for experimentation, adventurism, idealism, autonomy, mobility, change) that are associated with the sociological fact of 'being young.'"[2] Following Bayat's argument, it was the state's restriction of these youthful claims—as reflected in youth grievances such as the government's failure to enable their financial self-sufficiency by addressing high unemployment, the suppression of basic rights like freedom of expression and association, and their vulnerability to increasing police intimidation and brutality—that turned this collective into a political, socially transformative force. It was members of this youth population who, driven by their grievances, imagined changing the regime, not the defeated and succumbing generation of their parents, and not the workers, whose struggle was still limited to the realm of trade unionism.[3] And on January 25, they collectively took that crucial first step into the streets, deciding they would rather risk death in the fight against an oppressive regime than suffer through a hopeless future. This was supported by an organized cadre of youth with a compelling story particular to Egypt who were acting specifically in the name of their "generational aspirations and discontents."[4] It is also worth underscoring that central to the revolution was a defiance of the patriarchal political order in which old men held power and excluded and patronized the young, along with women and other marginalized groups. This theme courses through the narratives of youthful resistance set out in the previous chapters and was expressed during the uprising by many young protesters who said they had taken to the streets because they resented the fact that Mubarak had ruled over them against their will for their entire lives.

Moreover, the association of youth with the revolution served as a crucial frame for mobilizing protesters and supporters. The "January 25 Youth" brand—*shabab khamsa-wa-ishrin yanayir* in Arabic, commonly interchanged with *shabab al-thawra* (the revolutionary youth)—was a potent construct that captured popular imagination, having quickly become synonymous with courage, promise, and national salvation. This is reflected in the many chants that showed the youth's commitment to Egypt's liberation,[5] as well as the remarks of many older protesters who claimed solidarity with the youth in their struggle, even calling themselves "January 25 Youth" as a gesture of support and encouragement. These monikers are evidence of both the youth's understanding of themselves and the public's recognition of them as a novel collective political actor—one with particular outlooks, ideals, aspirations, and practices that distinguished them from others and, importantly, established their legitimacy as the carriers and leaders of the revolution.

In sum, to dismiss a reading of the revolution through the lens of youth is to undermine the agency of a critically important group of actors whose stories are integral to the revolution. Without the youth's role, neither the eighteen-day uprising nor the collapse of the Mubarak regime would have happened.

Leadership and Gender

My observations in the field and conversations with my interlocutors revealed that although men and women were equally engaged in organizing the movement, their leadership roles were gendered.[6] As we have seen with the RYC, for instance, of the thirteen official executive committee members (which increased to seventeen after February 11), only one was a woman, and she came to occupy her position through the recommendation of her male colleagues, who agreed on the need to have women among them, even as they rejected gender quotas as undemocratic. Several of the male activists I interviewed asserted that those who came to occupy positions as leaders in their group had distinguished themselves over the years through their street activism; that is, through their commitment and organizing skills, they naturally became leaders in youth activist circles. While this line of analysis might capture how activists are socialized into leaders, it fails to account for *who* gets socialized as such in light of structural factors like gender, class, and religion. The path to leadership for women, as my study suggests, was fraught with many more obstacles than it was for men, particularly for women who were less privileged. Had the male activists in the RYC not felt compelled to invite female leadership, it is likely that women would not have made their way into the RYC's leadership through the same socialization process.

The roles and positions of the women in the RYC and its constituent organizations and movements appears to be consistent with the position women have historically occupied in male-dominated movements, like the US Civil Rights Movement, and even in those with heavy participation from both genders, like the Algerian War for Independence. The RYC women appeared to be valued more for their leadership in field organizing, such as everyday mobilizing on the ground, than for their visionary or strategic leadership. But in this area they appeared to wield considerable power within their respective movements under the RYC umbrella. In many ways, their engagement was consistent with that of Robnett's conceptualization of women as "bridge leaders," those crucial but less visible leading organizers who mediate between the top leadership and the majority of followers, turning the visions and aspirations of the movement into on-the-ground, grassroots realities by "making connections between groups and networks and acquiring needed resources."[7] Moreover, the RYC women also found themselves at odds with gender dynamics within their movements. In this sense, their revolutionary struggle as women was nested: as members of the revolutionary youth, they resisted the regime and faced off with the oppositional old guard; as women they also struggled to varying degrees within their own organizations to be heard and respected by their male counterparts.

When the revolution first erupted in Egypt, it was celebrated for the equal participation of men and women from all walks of life.[8] The narratives I present here offer a more nuanced picture of what that participation looked like, one that is less romantic, especially in terms of leadership. They suggest that while women's leadership was not entirely absent, it was constrained by patriarchal norms. They also highlight the problematic suggestion that "youth" is a gender-neutral category, when in fact, in the Egyptian revolution and the wider Arab context in general, the term tends to have masculine connotations. This is underscored by the absence of women from the delegation that met with SCAF after Mubarak's ouster and their poor representation in subsequent youth meetings with authorities. It is also underscored by the absence of young Muslim Sisters from the cadres of youth representing the Muslim Brotherhood organization in the RYC.[9] Indeed, one might argue that the very label *shabab al-Ikhwan al-Muslimeen* (the Muslim Brotherhood youth) is compounded in its gender exclusivity.

As discussed in chapter 5, when I asked the former Muslim Brothers Abbas and Qassas why there were no Muslim Sisters in the RYC's leadership, they said that young women in their organization had not been particularly politically active before the revolution and suggested that they had even resisted political engagement. According to them, the Sisters' reluctance had something to do with the organization's conservative attitudes and religious beliefs about the boundaries of appropriate behavior for women in public life as well as gender roles and inter-gender interaction in general. Incidentally, there were very few politically active young Sisters before the revolution, let alone any that were able to advance as its youth leaders. This was the perspective of the former Brothers I interviewed. The Muslim Sisters I spoke to, however, had a more nuanced explanation for this apparent lack of feminine representation among the Brotherhood leadership in the RYC.[10] They stressed that women had long played a critical role in the Brotherhood's history of political struggle, but mostly behind the scenes as foot soldiers rather than at the forefront as leaders and decision makers.[11] They supported the Brothers as "silent partners," participating in student protests but not taking the lead, accompanying them at public events, and mobilizing to campaign for the organization's mostly male candidates in parliamentary elections starting from the mid-1990s.[12] They also supported the organization with their extensive community and charity work. While not outwardly political, this feminine grassroots social activism served an important political purpose insofar as it fostered a broad support base of loyal constituents for the organization. Still, the leadership activities of Muslim Sisters within the organization were largely limited to women's neighborhood and university chapters, and even then they were subject to the oversight of a Brother above them in the hierarchy. The Sisters I spoke to agreed that the absence of women in the Brotherhood's leadership and their marginal public role was a reflection of the organization's conservative, patriarchal culture, but they also attributed it to a very real concern for women's safety, given the oppressive sociopolitical context under successive regimes and the constant threat of crackdown on Islamists.[13] Still, it is important to highlight what my research participants saw as the failure on the part of the Brotherhood to empower women as political leaders due to their normative understanding that the public domain is masculine territory. In many ways, the absence of Muslim Sisters in the RYC leadership was an outcome of gendered hierarchy in the Brotherhood.[14]

Any analysis of the Egyptian revolution that degenders, declasses, or overlooks any other structural differences between participants, such as religion, generation, and the urban/rural divide, does not fully capture it. These factors are important for the multiple, if unevenly distributed, strengths and vulnerabilities they engender, especially as they intersect. As Maya Mikdashi[15] argues, neglecting these factors ultimately depoliticizes the variety of costs and rewards different actors faced for their participation. This point is even more worthy of contemplation today. Shortly after Mubarak's resignation, one of the main consequences for women who participated in the revolution was reputational damage—the perception that they were loose women. As the revolutionary struggle continued, however, and when it started to take a turn for the worse, sexual assault and organized gang rape emerged as the counterrevolution's tactics of choice to cow women revolutionaries, reassert control over public space, and restore the patriarchal, authoritarian order. From the beginning of the revolution, Ola, my female respondent, was subjected to both attacks on her reputation and sexual assault (which will be discussed in more detail in the next chapter). The counterrevolution's ability to use gender as a brutal mechanism of intimidation and control was fueled by the normative dichotomous understanding that the private domain is feminine and the public domain is masculine. It was a reflection of how deeply embedded this revolutionary movement was in a gender normativity that excluded women from the public sphere. Through a gendered analysis of the revolutionaries and their struggle, we learn as much about the movement and its obstacles as we do about the actors and their drives to push forward.

Leadership and Class

One of the enduring tropes associated with this revolution is that the youth who led it were middle and upper-middle class, if not from among the elite. The image that was often promoted in Western media outlets was that of the urban, Internet-savvy, highly cosmopolitan, English-speaking youth, many of whom might have gone to the American University in Cairo and come from families that were financially comfortable if not affluent.[16] This was epitomized in the iconic image of Wael Ghonim, the Google executive behind the We Are All Khaled Said Facebook page, who the media cast as "the face" of youth revolutionaries.[17] My findings, however, illustrate that this image belied the reality. Many of the youth leaders I interviewed who were behind the initial revolutionary spark did not fit this profile. They might have been proficient Internet users, but most did not speak English, and if they did, certainly not fluently. Moreover, although nearly all had received a college education, most were part of the first generation in their family to do so and completed their degrees at public Egyptian universities. And while they might be considered middle or lower-middle class according to the average annual income of Egyptian families, I contend that using the "middle-class" construct to describe Egyptian revolutionary youth is problematic for several reasons.

"Middle-class" seems to connote Western—and perhaps more specifically, American—notions of financial stability, suburban comfort, and privileged ways of being. It obscures the reality of what a middle-class existence looks like in contemporary Egypt in terms of place and space; that is, it masks the fact that the majority of Egypt's middle and lower-middle economic classes live in densely populated, deteriorating urban quarters— spaces they share with the urban poor (see figure 8). These social conditions began to take shape under Nasser. His educational and economic policies initially provided unprecedented opportunity for the underclass. Later, however, they revealed themselves to be flawed and resulted in a mismatch between the increasingly educated population and the actual employment opportunities that had been promised and that had been meant to improve living standards, create prosperity, and facilitate upward mobility. This gap was dramatically exacerbated with the country's turn to neoliberalism with Sadat's *infitah*, when the government started to cater less and less to the needs of the lower and middle strata of society. The neoliberal state's persistent inability—indeed, unwillingness—to fulfill its duty to provide housing and order urban development gave way to chaotic urban formations with large segments lacking access to basic services. In light of this reality, it would be more accurate to refer to these youth as members of the "middle-class poor," a term coined by Asef Bayat,[18] or perhaps even more appropriate, the "popular class" (*al-tabaqa al-shaʿbiya*), a term many of my respondents used to describe their socioeconomic position and distinguish

Figure 8. A glimpse of popular-class life in Dar al-Salam, Cairo. Photograph by Joseph Hill.

themselves from those they referred to as "the upscale class" (*al-tabaqa al-raqiya*), that is, those who live in more affluent areas. These terms are more useful than the generic "middle class" for understanding the revolutionary impulse and engagement of activists, as they more adequately capture the local, socioeconomic, subaltern milieu that shaped their respective trajectories and their determination to see social change. For the youth who grew up in informal working-class areas, it suggests that growing up in an area where they experienced the neglect, corruption, and repression of the state played a more crucial role in their consciousness formation than their family's economic status.

As the literature on leadership in social movements suggests, there appears to be a correlation between higher education and leadership for activists from this background. As noted earlier, most of the activists who identified as members of the popular class were among the first in their respective families to receive an education. Had they not received higher education, it is likely they would not have been able to rise to the status of leaders in their respective youth movements, and later in the RYC.

Again, social movement scholars see education as a critical determinant of leadership because the tasks involved in leading social movements, such as recognizing opportunities, devising tactics and strategies, and framing grievances and demands, are seen as intellectual in nature, and the reading, writing, analyzing, and public speaking skills required to carry out these tasks effectively are usually honed through higher learning.[19] Of course, this is not to say that all movement leaders have university degrees or even certain levels of formal education short of this; for instance, some leaders acquire their political education growing up in "movement families." This was the case with my interlocutor Abdelrahman Faris, for example, the RYC leader of modest economic means from Fayoum who opted out of going to college; having been raised in a Muslim Brotherhood family, he gained much of his social awareness and political knowledge through the exposure provided by his kin. But generally speaking, leaders tend to have more formal education than their followers or the constituents their movements represent,[20] and the overall experience of the RYC reflects this.

Class and gender intersected in different ways to determine the leadership of young men and women in the revolution. The vast majority of the activists who hailed from the popular class also happened to be men. In other words, membership in the popular class did not seem to preclude educated young men from leadership. In contrast, the two women who played leadership roles in the RYC were from the upper class. They both spoke English fluently and received their graduate education from elite universities in the West. The point here is that women from the popular class, though active in the youth movements, did not appear to play central leadership roles. This is not to say that non-elite women did not enjoy the limelight. Asmaa Mahfouz and Nawara Negm,[21] for example, were middle-class women who were counted among the *rumuz* (symbols) of the Egyptian revolution, but it is worth noting they made a name for themselves independent of organized movements, largely through social media networks and channels. As influential Facebook and Twitter users, these women were among those who contributed to the creation of what Paolo Gerbaudo calls a "choreography of assembly." In this capacity, they leveraged these platforms in "directing people toward specific protest events, in providing participants with suggestions and instructions about how to act, and in the construction of an emotional narration to sustain their coming together in public space."[22] Further research is needed to better gauge the participation of young women in the revolution and their movement organizations and to understand why higher positions of influence were not as accessible to them. From these initial observations, however, we can deduce a positive correlation between class and female active political participation: the higher the class position of the family, the higher the participation of women. This could be owing to a combination of traditional gender normativity strongly enforced at the bottom ranks of the social ladder and more Westernization of gender relations the higher one moves up.

Leadership, Religiosity, and Secular Ideology

I went into this research wanting to understand the role religiosity played in determining the revolutionary leadership of the youth and shaping their political attitudes. Were secular or progressively minded religious youth more likely to be revolutionary leaders than their conservative religious peers? In the field, however, I quickly realized that this question rested on the problematic assumption that secularism equates with political progressivism, while religiosity equates with political conservatism; moreover, it understands them as binary categories into which activists might neatly fit. My findings suggest that, on the contrary, these categories are relative and neither bounded nor mutually exclusive. For example, some of my interlocutors identified strongly as Muslims, yet admitted their religious practice did not meet minimum obligations of religious observance (some said they fasted during the month of Ramadan, for example, but did not regularly perform their daily prayers). Being so difficult to define, religiosity was almost impossible to test as a variable in determining the leadership of youth.

Moreover, my question was also problematic in that it assumed a strong correlation between personal religious observance and attitudes about the role of institutional religion in the political sphere. Again, this was not what I observed. Personal religiosity was not necessarily an indicator of political values. Among my interlocutors, for example, were activists who identified as devout, traditionalist Muslims, yet they advocated for a pluralist, secular nation state that would be agreeable to religiously grounded Egyptian cultural sensibilities. They also included those who characterized themselves as semi-practicing Muslims who sought to chart a new leftist platform that accommodated Egypt's Muslim identity. Here it is important to highlight the significance of these subjectivities, particularly in a post-Mubarak context in which the short-lived Islamist government and its supporters used identity politics to establish their hegemony and discredit the opposition as secularists, which they conflated in their discourse with atheists, infidels, and anti-Muslim Copts. It points to the creative ways in which these youth subjects tried to reclaim the discourse on religion and politics from sectarians and to mold it to agree with their revolutionary vision.

In light of my research findings, it made more sense to question youth's propensity toward revolutionary leadership in terms of their political ideology—from the far left to the Islamist right—than their personal religious practice. What I found was that Islamist youth—specifically, former members of the Muslim Brotherhood—had stepped up to the plate as revolutionary leaders as earnestly as their leftist and liberal-leaning peers. The strong presence of young Brothers in the RYC was especially intriguing. One might think it likely that these youth would have subscribed to a reformist rather than a radical, revolutionary approach, since this was their organization's preference. In fact, the more critical variable appears to have been the activists' particular histories of persecution, repression, and political engagement—stretching as far back as high school and college—in conjunction with generational differences and an evolving understanding of what it meant to be a Muslim and an Islamist. These young Brothers joined as initiators and leaders of this movement precisely because they were willing to question their organization's established ideological positions. Moreover, they had the audacity to chart a new orientation based on the same Islamic tradition that legitimized their revolutionary aspirations and intentions. Still, more research is needed to understand the variables at play, because there were many other young Brothers who experienced the same circumstances but did not incline toward revolution like the Brothers who joined the RYC, but remained loyal to the Brotherhood's reformist orientation.

On Revolutionary Becoming

Revolutionaries are not suddenly born; they are forged by the historical processes taking place around them. My discussions with the activists revealed that beyond dynamics of class, gender, and religion, there were other important structural factors that prompted and shaped the political engagement of youth and engendered their revolutionary mindset and leadership initiative. Their experience of these factors was crucial to the perceptions, leanings, and motivations that led to their engagement in the decade preceding the revolution. For example, the university was a recurrent theme in the activists' narratives. For some, it was where they first found themselves in direct confrontation with the state over policies that censored and repressed their student activities, making it the site where their engagement was first activated. For others, it was where they experienced the intellectual awakening that sparked their political engagement, in the classes they took or guest lectures they attended. For those from privileged backgrounds, the public university was a space where they could interact closely with and appreciate the struggle of Egyptians of lesser means and develop a sense of solidarity with them. Of course, all of these stories are reflections of their embeddedness in the same historical phenomenon: Nasser's populist educational policies that sought to extend opportunities to the lower classes.

Likewise, the Muslim Brotherhood emerged as a major theme in the narratives of these young activists. Whether they experienced the organization as official members or interacted with it indirectly through their family histories, college campuses, local communities, or the general political arena, the outlook and engagement of these youth activists were shaped by its history and its status as the largest and most organized opposition group in Egypt for more than half a century. The question of Palestine is another example. As noted in chapter 3, most of the activists I interviewed cited the Second Palestinian Intifada in 2000 as the event that marked their official entry into the political activist scene. However, the wave of solidarity protest it inspired among them and thousands of other Egyptians was not new: it drew its strength from a popular commitment that had existed between Egyptians and Palestinians since the creation of Israel in 1948. Similarly, the motivations that drove their participation, while diverse, were also historically rooted. Former young Brothers, like their predecessors, were moved to action by a religious obligation to support their Palestinian brethren and the Holy Land in their struggle against the Zionist threat. Meanwhile, left-wing youth followed in the footsteps of the 1970s student generation that shook Egypt's streets in solidarity with Palestine as they demanded a military recovery of the Arab territories lost to Israel in the 1967 War. Later, their broad-based, pro-Palestinian movement grew into an anti-imperialist, anti-regime struggle as they began to draw links between policies abroad and at home. This occurred alongside the US invasion of Iraq and a growing understanding that the political repression, socioeconomic marginalization, and humiliation they were experiencing as a nation globally and as citizens at home were generated by the mutually beneficial arrangement pursued by the Egyptian elite and foreign powers to protect their respective interests. Again, these multiple dimensions were experienced differently by different activists who became politically engaged through different sources: out of a religious obligation to fight injustice, or a liberal conviction to open up opportunities, or socialist ideals of equality. Despite these differences, what they had in common was their eagerness and commitment to change society for the better in the face of a corrupt, repressive, authoritarian regime.

Writing about secular women activists in Egypt, Nadje Al-Ali argues that life stories are crucial to our understanding of how activists and their movements evolve because they reveal how

> particular historical conjunctures, and experiences embedded in them, might inflect and colour ongoing political involvement. These conjectures are not merely contingent in the lives of . . . activists but have a meaningful relation to them. They do not determine political action, but they shape likelihoods, suggest possibilities, generate tendencies and frame choices. Political orientation, goals, agendas, and forms of engagement [in movements] . . . as well as in national and international agendas, are all affected by general trends and historical events. Family relations, friendships and support networks are not happenstance either, but are subject to the same social and political change that have affected each of the activists.
>
> Ideas come and go. People are not static in their beliefs, and beliefs and practices are not always mutually congruent and consistent. All activists have continuously accumulated new experiences, which further shaped their involvement. However, what has become evident in the cases of these activists is that their formative experiences appear to have left a particularly enduring mark.[23]

This has been my observation of Egyptian revolutionary youth leaders. Their politicization and subjective development first as activists, then as revolutionaries, was the consequence of formative experiences that stemmed from their embeddedness in Egypt's historical processes. These accumulated experiences have in turn continued to inflect their outlook and the iterations of their resistance. In this sense, the post-uprising subjectivities of these activists highlighted in the previous chapter are significant: they give us a sense of where they were coming from and where they and their movements might be headed. In short, activist orientations are processual. Early experiences leave an enduring mark, but the subsequent evolution in their positioning is contingent on historical processes as they unfold. This is illustrated in the next chapter, which charts the activists' trajectory through the Muslim Brotherhood's rise to the presidency and the military coup that removed them from power.

On Revolutionary Organizing and Constructing a Vanguard

Although several years have passed since the youth-initiated January 25 uprising shook Egypt's streets, the social revolution that protesters clamored for has not materialized, and indeed seems an even more distant prospect now than it was back then. While popular pressure during those suspenseful eighteen days might have achieved Hosni Mubarak's resignation, the movement fell woefully short of realizing its stated goal: to dismantle the oppressive regime. Indeed, it is now clear that the institutions that propped up Mubarak and constituted his authoritarian state—the military, the intelligence and security apparatus, and the political establishment—escaped the threat of revolutionary havoc largely intact.

Mubarak's removal, it turns out, was not accomplished through the people's persistence alone. According to Hazem Kandil,[24] it was maneuvered by a military that capitalized on the revolution to break out of its marginalized position in the tripartite ruling power bloc, bent on recovering its former power and influence. Throughout the transition period under SCAF, and later, behind the facade of a new democratic system and Egypt's first freely elected leader, President Morsi, the balance of power was constantly being negotiated and reconstituted within this triangle as each institution labored to protect its respective interests while attempting to create some outward semblance of a civilian government that would satisfy the public. Meanwhile, the organized youth who had been the movement's celebrated leaders fell by the wayside, the opposition persisted in its ineffectiveness, and episodes of local resistance grew increasingly violent as popular demands for bread, freedom, and human dignity went unrealized. It remains to be seen whether the sweeping political and social transformations for which Egyptians fought heroically will ever take place. For now, however, we can say what was once heralded as an ambitious, seemingly unstoppable revolution did not succeed in transforming social relations or radically changing the power structure as it had sought to do, notwithstanding the new political subjectivities it produced.

Organization was a key problem, as youth operations during the Tahrir occupation show. Even before the uprising, systematic regime repression and destruction of civil society made it impossible for radical, charismatic political leadership to emerge or a united, cohesive opposition vanguard to coalesce. But repression aside, oppositional activism in Egypt at the time also reflected wider global trends in anti-systemic movements, which in recent decades had moved away from the centralized organizational structures characteristic of twentieth-century struggles.[25] Organized as parallels of the state, these earlier movements were laser focused on the objective of seizing conventional power and using it to achieve their vision of change. The Leninist revolutionary vanguard party—with its centralized power, rigid hierarchy, and highly disciplined membership under the leadership of a professional elite and charismatic figure—epitomized this old-school trend. In contrast, New Social Movement (NSM) models, which regime opponents in Egypt were drawn to, set themselves apart as the antithesis of these traditional movements. NSMs emerged from popular and activist disillusionment with the performance of traditional movements after they got into power, a result of the de-radicalizing and corrupting nature of party politics.[26] Having lost faith in the potential of the state to serve as a vehicle for fundamental social transformation, activists around the globe shifted their focus from capturing the state to advocating for specific issues while pushing the boundaries of traditional politics and pressing for decentralized alternatives to the existing order. They rejected oppressive hierarchies, "great man" leaders, and doctrinal blueprints, on democratic principle; instead, they favored decentralized organization and distributed forms of leadership that accommodated the spontaneity, creativity, and autonomy of activists and protesters.[27] These NSM criticisms of the state and the political parties associated with it were consistent with young Egyptian dissidents' experience of the neoliberal authoritarian establishment under Mubarak and the co-opted political parties that toadied to it. Their grim outlook fueled their adoption of similar horizontal, rhizomatic movement structures in their effort to reclaim politics for the masses and draw them into a popular struggle on the street to undermine the status quo.

All of this explains why, when the people rose up in rebellion on January 25, no one emerged to lead them. As it had done before the revolution, resistance persisted in an increasingly diffuse and undefined manner, guided by the movement collective's emergent moral ethos, street logic, and imagination of what was possible. This was consistent with the format adopted in the years before the uprising by the youth who had staged the rebellion. Their social movements—Kefaya, Youth for Change, April 6, Youth for Justice and Freedom, and the ElBaradei Campaign, just to name a few—were characterized by extreme fluidity and flexibility in both membership and organization, which would incidentally prove to be a double-edged sword. On the one hand, flexibility and interchangeability in membership meant movements accommodated various ideological leanings, permitted belonging to multiple groups, and facilitated solidarity work with members of other organizations, all of which contributed to their efficacy. Likewise, their loose, decentralized, horizontal organization translated into efficient decision-making among members and facilitated their easy circumvention of security forces. On the other hand, this same fluidity and flexibility made these movements less stable, less cohesive, and less able to grow in strength and numbers, making them vulnerable to the kind of rapid fragmentation they experienced after Mubarak's resignation.

We see these dynamics play out during the eighteen-day uprising and in the months after. Certainly, this informality and extreme decentralization contributed to the revolutionary movement's effectiveness in its first few weeks and helped it secure significant gains in the following months. Its popular and scattered nature made it unpredictable and impossible for security forces to repress effectively. A more coherent movement with a clear figurehead might have been easier to quash or co-opt. Nonetheless, as it became clear that organization and coordination on a higher level were desperately needed to ensure the capture of the state after the anticipated fall of Mubarak, their absence proved to be a liability—and ultimately fatal. In the end, the failure of revolutionaries to organize themselves into a concrete, unified power bloc—one with a common political agenda and capable of contesting establishment power and providing a viable political alternative—was one of the main reasons the authoritarian state survived, albeit in democratic disguise. History has shown that successful revolutions are those in which regime opponents create a dual power scenario, positioning their threat through a format such as a revolutionary council with a mandate from the people to enforce the desired change on their behalf.[28] Instead, the approach of Egypt's opposition forces was more reactive than proactive; incapable of getting ahead of the competition because of their disorganization, they found themselves stuck trying to block the counterrevolution's moves and advances. As Hazem Kandil argues, ultimately, revolutions are wars, and winning them requires cohesion, method, and strategy, not just endurance and tenacity. It is for this reason that the highly organized Muslim Brotherhood was able to capitalize on the sacrifices of the youth to seize power in the first post-Mubarak elections.

While the youth were leaders of the January 25 uprising insofar as they mobilized it and attempted to nurture and direct it, the revolution remained without leadership in the traditional, Leninist sense. However, my study of youth organizing during the eighteen-day occupation of Tahrir suggests that the failure of revolutionaries to consolidate an official vanguard organization was not for a lack of trying. They faced many challenges. First, the movement itself was a popular one that fetishized its leaderless, organic nature and disinterest in seeking power. In fact, popular opinion reprimanded anyone who sought or was in some way accorded celebrity or leadership status. Revolutionary actors even insisted that the movement's leaderlessness is what made it legitimate. As Zyad's comments in chapter 4 illustrate, it was their way of assuring the public and the government that this was a legitimate people's movement, that no special interests were behind it, and that no group would be permitted to exploit it. This assertion was voiced by the entire range of participants in this movement, from the non-organized part-time protesters to those who were more embedded in institutions. Ironically, it was also made by the RYC youth, although it was also a source of conflict for them. While they might have idolized the idea of the people's spontaneous leadership along with everyone else—even insisting on working behind the scenes to direct the revolution in order to preserve this image, as the celebrated revolutionary Antonio Gramsci would have advised[29]—they also knew that failing to form a revolutionary coalition or council that subsumed and directed the will of the people could put them at risk of losing the street and the chance to fill whatever power vacuum would be left by Mubarak's pending departure.

The second challenge relates to the fractured, broad-based nature of the movement. The diverse backgrounds and ideological currents represented in the square were too many to encompass under one unified leadership. It was one thing for this heterogeneous group to assemble in solidarity behind the objective of toppling Mubarak; it was another matter entirely trying to unite them over a single alternative political vision or get them on the same page regarding what they should do next and who should lead that effort. There were also intergenerational tensions that had spilled over from the period before January 25. As discussed in previous chapters, youth organizing in the years leading up to the revolt developed in defiance of older generations' dominance over political life. This included not only those in the regime, but also those in the defunct mainstream opposition who provided little room for youth maneuverability in formal politics and even less hope for change. Rescuing the future, it became increasingly clear, required a revolutionary initiative that would disrupt their order and wrench the country from their stranglehold. Organized youth took that initiative and thus became the movement's effective leaders and most legitimate representatives. While some segments of the opposition accepted the youth's newfound role, the announcement of the RYC would disgruntle many elements of the old guard, who felt upstaged by the youth and more entitled to leadership because of their seniority and experience. This friction greatly hindered efforts to produce leadership and build revolutionary organizations, as did the long-standing antagonisms between members of the opposition, who did not want to see their rivals assume power or the limelight. Why the youth felt they had to work with the political old guard to appear more legitimate is one of the more curious paradoxes of the revolution, as it was precisely their break from established factions, perceived as corrupt and ineffective, that had earned them legitimacy in the eyes of the public. Perhaps their inability to act completely on their own, independent of these senior figures, speaks to the inherently limited nature of their political power and agency as young people in this revolutionary moment.

This brings us to the third challenge, which relates to participatory democratic practice—in contradistinction to Lenin's highly centralized, top-down bureaucratic approach—as the chosen method of revolutionary organizing, decision-making, and building vanguard structures during the eighteen-day uprising. The Egyptian revolution might be the most notable—if not the only—example of a revolutionary movement that categorically rejected hierarchy as a strategic organizing framework. Rather, bottom-up consensus building was the movement's staunchly preferred modus operandi, arguably to a fault. The approach was certainly understandable. As a movement that aspired to genuine democratic governance, it made sense to practice the kind of egalitarianism they envisioned. This approach was also inspired by a fear of reproducing the same sort of tyrannical elitist structures people were revolting against, as well as the concern that centralized forms might suffocate popular spontaneity, creativity, and radicalism. But while participatory democracy might be appropriate for issue-based movements like the Civil Rights, women's liberation, and the more recent anti-capitalist globalization movements, it could easily be suicidal for revolutionary struggles. I am referring to the kind of limitations Francesca Polletta highlights in her study of the development of participatory democracy through previous struggles in her book *Freedom is an Endless Meeting*, many of which have proven applicable to the Egyptian case as discussed next. I would argue that while there was certainly a place for participatory democracy in the Egyptian revolutionary movement, their version of it did not exemplify the best use of the form and led them to fall into some of the traps associated with it.

The youth groups that comprised the RYC, for example, were hindered by what Polletta refers to as invisible relational structures, which tend to flourish in horizontal, informal, structureless social movements if not properly managed, frustrating activists' ability to fully practice participatory democracy. Citing the example of the women's liberation movement and observations made by feminists like Joe Freeman who were active in it, Polletta speaks to how these loose arrangements can be problematic.[30] Movement decentralization gave rise to intimately woven communities built on camaraderie and trust. While this might have helped the women's movement by cultivating unity among activists and securing their commitment, it also translated into a degree of exclusivity, crippling the movement's ability to integrate new activists and develop leadership among them. This is precisely what occurred with the RYC leaders. The bonds they had forged in the universities and the street in the decade before the revolution structured their interpersonal relationships, networks, and organizing. This fellowship made it difficult for them to accommodate new groups into the RYC when the movement demanded it of them. Their exclusivity subjected them to criticism and diminished their legitimacy in the eyes of other revolutionary actors, who saw their actions as a disservice to the larger movement. Within the group, given the ideological diversity of its members, these structures prevented them from selecting one among them as a leader to help centralize and speed up their decision-making, which many RYC members felt made them less effective as a group. The fear was that if opened, this door would lead to intra-group competition driven by their ideological differences and would break them apart. In this sense, participatory democracy thwarted their leadership initiatives.

Another important limitation of participatory democracy derives from what some argue is the inherent tension between democracy and efficacy. According to Polletta, participatory democracy can be extremely unwieldy. For it to be effective, then, it must be guided by a clearly defined methodology for decision-making, overcoming conflict, dividing up tasks, and ensuring accountability. Given the massive ideologically diverse oppositional base of the Egyptian revolution, these processes were vitally necessary if they were going to operate democratically and do so successfully. But these processes were not established, and perhaps could never have been given the sheer number of revolutionary actors. As a result, they suffered from the kind of endless meetings Polletta refers to, many of which ended in infighting and led to nowhere.

Lastly, there was the problem of time. Simply put, they did not have time for the exhausting deliberations that participatory democratic practice required, especially since their attention was needed to sustain and escalate the movement practically in the immediate present. Social movement theorists might challenge the notion that the principles of democratic participation and inclusiveness do not have to be practiced at the expense of strategy. And while this might be true of issue-based social movements, it is a difficult argument to make for revolutions. This is because revolutionary struggles are significantly more defiant and demanding, determined as they are to go far beyond social reforms to fiercely challenge and radically transform state and social structures. Not only are they more threatening to the elite, but they also expose participants to a far higher level of threat and hostility from the state's security apparatus. As such, revolutionary environments are characterized by a greater degree of urgency. This was the experience of Egyptian revolutionaries during the eighteen-day uprising. The rapid pace of change; the extreme instability, fragility, and unpredictability; and the scattered and disorienting nature of the revolutionary context demanded focus, efficiency, and political expediency of its protagonists if they wanted to outmaneuver the elite and achieve their goals. Instead, young activists and other revolutionary actors who came together to figure out next steps and tried to build vanguard organizations were trapped in unproductive, endless meetings, the consequence of an ineffective bottom-up consensus-building process unresponsive to the time pressure they were under.

In the end, all of these processes culminated in the inability of the RYC youth and opposition to produce any radically constructive organizations or leadership that could collect popular energy and channel it into a focused and sustained challenge of the state. The failure of the RYC and other groups from the revolutionary camp to work together to structure the broader movement meant that they acted incoherently, and sometimes at cross-purposes. Thannassis Cambanis aptly likened the revolutionary movement to an archipelago, with leadership groups like the RYC emerging on different islands; often acting in isolation and unaware of each other's activities, they never tried to make themselves leaders of the whole.[31] The outcome of this, as we have seen, was that the movement continued to decentralize and fragment, until it escaped from the youth and other revolutionary forces completely, leaving the political playing field open to the two stronger forces, the Muslim Brotherhood and the military, both of them reactionary. The opposition's failure to assume the historical responsibility to produce coherent and effective leadership is something activists would voice regret about. "This was a mistake," Basem lamented.

> I mean, this was a huge mistake. This was a mistake on the larger scale [of the revolution] in that we didn't choose someone and stand behind them, and at the same time, the mistake was that we didn't put forward someone from among ourselves [from the RYC] and walk behind him. If we had agreed on a name, and said, "So-and-so is the one representing us, he is the one who speaks on our behalf, he is the one that is our leader," the world would have been totally different!

Conclusion

The story of the RYC turns more tragic in the transitional period leading up to the 2012 presidential election. During this time, the youth were so embroiled in their battle with SCAF and the Muslim Brotherhood that they were sidetracked from what was perhaps the more critical task of entrenching their movement in the hearts and minds of common Egyptians through grassroots political and community organizing.[32] Many argue that the RYC groups lost their connection to the street—especially the poorer segments of the population who were not in tune with the revolution—when they should have continued to build the revolution's support base, to develop the revolutionary consciousness of the masses from below and organize them into a single, coherent movement as they consolidated themselves as its leadership. Instead, they got caught up in the media frenzy that surrounded the revolution, jumping from one satellite program to the next as revolutionary youth pundits and celebrities. In fact, their newfound role earned them the pejorative label "Coalition of the Camera-obsessed Youth" (*I'tilaf Shabab al-Kamira*). Meanwhile, their relentless street action throughout 2011 frustrated and alienated once-sympathetic Egyptians, who struggled to understand the purpose of continued protests. Yearning for stability and a return to normalcy, they grew increasingly receptive to SCAF's narrative, which blamed the youth and their alleged foreign bankrollers for the continuous turmoil and violence. The RYC and the wider revolutionary camp had trouble reading and reconciling themselves with public opinion, which reduced their ability to sway it.

Also contributing to this shift in popular support was the failure of the youth to translate their revolutionary demands into a practical political project the public could potentially rally behind. Along with the rest of the opposition, they failed to articulate an alternative vision for post-Mubarak Egypt that was actionable.[33] The narratives in the previous chapter illustrate the kind of grand ideas about Egypt's future that emerged from Tahrir and other city squares. The activists I spoke to expressed their hopes for the collapse of authoritarianism and the birth of a new democratic order. They imagined a government that did not infantilize them as subjects but respected them as citizens. They wanted a transparent system that was accountable to its people. They envisioned a government that protected freedoms and delivered political, social, and economic justice. Ultimately, what they sought was a life of dignity for Egyptians, the kind that came with the rule of law and the meeting of their basic needs—food, housing, education, employment, security, and health care. The order they wanted incorporated some elements from systems in Europe and the United States, but leaned more on their own national and regional history for inspiration. These were profound goals, but they were also vague and abstract. Tragically, in the transition period following the eighteen-day revolt, these thoughts never hardened into a concrete, coherent revolutionary program that might draw public backing and empower the revolutionaries over the military and the Brotherhood in the competition for Egypt's future. Some, like Basem, tried to craft platforms that spoke to these aims through their work in political parties in the run-up to the first post-Mubarak elections, but on the whole, the youth mostly avoided these more difficult questions and failed to coalesce around a coherent agenda. Instead, they spent most of their energy opposing the military and Islamists. As a result, it became increasingly difficult for the public to identify what the revolutionaries aspired to, let alone support them in their venture. In the end, the youth would learn the hard way that revolutions are about competing political projects, and if you do not have one to offer, you lose. Bread, freedom, and social justice were noble ideals, but in the absence of a constructive political program that could operationalize and expand upon them, they started to ring hollow.

The revolution also suffered because its protagonists never became comfortable with the idea of compromise and politics. The morally pure revolution espoused by many of the Tahrir activists precluded them from acting strategically to win the power necessary to advance the aims of the revolution. Early on, the RYC leaders stood out from their peers in the larger movement in their willingness to take a more pragmatic approach. After February 11, for example, they agreed to meet with military figures and other state officials, their idea being that they should communicate their views to the country's power brokers and push for reform through whatever openings they could find. But their critics—most notably a small but outspoken group of hardcore leftists who set the tone for the rest of the revolutionary camp—accused them of betrayal and warming up to power for their own personal gain.

These Marxist ideologues also chided the RYC activists for fielding candidates in the parliamentary elections. They pointed to the ways in which the so-called democratic transition was becoming a ploy designed by reactionary forces to capture and control the movement for sweeping change by disciplining it into something much more procedural, muted, sanitized, and ineffectual. They wanted activist energy to maintain its focus on agitating for radical socioeconomic and political transformation through sustained mass street mobilization and a boycott of the formal political arena. While RYC activists like Basem, Zyad, and Amr sympathized with this view, they argued that it was important for revolutionaries to gain formal political power and agitate for change within official institutions as well as in the street. For them, revolution and formal politics were not binary or mutually exclusive; they saw that the battle should be fought simultaneously on both fronts. Even so, most of the RYC leaders who decided to run for elections were conflicted about their choice and unable to embrace the process fully. While they agreed it was important to offer the public choices on the ballot that represented the revolutionary youth and their vision of change, winning elections also required well-funded campaigns which could only be achieved by playing politics. Many of the revolutionaries refused to make the moral compromises required by this game, such as pursuing alliances with wealthier but less principled political parties. When a new round of street protests erupted in November 2011, many of them seemed relieved to shelve their campaigns and return to the good fight against police in the streets. Their distaste for conventional politics had grave implications for the kind of influence they could expect to have in the next stage of the struggle for Egypt's future: out of 508 members elected to Parliament, only three were youth revolutionaries.[34] The rest were mostly Islamists.

Other factors contributed to the weakening of the RYC. First there were the external challenges posed by the wider context. In the year following Mubarak's ouster, state political forces and the socioeconomic elite regrouped and returned with a vengeance, launching a counterrevolutionary movement that grew increasingly fierce and unrelenting. Moreover, the sudden emergence of countless youth coalitions and unions on the revolutionary scene rendered the RYC obscure and therefore less influential. Internally, the RYC itself sustained several crippling splits within its constituent movements that reduced its effectiveness. After the fall of Mubarak, the April 6 movement cleaved in two, the ElBaradei Campaign became defunct, and the Muslim Brotherhood youth were excommunicated from the movement, leaving several RYC leaders with little to no organizational backing and seriously reducing the number of people they could legitimately claim to represent. More tragically, rifts and distrust among RYC members started to appear along the old lines dividing secularists and Islamists, leftists and liberals. The group started to splinter during the 2011 parliamentary elections, when ideological competition, personal ambition, and egotism prevented them from agreeing on an electoral strategy and agenda. The tensions among them grew as they joined different political parties and ran on separate slates, sometimes against each other in the same district. During the heady days of Tahrir and in the months afterward,

Figure 9a. RYC executive committee member Sally Tomah speaks at the press conference in July 2012 in which the coalition announced its dissolution. Photograph by Salma Alaa Akl.

Figure 9b. Group photo of RYC leaders and key members, taken after their press conference in July 2012 announcing their dissolution. Top, left to right: Mohammed Al-Qassas, Nagy Kamel, Khaled Tallima, Ahmed Eid, Tarek El-Khouly, Zyad Eleleimy, Abdelrahman Faris, Mostafa Shawky, Amr Ezz, Nasser Abdel-Hamid, Shady ElGhazaly Harb, Hossam Moanes. Bottom, left to right: Yasser El Hawary, Islam Lotfy Shalaby, Mohammed Abbas, Khaled Elsayed, Basem Kamel, Sally Tomah, Amr Salah. Photograph by Salma Alaa Akl.

these youth had set an example for Egyptians in how to overcome political differences and find common ground to work for the greater good. Now they too were being undone by the same forces that had long rendered the opposition ineffectual. In the end, the RYC would vote to disband. They made the official announcement after Morsi's election to the presidency on June 30, 2012 (see figures 9a–b).[35]

The genesis of this revolutionary movement, as outlined in earlier chapters, helps us understand both the increasing marginalization of the movement after the eighteen-day uprising and the ascension of the Muslim Brotherhood. The fluidity, structurelessness, informality, and pragmatism of these movements—the individual youth movements, the RYC, and the wider revolutionary movement—allowed them to draw in a wide array of participants, securing the numbers necessary to pressure Mubarak to resign. In the following months, these same characteristics allowed it to secure many gains, including the trial of Mubarak and his associates and a fixed date for the presidential election, which SCAF had continued to delay. However, they also made these political formations highly vulnerable, unsustainable, and ultimately, incapable of capturing the state, if this had indeed ever been their goal. In comparison, the Muslim Brotherhood, with its highly bureaucratic structure and extensive organization, was able to mobilize quickly and successfully take advantage of the new opening in the political system to try to entrench itself in the state power structure, a mission that would ultimately prove fatal for the revolution.

7
The Revolution Continues?

Amid the deafening cheers and jubilant celebrations that rocked Tahrir well into the evening of February 11, 2011, following the earthshaking news of Mubarak's exit, the RYC leaders, who had helped set the wheels of their nation's history in motion, took a moment to mark the occasion. Emotions ran high in the green tent that had served as their operations base in the square as they huddled to draft a magniloquent communiqué immortalizing the people's achievement. They also articulated their hopes in the military's neutrality and paid homage to those who gave their lives for the cause. None of them could have imagined back then that "The Birth Certificate of a New Egypt," as they called it, would one day make for a heartrending read. "The people have finally toppled the regime!" it declared, invoking the sonorous cry of Egyptians that night.

> With all pride, we announce we are on the brink of the new Egypt we have always dreamt of! An Egypt free of fear, oppression, and tyranny! An Egypt of safety, transparency, and tolerance! This is a great awakening, and the Egyptian people will no longer allow a tyrant or a corrupt ruler to lead. Therefore, we declare that the first urgent step is to ensure the civility[1] of the Egyptian State. The brave Egyptian army will secure the gains of this revolution, that it will not be aborted by the remnants of the previous regime. And then they will return to their position as the protector of Egypt—the land and the people—from every aggression or instability. History will not forget how the army stood by its people, without any hesitation. The annals of history will remember the martyrs of Egypt, those who wrote with their blood the birth certificate of a free Egypt. Long live the struggle of the free Egyptians![2]

Several years on, the dream of a "new Egypt" is yet to be realized, and the triumphant spirit surging from the RYC's declaration is nowhere to be found among Egypt's January 25 revolutionaries. Instead, the mood is one of defeat and resignation as they face a resurgent authoritarianism under Abd al-Fattah al-Sisi arguably more repressive than Mubarak's. Indeed, the attack on basic freedoms has been breathtaking in its scale and severity. Over a thousand political protesters have been killed and many more imprisoned. The number of those who have been arrested and jailed on political grounds is estimated in the tens of thousands and includes protesters, activists, opposition figures and supporters, human rights workers, and journalists, as well as former president Muhammad Morsi, who died in custody.[3] Leading youth revolutionaries have been locked up for allegedly violating the draconian protest laws enacted in 2013, while Mubarak, his sons, and ex-interior minister Habib Al Adly were left to walk as free men, acquitted of the charges laid against them in 2011 in relation to corruption and the killing of protesters during the eighteen-day uprising. Prison torture continues unabated, and sexual violence became state agents' tactic of choice for silencing female activists.[4] Human rights groups and NGOs are suffocating under restrictive laws that have brought their funding, operations, and activities under scrutiny, if not to a complete halt. The courts renege on the law, with judges presiding over patently unfair trials, issuing arbitrary verdicts, and doling out mass death sentences.[5] Regime loyalists dominate the airwaves, while critical voices are demonized and excluded—gone are the days when robust political debate lit up television screens across Egypt in the two and a half years following Mubarak's ouster. Likewise, independent news sites have been heavily censored.[6] As for the martyrs who gave their lives to rescue Egypt from a bleak future under military rule, the memory of their sacrifice continues to haunt their fellow revolutionaries who survived them and lived to see their shared dream of a more open, egalitarian, and just society crushed.

How did it come to this? How did the January 25 uprising fall so short of its goals, especially when its prospects for ushering in radical change seemed so promising when it began? Why did the revolutionary movement fail to gain a foothold in governance or acquire any real political clout? There are many answers to these questions. High on the list of challenges that the architects of this struggle faced early on and never managed to resolve was their inability to constitute themselves as an alternative, cohesive political force backed by the public. This failure rendered them incapable of effectively confronting and ultimately overpowering the forces of autocracy and reaction. A cursory look at how Egypt's leading revolutionaries fared through the tumultuous years between Mubarak's resignation and Sisi's ascent will shed some light on how the current counterrevolutionary status quo came to be and offer insight into what the future might have in store for this movement and the country.

Revolutionary Youth and Counterrevolution

"I still have hope," Abdelrahman sighed wistfully, his hushed tone betraying a sense of defeat and resignation. "Of course," he confessed, "I'd be lying if I told you it was the same hope I had before."

It had been two years since I ended my fieldwork in Egypt when I had this Skype conversation with Abdelrahman—the activist who grew up in a Muslim Brotherhood family but left the organization in his early teens in pursuit of a more secular political path—but I had remained immersed in the country's political developments from California through social media and regular contact with the revolutionaries I befriended through my research. I had just begun the process of reaching out to the now-former leaders of the RYC for follow-up interviews when tensions between Morsi, Egypt's first freely elected president, and his opponents began to escalate in June 2013, following Egypt's tumultuous first year experimenting with democracy. By then, a new movement had gathered force demanding Morsi's resignation and an early presidential election. Protests against the president were set to take place on June 30 in Tahrir and other city squares across Egypt. Meanwhile, counter demonstrations in support of Morsi, which later evolved into open-ended sit-ins, began sprouting in Cairo's Rabaa and Nahda Squares. Tensions ran high as both sides became increasingly radicalized and uncompromising in what quickly became a zero-sum battle of political wills. Egypt was dangerously divided against itself. An implosion felt imminent.

In a way that was reminiscent of my attempts to secure interviews in the early days of the revolution, the unpredictable unrest forced me into standby mode as I tuned in with bated breath along with observers around the world to see how Egypt's political crisis would unfold and what would become of the revolutionary dream. I was particularly struck by the radical difference in the ways my research participants were reacting—not just compared to each other, but compared to the way they responded to similar events two years earlier—on Facebook and Twitter to developments as they unfolded. At a loss for how to reconcile the latest iteration of this group of revolutionary subjects with the ones I had come to know in 2011, I was eager to hear more about how they had experienced the political developments of the last few years and how this might have informed their subjectivities during this time of counterrevolution. The conversations I had with Abdelrahman and some of the other former RYC activists following the vortex of events in the summer of 2013 were the most sobering yet, but no less fascinating and instructive.

This particular Skype call with Abdelrahman took place on October 22, 2013, about two months after the bloodiest event in Egypt's recent memory. It was August 14 when security forces raided the sit-ins in Rabaa and Nahda Squares, where Morsi supporters—including some of Abdelrahman's family and friends—had been camping out for six weeks, demanding that he be reinstated; the military had ousted him on July 3, after massive protests on June 30 demanding his resignation. Supported by armored vehicles and rooftop snipers, police in menacing riot gear moved in on protesters, deploying tear gas, rubber bullets, and live ammunition as bulldozers razed the barricades and tents to clear the way, all to the cheers of much of the non-Islamist public. Emboldened by the nationalist fever that gripped the nation and the calls for a violent solution that accompanied it, the security forces cleared the massive sit-in in front of Rabaa mosque in a matter of hours. It was a bloodbath, carried out in broad daylight and plain sight, that left hundreds dead and thousands injured. So horrific was it that Human Rights Watch called it "the most serious incident of mass unlawful killings in Egypt's modern history" and a crime against humanity comparable to the 1989 massacre in Tiananmen Square.[7]

I had expected that Abdelrahman's mood would be sober when we spoke, having learned from Facebook that he had tragically lost his eldest brother, Mohammed, in the state violence waged against Morsi supporters that summer. But Abdelrahman was in a worse state than I had imagined. He appeared on camera depressed and utterly broken. After learning the harrowing details of his brother's death and the larger impact the summer events had had on him, I could understand why. A gentle, upstanding working-class man in his late forties, Abdelrahman's brother Mohammed went to the Brotherhood protest areas to search for his teenage son, who had been missing since the violent Rabaa dispersal two days earlier. Along with another one of their brothers, Mohammed went looking for his son in the hospitals around Ramses Square, where a new round of violence was being unleashed on the Brotherhood's anti-coup protest marches. On their way to the last hospital, Mohammed decided they should take a break from their consuming worry and help those injured in the clashes, much as he had done during the many other clashes between protesters and security forces that had taken place since early 2011, when he frequently volunteered to transport the injured with his motorcycle. "Thirty minutes had not passed," Abdelrahman told me, "before he became a victim himself." He died from a police bullet to the chest without knowing whether his son was dead or alive. Someone had posted a picture on Facebook of Abdelrahman grieving as he knelt beside his brother's pale corpse shrouded in white, lying in the mosque among hundreds of other bloodied and burnt corpses and surrounded by mourning families.

It was more than just his brother's death that shattered Abdelrahman; he was traumatized by the agonizing ordeal he and so many other bereaved Egyptians were subjected to before they could bury their dead. A lack of ambulances meant he had to solicit help from a friend with a car to transfer his brother to a hospital. He had been forced to sit in the back seat with his brother's limp body, his brother's head resting on his lap and his feet dangling out the far window. If this were not torment enough, they also had to endure the harassment of pro-military plainclothes police and hostile neighborhood watch brigades (*ligan sha'biya*), which had a habit of emerging in moments of deteriorating security following the eruption of the revolution.[8] At checkpoint after checkpoint, they searched his car, poked at his brother's corpse, and interrogated Abdelrahman and his friend about how Mohammed had died and what their political affiliations were. To make matters worse, many of the hospitals refused to receive his brother's body, overwhelmed as they were with the number of dead flooding in from the violence and lacking sufficient refrigeration facilities to accommodate them. At Zeinhom, the state morgue where the hospitals had directed them, Abdelrahman became unhinged by the sight and stench of hundreds of decaying dead strewn around the morgue and the callousness of the medical examiners who, under state orders, refused to release bodies to the families for burial unless they signed forensic reports citing "suicide" as the cause of death. Refusing to subject his brother to Zeinhom's wretched conditions, Abdelrahman pursued his connections until he was able to find a doctor at Ain Shams hospital who agreed to examine the body and helped produce a police report confirming that Mohammed had died from a bullet wound. This report, along with the bullet they left in his chest when they buried him, was the one thing that gave his family hope that one day, when the political circumstances were less bleak, they might be able to exhume Mohammed's body for a proper autopsy and bring his killers to justice.

As if this tragedy were not enough, several of Abdelrahman's relatives were unjustly arrested as part of the state's sweeping post-coup crackdown on the Muslim Brotherhood. These included two of his uncles in Fayoum, his brother-in-law, and Mohammed's son (it turned out he had not been found on that fateful day because he had been arrested). Abdelrahman also lost several friends and close acquaintances in the clashes. When I asked him how many people he knew had been killed, he said he had stopped counting after he reached thirty.

Activism appeared to be the last thing on Abdelrahman's mind. He told me that the amount of blood and death he had witnessed had made him completely numb, depressed, and devoid of any desire for anything in life. He was also deeply disturbed by the enthusiasm many Egyptians showed for the killing of Morsi supporters and their callous disregard for the loss of human life. He had nightmares regularly, he told me, and it had reached the point where he had been driven to alcohol a few times to take the edge off, which was telling, given that he was a practicing Muslim who had always abided by Islam's prohibition of alcohol. He had even sought out psychological therapy. The only thing that kept him going, he told me, was the anticipated birth of his first child, a baby girl (he had married since I had met him in 2011). Even so, he was immensely distressed by the Egypt she would be born into and was looking for work opportunities abroad that would provide them a way out.

In stark contrast to Abdelrahman's gloom, Tarek's mood when we spoke on Skype was buoyant and upbeat, his outlook positive and optimistic. He beamed with pride at the fact that as revolutionaries, they had now toppled two dictators. This version of Tarek was a far cry from the die-hard April 6 revolutionary from Sharabiya I had come to know in January 2011. Back then, Tarek had been a staunch adversary of the authoritarian police state, given his own personal experience with police abuse and government corruption. His enmity had been stoked by several experiences: the police extortion of bribes from his father as a small business owner in the informal economy; his inability to obtain justice for his brother, who had been callously run over by a driver with personal connections to authorities; and having been banned for years from receiving his degree because he had publicly criticized a university administrator affiliated with Mubarak's corrupt ruling party. But none of these experiences seemed to deter him from aligning with old state actors against Morsi in this latest political standoff. A self-described liberal and defender of democracy, he was among those who fully supported the military's intervention and the dispersal of Rabaa Square. His visceral contempt for the Muslim Brotherhood, shared by a large number of Egyptians at the time, was palpable. With unapologetic frankness, he told me, "I was one of those who was encouraging the Ministry of Interior to clear them out of the square. I got on more than one important talk show, and I appealed to the Ministry of Interior to go in and to disperse them by force, in the manner that they actually did, and I'm pleased with the way they did it." With half-suppressed laughter, he then joked: "I've become very sadistic, but I'm pleased. I've become sadistic and violent."

Unlike Abdelrahman, Tarek's life post August 2013 was looking up. Following Morsi's ouster and Tarek's alignment with the military, he continued to enjoy access to the Egyptian public as a guest commentator on talk shows and a weekly columnist for the avowedly liberal newspaper *Al-Masry Al-Youm*. With a tone that revealed a new sense of confidence and self-importance, he also boasted about having direct access to people in high places—ministers, state officials, and other decision-makers in the military government—who regularly reached out to him and some of his peers for their views. "We've become people of influence," he told me matter-of-factly. In the fall of 2013, he had joined a public diplomacy delegation to Iran organized by the Egyptian Ministry of Foreign Affairs, the purpose of which was to emphasize to Iranian leaders sympathetic to the Brotherhood that June 30 had in fact been a legitimate popular revolution, not a coup, as some critics inside and many outside of Egypt were calling it. Tarek was also engaged in building a new liberal political party with other colleagues, including Amr, his former April 6 collaborator who had also aligned himself with the military against the Brotherhood. Tarek had married in December of 2013—incidentally, to a member of April 6, breaking his earlier vows to never marry an activist—and now worked as a lawyer for a well-known attorney, a position he had secured earlier that year. Tarek had undergone an ironic shift. He still claimed solidarity with the revolution, but had now become an ally and strong supporter of a regime seen as even more repressive than the one he had actively opposed three years earlier. Whatever his reality and motivations, Tarek appeared to be happy, stable, upwardly mobile, and notably unvexed by the current state of affairs.

Abdelrahman's and Tarek's positions are representative of the splits that appeared between previously united revolutionaries once the dust from the 2013 summer crisis had settled. Several of the other activists I caught up with had assumed similar positions. They were either disturbed by the turn of events and feeling dejected about the unraveling of the revolution, or they were pleased with developments and feeling politically rejuvenated. But how had they ended up in such different places?

The Brothers, the generals, and the revolutionary youth

In trying to make sense of the divergent trajectories of the youth revolutionaries in mid-2013, it helps to understand their shifting location within the changing alliances among key political players that emerged at different junctures after January 25 to steer Egypt's future. Relations were not always sour between the Brothers and the revolutionary youth. They enjoyed a brief partnership in the heady days of early 2011, when they united along with an amalgam of other secular forces to bring down Mubarak. Although the Brotherhood was at first reluctant to join the youth-initiated effort, it got on board after it became clear the protests could be consequential, and it helped the movement reach critical mass.[9] But rifts between the revolutionaries and the Brotherhood would appear soon after, as the Brotherhood began to put its own interests ahead of the revolution's and pursue a mutually beneficial relationship with SCAF in the hope that it would empower them as leaders in the post-Mubarak order.

As it turned out, the hope the revolutionaries had put in the generals on February 11 was misplaced. Indeed, whether or not the self-described "protectors of the revolution" ever intended to usher in a genuine democratic transition when they intervened to end the eighteen-day standoff is unclear. Self-preservation and maintenance of the status quo were certainly high on their agenda. At stake for the army's leaders, should revolutionary resolve continue to intensify and press for a complete overhaul of the state, was an entire sociopolitical and economic order forged over the course of six decades—one in which they ranked above civilian officials and had been afforded many privileges. The main goal of the military elite was to avoid civilian oversight of its internal affairs and budget, which it had kept classified up to that point. Above all, they were keen on protecting their vast, multibillion-dollar economic empire, which would undoubtedly become a target of popular calls for fiscal reform.[10] So, instead of facilitating the consolidation of an open and representative system as they had promised, the generals attempted to shape a new order that was sufficiently more democratic than Mubarak's to appease the public's demands for change, but limited enough to protect the corporate interests of the military, political, and economic elites. In time, it became clear that what SCAF sought was an arrangement in which a newly elected government would relieve them of the enormous challenges and political liabilities of day-to-day governance, allowing the military to retreat from the public eye but remain in control behind the scenes as the state's most powerful actor.[11] The Brotherhood stood out as the most practical partner.

Much more organized, ideologically coherent, and broadly supported by the public, the Muslim Brotherhood easily displaced the revolutionary youth and the secular forces during this period as the opposition group with the most bargaining sway, which they used to play the political field to their advantage. Hoping to secure their position as leaders in the new order and realize their vision of an Egyptian state governed by Islamic law, the Brothers played on SCAF's assumption that the revolutionary movement would be toothless and fickle without their participation. For their part, SCAF had assumed leadership after Mubarak's ouster with virtually no experience of civic governance or politics, and they found themselves in over their heads as they struggled to maintain order in the face of an increasingly unruly public. Eager to contain the revolutionary movement and stabilize the political arena, SCAF began to accommodate the Brothers, who readily obliged by complying with SCAF's plan. The Brotherhood's conduct during the turbulent transition led many to speculate they were engaged in backdoor dealings with the generals.[12] This was apparent in their willingness to "play by their rules" in the lead-up to elections, the blind eye they turned toward the army's abuses, and their refusal to participate in or support the many revolutionary mobilizations against military rule—unless their own interests were being threatened.[13] In hindsight, it appears that this SCAF–Brotherhood marriage of convenience was based on shared, if somewhat conflicting, interests, the former seeking to maximize its power and privilege in the new order, the latter eager to sideline the progressive movement, take control of the state's governing institutions, and realize its reformist, Islamist agenda. Effectively, this pragmatic alliance succeeded in undercutting the revolutionary movement by legitimizing the military's management of the transition and undermining the position of the youth, while eroding public support for their cause.

This modus vivendi between the generals and the Brothers was discernible almost immediately after Mubarak stepped down. In February 2011, SCAF appointed several Brotherhood sympathizers—and not a single revolutionary—to a committee of jurists responsible for drafting a series of constitutional amendments that would play a decisive role in shaping the new Egypt. The amendments provided guidelines for the democratic transition and favored holding parliamentary and presidential elections before the drafting of the new constitution. The Brotherhood backed the amendments in a referendum held on March 19 of that year, turning their back on the revolutionaries, who opposed the new clauses on the grounds that early elections would give the Brothers an unfair advantage over less established political forces and guarantee Islamist domination of the constitutional drafting process. The RYC and other revolutionary forces wanted the existing constitution scrapped altogether and rewritten ahead of parliamentary elections by a council representative of Egypt's diversity to ensure deep, radical changes in the political order. They believed it was necessary to agree on the rules of the political game, as set out in the constitution, before they became embroiled in divisive electoral politics. Moreover, the revolutionaries distrusted the military and wanted the Islamists to support them in pressuring the military to relinquish oversight of Egypt's transition to a civilian council. But the Brotherhood could not see past the immediate advantages the amendments gave them over the other political forces and chose to align with the military. Their aggressive pursuit of their short-term prospects at the expense of the revolution soured the youth forces and generated the first rifts in their alliance.

This maneuver by the Muslim Brotherhood was just the first in a series of blows to the movement. Meanwhile, the January 25 forces including the RYC continued to descend into the streets to protest SCAF's repression, reluctance to implement reforms, and repeated extension of the transitional period well beyond the six months of military rule they had initially promised. They pressed for an end to the Emergency Law and military trials for protesters, justice for those killed by security forces in the eighteen-day uprising, and the immediate prosecution of the deposed president and those of his associates who were implicated in corruption and crimes against protesters. Not only did the Brotherhood boycott most of these protests, but they also called them illegitimate and generally sided with the military junta. Even as protesters experienced some of the worst violence from the state yet in a series of clashes between October and December 2011, the Brothers avoided serious criticism of the military leaders and toed the official state line, blaming undefined sinister forces attempting to divide Egypt. Perhaps the biggest stab in the back of the secular opposition forces was when the Brotherhood refused to stand by the revolutionaries in the infamous Muhammad Mahmud Street battle with police that took place from November 19 to 24, 2011, and left fifty-one dead and three thousand injured.[14] These events presented revolutionaries with the first real chance to force the military to relinquish power to a civilian council and reset the transition process, but the Muslim Brotherhood thwarted it. Bent on taking power as soon as possible, the Brothers shunned the protests, fearing the upheaval might lead to the postponement or cancellation of the upcoming parliamentary elections in which they intended to dominate. They continued to focus on campaigning and went so far as to criticize protesters as "groups trying to sow chaos in Egypt,"[15] lending legitimacy to SCAF's narrative branding the protesting youth as thugs, anarchists, and foreign agents. It was at this point that the revolutionary movement began to define itself in opposition not only to SCAF but also to the Muslim Brotherhood, which in the eyes of activists had officially sold out their struggle for change and was now an accessory to the counterrevolution.

The revolutionaries were incensed by the Brothers' refusal to criticize SCAF except when it suited their purposes, and by their blatant attempt to monopolize political discourse and power. The Brotherhood's hunger for power was most apparent in the parliamentary elections, when it began to reap the rewards of its strategy with SCAF. Although early on the Brothers and their Freedom and Justice Party had promised not to contest more than 25 percent of the seats in the People's Assembly (the lower house of Parliament), to the activists' chagrin, they went on to take almost half of the seats (47 percent) with their Islamist allies. They also competed for and won 58 percent of the seats in the upper house. Basem, the forty-two-year-old architect-turned-politician from the RYC, was one of the few revolutionaries to win a seat in the Islamist-majority Parliament, having run on the ticket of the Egyptian Social Democratic Party, which he helped found following Mubarak's removal. The contempt he developed for the Brotherhood grew out of his engagement with them and other allied Islamists in the corridors of power. The Islamists continuously thwarted the attempts of Basem and other like-minded MPs to implement far-reaching reforms and advance the revolution's agenda. He tried to push a bill that would ban military trials for civilians and curb torture in prisons by introducing a system of independent monitoring. His colleague Zyad, the only other RYC activist to win a seat in Parliament, introduced a bill instituting a minimum wage and another eliminating the military code of justice. The Brotherhood lawmakers killed both bills, presumably to avoid provoking SCAF. When I interviewed him in late 2013, Basem told me he found the experience so disagreeable that he was actually pleased when the military-aligned Supreme Constitutional Court dissolved Parliament six months later on constitutional grounds and SCAF assumed legislative powers in its absence; it hardly mattered to him at that point that SCAF's move was effectively a judicial coup and a clear sign that elements from the old regime were actively working to undermine the democratic experiment he was so invested in.[16] When we spoke, more than a year had passed since Basem's sour experience, but the memory of it still aggravated him. "They weren't working in the genuine interests of the country," he protested, referring to the Islamists.

> Their main objective was to secure control of the state. They weren't prepared to compromise, come to an understanding, or cooperate. Their understanding of democracy was limited to majority rule. This is the only democracy they understand, that "We have the majority, so we can do whatever the hell we want." ... So that was it. We weren't able to create any laws related to social justice, we weren't able to initiate any laws related to the revolution. ... We weren't able to work on anything! ... We seriously weren't able to get anything done! They were the majority and they operated like a machine—someone raises their hand, everyone raises their hand, someone drops their hand, everyone drops their hand. ... It was as if they were robots. None of them acted out of their individual, personal will.

In the end, Basem felt that the dissolution of Parliament was for the best, because the Islamists "didn't truly speak on behalf of the people" or "represent the revolution."

The Brotherhood had also vowed not to field a candidate for president, but they broke that promise too. Emboldened by their success in the parliamentary elections, they now felt confident they could rely on their supporters to win the top elected office and achieve total political control.

Meanwhile, even at this critical juncture, the revolutionary camp remained disorganized, with devastating consequences for their movement. Failing to coalesce around a single candidate in the primaries, they effectively split the revolutionary vote,[17] which led to a runoff between Morsi, the conservative religious candidate who represented the Brotherhood, and Ahmed Shafik, Mubarak's last prime minister who represented a return to the old order.

Morsi and his party would go on to win the presidential bid in June 2012, but not without help. They slid past Shafik with just 51.7 percent of the vote, a slim victory that was only achieved with the critical backing of the multi-ideological revolutionary coalition, which rallied voters in Morsi's support in exchange for promises from him to create an inclusive government and share power. Hardly a ringing endorsement, the narrow margin confirmed that Egypt was deeply divided and, according to the revolutionaries, should have been recognized by the president elect and his party as a mandate to close the rifts across the sociopolitical divide. Instead, Morsi and the Brotherhood would adopt a policy of unilateralism, showing little regard or tolerance for their ideological opponents throughout their first year in office, effectively uniting these forces against them in a bid to remove them from power.

The Muslim Brotherhood in office: the lesser of two evils?

Although they had grown completely disenchanted with the Muslim Brotherhood over the course of the transition period, several of my interlocutors voted for Morsi over Shafik in the 2012 second round of the presidential race, considering him the lesser of two evils. They were choosing to follow the collective strategy negotiated with the Brothers to prevent the old regime from returning to power. In this begrudging group were Abdelrahman, his colleague in the Egyptian Current Party and former Muslim Brotherhood member Abbas, and Ola from the leftist Youth for Justice and Freedom Movement, all of whom had supported the moderate Islamist Abd al-Mun'im Abul-Futuh in the primaries. Others, such as Basem and Tarek, who had supported the Nasserist Hamdeen Sabbahi, were dissatisfied with both candidates and spoiled their ballots.

Still, irrespective of whether or not they voted for him, when Morsi was elected, most of the activists I spoke to said they were relieved they had dodged Shafik. They recognized Morsi's legitimacy as the newly elected president and hoped he and his party would keep their electoral campaign promise to work with the secular opposition to achieve the goals of the revolution in exchange for their constituencies' votes. They imagined that Morsi would navigate the political landscape cautiously, given the vulnerability of the budding democratic project to counterrevolutionary threats and how eager the Islamists were to stay in power. Even in the absence of those threats, he would still be facing reelection in four years' time and would have to govern wisely if he wanted voters to give him a second term. The activists, in a premature show of political trust, even voted to disband the RYC. Most of them assumed the handover of power to a civilian government meant that the old order had been permanently forced into retreat and that the time was now right to focus on building their political parties, preparing for the next parliamentary and presidential contests, and pursuing whatever goals of the revolution remained through electoral politics. But their cautious hopes in Morsi and the Brotherhood leaders were soon dashed as these new incumbents quickly began to break their promises. They abandoned their pledge to collaborate with the secular opposition in favor of a working relationship with the military and police and showed that they were more interested in replacing Mubarak than seeing the authoritarian state dismantled and rebuilt as a genuine democracy. Increasingly, it became clear that they had never been truly vested in restructuring the corrupt state institutions or bringing about real change. Instead, they seemed determined to infiltrate these establishments and mold them to suit their Islamist agenda.[18]

Morsi's transgressions began to pile up almost as soon as he stepped into power. He had promised to form a national unity government representing Egypt's diverse political factions. Instead, he packed Brotherhood loyalists and old regime figures (the latter, many presumed, to appease SCAF) into his Cabinet and gave them other leadership positions in government institutions, such as state media.[19] Meanwhile, he squeezed opposition voices out of any decision-making. All of this raised fears that he was "Brotherhoodizing" the state.[20] Crucially, Morsi and the Brothers shrugged off one of their most pressing obligations: to reform the police and the Ministry of Interior.[21] This angered many revolutionaries, among them Tarek, whose fellow April 6 activist Gaber Salah, also known as "Jika," was one of the many victims of Morsi's neglect. Jika died of a police bullet to the head during a demonstration commemorating the first anniversary of the Muhammad Mahmud Street protests, and he was the first protester killed on Morsi's watch. Tarek cited this as the incident that sealed his enmity toward the Brotherhood.²² From this point forward, he resolved to work to bring down Morsi and his cohort.

The drafting of the constitution under Morsi's stewardship was another point of dispute. The Constituent Assembly responsible for the draft was dominated by the Brothers and their more conservative Salafi allies. Together, they monopolized the drafting process, provoking the walkout of key stakeholders including secular liberals, Coptic Christians, and human rights organizations. The draft constitution that Morsi signed into law after securing majority approval in a rushed public referendum was a seriously flawed document that failed to reflect a national consensus and fell woefully short of the revolutionary ideals it was supposed to embody.²³

For the former RYC activists and the rest of the secular opposition forces, the official turning point came with Morsi's November 2012 constitutional declaration, in which Morsi claimed unchecked powers for himself by declaring presidential immunity from judicial oversight. Although he justified this as a temporary measure necessary to protect the revolution, it cost him his legitimacy in the eyes of the secular opposition. Having already claimed the legislative powers of the SCAF-dissolved parliament until a new one was elected, he had now also snatched the powers of the judiciary, giving himself sweeping dictatorial powers unknown even to Mubarak.²⁴ The act shocked and infuriated the opposition and precipitated a new wave of unrest, much to the frustration of the military, who had thought they could rely on the Brotherhood to keep a lid on the revolution and maintain order.²⁵ Once more the opposition united, but this time in protest against the first freely, democratically elected president in Egypt's history.

Many of my interlocutors participated in the December 2012 demonstrations and the peaceful sit-in outside the Ittihadiya presidential palace to protest the decree and were later embroiled in the violent street battles that ensued after Morsi called on Brotherhood partisans to come defend his legitimacy. This alarming turn toward vigilante justice revealed the worst of the organization's exclusionary politics and the extent to which it would go to secure its hold on power. Ola was one of the many opposition activists who fell victim to the Brotherhood's vigilantism. Not only did the Islamists hold her captive, interrogate her, and brutally beat her along with other revolutionaries, they also sexually assaulted her, something she had never imagined possible from those who publicly aligned themselves with notions of morality and piety. Ola described the brutal assault in detail. Her face was bruised and swollen and she had a black eye. On her Facebook page, she wrote:

> They pulled me and they pulled each one of us in a different direction. I then found myself surrounded by many people who began beating me. One of them tried to force his finger through my behind.[26]

And in a televised interview on the popular show *Akher Kalam* (The Last Word) with host Yosri Fouda, she went on to say:

> As they were cursing at me I understood that they thought I was a man. I was wearing a helmet [a sweatshirt hood], so they didn't know that I was a woman. When they took off my helmet and realized that I was a woman, then, the unthinkable happened. I always thought that something like that could have happened on the day of the Battle of the Camel, if I had fallen on the hands of our attackers. I did not imagine that I would be sexually harassed at the hands of those adhering to political Islam. They started harassing me and touching my body and my breasts. I then decided to sit to the ground and stop moving and started shouting, "No one touches me!"[27]

The attacks on Ola and other women protesters drew the ire of revolutionaries. For them, it was telling that Islamists were just as quick to use sexual violence to discipline women like Ola for protesting as the military had been to subject Samira Ibrahim and other detained women protesters to "virginity tests" in 2011. The continuity in the use of gender-based violence to punish, intimidate, and delegitimize women protesters made it clear that far from being partners in revolutionary change, the Islamists were committed to preserving the authoritarian status quo and the unjust patriarchal order in which it was grounded.

For Ola and the other revolutionaries, what added to their shock and anger was that they had been betrayed by Brotherhood supporters whom they had fought alongside during the eighteen-day uprising against a common enemy for their mutual good. Now that the Brothers were in power, they were attacking, beating, and molesting their former partners in the revolution. Ola told me she had begged her captors to hand her over to the police, arguing she would rather be shot and killed at their hands than suffer abuse from her former comrades in the revolutionary struggle: "I never wanted to see the people I stood side by side with protesting [during the eighteen days] hitting and harassing and beating me themselves. I didn't want that."

Equally upsetting for Ola was the sectarianism underpinning their violence against her. She described it on *Akher Kalam*:

> As I was being pulled away by them, I noticed that they were pulling my hands strongly and I did not understand why, until I realized that they were looking for a tattooed cross on my hand.[28] They asked where the cross was, and I decided to remain silent. I do not know why, but I was probably overwhelmed with grief at the thought of them caring about whether I was Muslim or Christian.[29]

Ola's experience was consistent with the wider tendency of Morsi and the Brotherhood during their stint in power to dismiss the secular opposition as Christians, infidels, and enemies of Islam—even those among them who were Muslim—whenever they turned out to criticize and challenge Brotherhood positions. It was exactly this kind of sanctimonious, divisive sectarian discourse and utter disregard for the opposition that alienated the youth activists and the rest of Morsi's reluctant supporters and later drove them to rebel against him.[30] This was true for Abdelrahman and Tarek. Abdelrahman held the Brotherhood responsible for the political turmoil Egypt had been embroiled in since the summer of 2013: "They are to blame for where we are today. It's because of their insolence, their selfishness, their disrespect for and refusal to cooperate with the opposition and their contempt for the people." Tarek agreed and went further to claim that the Brotherhood was not just a self-interested organization, but unpatriotic. For him, Morsi's leadership was undemocratic because it was partial to his group; he did not present himself as a leader for all Egyptians:

> We would take part in protests and we were prepared to die so that Egypt could be better. But the Brothers would go down to protest, prepared to send their youth to die, for the sake of the Brotherhood, because they only have the interests of their organization in mind.... I know them well because I saw them in all three periods: before January 25, during the transitional period, and in executive leadership.... They became plagued with a sense of insolence and arrogance, and a lack of concern for the others, as in there's no need to take the rest of us seriously.

Like Abdelrahman, Tarek emphasized the manner in which Morsi and the Brotherhood mishandled the secular opposition. Democracy, Tarek argued, was supposed to be a practice of give and take, of compromise and negotiating opposing interests, of governing by consensus; instead, he lamented, the Brotherhood played the political field with a winner-takes-all mindset, as if their election victory had given them license to sideline their opponents and push through whatever laws they fancied.

Adding to popular frustration and impatience, Morsi's administration proved grossly inept at running the country's affairs, especially in managing the debacle that was the economy. Of course, the economy had been ailing before Morsi stepped into power, but its free fall accelerated on his watch and further undermined his credibility. That said, it is important to note that Morsi was not entirely to blame for the instability; it later emerged that elements of the traditional elite bent on restoring the old order had played an incendiary role in fomenting popular anger against him and the Brotherhood by actively undermining the quality of life during his presidency, for example, by intentionally causing public fuel and electricity shortages. The sudden return of both after Morsi was ousted suggests that state utility agencies had intentionally rolled back public fuel and electricity supplies; the shortages resulted in panic, endless lines at gas stations, and a crippled public transportation network. The police, who had long been groomed to hate the Islamists, also appeared to have purposely withdrawn from the streets to create a security crisis, allowing the crime rate to rise.[31] Still, the consensus was that Morsi's government and his policies were failing miserably.

Even as sentiment against him started to intensify in June, the president only appeared more uncaring. Instead of trying to calm an already tense political crisis, he and his supporters inflamed it further. In mid-June, he tactlessly appointed a member of al-Gama'a al-Islamiya to the governorship of Luxor, the very city where this hardline Islamist group carried out a terrorist attack in 1997, killing fifty-eight foreigners and four Egyptians, sabotaging the country's tourism industry. Around the same time, at an Islamist-organized rally in support of Syrian rebel fighters, Morsi shared the stage with extremist preachers who gave speeches in which they cursed his opposition as infidels. The president also appeared to endorse calls from some of the speakers for Egyptians to join the jihad in Syria, alarming the army and security forces, who were concerned about civilians going abroad to train in arms and guerrilla warfare alongside extremists only to return home as militant jihadis.[32] Equally serious was the disturbing rise in violence against religious minorities, fueled by sectarian hate speech by Brotherhood members and their ultraconservative Salafi counterparts. In his failure to condemn the string of anti-Christian attacks carried out during his presidency by radical Islamists, or the lynching of four Shia men in a Cairo neighborhood, Morsi appeared unconcerned with the security of religious minorities in Egypt.[33]

With so many mistakes and failures after just one year in power, it became nearly impossible to find anything redeeming in Morsi's leadership. The president and his support base managed to provoke nearly every part of Egyptian society: their former revolutionary partners and allies in the election, the army and the police (even taking into account their long-standing vendetta against the Brotherhood), the judiciary, Coptic Christians, al-Azhar clergy leaders, the Salafi al-Nour Party (the second-largest Islamist party after the Muslim Brotherhood),[34] the secular opposition, human rights groups, the media, many members of the business class, and finally, the vast majority of citizens, ranging from the poor to the well-heeled.[35] By the end of Morsi's first year as president, many Egyptians had come to see the Brotherhood's religious project as a threat to the Egyptian state and were ready to embrace the campaign calling for an end to his rule.

June 30: a new rebellion, a new alliance

The movement that capitalized on this popular discontent was called Tamarod, the Arabic word for "rebellion." It was launched in April 2013 by five young organizers who cut their teeth on the Kefaya and April 6 movements. The campaign revolved around a petition drive presented to citizens as a chance to show their lack of confidence in Morsi's leadership. Tamarod demanded Morsi's resignation and an early election but offered no plan for how to achieve them. By the end of June, what had started as a small grassroots operation to which few paid much heed quickly evolved into an extensive, decentralized network of volunteers with stunning reach across Egypt. Tamarod claimed they had secured as many as twenty-two million signatures,[36] dramatically exceeding the thirteen million who had actually voted Morsi into office in 2012[37]—a staggering claim that was never substantiated and likely exaggerated, as the math simply did not work.[38] Still, there was no denying the sweeping popular disenchantment and anger with Morsi one year into his rule.

Tamarod's speedy success provoked suspicions that it was being facilitated and braced by deep-state actors like the military and security forces, old establishment forces like members of the former ruling NDP, and other opportunist groups. Not only did the police give Tamarod activists the freedom to carry out the campaign, but Interior Ministry officials even helped distribute petitions and collect signatures.[39] Members of the business and secular political elite with ties to the Mubarak regime offered them funding and other resources, like free workspaces and media publicity.[40] All of this propelled Tamarod forward. Now, riding its momentum at full speed, the movement began plotting what it hoped would be an epic day of mass action against the president on June 30, the first anniversary of his inauguration. Their goal was to organize protests so large Morsi would have no choice but to step down and hold a new election.

Although they were not among those who founded and led the Tamarod campaign, the former RYC activists readily offered their signatures, and many joined the effort to distribute and collect signed petitions. Basem, for example, worked diligently on the campaign from the Downtown Cairo headquarters of his Egyptian Social Democratic Party, which opened its office as one of the campaign's informal operation sites. Along with most of the other activists, he also endorsed—and in his case, even helped plan—the June 30 protests to overthrow the country's first democratically elected president, a highly controversial undertaking that would put January 25 partisans in the same camp as their adversaries from the old regime, entangling the revolutionary with the counterrevolutionary in an incongruous mix of political resistance and restoration.

The turnout across Egypt was massive. Although the numbers were not as high as the wild estimates ranging from seventeen to thirty-three million that were being propagated by questionable sources,[41] the demonstrations were clearly larger and more widespread than those seen during the eighteen-day uprising against Mubarak. Protesters cut across social classes and age groups, from secular liberals to Salafi Islamist conservatives. In attendance were hardcore revolutionary youth as well as *felool*, reactionaries who had long been hostile to their cause. June 30 even mobilized *hizb al-kanaba* (the sofa party), a catch-all phrase coined to describe those middle- and upper-class Egyptians constituting the politically unaffiliated silent majority; these are the people who chose to sit out the January 25 protests and every revolutionary mobilization since in favor of calm and stability, but now, even they felt compelled to demonstrate. The police had made a comeback too, the same police whose impunity provoked the initial uprising in 2011. They joined in the protests, audaciously chanting, "The army, the police, and the people: we are one hand!" And then there was the suspect participation of the military in the form of helicopters showering crowds in Tahrir with Egyptian flags and fighter jets painting the sky over the square with Egypt's national colors and giant, tender hearts.

This peculiar arrangement of political forces was just the latest in the fluid crisscross of temporary alliances that had emerged at critical junctures during the struggle since January 25 to direct Egypt's future. Oddly, secular and revolutionary forces would find themselves on the side of the military once again, this time standing shoulder to shoulder with the police and the *felool*, their old state foes, in a face-off with the Brothers, their former allies. Both groups sought the end of Morsi's regime, but their coming together was inherently problematic because their interests were diametrically opposed. While the activists were denouncing the Brotherhood's betrayal of the revolution and calling for a "do-over" transition in the hopes of electing a more democratic government than Morsi's and correcting the course of the revolution, the state and economic elite had demonstrated time and again their preference for restoring the status quo. Indeed, the convergence of these opposing, rival forces in this temporary alliance against the Muslim Brotherhood speaks to how complicated and confusing the political scene had become by the summer of 2013, not just to outside observers, but even to participants within Egypt.

There was a lot of uncertainty and speculation in the lead-up to these protests about how events would unfold. In light of all the risks, many observers criticized the decision of the revolutionaries and liberal opposition forces[42] to jump on the June 30 bandwagon. Given Morsi's expected refusal to concede to their demands and the political impasse this would likely produce, there was the very real prospect of unprecedented violence breaking out between Brotherhood supporters and the opposition, as well as a return to military rule.[43] Also worth noting—and a reminder of what had happened after the fall of the Mubarak regime—was the opposition's failure to articulate a clear plan for the protests and what might follow. Instead, there were implicit and explicit calls on the military to "carry out the people's will" coming from the opposition's ranks. This was all the more perplexing considering the regret many had expressed after February 11 about putting their faith in the military to guard the gains of the revolution. Though critics recognized that the situation under Morsi had indeed grown increasingly intolerable and saw that the protests against him were understandable, the concern was that bypassing the ballot box came with its own set of risks that could lead to outcomes more detrimental to the country and the revolutionary cause than Morsi's presidency. None of this seemed to bode well for Egypt and its fragile democratic experiment. So what were the revolutionaries thinking going into June 30?

My conversations with my interlocutors revealed that they were of two different mindsets. On the one hand were those who were fully invested in the rebellion. On the other were activists who were much more conflicted and wary about where the unfolding drama was heading.

Basem and Tarek were among the former. Both activists were energized ahead of the protests—even euphoric—as they worked on the campaign against Morsi. In their minds, they were continuing the same revolutionary struggle against authoritarian rule they had started two and a half years earlier. They insisted Morsi had to go immediately; they were not out to pressure the incumbent president into concessions and negotiations. As far as they were concerned, allowing Morsi to complete his four-year term and possibly wreak more havoc was not an option. Neither was pursuing his removal through the legal route—a parliamentary impeachment—which would require them to defeat the Brotherhood's Freedom and Justice Party in the upcoming fall elections. Tarek believed waiting for elections was too risky, and besides, there were no guarantees the Brotherhood would not rig them, since they had rebuffed the opposition's demands to provide guarantees elections would be free and fair. Another plausible explanation that Tarek might not have been willing to admit was one making the rounds among June 30 critics—namely, that the opposition's disorganization and inability to compete with the Islamists at the polls were the real reasons behind their decision to abandon formal democratic mechanisms to oust the president. A few lonely, cautionary revolutionary voices expressed reservations about an open revolt against a democratically elected president, expressing concerns over the precedent it might set and the very real possibility it might lead to a return to military rule and the death of their nascent democracy. But Basem and Tarek saw the situation differently. They seemed unconcerned about the overt support the military, police, and other old regime forces were lending the protests. In their minds, this just proved the justice of their cause: even the official arms of the state, including the military who were supposedly bound to Morsi and the Brothers in a pact, felt that Morsi and the Brothers could no longer be trusted to maintain security and stability. In revolting against Morsi and the Brothers, they had no plan as to how they would prevent the military's return to power.

Perhaps in the extreme confusion and volatility of the moment, it was too much to account for more than one threat at a time, if they considered a return to military rule a real threat in the first place.

Basem and Tarek expressed many reasons for protesting. Their many legitimate grievances aside, what stood out about some of their arguments was their conspiratorial bent. The xenophobic nature of their remarks echoed some of the anti-Brotherhood propaganda disseminated in the lead-up to June 30 by independent satellite network stations and newspapers, many of which were owned by businessmen with ties to the old regime and demonstrated clear bias against the Islamists.[44] These media outlets worked tirelessly in the months before the protests to demonize Morsi and the Brotherhood and turn public opinion against them. Tarek in particular referenced many unverified claims about Morsi's and the Brotherhood's relationship to Hamas, their desire to sell Sinai to the Palestinians in Gaza, their links to the jihadist insurgency in Sinai, and their transnational loyalties to the international Brotherhood organization and concern for its agenda over Egypt's national interest. In their minds, all of this amounted to an existential and security threat to the country so serious that it justified Morsi's extra-legal overthrow. Both Basem and Tarek went so far as to insist that the country had been better off under Mubarak, that the Brothers were much more dangerous. "I mean, what's worse?" Tarek asked me rhetorically. "Having a repressive regime or a regime that fulfills foreign agendas or the agenda of an international organization?" Basem agreed, "Mubarak might have been corrupt, but Morsi was corrupt and treasonous." Like talk show hosts and their guest commentators, they spoke of Morsi and the Muslim Brotherhood as foreign occupiers and Egypt a land that needed to be liberated from their rule.[45] They invoked the visceral fears many Egyptians had expressed that the country would descend into chaos and become another Syria or Libya. The situation was so dire in their minds that it warranted the intervention of the military, and both of them called for it ahead of June 30 on the condition that the military stay out of governance thereafter. Incidentally, they would later disagree about what this meant when General Sisi decided to run for president.

On another level, the opportunity to relive the intoxication of people power appears to have been enough incentive for many to protest. There was a palpable excitement in the lead-up to June 30 about the prospect of toppling yet another leader, and I heard as much in Tarek's animated voice after the fact when he boasted about the unstoppability of Egyptians who had set some kind of world record for revolutions by ousting three regimes in three years. The nostalgia for the glory days of the January 25 uprising that fed into June 30, along with the romanticization of "the people" and blind deference to their leadership and will, were traps revolutionaries repeatedly fell into after they ousted Mubarak. They were the source of much of the dysfunction of the revolutionary youth, distracting them from the unglamorous but critical work of visionary leadership, constructing a political program, and grassroots organizing.

Much less spirited than Basem and Tarek about the June 30 protests were left-leaning activists like Ola and Abdelrahman. They were torn about participating, sensing that the prevailing mood would likely be pro-military, that the day would not be theirs. Theirs was a terrible dilemma. They felt they had no choice but to protest but could not shake the feeling that this could turn out badly for the revolution and Egypt in the long run. They wanted to bring Morsi down because he was an inept leader who was unresponsive to their revolutionary demands and had driven the country to the brink of civil war. But they also did not want the military to overthrow him and resented those in the opposition championing this as the way out. Still, they decided to protest, convinced that the status quo under Morsi could not continue, that the president who was sabotaging their revolution needed to be challenged. As averse as they were to the military, they went down to demand a snap election, aware that their goal could only be achieved with the generals' intervention since Morsi was unlikely to step down voluntarily. And so these activists wound up protesting, albeit reluctantly, alongside the masses, old elites, and *felool* (old-regime loyalists) on the path toward the July 3 coup. Yet, they refused the suggestion that they bore responsibility for what followed, since it had not been their objective.

Abdelrahman, for instance, believed that he was justified in taking to the streets on June 30. Ultimately, like Basem and Tarek, he did not think the revolutionary legitimacy of the day of protest was compromised by the reactionaries expected to participate. What mattered was his intention. He argued he had every right as a citizen to exercise his freedom to petition his president to step down and facilitate an early election; his purpose had never been to ask the army to depose him. On the contrary, he joined Ola, Abbas, and other comrades marching to Tahrir under the banner rejecting all three counterrevolutionary forces, the demonstration being their attempt to wiggle their way out of the dilemma of wanting to protest, but not alongside the *felool*. They marched to the cry, "*Yasqut yasqut kullu man khan! Askar wa felool wa ikhwan!*" (Down, down with the traitors! The army, the *felool*, and the Brotherhood!). But their march was a relatively small current obscured by the popular energy overwhelming the streets in favor of restoring the status quo. Whether or not they had intended it, their participation that day would end up serving the interests of those who shared their immediate anti-Brotherhood cause, but certainly not their progressive, revolutionary agenda. That said, it is important not to assign the revolutionaries more influence than they actually had at this juncture. The June 30 outcome, as time would reveal, was in large part orchestrated by the networks of power aligned with deep-state interests and would likely have been the same whether or not they participated. Nevertheless, their impotence and irrelevance was a reflection of how weak and fragmented they had become as a movement by this point; had they managed to constitute themselves into a cohesive revolutionary force of consensus capable of speaking with one voice, as H. A. Hellyer argues, they might at least have been able to agree upon and press for alternatives to military intervention ahead of the demonstrations, even if they lacked the power to ultimately implement them.[46]

A second revolution? Or a military coup?

Events escalated quickly after June 30. The following day, the military did in fact intervene: it issued Morsi an ultimatum threatening to impose its own "roadmap" to end the impasse should he fail to address the demands of protesters and resolve the crisis with the opposition within forty-eight hours. But the president remained defiant. He continued to insist on his legitimate authority as Egypt's democratically elected president, ignored the protesters' grievances, railed against the opposition forces for conspiring to undermine him, and offered no concessions, plunging Egypt into a state of greater uncertainty. The crisis came to a head on July 3, when General Sisi declared Morsi's removal from power on live television and announced plans for the immediate formation of a transitional technocratic government. The General—who had, ironically, been handpicked by Morsi to replace the despised General Muhammad Husayn Tantawi as defense minister on the assumption that he would be loyal—assured the public that the army had no interest in taking power and was merely performing a public service by carrying out the will of the Egyptian people. Within hours of the ouster, Morsi and other leading Brothers were arrested and Brotherhood satellite stations were raided and shut down. Anti-Morsi protesters in

Tahrir celebrated their deliverance from the Brotherhood and newfound military hero and savior Sisi. Meanwhile, angry Morsi supporters cried coup, vowing to remain in Rabaa and Nahda Squares, where they had been holding counter demonstrations, until the military reinstated him. The event marked the restoration of the junta's role as ultimate arbiter in the nation's political affairs. Egypt seemed to be on a fast track back to square one.

None of the former RYC activists were surprised when Sisi ousted Morsi on July 3, but their reactions were profoundly different and marked the deepening of the split in the revolutionary ranks. While the non-Islamist public celebrated their June 30 "revolution," as they now called it, Abdelrahman and Ola were notably less enthusiastic, recognizing the intervention as a military coup they feared would undermine all the progress Egypt had made toward a new democratic order. Basem and Tarek, in contrast, were among those who celebrated the intervention as a positive development and rejected the notion that it was a coup on the grounds that this framing undermined their agency. They based their argument on the fact that the intervention was popularly mandated and that Sisi and his fellow generals had not usurped executive authority for themselves as SCAF had done back on February 11, 2011. Instead, the military—operating under what Asef Bayat calls "revolutionary coercion"[47]—had enforced the will of the people, who had turned out in unprecedented numbers on June 30, and created in concert with the secular opposition a roadmap out of this crisis that did not involve them as political leaders. For them, the fact that respected civic leaders like ElBaradei were involved in leading the transition as members of the post-Morsi Cabinet only evinced this. What they sought at the time with the help of such leaders, they claimed, was a civilian-led transition that would be inclusive of everyone, including the Muslim Brothers.[48] "If we're going to say this was a coup," Basem insisted,

> then we'd have to call February 11 a coup. In February, they came to power and sat in power. SCAF removed Mubarak and they sat in power, and no one said it was a coup. And we said, yeah, this is a blessed revolution and a glorious revolution. But now, Sisi came and removed Morsi and created a roadmap that we agree on. There is a plan that we are following in which we create a constitution, followed by parliamentary elections then the presidential election, and then that's it. So the army isn't ruling, in the way we tend to think of military rule. I don't believe that this is a coup at all.

Basem and Tarek insisted that Egypt's experiment with the military would be different this time because the military itself was different. Along with many others in the opposition, they seemed to have been operating under the belief that they had tamed SCAF. The assumption was that the generals had no interest in assuming executive power after SCAF's difficult experiment with interim governance from 2011 to 2012. They believed the military had only intervened to referee the standoff because the people had forced them to; few entertained the notion that the military was appropriating the movement for its own regressive agenda. This time, they seemed certain the army would not dare to overstep its bounds and repeat the mistakes of the transition period, knowing that the people could easily turn against them. "The army knows that without a popular force backing it, its enemies both inside and outside will increase and bring them down," said Tarek. "So they also changed." What was remarkable about Tarek's and Basem's positions was the degree of trust they had in the military's intentions. Their willingness to believe the army would usher in a fast and robust democratic process—when their own very recent history with the military after the fall of Mubarak evinced otherwise—spoke to the kind of dissonances that characterized these new political developments and were difficult to understand.

Breaks in the revolutionary ranks

From this point on, the politics of the former RYC activists diverged in two radically different directions, as Brotherhood supporters in Rabaa and Nahda Squares persisted in their calls for Morsi's reinstatement, and the public, growing increasingly fed up with their endless sit-ins and threatening rhetoric, began to call on the military to disperse their encampments, raising the specter of cataclysmic violence.

Despite their political differences with Morsi supporters, Abdelrahman and Ola argued that they had a right to continue peacefully protesting after the coup. In fact, Abdelrahman went to the Rabaa sit-in for the first time the day after the July 3 military intervention and met with Brotherhood leaders to make clear that he and many others were against the army and would advocate to protect the protest. He was disturbed by the increasing military aggression against Brotherhood supporters, especially the killing on July 8 of over fifty protesters camped outside the Republican Guard headquarters, where Morsi was thought to be held. The officers claimed that the Brotherhood had initiated the violence and defended their actions as self-defense, but eye-witness reports asserted that it was a coordinated assault on unarmed civilians. Meanwhile, private and state media quickly revealed their bias, spinning the clashes as acts of Brotherhood terrorism against the state and engaging in other Islamist fear-mongering to generate public support for the army and police.[49] Following the attacks, Abdelrahman declared his solidarity with the Rabaa occupation on his Facebook page. He even gave a speech at the Rabaa sit-in condemning the coup, the state violence against protesters, and what he feared would be more violence to come, all while maintaining his stance against Morsi's and the Brotherhood's conduct in power, his commitment to an early election, and his opposition to the idea of Morsi's reinstatement.

In contrast, Basem and Tarek blamed the rising death toll of Brotherhood supporters on their intransigent, fanatical leaders. On his Facebook page, Basem criticized these senior figures for sending their youth into clashes with the military to press for Morsi's reinstatement knowing it was a lost cause and would only lead to their death. Initially, Basem and Tarek had supported their right to continue to protest, but as media allegations of weapons and torture camps within the sit-ins began to mount, they veered to the political right, aligning themselves with the politics of those whom critics were calling pseudo-liberals, opportunists, and even fascists.[50] Going against their professed liberal and pluralist values, they joined the many Egyptians who took to the streets on July 26 in response to General Sisi's surprising appeal two days before for mass rallies that would give him a mandate (*tafwid*) to fight "terrorism," a development that signaled to many that a crackdown on the Brotherhood camp was imminent. The media, liberal opposition, and public embraced the general's cause with gusto. Millions flooded Tahrir and other city squares carrying Egyptian flags and posters of the army-chief-turned-savior in a show of nationalist fervor. Few seemed to question how a movement demanding an early presidential election had suddenly become a "war on terror," including Basem and Tarek, who were now going well beyond their appeal for a snap election to endorse the exclusion of their ideological opponents from the political process, and possibly even worse, the use of punishing state violence against them. Meanwhile, Abdelrahman and Ola clung to the small minority who rejected the military's intervention and the false binary being peddled to the public casting the military and the Brotherhood as Egypt's only options. In a desperate attempt to make themselves heard and avert bloodshed, they joined the breakaway core revolutionaries congregating in Sphinx Square in Mohandiseen, a third space free of Islamists and *felool*, to call on citizens to rise above the fray and recommit themselves to the January 25 vision of an inclusive Egypt.

When the security forces began their raid on Morsi supporters in Rabaa Square on August 14, Tarek and Basem voiced no objections; given the national security threat they had come to believe the sit-in posed, both had pressured for state action. Having been among those who called for a forced clearance, Tarek especially was supportive of the operation and showed no sympathy for the protesters who were injured and killed. For him, these were no longer Egyptians whose political and human rights should be safeguarded—they were criminals, traitors, terrorists, and enemies of the state who should be dealt with accordingly. His indifference toward the indiscriminate nature of the assault was evident when I tried to ascertain how he felt about women and children being among the victims. He avoided my question about children and instead focused on the young adults he said the Brotherhood leaders "brainwashed" and used to carry out their confrontations in the streets. Since these young people were acting on behalf of their leaders, he argued, they had to be treated as the leaders' proxies and not on the basis of their own humanity. It is worth noting that at the time Tarek shared his position with me, there were reports from the state and rights organizations in circulation, along with eye-witness accounts, substantiating the claim that the vast majority of Brotherhood protesters were peaceful and unarmed and posed no threat to police during the dispersal.[51] Whether or not he was aware of them, he showed no sign of being open to changing his position, claiming he had seen pictures with convincing evidence of the Brotherhood's crimes related to torture at the sit-in.

As for Basem, initially, he had been opposed to shutting down the Rabaa sit-in using force. He had believed a gradual clearance, achieved through a nonviolent siege in which security forces established checkpoints to search for weapons and control the flow of food and medical supplies, was the appropriate approach, and he called for as much on Facebook. Later, however, once the action was underway, Basem was not against it. He trusted in this instance that state officials were basing their decisions on sound intelligence about the threat and acting in the interest of the greater good. This was a striking departure from the mistrust of the establishment—especially the security arms of the state—that had up until this crisis point generally characterized the revolutionary subjectivities of Egypt's January 25 youth, which emerged in response to police brutality. Moreover, in his earlier Facebook posts, Basem conditioned his support for a Rabaa dispersal on authorities abiding by the law and exercising restraint. However, in the wake of the operation, he did not question its lawfulness nor was he critical of the amount of force deployed against protesters. In this way, he was unlike those among his former revolutionary comrades who shared his enmity toward the Brotherhood but remained consistent on the issue of human rights abuse no matter who the perpetrator or the victim; they swiftly decried the force used as excessive and intentionally lethal. Basem, on the other hand, offered alternative explanations for the security forces' actions—citing their limited training in how to minimize casualties, for instance—and continued to blame the Brotherhood leaders for the bloodshed.

When Basem and I spoke, he mentioned the Brotherhood had claimed the civilian death toll from Rabaa to be five thousand, which he rejected as one of their many lies and exaggerations. Echoing the state narrative, he submitted that the number was closer to five or six hundred according to his recollection, and he justified those deaths as proportionate to the hundred or so police allegedly killed by armed Brotherhood aggressors. He reasoned that for that many policemen to have been killed, there must have been a significant number of protesters with heavy weaponry among those who were peaceful; the police must have been met with considerable violence from the other side, warranting their use of heavy force. In fact, Human Rights Watch later confirmed 817 casualties from the massacre and asserted the actual count was likely well over a thousand; they also only verified eight police fatalities.[52] But accurate numbers aside, Basem's acceptance of the massacre and ability to rationalize, in this calculated manner, the killing of civilians speaks to the tragic extent to which state violence had become normalized and legitimized in Egyptian society three years into this struggle, and the kind of moral sacrifices many were making in the thick of this crisis. In the end, the counterattacks allegedly carried out by the Brotherhood on police stations and churches across Egypt in the wake of the massacre[53] only hardened Basem's belief that the violent dispersal was justified and warranted the outlawing of the group as a terrorist organization. "There can be no reconciliation with those who kill and act treacherously," he proclaimed on Facebook on August 30, 2013, backtracking from his calls immediately after the coup for a rapprochement with the Brothers.

I found Basem's positions in this moment of crisis—including his new support for the military and tolerance for state-led violence against civilians—difficult to reconcile with those of the staunchly principled, level-headed revolutionary activist I had come to know two years earlier. His views illustrate the kind of currency anti-Brotherhood, "war on terror" military propaganda had among many secular and liberal Egyptian intellectuals, whose critics lamented that they should have known better. Even harder to grasp was the strong pro-state stance I observed in Tarek, who had been tenacious in his opposition to SCAF rule and police brutality in 2011 when I first began to engage with him. Ironically, Tarek was now appealing to the security arms of the state to do his bidding and clear the square, including the police force he had criticized Morsi for not reforming—the same police who killed his friend Jika. I questioned him about his inconsistency, but he seemed unwilling to consider how his actions might empower the Interior Ministry and undermine the demands for security reforms that had driven the January 25 uprising he helped incite two and a half years before. I also asked him about his apparent double standards regarding liberal democracy and human rights as they applied to Brotherhood supporters. He skirted my question and instead offered this reply:

> The lesson we learned is that if we're going to rule, we must do what the Brotherhood did and work with the army to get ahead. The Brothers didn't like the military, but in the transitional period, they worked with them because it was in their interest ... until they achieved power, and then they were able to do whatever they wanted. So we're thinking with the same logic, and this isn't the logic of opportunism, but it's the logic of "how do we make this revolution succeed?" ... We're operating with this logic right now, that my enemy's enemy is my friend—not my friend so much, but the idea is that I'm dealing with him as long as he is doing what I want him to do. Because what's new this time is that they haven't done anything we don't want.

The irony is that Tarek could not see how poorly this logic had served the Brotherhood, who had indeed aligned with the military against the revolutionaries to attain power. The argument that the revolutionaries' alliance with the military was different from the Brotherhood's because they had the revolution's best interest in mind and therefore occupied the higher moral ground in this battle of the wills reflects just how convoluted revolutionary politics had become by 2013. Tarek seemed genuinely convinced that they had tamed the army because "they haven't done anything we don't want" and that they were therefore inoculated from the same fate as their Islamist opponents.

On the other hand, despite Basem's support for the military's actions against the Brotherhood, there was some clear incongruity in his remarks, reflecting an inability to completely reconcile his revolutionary principles with his support for the military intervention and the sweeping political repression it gave way to. He made a point of emphasizing that although he supported the military's removal of Morsi, its actions in ending the Rabaa Square occupation, and the subsequent crackdown on the Brothers, his support stopped there. When we spoke, he was not among those who were imploring Sisi to run for president. He argued that the military should have no place in governance and was frustrated with the media for distorting the public political discourse by branding as a traitor or foreign agent anyone who criticized Sisi. He held Sisi responsible for this. "I can't say that because you did something really great [meaning deposing Morsi] I'll forgive you for anything else you do," he said, speaking of Sisi. "I'm not like this." He also lamented that the revolution was far from being achieved and had in fact fallen back many steps, but he spoke as if he and his party bore no responsibility for this outcome, even though they had supported the Tamarod protests, the coup, and the Rabaa crackdown that led to it. Citing the new draconian protest law passed in late 2013 as an example, he recognized Sisi's effort to reestablish Mubarak's police state and feared that Sisi would ban all dissent. Yet, in the same breath, he insisted the political situation was still better than it was under Mubarak, given that people had not lost the freedom they gained since January 25 to organize political parties and openly voice their views. Then he took a step back and admitted that this free space was diminishing.

While Basem labored to articulate a position that comfortably accommodated his conflicting views, Tarek showed no signs of such inner conflict. In fact, he campaigned for Sisi during the 2014 presidential election and would go on to run for and win a seat in the first post-coup—and decisively nonrevolutionary—Parliament shortly thereafter, inviting a storm of attacks from his former comrades who accused him of selling out.[54]

Indeed, the events of 2013 generated deep rifts among the activists who had formed the RYC, many of whom were no longer on speaking terms with each other when I caught up with them. Basem, for example, told me he had no problem with former young Brothers like Abbas and Qassas on a personal level, but that he had lost all confidence in their politics; he believed that positions they had taken revealed their enduring loyalty to the Brotherhood and, on that basis, he refused to collaborate with them on future organizing initiatives. Similarly, Abdelrahman had completely cut off ties with Basem, Tarek, and the rest of his former revolutionary allies who took to the streets on July 26 to license Sisi to fight "terrorism." He blamed them for the death of his brother and friends. Even within political groups that shared the same ideology, like the Egyptian Current Party[55] and the Popular Socialist Alliance Party, members started falling out with each other after the coup as some shifted to the left or right of their original revolutionary positions. In short, the landscape of the opposition was undergoing rapid fragmentation and atomization, and the leading youth movements were not immune to these effects.

Back to the margins
In the aftermath of Morsi's fall and Sisi's ascent to power, Egypt's core revolutionaries found themselves a lonely, shrunken, persecuted minority. Predictably, the crackdown on the Brotherhood led to a wider assault on public dissent in the name of stabilizing Egypt and fighting terrorism. As someone who had appeared regularly on television since January 25 as a face of the revolutionary youth, Abdelrahman found the public hostile to him and feared for his and his wife's security. In fact, he had been attacked by thugs on one occasion and said he could no longer show his face Downtown, where he used to meet up regularly with other activists and intellectuals, for fear of being picked up by State Security. For months following the summer of 2013 unrest, his mother had forbidden him to visit her in Fayoum, the city where he had grown up, because his uncles had been arrested there and she feared he would be too. When we spoke, he told me he believed it was only a matter of time until he was arrested or killed.

Abdelrahman and his peers had also been completely shut out by the media, except for those who had aligned themselves with Sisi's actions, like Tarek and Basem. To get around this media blackout, Abbas, Abdelrahman's former colleague from the RYC and the Egyptian Current Party, traveled to Doha, Qatar, to appear on the satellite station Al Jazeera Arabic hoping to make the revolutionaries' views heard in Egypt and around the globe. This was a risky move since, by that point, Al Jazeera and its patron

Qatar had made many enemies in Egypt, especially among the authorities. Although the network claimed its treatment of political developments in Egypt had been even-handed, many viewers felt that its coverage had been biased toward the Muslim Brotherhood, and government officials accused it of promoting the Brotherhood's activities and sowing trouble in Egypt. According to Abbas, for him to criticize the military on Al Jazeera in that context would have been interpreted by many Egyptians as treason. His fierce and unapologetic criticisms of the coup, the Rabaa massacre, and the state's ongoing assault on human and civil rights have made it impossible for him to return home without danger to himself. Abbas is now one of many January 25 revolutionaries who are living in exile. Some are with him in Doha, including Abdelrahman, who managed to join him later with his wife and baby daughter. Others have fled to Turkey, the United States, and different parts of Europe.

The intensity and scale of state tyranny following the 2013 rupture left Egypt's leading youth activists feeling dejected, jaded, traumatized, and utterly fatigued. In contrast to Basem, Abbas argued that the situation was much worse than it had been under Mubarak because the current ruling bloc had the support of a vast swathe of the Egyptian public ready to sacrifice the activists for the sake of political stability. Abbas shared how many young people, particularly the revolutionaries, experienced what they saw as a betrayal from their fellow Egyptians and the bitterness and disillusion it engendered in them. His words dripped with dolefulness:

> There is an internal struggle inside people. They're saying things like, "The country deserves what's happening to it. The people deserve this." There are questions running through people's minds like, "Why should I die for the sake of these people? They want to be slaves, so why should I die for them? Why should I die for a country that doesn't give me anything and accuses me of treachery and tortures me?"

Holding on to hope

The story of Egypt's revolutionary struggle and the youth activists who championed it has been a tragedy in the heaviest sense of the word. Four years of heartfelt struggle and enormous sacrifice failed to produce any meaningful political and social change. To the contrary, the police state is stronger than ever, and the old regime forces have tightened their grip on the country's power centers.

And yet, despite their painful circumstances, Abbas and his comrades have not lost hope. For them, the hope lies in the persistent crisis. They were convinced when we last spoke that the story of their revolution was far from over; after all, the core grievances that drove the initial uprising remained unresolved. As they saw it, General Sisi's aura of invincibility would fade sooner or later as he came under the same kind of scrutiny from the public as his predecessors over his performance in office. Indeed, well into his second term in power, the president and his regime have already had to deal with considerable discontent. The expressions of this were many—the bread riots following his introduction of austere economic reforms;[56] popular protests against continued policy brutality;[57] and acts of civil disobedience from students, professionals, and workers[58]—but three episodes stand out in particular.

The first of them was Sisi's controversial handover of Tiran and Sanafir islands to Saudi Arabia. The event provoked mass outcry from Egyptians and even compelled some of Sisi's loyal apologists in state media to daringly pull back from their unquestioning support and take him to task for his actions.[59] State repression intensified considerably thereafter, but that did not prevent Egyptians from speaking out. A clear example of this was the public reaction to the controversial constitutional amendments that would allow Sisi to stay in power until 2030. Quite telling was the number of Egyptians who, despite the extreme security risk, registered their opposition online and at the polls. Social media lit up with calls to "vote no," with tangible results: the state was forced to admit that three million (11 percent) of those who turned out to vote in the referendum objected.[60] And just when it seemed like Sisi's repression had finally succeeded in instilling in Egyptians the fear of protesting by late 2019, remarkably, claims from an unlikely whistleblower that the president was misappropriating public funds for multimillion-dollar vanity projects like presidential palaces for his family triggered their eruption onto the streets once again.[61] The president's unapologetic admission that he was indeed building palaces was seen as a slap in the face by many Egyptians who were struggling to make ends meet under austerity measures his government enforced.

Meanwhile, a violent Islamist insurgency continues to rage in the Sinai, testing public confidence in the ability of Sisi and his military to deliver on their promise to provide stability and security. And then there is the silent rebellion Sisi has faced from the country's youth, who have shown little interest in the political process since he took power, boycotting his two elections, for example, and depriving him of the youth validation he has needed to claim legitimacy as Egypt's democratically elected leader.[62]

What all of this suggests for Egypt is that more turbulence might yet be in store. Many have been speculating that it is only a matter of time before popular patience with the government runs out again, giving way to a social upheaval more desperate, angry, and unforgiving than the January 25 uprising—something akin to what Egyptians call *thawrat giya'*, a "revolution of the hungry."

This is how the revolutionaries see it. Ola was firm in her belief that although the people had taken the side of the regime, their support would not last: "I don't feel like it's the end of the game because this dictatorship . . . will not really improve the lifestyle of people, will not really invest in making their daily life easier. . . . Soon, social needs will push people to demand change and move again." Abbas agreed, citing the limitations of the state's tendency to use security measures to deal with social problems that are symptomatic of failed economic and political policies. "In the end, they're not giving me a solution," he told me. "Popular anger will erupt again. They're going to bring themselves down."

Getting Organized

If all the indicators hold, and the youth are right in their assessment that another major popular challenge to the regime is likely, a number of questions naturally follow: What are they doing to prepare for this next popular eruption? How do they plan to guide it and support it to realize their revolutionary ends? If the revolutionary movement is going to reemerge at some point in the future, will it be the same horizontal, segmented configuration characteristic of NSMs these revolutionaries adopted in the past (even though this led to their current status)? To what extent are the "old" movement organizing structures presented by traditional Marxist theorists like Lenin or Gramsci the way forward?[63] How viable will participatory democracy be as a revolutionary organizing process? Is it time to consider more conventional or innovative leadership models from different movements around the world?

These are all questions the activists will have to grapple with in the next stage of this struggle if there is any hope for genuine, far-reaching transformation in Egypt. So far, Egypt's experiment in revolution appears to have validated Lenin's and Gramsci's arguments that sustainable organizational structures are needed to reach out to and secure the commitment of the masses, continuously cultivating them into a counter-hegemonic force capable of undermining and replacing the state. It might be the case, as Luxemburg suggests, that the masses are capable of developing a revolutionary consciousness independently without the intervention of leaders, much as Egyptians did when they erupted onto the streets on January 25. However, the notion that they can *maintain* a revolutionary consciousness and will on their own has been disproven by the fact that Egyptians were so easily won back by the army. The solution may not be in the iron discipline and rigid, centralized design of the bureaucratic Leninist vanguard party, but clearly, some form of durable, recognizable organization is needed, complete with a long-term vision, concrete political objectives, and a far-sighted strategy for building and sustaining grassroots revolutionary sentiment and momentum.

Why was creating this sort of organization consistently a challenge for Egypt's revolutionaries? As alluded to in chapter 6, the answer lies partly in the decade-long history of political activism that preceded the revolutionary movement, but also, more significantly, how it was circumscribed by neoliberal dictates. As relentless and fervent as this resistance movement was in challenging the abuses of the authoritarian state, the activists driving it never entertained the idea of taking over state power—a prospect which, while a dream for many, seemed absurd, given the regime's seemingly unshakable grip—and therefore never developed the organizational capacity or undertook the long-term strategic planning necessary for such an endeavor. Indeed, notably absent from the politics of the activists in the lead-up to the revolution was the kind of radicalism that characterized the activity of their twentieth-century counterparts, who thought and strategized in terms of revolution; this is a phenomenon Asef Bayat attributes to the de-radicalizing effect of neoliberalism on the political class and its idea of change. As marketization "caused social exclusion and dissent among the grassroots," he argues, it simultaneously "conditioned the activism of groups like youth, women, and the political opposition, including the Islamists," constricting their political imagination and limiting their change efforts to reforming the existing order instead of transforming the governing power structure and bringing about a completely different social older.[64] Although they were outspoken in their critique of government corruption and despotic rule, few Egyptian dissidents had deliberated on the workings of state power under neoliberalism to decide how they might address it, let alone usurp it, to effect sweeping change.[65]

Scholar Maha Abdelrahman provides some additional insight on this perspective, elucidating how the activists' experience of power and the way it was structured under neoliberalism influenced their organizing and dissent. She submits that not only was the idea of capturing state power impossible for Egyptian activists to contemplate under regime repression, but that it also did not fit with the fluid notion of power or the vision for social transformation they had developed through their activism: power, as they implicitly understood it, was not a bounded object to be pinpointed and captured, but a diffuse and complex system involving the domestic, regional, and global—an elaborate network of vested interests and exploitative relations—that needed to be resisted and dismantled at these multiple levels. The revolutionary movement, with its expansive set of demands and grievances and multiple targets, reflected this understanding. So, too, did its loose, decentralized, horizontal structure, which accommodated a diverse range of actors working autonomously to advance these different causes.[66]

It is no surprise then that the youth activists and the rest of the opposition forces struggled to compete with the state as a cohesive revolutionary vanguard when the opportunity suddenly presented itself. Given their earlier short-term efforts and their inexperience with this level of organizing (which was not necessary, as their organizing objective had not been to capture state power), they persisted in the kind of decentralized contentious street action that marked their pre-January 25 resistance, even as they struggled to live up to the new responsibility history had placed on them as revolutionary leaders. In the early days of the revolution, the diffuseness, informality, and extreme decentralization the activists carried over from their earlier attempts at resistance were an advantage, making it easy for them to mobilize the masses and impossible for counterrevolutionary forces to subdue the movement. But these same features became a liability when it came to contesting power among old and new actors after Mubarak's fall, a battle for which the revolutionaries were unprepared. This is how Basem saw it:

> In the eighteen days, we weren't prepared to seize power. I mean, who was going to take power, and how? But if there had been a strong organization before January 25 started, if there had been a clear and strong organization that mobilized people and catapulted them to

power, we would have been able to sit down and cross our legs and the Brotherhood wouldn't have come and stolen the revolution.

Tragically, the young architects of this movement lost their position as leaders and were sidelined in the struggle, reduced to a force incapable of doing more than rejecting the advances of their more organized, formidable political foes, or together acting as kingmakers between them. By the summer of 2013, the early lack of cohesion among revolutionary opposition forces had proved near-fatal for the struggle. Whatever remained of the movement following those volatile summer months only continued to fragment, rendering it that much more incapable of solidifying into a unit that could lead Egypt to a revolutionary outcome. The byproduct was a situation of intense political flux that, in the absence of organized intervention, only continued to intensify, opening the door to the military to take full control in the name of stability.

Something must also be said of the organizing mechanisms that activists continued to rely on after Mubarak's ouster. In part, the revolutionaries' struggle to maintain a connection to the street stemmed from their structural dependence on social media as a main platform for organizing and mobilizing following the eighteen-day uprising. Paolo Gerbaudo rightly argues that "short-termist over-reliance on the power of social media . . . contributed to a neglect for the question of long-term organization, ultimately leading to the incapacity in constructing a credible leadership for the revolutionary youth."[67] Following the example set by the We Are All Khaled Said Facebook page, a plethora of campaigns and groups emerged onto the political scene by way of social media, such as al-Askar Kazeboon (The Army Generals are Liars) and al-Ikhwan Kazeboon (The Brothers are Liars). The former was a public awareness campaign launched in late 2011 to expose SCAF's abuses during its post-Mubarak rule with the goal of removing them from power; the latter was a campaign against the Muslim Brotherhood that called out its counterrevolutionary transgressions between 2011 and 2013 as it acquired more and more state power. Another group was the Black Bloc (al-Kutla al-Sawda), an upstart anarchist group that appeared during Morsi's tenure seeking to challenge his authority. Through their Facebook pages and Twitter accounts, such initiatives achieved increasing visibility and online influence until the number of their likes, followers, and shares peaked, sometimes attaining a critical mass that spilled over into popular street action. And then, as if vulnerable to the same obsolescence fixed into the life cycles of the very software and technology they relied on, these revolutionary fads declined in popularity, losing the attention and interest of their followers to the next online political trend, and faded into the cyber abyss.[68] For the activists, this perishing effect of social media on their digitally dependent political initiatives suggested the need to shift into developing longer-term projects dependent on offline organizational structures and mechanisms to draw in the masses and sustain the revolutionary process into the future.

It is crucial to note that the fleeting nature of these organizations, which became a fixture in the post-Mubarak revolutionary scene, was also a product of their "anti-" dispositions. Their objectives tended to be oriented toward rejecting and challenging the latest counterrevolutionary developments rather than pursuing alternatives and long-term, constructive goals that would build and strengthen the movement. This is not to say that resisting these developments was unnecessary, but all too often, the revolutionary movement's almost exclusive focus on reacting to and resisting the immediate came at the cost of articulating a far-sighted vision of the future it actually did want for Egypt and organizing to achieve it. Most of the revolutionary campaigns and organizations that appeared on the political scene following Mubarak's exit reflected this trend. In addition to initiatives like al-Askar Kazeboon and al-Ikhwan Kazeboon, there was also the National Salvation Front, Tamarod, and the Way of the Revolution Front. Each of them coalesced around rejecting the ruling power—whether it was the military, the Muslim Brotherhood, or both—and failed to provide a constructive, alternative idea of governance or a positive revolutionary agenda. The National Salvation Front (NSF), formed by a medley of avowedly liberal, secular forces in reaction to Morsi's constitutional decree, was particularly problematic. Morsi's violation of constitutional norms gave the secular opposition an opportunity to present a clear governing agenda that would appeal to moderate Egyptians—one based on freedoms, individual rights, the rule of law, and the subservience of the army to elected civilian government. But this liberal rhetoric was notably absent from the NSF's discourse. Instead, they railed against the Islamist dictator and focused their energy on trying to thwart him, proving just as willing as the Brothers to lean on the military to do their bidding.[69] As for the Way of the Revolution Front, established in the summer of 2013 by leading revolutionaries to break the polarization of the political space between the military and the Brotherhood and serve as a third, revolutionary option for the public, it also collapsed because it had no compelling, constructive political project ready to market and lacked a strong organizational structure.[70]

But of all the initiatives, Tamarod deserves particular attention for illustrating the most serious drawbacks of the diffuse, pragmatic, agendaless, leaderless movement model—most notably, its vulnerability to being coopted.[71] Without recognizable leaders giving it clear direction or structure, this protest movement continued to grow in hazardous directions, opening within its folds spaces for deleterious, anti-democratic forces with counterrevolutionary interests ready to exploit the movement's incoherence and rudderlessness to advance its own agenda. Whether or not the revolutionaries intended it, the Tamarod movement they supported ended up serving as a vehicle for reviving the political legitimacy of old regime forces and restoring the status quo—again, in large part because they abstained from giving it any direction. In this respect, Tamarod serves as another instructive example of how the organizing logic that gave rise to the revolution on January 25 and was its biggest strength proved ineffective for the movement in the long run and turned out to be its greatest weakness, ultimately leading to its collapse.

The activists I interviewed readily admitted that political organizing and planning had long been their Achilles heel. Now, as they bide their time in the margins, they have been slowly coming to grips with their failings and are trying to address them. Along with the wider network of leading activists and intellectuals—some of whom are in prison, many others in exile—they have started to conceive new ideas of governance and alternatives to status-quo rule that might one day win them the support of the masses, should they find themselves ready to take on the authoritarian state again. The fight for Egypt's future will continue to be a monumental challenge, but what the activists have going for them is the invaluable knowledge and experience they gained over the course of the revolutionary period that might feed back into and strengthen a resuscitated movement. They organized mass protests, built extensive networks, founded coalitions, developed creative campaigns, launched political parties, ran in elections, engaged with the country's power brokers, interfaced with private and state media. They now have a better sense of how the power balance at the top is negotiated as well as a more intimate, nuanced understanding of the mechanics of public opinion—how it flips and fluctuates to fuel or undermine resistance. No one knows what the future will bring, but they are not prepared to waste all their effort. "There isn't a vision for where we're headed," Abbas told me, "but we're still working." Ola, staying true to her Trotskyist streak, emphasized the permanency of revolutionary struggle and the iterative nature of the process:

> I think revolution is still achievable. But I've always thought that it takes a process and it's not that easy or that fast, so we're still there. . . . We believe in continuous revolutions, we always thought it would take a while . . . I don't think of it [the turn of events in 2013] as a step back, I think of it as a process, that we've always realized it will be ups and downs. It's a very bad moment where people are willing to nurture fascism, just to see their enemy brought to their knees. But at the same time, I think we had to go through this. It had to come out on the surface and be dealt with. So let's see. We're hoping it doesn't bring us down.

Ola and her peers have always recognized the road ahead of them is long, yet they have remained committed, even as they have noticeably scaled back their expectations for success since they embarked on this journey in early 2011. They realize that the counterrevolutionary developments since 2013 mean they have lost a major battle with the regime, but they refuse to admit defeat in the war. Their biggest challenge in the period ahead will be figuring out how to organize to revive the revolutionary consciousness in the masses under the prohibitive circumstances of intensified state repression and far-reaching surveillance. In the meantime, their focus has narrowed to more targeted issues that might collectively build up to a new revolutionary uprising one day against the authoritarian state: the war on sexual harassment, efforts to free political prisoners and to document and raise awareness about the state's egregious human rights violations for audiences at home and abroad, and indirect agitation through adversarial journalism. Remarkably, despite the crackdown, revolutionaries continue to work and voice their dissent, albeit it much more cautiously.

Equally significant, if not more, have been the protests among high school and university students. The former, at one point, took to the streets in several major cities to demand sweeping education reform. The latter have tried to continue the tradition of resisting state repression and interference in the administration of their campuses.[72] The politicization and radicalization of this new generation of students post 2013 speaks to the same processes that primed the RYC activists at the forefront of January 25 and signals another wave of righteous, youthful fury possibly yet to come. In short, the revolution might have been subdued, but its legacy is still alive and shaping actors and realities on the ground in ways that might prove to be profound.

January 25 in the Balance

As important as it is to interrogate the activists' failings, strategic errors, and missed opportunities, it is vital that we not lose sight of what they accomplished. Egypt's young dreamers provoked the possibility of change in their country at a time when their people were losing hope. January 25 opened up Egyptians' imagination of what was socially and politically possible. The utopian eighteen days in Tahrir showed them their potential as a nation and as a people. It empowered them with the knowledge of their agency. As a result, Egyptians are no longer the same, and neither is their relationship with their government. The proof is in the myriad protesters who took down three successive regimes in three years: a police state, a military state, and a religious state. Because of the youth effort, Egyptians today know very deeply and fundamentally that they have rights. And they know they will always have their voice. Combined with the memory of their January 25 people power, which will always be available to them to draw on for inspiration, none of these factors should be discounted when considering possibilities for how the future might unfold.

No less significant is the impact Egypt's youth had globally. Not only did they rouse their countrymen to action, they emboldened Arabs across the region and exhilarated disaffected citizens around the world. The spark of hope might have started in Tunisia, but Egypt turned it into a fire. On every continent, movements and protests erupted looking to bring down entire political systems or to pressure incumbent governments to reform unjust policies. From the Arab uprisings in Libya, Syria, Bahrain, Jordan and Yemen; to the Occupy Movements that swept through North and South America and Europe; to the Indignados movement in Spain; to the courageous attempt by Chinese activists to start a "Jasmine Revolution"—each of these cited Tahrir as their inspiration.

Enough cannot be said about the impact Egypt's young revolutionaries had on Arabs' perception of themselves and on the way they were perceived globally, especially in the West. It might sound cliché, but the energy and determination that emanated from Tahrir truly moved Arabs to believe in themselves, assert their dignity as citizens, and find the courage to speak truth to power. In the process, they collectively overturned the offensive notion that Arabs were averse to or unready for democracy and exposed it for what it really was: a fallacious argument rooted in a long-standing Orientalist discourse spun by Western imperialists and later adopted by their authoritarian Arab clients to justify subjugating the populations of Arab states. Indeed, if anyone was unprepared for democracy in the Arab world, it was the anciens régimes and their Western democratic patrons, whose hegemony and interests were at stake. While these movements might since have been appropriated or redirected by notably less moral forces, the original impulse that fueled this emancipatory wave was righteous and noble.

The myth that Arabs were innately opposed to freedom and democracy was just one of the many dispelled by images that emanated from Tahrir and other Arab squares. Images of peaceful protesters from all walks of life—young, old, men, women, children, Muslim, Christian, rich, poor, students, professionals, and laborers—working in concert to achieve ideals of dignity, social justice, and self-determination, challenged the prevailing stereotypes that Arabs were angry, violent, and uncivilized. Scenes depicting interfaith community and Christians forming circles around their Muslim brethren while they prayed countered the stereotype that all Arabs were Muslims intolerant of other faiths. Arab women, both veiled and non-veiled, spoke articulately and passionately, led inter-gender protests, and fought against the police, invalidating Western claims that associated them with oppression and subservience. In short, the youth-initiated movement performed an immense service in challenging the perceptions of Arabs and Muslims in Western publics that have led them to support their governments' imperialist policies in the region. Those arresting images will forever continue to undermine the discourses used to legitimize imperialist practices.

One of the greatest achievements of Egypt's revolution was that it politicized and transformed legions of apathetic young people, myself among them. The January 25 uprising snapped me out of my prior political indifference and purged me of the cynical belief that people were powerless to effect real change and overhaul the systems that neglect, marginalize, abuse, and exploit them. Seeing the people of my native Egypt so movingly shed their fear and empower themselves transformed my outlook of what was possible for humanity and invited me to think more positively about my own agency and ability to effect change, as both a scholar and a transnational citizen. It was this newfound sense of obligation that motivated me to pursue this research in 2011 as an expression of my solidarity with my fellow Egyptians and the excluded around the world. My hope is that this book will not only contribute to our understanding of the Egyptian revolution through the stories, hopes, and struggles of the young people who dreamed it up, but also offer lessons in what it takes to build and sustain revolutionary movements in the twenty-first century, and conversely, highlight the challenges and threats that could lead them to unravel.

Will Egypt's revolutionaries win? Not necessarily. In fact, the kind of idealism that spurred them early on is mostly gone now among Egypt's January 25 youth, and perhaps for the better. Their more sober outlook might yield a clearer set of aims and a more strategic approach to their revolutionary politics. In the meantime, Egypt's activists and ordinary citizens will have reasons to keep resisting.

Ultimately, however, no one knows how this story will end. At the time of writing, it is difficult to speak of the revival of the revolutionary movement that was born on January 25, since it has more or less ceased to exist. It is even more challenging when considering how the securitization of the growing conflict between the military and underground groups that supported the ousted president Muhammad Morsi—the "war on terror"—has trumped the importance of real politics for many Egyptians and pushed revolutionaries to the margins, making them and their cause even more irrelevant than they had already become after the June 30 protests. The battlefield has certainly changed, and the entry of new players, the evolving dynamics on the ground, and changing geopolitical constraints could take Egypt and the fight for its emancipation in many different directions. But what we do know from Egypt's trajectory through the revolutionary period is that the future has a way of shifting things around to provide second and third and fourth chances, as if history wants us to get it right. Whatever the outcome, the activists appear to have no regrets about what they started. I posed the question to Abdelrahman specifically: Looking back at all the blood and sacrifice of the last several years, and the personal loss he sustained with the death of his brother and friends and imprisonment of his family members, was January 25 a mistake?

"Absolutely not," he retorted emphatically without a moment's hesitation. The memory of that day seemed to breathe back some of the life that had been drained from him. "It reflects the purest of what's inside us. It's the best thing we ever did.... Even if we did nothing else in our lives but contribute, even in a small way, to the making of January 25—I mean, I don't see that I've really done anything more worthwhile in my life."

The revolutionaries coined a saying, an assertion they repeated as a kind of mantra in the first two and a half years of the struggle whenever reactionary forces challenged their will to see their vision for a brighter Egypt through: *al-thawra mustamirra*, they would say, the revolution continues. Those words have barely been invoked since the tragic turn their movement took in 2013. But who is to say Egyptians will not find a way to make them meaningful once again?

Reference Matter

Appendix

The following is an overview of the data set collected for this study:

- Over sixty recorded hours of in-depth interviews conducted face-to-face with twenty-five youth activists, eighteen men and seven women, in 2011 (including RYC and non-RYC activists). Interviews with the activists ranged between forty five minutes to six hours, and longer sessions were usually conducted in two or three sittings. Follow-up interviews totaling over fifteen recorded hours were conducted by Skype in 2013 and 2014 with five of the ten RYC activists whose narratives are emphasized in this study.

- Over fifteen recorded hours of in-depth interviews conducted face-to-face with ten key informants, five men and five women, including academics, journalists, politicians, human rights activists, and patrons of the RYC. Our discussions covered a range of topics, including the political context around the revolution, historical processes leading up to it, analysis of current events, and their observations of the RYC and its significance.

- Detailed field notes and recordings from over thirty events and actions in which I participated, including youth movement meetings, coalition press conferences, and observations during protests, marches, extended sit-ins, and parliamentary election campaign events for RYC candidates.

- Social media sources, such as the Facebook pages and Twitter feeds of activists; statements issued by the RYC and its member organizations; and secondary media sources like Al Jazeera documentaries and TV talk show programs featuring activists as guest interviewees and commentators.

Notes

Introduction

1. *Amnesty International Report 2012: The State of the World's Human Rights* (London: Amnesty International, 2012), 136.
2. For exceptions, see Jeroen Gunning's and Ilan Zvi Baron's *Why Occupy a Square? People, Protests and Movement in the Egyptian Revolution* (Oxford: Oxford University Press, 2014) and Anne Rennick's *Politics and Revolution in Egypt: Rise and Fall of Youth Activists* (New York, NY: Routledge, 2018).
3. Quintin Hoare and Geoffrey Nowell-Smith, *Selections from the Prison Notebooks* (London: Lawrence and Wishart, 1971), 196–97.
4. Immanuel Wallerstein, "New Revolts against the System," *New Left Review* 18, November–December, 2002; Maha Abdelrahman, *Egypt's Long Revolution: Protest Movements and Uprisings* (New York, NY: Routledge, 2015), 81.
5. Theda Skocpol, *States and Social Revolutions* (Cambridge: Cambridge University Press, 1979), 5.
6. Examples include transitions to democracy in Europe, anti-colonial and anti-dictatorial revolutions in the third world, and Islamic revolutions in the Middle East (Jack Goldstone, "Toward a Fourth Generation of Revolutionary Theory," *Annual Reviews of Political Science* 4 [June 2001]: 141).
7. Goldstone, "Toward a Fourth Generation," 141.
8. Charles Tilly, *From Mobilization to Revolution* (Reading, MA: Addison-Welsley, 1978).
9. Analyzing Tilly's concept of revolution, Jésus de Andrés and Rubén Ruiz Ramas explain, "A revolutionary situation arises from the sum of three causes: the appearance of two or more contending blocs who aspire to control the state, citizen support for this aspiration, and the rulers' inability to suppress the alternative coalition. A revolutionary outcome results when a transfer of power takes place—from the hands of those who had it before a situation of multiple sovereignty arose—leading to a new governing coalition. Hence, Tilly's main contribution is his characterization of revolution as a political event, a perspective which would deprive the great revolutions of their conceptual monopolization of the term" (Jesus De Andrés and Rubén Ramas, "Charles Tilly's Concept of *Revolution* and the '*Color Revolutions*,'"

in *Regarding Tilly: Conflict, Power, and Collective Action*, edited by Maria J. Funes [Lanham: University Press of America], 2016, 137).
10 See Gilbert Achcar, *The People Want: A Radical Exploration of the Arab Uprisings*, trans. G.M. Goshgarian (Berkeley, CA: University of California Press, 2013); De Smet, *A Dialectical Pedagogy of Revolt; Gramsci, Vygtosky, and the Egyptian Revolution* (Leiden: Brill, 2014); Asef Bayat, *Revolution without Revolutionaries: Making Sense of the Arab Spring* (Stanford, CA: Stanford University Press, 2017). In his analysis of the Egyptian revolution, Brecht De Smet makes the distinction between the "*object* produced by mass political activity" and the "*activity itself*" as a way of separating between process and outcome. For him, the emergence of *al-sha'b* (the people) as a new collective subjectivity is what makes this activity revolutionary (De Smet, *A Dialectical Pedagogy of Revolt*, 105). As for Asef Bayat, his analysis of the revolutionary movement led him to coin the term "refolution" to capture its peculiar nature: "revolutionary in terms of movement and mass mobilization, but reformist in terms of strategy and change" (Bayat, *Revolution without Revolutionaries*, 159).
11 Jack Goldstone, *Revolutions: A Very Short Introduction* (Oxford: Oxford University Press, 2014), 21–23.
12 Eric Selbin, "Revolution in the Real World: Bringing Agency Back In," in *Theorizing Revolutions*, edited by John Foran (London: Routledge, 2005), 121 (emphasis added).
13 Selbin, "Revolution in the Real World," 118.
14 Some of the most notable of these organizations include the Hisham Mubarak Law Center, the Nadim Center, and the Egyptian Initiative for Human Rights.
15 Alan D. Morris and Suzanne Staggenborg, "Leadership in Social Movements," in *The Blackwell Companion to Social Movements*, edited by D. Snow, S. Soule, and H. Kriesi (Malden, MA: Blackwell Publishing, 2004), 171.
16 Goldstone, "Toward a Fourth Generation," 157; Aminzade et al., "Leadership Dynamics and Dynamics of Contention," in *Silence and Voice in the Study of Contentious Politics*, edited by Ronald Aminzade et al. (New York, NY: Cambridge University Press, 2011), 129–33; Sharon Erickson Nepstad and Clifford Bob, "When Do Leaders Matter? Hypothesis on Leadership Dynamics in Social Movements," *Mobilization: An International Journal* 11, no. 1 (February 2006): 3–4. Some scholars believe these two forms of leadership can be combined in one individual; others see that two or more individuals or groups are generally required to fill these visionary organizer roles, though in practice the division of tasks might not always be clearly distinguishable (Goldstone, "Toward a Fourth Generation," 157).
17 Marshall Ganz and Liz McKenna, "The Practice of Social Movement Leadership," *Mobilizing Ideas*, June 23, 2017.
18 Max Weber, "The Types of Authority and Imperative Coordination," in *The Theory of Social and Economic Organization*, edited by T. Parsons (New York, NY: Free Press, 1964), 324–423; Todd Gitlin, *The Whole World is*

Watching: Mass Media and the Making and Unmaking of the New Left (Berkeley, CA: University of California Press, 1980); Jo Freeman, "The Tyranny of Structurelessness," in *Radical Feminism*, edited by Anne Koedt, Ellene Levine, and Anita Rapone (New York, NY: Quadrangle, 1972), 285–99; Helen Brown, "Organizing Activity in the Women's Movement: An Example of Distributed Leadership," *International Social Movement Research* 2 (1989): 225–40; Belinda Robnett, *How Long? How Long? African-American Women in the Struggle for Civil Rights* (New York, NY: Oxford University Press, 1997); Ann Herda-Rapp, "The Power of Informal Leadership: Women Leaders in the Civil Rights Movement," *Sociological Focus* 31, no. 4 (November 1998): 341–55; Ganz and McKenna, "The Practice of Social Movement Leadership"; Jennifer Leigh Disney and Joyce Gelb, "Feminist Organizational 'Success': The State of US Women's Movement Organizations in the 1990s," *Women and Politics* 21, no. 4 (October 2008): 39–76; Simon Western, "Autonomist Leadership in Leaderless Movements: Anarchists Leading the Way," *Ephemera* 14, no. 4 (November 2014): 673–98; Goldstone, "Toward a Fourth Generation"; Marshall Ganz, *Why David Sometimes Wins: Leadership, Organization, and Strategy in the California Farm Worker Movement* (Oxford: Oxford University Press, 2010).

19 Colin Barker, Alan Johnson, and Michael Lavalette, "Leadership Matters: An Introduction," in *Leadership in Social Movements*, edited by Colin Barker, Alan Johnson, and Michael Lavalette (Manchester: Manchester University Press, 2001), 16.
20 Robnett, *How Long? How Long?*; Morris and Staggenborg, "Leadership in Social Movements," 177.
21 Morris and Staggenborg, "Leadership in Social Movements," 174–75. Of course, this is not to say that all movement leaders have university degrees or even high school diplomas. See chapters 5 and 6 for more on this subject.
22 Since the activists I profile in this book are all Muslim (see the section on my sample in chapter 1 for my reasons), the focus of this study is on Muslim religiosity, but this is not to diminish the experience of Coptic youth activists and how their religion might have informed their ideologies and participation in the revolution.
23 Goldstone, "Toward a Fourth Generation."
24 João Biehl, Byron Good, and Arthur Kleinman, "Introduction: Rethinking Subjectivity," in *Subjectivity: Ethnographic Investigations*, edited by João Biehl, Byron Good, and Arthur Kleinman (Berkeley: University of California Press, 2007), 6.
25 Sherry B. Ortner, *Anthropology and Social Theory: Culture, Power, and the Acting Subject* (Durham, NC: Duke University Press, 2006), 107.
26 Ortner, *Anthropology and Social Theory*, 110.
27 R.W. Connell, *Masculinities* (Berkeley, CA: University of California Press, 2005), 35.
28 For excellent examples of how this gendering dynamic plays out in other movements, see Say Burgin, "Understanding Antiwar Activism as a

Gendering Activity: A Look at the U.S. Anti-Vietnam War Movement," *Journal of International Women's Studies* 13, no. 6 (December 2012): 18–31; Julia Peteet, "Male Gender and Rituals of Resistance in the Palestinian *Intifada*: A Cultural Politics of Violence," *American Ethnologist* 21, no. 1 (February 1994): 31–49.

29 Connell, *Masculinities*, 43.
30 Ted Swedenburg, "Imagined Youths," *Middle East Research and Information Project* 245 (Winter 2007); Asef Bayat, "Muslim Youth and the Claim of Youthfulness," in *Being Young and Muslim: New Cultural Politics in the Global South and North*, edited by Asef Bayat and Linda Herrera (Oxford: Oxford University Press, 2010), 6–7.
31 Diane Singerman, "The Negotiation of Waithood: The Political Economy of Delayed Marriage in Egypt," in *Arab Youth: Social Mobilization in Times of Risk*, edited by S. Khalaf and R. Khalaf (London: Saqi Books, 2011), 67.
32 Karl Mannheim, "The Problem of Generations," in *Essays on the Sociology of Knowledge*, edited by P. Kecskemeti (London: Routledge and Kegan Paul, 1952), 276–322.
33 Mannheim, "The Problem of Generations," 291.
34 Mannheim, "The Problem of Generations," 302-304.
35 Herrera, "Youth and Citizenship in the Digital Age: A View from Egypt," *Harvard Educational Review* 82, no. 3 (September 2012): 333–52.
36 Constance A. Flanagan and Amy K. Syversten, "Youth as Social Construct and Social Actor," in *Youth Activism: An International Encyclopedia*, vol. 1, edited by Lonne R. Sherrod (Westport, CT: Greenwood Press, 2006), 17.
37 Mannheim, "The Problem of Generations," 294.
38 Mannheim, "The Problem of Generations," 303.
39 Mannheim, "The Problem of Generations," 304.

Chapter 1

1 I decided on an ethnographic methodological approach for my inquiry for a number of reasons. First, given my research interest in how youth were operating as leaders in the revolution and the transformations they went through as its proponents, it made sense to study them ethnographically, that is, in real time in the revolutionary context they helped engineer. In this sense, an ethnographic approach would provide me with a richer, more holistic perspective by allowing me to engage with the revolution and experience its effects as a researcher and a participant as I observed my interlocutors in it. Second, this perspective would also be enriched by the flexibility and multiple methods at the disposal of an ethnographer, such as interviewing, participant observation, and the use of secondary sources. Lastly, it would allow me to reflect the most important issues emerging from the field by providing a platform for my respondents from which to project their voice and tell their story.
2 My initial sampling process was necessarily biased because I had relied, in the beginning, on English-language media sources. Given that I was

largely following English news sources and Tweets, my preliminary list of potential interview subjects was limited to English speakers. In Egypt, as in most developing countries, English proficiency indicates a certain level of privilege. In other words, my initial sampling was biased because it excluded from my list the names of those who only spoke and tweeted in Arabic and were mentioned in Arabic media only. These activists would likely have come from more varied class backgrounds and have had more diverse histories and narratives. Evidently, this bias needed adjusting.

3   For example, impressing one of my activist acquaintances from Imbaba with the intimate knowledge of children's street games I had gained in my parents' village when I was young helped take our relationship to the level of friendship.

4   I recall how a misuse of some Arabic words sent my new acquaintances into uproarious laughter. Apparently, I reminded them of an iconic character from a popular contemporary film called *'Asal iswid* who had, like me, lived most of his life in the United States, only to suffer the consequences upon his return to Egypt for being out of the loop for so long.

5   Disencounters are failed encounters, which "lack mutual resonance and shared understandings of what is at stake in the encounter" (Astrid B. Stensrud, "'You Cannot Contradict the Engineer': Disencounters of Modern Technology, Climate Change, and Power in the Peruvian Andes" *Critique of Anthropology* 39, no. 4 [2019]: 422).

6   Mona Abaza, "Academic Tourists Sight-Seeing the Arab Spring," *Ahram Online*, September 26, 2011.

7   These events included the Israeli embassy protests in September, the Maspero Massacre in October, the Muhammad Mahmud Street clashes in November highlighted in the Introduction, the Cabinet clashes in December, and the chaotic parliamentary elections and campaigning that spanned all of these months.

8   For a good discussion on the history of Egyptian anxieties about the foreign threat, see Bel Trew, "The Third Man: Egyptian Fears of the Foreign Plot," *Ahram Online*, February 24, 2012.

9   The Occupy Movement was a progressive sociopolitical movement that began as a protest in Zuccotti Park in Manhattan, New York, and quickly spread across the US and around the world. The movement drew inspiration from the Egyptian Revolution. In particular, the practice of occupying public spaces as a protest tactic was modeled on the occupation of Tahrir. The movement's demands were many, but among its chief concerns was the concentration of wealth in the pockets of the top 1 percent of income earners compared to the bottom 99 percent, as well as the corrosive influence of big money on the political process. The pepper-spray incident took place at UC Davis on November 18, 2011, during a student-organized Occupy protest. After asking a group of protesters sitting on a paved path several times to disperse, university police pepper-sprayed them in the face. The video footage went viral and sparked a heated public debate about the militarization

of the police, a theme that resonated with the Egyptian experience. The incident spoke to the shared struggles of citizens of the Global North and Global South under the neoliberal order. See Sunaina Maira and Julie Sze, "Dispatches from Pepper-Spray University: Privatization, Repression, and Revolt," *American Quarterly* 64, no. 2 (2012): 315–30.

10   I was, however, able to refer to Wael Ghonim's memoir *Revolution 2.0: The Power of the People is Greater than the People in Power* (Boston, MA: Houghton Mifflin Harcourt, 2012), which was published after my requests for an interview.

11   I echo the sentiments that anthropologist Nadine Naber expresses in her book after she shares the story of an important respondent who refused to sit with her for follow-up interviews following September 11, 2001. Discussing the implications of this missing narrative for her work, she says, "My book is less compelling without her voice, but her decision contains its own power and makes its own statement" (Nadine Naber, *Arab America: Gender, Cultural Politics, and Activism* New York, NY: [New York University Press, 2012], 24). The statement made by the absence of Sally's voice from my book speaks to the intensity of the revolutionary setting and the emotional toll it took on activists, particularly women like herself, as discussed in chapter 5.

12   As prominent activists who were widely known during the revolutionary period due to the frequent media attention they received, they saw no need to conceal their identities. Their concern for preserving the historical record trumped any safety concerns.

Chapter 2

1   Zeinab Abul-Magd, "Understanding SCAF," *The Cairo Review of Global Affairs*, Summer 2012.

2   Bruce Rutherford, *Egypt after Mubarak: Liberalism, Islam, and Democracy in the Arab World* (Princeton, NJ: Princeton University Press, 2008), 135.

3   Raymond A. Hinnebusch, "The Foreign Policy of Egypt," in *The Foreign Policy of Middle East States*, edited by Raymond A. Hinnebusch and Anoushiravan Ehteshami (Boulder, CO: Lynne Rienner Publishers, 2002), 96; Rutherford, *Egypt after Mubarak*, 135.

4   William Joseph Burns, *Economic Aid and American Policy Toward Egypt, 1955–1981* (Albany, NY: State of New York Press, 1985), 181; John Waterbury, *The Egypt of Nasser and Sadat: The Political Economy of Two Regimes* (Princeton, NJ: Princeton University Press, 1983), 134; Hazem Kandil, *Soldiers, Spies, and Statesmen: Egypt's Road to Revolt* (London: Verso, 2012), 148.

5   Tarek Masoud, "Egypt," in *The Middle East*, edited by Ellen Lust (Los Angeles, CA: Sage CQ Press, 2013), 455; Raymond A. Hinnebusch, *Egyptian Politics under Sadat* (Cambridge: Cambridge University Press, 1985), 59. Sadat introduced a more liberal constitution, eliminated Nasser's totalitarian single-party system, and legalized political parties. As part of his political posturing, he also changed the name of the ruling party from the Arab Socialist Union to the National Democratic Party.

6 Waterbury, *The Egypt of Nasser and Sadat*, 134.
7 Dina Jadallah, "Economic Aid to Egypt: Promoting Progress or Subordination?" *Class, Race and Corporate Power* 3, no. 2 (2015).
8 Jadallah, "Economic Aid to Egypt"; Kandil, *Soldiers, Spies, and Statesmen*, 163.
9 Jadallah, "Economic Aid to Egypt."
10 Steven A. Cook, *The Struggle for Egypt* (Oxford: Oxford University Press, 2012), 232, 241. This was because the trilateral arrangement that constrained Egypt and curtailed its foreign policy enabled Israel to pursue its regional agenda at will. In the face of Israel's regional aggression—including two invasions of Lebanon, attacks on Iraq and Syria, the country's rapid growth of settlements in the Gaza Strip and West Bank, and the human suffering it inflicted with the killing and imprisonment of countless Palestinian men, women, and children—Egypt was powerless to act, lest such action jeopardize the flow of US funds (Cook, *The Struggle for Egypt*, 232, 302).
11 Tarek Osman, *Egypt on the Brink: From the Rise of Nasser to the Fall of Mubarak* (New Haven, CT: Yale University Press, 2011), 130–34; Omnia El-Shakry, "Egypt's Three Revolutions: The Force of History Behind This Popular Uprising," *Jadaliyya*, February 6, 2011; Hinnebusch, *Egyptian Politics Under Sadat*, 265–72.
12 Osman, *Egypt on the Brink*, 136.
13 Nadia Ramsis Farah, *Egypt's Political Economy: Power Relations in Development* (Cairo: The American University in Cairo Press, 2009), 42.
14 Angela Joya, "The Egyptian Revolution: Crisis of Neoliberalism and the Potential for Democratic Politics," *Review of African Political Economy* 38, no. 129 (September 2011): 374.
15 A. Hanieh, "Egypt's Orderly Transition: International Aid and the Rush to Structural Adjustment," in *The Dawn of the Arab Uprisings: End of an Old Order?*, edited by B. Haddad, R. Bsheer, and Z. Abu-Rish (London: Pluto Press, 2012), 24.
16 Joya, "The Egyptian Revolution," 374; United Nations Development Programme (UNDP), *Human Development Report 2007/2008*, 239.
17 Jason Brownlee, *Authoritarianism in an Age of Democratization* (New York, NY: Cambridge University Press, 2007), 124–25; Brownlee, "Democratization in the Arab World?" *Journal of Democracy* 13, no. 4 (October 2002): 7; Anthony McDermott, *Egypt from Nasser to Mubarak: A Flawed Revolution* (New York: Routledge, 1988), 75–77; Dalia Dassa Kaye et al., *More Freedom, Less Terror: Liberalization and Political Violence in the Middle East* (Pittsburgh, PA: Rand Corporation, 2008), 29–30.
18 Osman, *Egypt on the Brink*, 186; Dina Shehata, *Islamists and Secularists in Egypt: Opposition, Conflict, and Cooperation* (New York, NY: Routledge, 2009), 33–34.
19 Maye Kassem, *Egyptian Politics: The Dynamics of Authoritarian Rule* (Boulder, CO: Lynne Rienner Publishers, 2004), 55–57.
20 Robert Springborg, *Mubarak's Egypt: Fragmentation of the Political Order* (New York: Routledge, 2018), 184; Shehata, *Islamists and Secularists in Egypt*, 33–34;

Lisa Blaydes, *Elections and Distributive Politics in Mubarak's Egypt* (Cambridge: Cambridge University Press, 2010), 41; Kassem, *Egyptian Politics*, 55–59.
21 Mathieu Gudière, *Historical Dictionary of Islamic Fundamentalism* (Lanham, MD: Rowman and LittleField Publishing Group, Inc., 2012), 103–104.
22 Yasmine Fathi, "Torture in Egypt: Never Again?" *Ahram Online*, June 25, 2011. This security system was in part buttressed by the United States, which relied on Egypt to carry out the CIA's extraordinary renditions program. See Jane Mayer, "Outsourcing Torture," *The New Yorker*, February 6, 2005; Armit Singh, "Globalizing Torture: CIA Secret Detention and Extraordinary Rendition"; "Extraordinary Rendition in U.S. Counterterrorism Policy: The Impact on Transatlantic Relations," Joint Hearing before the Subcommittee on International Organizations, Human Rights, and Oversight and the Subcommittee on Europe of the Committee on Foreign Affairs, One Hundred Tenth Congress, April 17, 2007.
23 Kassem, *Egyptian Politics*, 112.
24 Osman, *Egypt on the Brink*, 85.
25 Mona Attia, *Building a House in Heaven: Pious Neoliberalism and Islamic Charity in Egypt* (Minneapolis: University of Minnesota Press, 2013), 42.
26 Attia, *Building a House in Heaven*, 43–44; Nancy J. Davis and Robert V. Robinson, *Claiming Society for God: Religious Movements and Social Welfare* (Bloomington: Indiana University Press, 2012), 33–36.
27 Hesham Al-Awadi, "Mubarak and the Islamists: Why Did the 'Honeymoon' End?" *Middle East Journal* 59, no. 1 (Winter 2005): 62–63, 74–77; Shehata, *Islamists and Secularists in Egypt*, 54; Osman, *Egypt on the Brink*, 93; Brooke, *Winning Hearts and Votes*, 49–55; Davis and Robinson, *Claiming Society for God*, 33.
28 For more on the Muslim Brotherhood's history with violence and representative politics, see Tarek Masoud, "The Muslim Brotherhood in Egypt," in *The Oxford Handbook of Islam and Politics*, edited by John L. Esposito and Emad El-Din Shahin (Oxford: Oxford University Press, 2013), 475–505.
29 Osman, *Egypt on the Brink*, 184.
30 Davis and Robinson, *Claiming Society for God*, 33, 49.
31 The idea behind Mubarak's expansion and empowerment of the internal security forces was not just to protect the regime from a challenge to its rule from below; the president, like his predecessors, saw the need to build the security apparatus into a loyal power center that could rival the mighty military establishment and protect him from being undermined by it. It is worth noting, as Shafeeq Ghabra points out, "that in the early 1980s, the army was 1.5 million strong, while internal security and the police numbered 250,000; but as the 2011 revolution approached, the army consisted of 250,000 troops and the security forces 1.5 million men" (Shafeeq Ghabra, "The Egyptian Revolution: Causes and Dynamics," in *Routledge Handbook of the Arab Spring*, edited by Larbi Sidki [New York, NY: Routledge, 2015], 200).
32 Kandil, *Soldiers, Spies, and Statesmen*, 218.

33 Hossam El-Hamalawy, "Egypt's Revolution Has Been 10 Years in the Making," *The Guardian*, March 2, 2011.
34 For a more detailed exploration of the genealogy of the January 25 revolt, specifically how the different waves of protest movements built on each other's tactics and frames, see Jeroen Gunning and Ilan Zvi Baron, *Why Occupy a Square? People, Protests and Movement in the Egyptian Revolution* (Oxford: Oxford University Press, 2014) and Maha Abdelrahman, *Egypt's Long Revolution: Protest Movements and Uprisings* (New York, NY: Routledge, 2015).
35 El-Hamalawy, "Egypt's Revolution Has Been 10 Years in the Making."
36 Shehata, "al-Harakat al-shababiya wa thawrat 25 yanayir," *Strategy Paper Series* 218. Cairo: Al-Ahram Center for Political and Strategic Studies, 2011.
37 Sherif Mansour, "Enough Is Not Enough: Achievements and Shortcomings of Kefaya, the Egyptian Movement for Change," in *Civilian Jihad: Nonviolent Struggle, Democratization, and Governance in the Middle East*, edited by Maria J. Stephan (New York, NY: Palgrave McMillan, 2009), 207.
38 Mansour, "Enough Is Not Enough," 207.
39 Nasser initiated the dramatic expansion of Egypt's public sector following his confirmation as president in 1956. It was the cornerstone of his state development project, which involved nationalizing private factories and industries and creating new ones. During this time, the military assumed management of these new state-owned enterprises as the protectors of the people's wealth, and it was through this new positioning that they began to appropriate public wealth through unethical means and build the vast business empire they maintain today. For more on the military and its entrenchment in the public sector and economy, see Shana Marshall, "The Egyptian Armed Forces and the Remaking of an Empire," Carnegie Middle East Center, April 2015.
40 Zeinab Abul-Magd, "Understanding SCAF," *The Cairo Review of Global Affairs*, Summer 2012; Zeinab Abul-Magd, *Militarizing the Nation: The Army, Business, and Revolution in Egypt* (New York, NY: Columbia University Press, 2017).
41 Nathan J. Brown and Hesham Nasr, "Egypt's Judges Step Forward: The Judicial Election Boycott and Egyptian Reform," Carnegie Endowment for International Peace, Policy Outlook, May 13, 2005.
42 Rabab El-Mahdi, "Does Political Islam Impede Gender-Based Mobilization?" *Totalitarian Movement and Political Religions* 11, no. 3–4 (2010): 385.
43 The Women for Democracy Movement was short-lived. For a detailed discussion of what led to its dissolution, see El-Mahdi, "Does Political Islam Impede Gender-Based Mobilization?"
44 Fawaz A. Gerges, *Obama and the Middle East: The End of America's Moment?* (New York: St. Martin's Press, 2012), 162; Juan Cole, "Democratisation, Religious Extremism, Fragile States, and Insurgencies: Bush's Legacies to Obama and the Challenges Ahead," in *American Democracy Promotion in the*

Changing Middle East: From Bush to Obama, edited by Shahram Akbarzadeh et al., (London and New York: Routledge, 2013), 11–12.
45 Mansour, "Enough is Not Enough," 211.
46 Shehata, "al-Harakat al-shababiya wa thawrat 25 yanayir."
47 Mansour, "Enough Is Not Enough," 208.
48 Leading the stoppage was a charge of three thousand women garment makers, in keeping with the long tradition of women's active participation at the forefront of movements dating back to the nationalist struggle in the early 1900s. The women shamed their male coworkers into joining them, quickly energizing the mill's twenty-seven thousand employees to take part in their industrial action (Hossam El-Hamalawy, "Resistance in Egypt," *MR Online*, August 18, 2008).
49 El-Hamalawy, "Resistance in Egypt"; Hossam El-Hamalawy, "Revolt in Mahallah: As Food Prices Rise in Egypt, Class Struggle Is Heating Up," *International Socialist Review* no. 59 (May–June 2008).
50 Hossam El-Hamalawy, "Egyptian Strikes: More Than Bread and Butter," *Socialist Review* no. 325 (2008).
51 Mansour, "Enough Is Not Enough," 214
52 El-Hamalawy, "Revolt in Mahallah."
53 The 2006 and 2008 industrial actions in Mahalla were part of a larger wave of labor strikes that brought out as many as two million workers between 2001 and 2008 (Kandil, *Soldiers, Spies, and Statesmen*, 217).
54 Shehata, "al-Harakat al-shababiya wa thawrat 25 yanayir."
55 Shehata, "al-Harakat al-shababiya wa thawrat 25 yanayir."
56 For an excellent discussion of the "loyal opposition" and the Mubarak regime's co-optation of political parties, see Holger Albrecht, *Raging against the Machine: Political Opposition under Authoritarianism in Egypt* (Syracuse, NY: Syracuse University Press, 2013), 38–59.
57 The seven demands for change were articulated by the Muslim Brotherhood and adopted by the National Association for Change (NAC) headed by ElBaradei. They included the following demands: "(1) Ending the state of emergency; (2) The empowerment of the Egyptian judiciary to supervise the full electoral process; (3) Monitoring of the elections by local and international civil society organizations; (4) Providing equal opportunities in the media for all candidates, especially in the presidential elections; (5) Enabling Egyptians abroad to exercise their right to vote in embassies and consulates of Egypt; (6) Ensuring the right to run for presidential elections without arbitrary restrictions, in line with Egypt's obligations under the International Convention for Civil and Political Rights and limiting the right to run for presidency to only two terms; (7) Elections by individual identifying social numbers" (Hussein Mahmoud, "MB and NAC's Petition 7 Demands for Change Approaches 1,000,000 Signatures Target," *Ikhwan Web*, October 5, 2010).

58 Much has been said about the mythologization of Khaled Said. See Amro Ali, "Saeeds of Revolution: De-Mythologizing Khaled Saeed," *Jadaliyya*, June 4, 2012.

59 Rabab El-Mahdi, "Against Marginalization: Workers, Youth and Class in the 25 January Revolution," in *Marginality and Exclusion in Egypt*, edited by Ray Bush and Habib Ayeb, (London: Zed Books, 2012), 139–40.

60 "Khaled Saeed: The Face That Launched a Revolution," *Ahram Online*, June 6, 2012.

61 Ashraf Khalil, *Liberation Square: Inside the Egyptian Revolution and the Rebirth of a Nation* (New York, NY: St. Martin's Press, 2011), 22.

62 Shereen El Feki, Farzaneh Roudi-Fahimi, and Tyjen Tsai, "Youth Revolt in Egypt, a Country at the Turning Point," *Population Reference Bureau*, 2011.

Chapter 3

1 Catharine Smith, "Egypt's Facebook Revolution: Wael Ghonim Thanks the Social Network," *Huffington Post*, February 11, 2011; Jose A. Vargas, "Spring Awakening: How an Egyptian Revolution Began on Facebook," *The New York Times*, February 17, 2012.

2 Giza borders Cairo along the western bank of the Nile River and is considered part of Greater Cairo.

3 Amr made a point of emphasizing that he intentionally chose law as a field of study because of its importance, not because his high school scores were not high enough for entry into more prestigious degree programs like medicine or engineering. Law had once been the most prestigious field of study before Nasser restructured the education system to serve his industrial revolution. Two important educational reforms stand out: (1) the prestige ranking of fields of study based on the needs of development and (2) the admission of students into them based on their general secondary exam scores rather than their career interests. This new system ranked "practical" faculties (colleges or departments), like medicine and engineering, at the top while relegating "theoretical" ones, like the social sciences and the once-proud law faculty, to the bottom. It also gave high-scoring students first choice in choosing their fields, which consistently reflected a preference for sciences because of its better career prospects. As a result of these reforms, the theoretical faculties became exceedingly overcrowded and, consequently, experienced the most significant decline in academic standards (Donald Malcolm Reid, *Cairo University and the Making of Modern Egypt* [Cambridge: Cambridge University Press, 1990], 15, 181–84, 189–92).

4 In the months after the fall of Mubarak, differences between activists in April 6 led to a split in the organization. The April 6 Movement Democratic Front was established in April 2011 by members who disagreed with some of the movement's leaders over their plans to turn April 6 into an NGO, a decision they criticized because it was not reached democratically. Amr and Tarek were among those who initiated the split.

5   In Egypt, it is common for parents to seek after-school private tutoring for their children. In fact, much of student learning tends to take place in these lessons, not in the classroom. The widespread practice is a symptom of the failing school system in which low-paid teachers provide a substandard education to students who are already disadvantaged by overcrowded classrooms. Often, the classroom teachers work as tutors to make up for their low pay, and many even intentionally reduce the quality of their classroom teaching to force students, directly or indirectly, to seek out their private lessons. Because academic success for students has come to depend on securing a good tutor, poor parents feel the same need as wealthy ones to enlist tutors for their children in the hopes of helping them to get ahead. Of course, this places an extra burden on the poor and contributes to the reproduction of class inequality (Sarah Ahmed Abdel Aziz, "Public Education and Private Tuitions: A System of Inadequacy," *Daily News Egypt*, December 26, 2015). See also Sarah Hartmann, "The Informal Market of Education in Egypt: Private Tutoring and Its Implications," Working Paper No. 88 (Mainz, Germany: Institut für Ethnologie und Afrikastudien, Johannes Gutenberg-Universität, 2008) and Sebastian Ille, "Private Tutoring in Egypt: Quality Education in a Deadlock between Low Income, Status, and Motivation," Working Paper No. 178, The Egyptian Center for Economic Studies, 2015.

6   Sadat's *infitah* program enabled Egyptians to travel more freely, and many went to the Gulf to work, where they reaped the rewards of the oil boom as laborers. It is worth noting that the remittances from these migrants decimated the purchasing power of those living in Egypt, contributing to the economic crisis that plunged many Egyptians into poverty.

7   David Sims, "The Arab Housing Paradox," *The Cairo Review of Global Affairs*, November 24, 2013.

8   Sofia Fenner and Mohamed Talaat, "Shaabi Cairo after June 30th: The View from Shubra," *Muftah*, November 14, 2013.

9   Marion Séjourné, "The History of Informal Settlements," in *Cairo's Informal Areas Between Urban Challenges and Hidden Potentials: Fact. Voices. Visions* (Cairo: German Technical Cooperation [GTZ], 2009), 17.

10 Elena Piferro, "Beyond Rules and Regulations: The Growth of Informal Cairo," in *Cairo's Informal Areas Between Urban Challenges and Hidden Potentials: Fact. Voices. Visions* (Cairo: German Technical Cooperation [GTZ], 2009), 22–23.

11 A prime example was Sadat's 1977 New Towns policy, which shifted government investment from the construction of affordable rental housing to the development of low-income homes for sale in new towns on the desert fringes of the city. The goal was to address the housing crisis and rescue agricultural land from urbanization, but the effort was largely unsuccessful. The high costs of homes in these towns, their lack of services, and their distance from the economic opportunities in the city center were no incentive for low-income and poor families (Séjourné, "The

History of Informal Settlements," 18–19). At the same time, state-imposed rent controls also led the private sector to withdraw from the production of rental housing and begin catering exclusively to the preferences of the upper class in the form of semi-luxury homes (Christian Arandel and Manal El Batran, "A Shelter of Their Own: Informal Settlement Expansion in Greater Cairo and Government Responses," *Environment and Urbanization* 10, no. 1 [April 1998]: 219; Piferro, "Beyond Rules and Regulations," 23). Meanwhile, the government failed to plan for the remittances flowing into Egypt from migrants to the Gulf who were reaping the rewards of the oil-boom as laborers, thanks to the *infitah* policy that permitted them to travel more freely. Discouraged by the strict planning and construction regulations surrounding formal real estate, they invested their savings in informal land and housing development (Arandel and El Batran, "A Shelter of Their Own," 219–20).

12 Piferro, "Beyond Rules and Regulations," 21.
13 Built during the Nasser era to house government bureaucrats and their families, the Ramses district today is a dense, popular area.
14 Salwa Ismail, "The Egyptian Revolution against the Police," *Social Research* 79, no. 2 (Summer 2012): 435–62.
15 Leela Jacinto, "Enter the 'Baltagiya': Egypt's Repression Spills Out of the Torture Chambers," *France24*, February 9, 2011.
16 Ismail, "The Egyptian Revolution against the Police," 443.
17 Ismail, "The Egyptian Revolution against the Police," 443.
18 Salwa Ismail, *Political Life in Cairo's Popular Quarters: Encountering the Everyday State* (Minneapolis, MN: The University of Minnesota Press, 2006), 13.
19 Stefan Malthaner, *Mobilizing the Faithful: Militant Islamist Groups and Their Constituencies* (Frankfurt: Campus Verlag Publishers, 2011), 127.
20 Ahmed Abdalla, *The Student Movements and National Politics in Egypt 1923–1973* (London: Al Saqi Books, 1985), 80–98, 119–137, 151–53; Betty Anderson, "The Student Movement in 1968," *Jadaliyya*, March 9, 2011.
21 Abdalla, *The Student Movements and National Politics in Egypt*, 189–92, 226–30.
22 Hesham Al-Awadi, *In Pursuit of Legitimacy: The Muslim Brothers and Mubarak, 1982–2000* (London: I.B.Tauris, 2004).
23 For more on this, see Hossam El-Hamalawy, "Comrades and Brothers," *Middle East Report* 242 (Spring 2007).
24 Dina Shehata, "Youth Movements and the 25 January Revolution," in *Arab Spring in Egypt: Revolution and Beyond*, edited by Bahgat Korany and Rabab El-Mahdi (Cairo: The American University in Cairo Press, 2012), 111.
25 "Al-Wafd Party," *Jadaliyya*, November 18, 2011.
26 Dina Jadallah, "Economic Aid to Egypt: Promoting Progress or Subordination?" *Class, Race and Corporate Power* 3, no. 2 (2015). A twenty-year contract was signed in 2005 guaranteeing the Egyptian provision of natural gas to Israel, but it was terminated early in April 2012 over a payment dispute. The agreement was highly controversial among Egyptians, who were upset that the gas was sold to Israel at rates significantly below international

market prices. This was all the more exasperating considering that Egypt itself was struggling with a growing natural gas crisis, which is what was leading to Egypt's electricity troubles in the form of power blackouts. It is worth noting that the gas pipes running through the Sinai desert to Israel were blown up by Egyptian insurgents at least fourteen times following the January 25 uprising. See Harriet Sherwood, "Egypt Cancels Israeli Gas Contract," *The Guardian*, April 23, 2012.

27 See note 57, chapter 2, for a list of the seven demands for change.
28 Sam Gustin, "Social Media Sparked, Accelerated Egypt's Revolutionary Fire," *Wired*, February 11, 2011.
29 Atef Said, "The Tahrir Effect: History, Space, and Protest in the Egyptian Revolution," unpublished PhD Thesis, University of Michigan, 2014, 81.
30 For more on this, see Marc Lynch, "Young Brothers in Cyberspace," *Middle East Report* 245 (Winter 2007).
31 Linda Herrera, *Revolution in the Age of Social Media: The Egyptian Popular Insurrection and the Internet* (Brooklyn, NY: Verso, 2014); Jeroen Gunning and Ilan Zvi Baron, *Why Occupy a Square? People, Protests and Movement in the Egyptian Revolution* (Oxford: Oxford University Press, 2014); Paolo Gerbaudo, *Tweets and the Streets: Social Media and Contemporary Activism* (London: Pluto Press, 2012); Said, *The Tahrir Effect*; Wael Ghonim, *Revolution 2.0: The Power of the People is Greater than the People in Power: A Memoir* (Boston, MA: Houghton Mifflin Harcourt, 2012).
32 In his famous *Prison Notebooks*, Antonio Gramsci differentiates between "traditional intellectuals," those who incorrectly imagine themselves as an autonomous, separate class from the rest of society, and "organic intellectuals," that is, the thinking members that emerge from the ranks of each class organically. We can think of them as intellectuals or professionals (that is, doctors, lawyers, teachers, and so on) who rise to their level "from within a social class that does not normally produce intellectuals, and remain connected to that class. In other words . . . they are not upwardly mobile and their concern is for the conditions of their class as a whole, not for themselves" (Ian Buchanan, *A Dictionary of Critical Thinking* [Oxford: Oxford University Press, 2010], 353). For more on how the concept of organic intellectuals fits into Gramsci's ideas for revolutionary strategizing, see note 63, chapter 7.
33 Imam Muhammad Ahmad Eissa, or Shaykh Imam (1918–95), was a famous singer and composer who was known for his political songs celebrating the poor and working class. He frequently performed with the folk poet Ahmed Fouad Negm (1929–2014). Both are seen as icons of political resistance in Egypt.
34 Marwa Awad and Hudo Dixon, "Special Report: Inside the Egyptian Revolution," *Reuters*, April 13, 2011.

Chapter 4

1. Simply defined, we can understand spontaneous activity as "unpremeditated events beyond human control" and conscious activity as "carried out in conformity with previously determined goals" (A.M. Prokhorov, ed., *The Great Soviet Encyclopedia* [New York, NY: Macmillan, 1974–83, 1979]).
2. Though these Marxist theorists were speaking in terms of class struggle and the proletarian revolution, their ideas are still relevant for the Egyptian case, which encompassed the middle as well as the working class.
3. Vladimir Lenin, *What Is to Be Done?* trans. S.V. Utechin and Patricia Utechin (Oxford: Oxford University Press, 1963).
4. Lenin makes the distinction between trade-union consciousness and revolutionary consciousness in his discussion on the need for outside leaders, or intellectuals, for revolutionary movements. Speaking in terms of class struggle, he argued that "the working class, solely by its own forces, is able to work out merely a trade-union consciousness, ie. the conviction of the need for combining in unions, for fighting against employers, and for trying to prevail upon the government to pass laws necessary for the workers" (Lenin, *What Is to Be Done?*, 63). He believed that mired in the daily drudgery of ten- to twelve-hour work days, these workers simply did not have the capacity to think beyond their immediate economic needs to conceive a radically different system—a socialist theory—that would abolish their position as hired laborers altogether; thus, they could not be expected to carry out a revolution without mediation from outside the class struggle. The way he saw it, Social Democratic intellectuals would need to take on the role of educating the masses in the laws of historical development and socialism, infusing them with a revolutionary consciousness as they organized them into a single, coherent movement while directing them toward their revolutionary mission.
5. Rosa Luxemburg, "The Political Leader of the German Working Classes," in *Rosa Luxemburg Gesammelte Werke* [Collected Works], vol. 2, edited by Annelies Laschitza and Eckhard Müller (East Berlin: Dietz Verlag, 1970–75).
6. Farrag Ismail, "Ex-minister Suspected Behind Church Bombing," *Al Arabiya News*, February 7, 2011.
7. For more on Ghonim and Mansour, the latter being the lesser-known administrator behind the We Are All Khaled Said Facebook page, see chapter 6.
8. Alcinda Honwana, *Youth and Revolution in Tunisia* (New York, NY: Zed Books, 2013).
9. Ashraf Khalil, *Liberation Square: Inside the Egyptian Revolution and the Rebirth of a Nation* (New York, NY: St. Martin's Press, 2011), 146.
10. The Ultras are not a political organization but are rebellious and anti-authoritarian by nature. Although they participated heavily during the eighteen-day uprising, it appears that they were present in an unofficial capacity (Robert Woltering, "Unusual Suspects: 'Ultras' as Political Actors in the Egyptian Revolution," *Arab Studies Quarterly* 35, no. 3 [2013]: 290–304). Of course, the Ultras would continue to play a significant role

in revolutionary street politics after the eighteen-day uprising. For a more thorough discussion of the Ultras, see Woltering, "Unusual Suspects"; Ashraf El-Sherif, "The Ultras' Politics of Fun Confront Tyranny," *Jadaliyya*, February 5, 2012; Wael Nawara, "Egypt's Ultras: Revolutionaries to Villains?" *Al-Monitor*, November 18, 2013.

11 Tarek El-Khouly interview, September 22, 2011.
12 In Arabic: "*Ehna min? Ehna min? Ehna kul al-masriyin!*" and "*Masr ya umm! Wiladik ahum!*"
13 "Asmaa Mahfouz & the YouTube Video That Helped Spark the Egyptian Uprising," *Democracy Now*, February 8, 2011.
14 Jack Shenker, *The Egyptians: A Radical History of Egypt's Unfinished Revolution* (New York, NY: The New Press, 2017), 129.
15 Neil MacFarquhar and Dina Salah, "Youth Leader in Egypt Straddles the Line of Revolution and Electoral Change," *The New York Times*, November 27, 2011.
16 Mohammed Abbas, Interview, October 2, 2011.
17 Activist estimates ranged from forty-five to eighty thousand and were impossible to verify. Accuracy aside, the high estimates reflect the activists' astonishment and sense of empowerment upon seeing such large numbers in a protest for the first time.
18 For an excellent discussion on the different factors that led Egyptians to overcome their fear of authorities and develop increasingly defiant stances vis-à-vis the state, ultimately culminating in their transformation into revolutionaries, see Jeroen Gunning and Ilan Zvi Baron, *Why Occupy a Square? People, Protests and Movement in the Egyptian Revolution* (Oxford: Oxford University Press, 2014), 203–39.
19 Mona El-Ghobashy, "The Praxis of the Egyptian Revolution," *Middle East Research and Information Project* 41, no. 258 (2011).
20 Tarek is likely referring to the protest organized by the Kefaya Movement on September 10, 2005 to contest the presidential election results and the election's mass rigging. There were a reported ten thousand participants in the Cairo protest and thousands more in demonstrations across Egypt's twenty-three governorates ("Kefaya: The Origins of Mubarak's Downfall," *Egypt Independent*, December 12, 2011). That said, the anti-Iraq War protests in March 2003 had brought out even larger numbers of protesters, upwards of twenty thousand, who had managed to occupy Tahrir Square for a whole day for the first time (Amira Howeidy, "A Day at 'Hyde Park,'" *Al-Ahram Weekly*, March 27–April 2, 2003). Tarek might have been referring to this larger protest.
21 "Protesters Torch Egypt Police Post," *Al Jazeera*, January 27, 2011.
22 Mohammed Bamyeh, "The Egyptian Revolution: First Impressions from the Field," *Jadaliyya*, February 11, 2011.
23 The one group that still abstained from participating in the protests at this point was the Coptic Church. See Mirette Bahgat, "Coptic Christians in Egypt Standing at the Crossroads," *Huffington Post*, May 6, 2011.

24 The riot police were not so much the object of the protesters' rage as were the higher-ranking officers of the Interior Ministry. The protesters sympathized with the former, who were mostly poor conscripts from the Delta and were underpaid and mistreated by their commanders.

25 For a fascinating discussion on the popular committees (*ligan sha'biya*) that explores their diverse positions vis-à-vis the Tahrir movement and their unrealized revolutionary potential as an emergent form of community organizing, see Atef Said, "The Tahrir Effect: History, Space, and Protest in the Egyptian Revolution," unpublished PhD Thesis, University of Michigan, 2014, 206–13.

26 Neil Ketchley, *Egypt in a Time of Revolution* (Cambridge: Cambridge University Press, 2017), 48. According to Ketchley, during the eighteen-day uprising, "fraternization performances initially emerged as improvised techniques of micro-conflict avoidance," first with the Central Security Forces (CSF) troops, then with the army. Later, fraternization was adopted by protesters as a way of making claims on army officers to ensure their security, especially during escalated conflict with pro-Mubarak forces (Ketchley, *Egypt in a Time of Revolution*, 49). For more on the protesters' mixed reactions to the army's arrival on the scene, also see Atef Said, "The Paradox of Transition to 'Democracy' under Military Rule," *Social Research* 79, no. 2 (Summer 2012): 397–434.

27 The youth activists were largely able to carry out these activities with the generous patronage of Mamdouh Hamza, a prominent engineer, industrialist, and political activist who was a strong supporter of the budding Tahrir movement. Hamza was politically active in the student movement of the late 1960s and early 1970s and had been an outspoken critic of the Mubarak regime before the uprising.

28 Aside from chanting in the name of the military and embracing soldiers, other fraternizing performances during the January uprising included "graffitting, climbing aboard military vehicles, sleeping in tank tracks ... and posing for photographs with soldiers" in and around Tahrir Square (Ketchley, *Egypt in a Time of Revolution*, 47).

29 The United States was in a particularly difficult quandary as the friend, patron, and weapons supplier of a regime that was denying its people their legitimate aspiration for a just and democratic society, a cause the United States supposedly championed in the Middle East. Washington struggled to save face with Egyptian protesters, who perceived it as complicit in their repression and suffering, by offering them moral support, but not enough support to actively undermine the government so critical to its security interests in the region. Throughout the eighteen days in Tahrir, protesters expressed their frustration with the United States for financing the regime that repressed them.

30 "Protesters Flood Egypt Streets," *Al Jazeera*, February 11, 2011.

31 "Egyptian President Mubarak Announces He Will Not Run for Reelection; Reaction from Prince Hassan Bin Talal of Jordan," *CNN*, February 1, 2011.

32 *Amnesty International Report 2012: The State of the World's Human Rights* (London: Amnesty International, 2012), 135.
33 For an excellent discussion of the factors that influenced the military's conduct during the eighteen-day uprising and transition period, see Said, "The Paradox of Transition to 'Democracy' under Military Rule."
34 See the earlier discussion in this chapter of Asmaa Mahfouz's YouTube video on pages 120–21 in which she challenges her male viewers to "man up" and join the movement.
35 Salwa Ismail, "The Egyptian Revolution against the Police," *Social Research* 79, no. 2 (Summer 2012): 435–62.
36 Leila Zaki Chakravarti, "Performing Masculinity: The Football Ultras in Post-revolutionary Egypt," *Open Democracy*, March 8, 2013.
37 Farha Ghannam, *Live and Die Like a Man: Gender Dynamics in Urban Egypt* (Stanford, CA: Stanford University Press, 2013).
38 Ghannam, *Live and Die Like a Man*, 125.
39 The first four groups were the main pillars of the RYC and are discussed more thoroughly in chapter 5. RYC members had reserved a seat for Wael Ghonim of the We Are All Khaled Said Facebook page, but he chose not to participate after being released from prison (he was arrested in the early days of the uprising). After the eighteen days, a few more groups were invited into the RYC, such as the youth of the leftist Unionist Party (Hizb al-Tagammuʻ).
40 Atef Said, "The Egyptian Revolution: Ethnographic Notes from Tahrir," *Footnotes* 39, no. 6 (July–August 2011).
41 John Chalcraft, "Horizontalism in the Egyptian Revolutionary Process," *Middle East Report* 42 (March 2012), 8.
42 My interlocutors Ola and Abbas told me they believed that activists from their group—which would later become known as the RYC—were behind this particular banner. Atef Said's study, however, led him to less conclusive answers to the question of the banner's origin and the process through which the demands it listed were decided and agreed upon. Based on his interviews, he suggests the banner could have been authored and hung by other groups besides the RYC, such as the National Association for Change and Kefaya. But at this stage, asking who crafted and unfurled the banner is less important than identifying why it was so quickly and widely embraced by protesters as the demands of the revolution. As Said put it, "It was likely the very anonymity of the banner that fueled its acceptance and power. With no one specific author or owner, the banner—and its demands—belonged to everyone and could thus be accepted as those of the revolution" (Said, "The Tahrir Effect," 148). See also Said's study for a compelling analysis of the role this banner played in circumscribing the revolutionary movement.
43 Abdelrahman Faris, Interview, October 28, 2011; Hawary Hawary, Interview, December 2, 2011; Momen el-Husseiny, Interview, February 23, 2013.
44 Hawary Hawary, Interview, December 2, 2011.

45 The activists I interviewed claim that many of these coalitions were created by SCAF to "represent" the revolution's youth at its meetings after RYC members refused its many invitations on ideological grounds. Ultimately, SCAF was able to exploit divisions among the youth activists and their inability to create a more inclusive revolutionary organization to diminish their legitimacy and undermine their influence.
46 Qassas said that the Revolutionary Salvation Front did not gain the prominence it should have because Mubarak's resignation the next day eclipsed it. He speculated that this organization would have played a more influential role in the revolution had Mubarak not resigned so soon.
47 Bassam Haddad, "English Translation of Interview with Hossam El-Hamalawy on the Role of Labor/Unions in the Egyptian Revolution," *Jadaliyya*, April 30, 2011; Joel Beinin, *Workers and Thieves: Labor Movements and Popular Uprisings in Tunisia and Egypt* (Stanford, CA: Stanford University Press, 2016).
48 Hazem Kandil, "Soldiers without Generals," *Dissent Magazine*, October 21, 2012.

Chapter 5

1 A full discussion of what it means to be a liberal in Egypt is beyond the scope of this study. Suffice it to say that "liberal" is a murky category that has historically encompassed diverse groups whose only commonality is that they are opposed to the Muslim Brotherhood and other right-wing Islamist groups. According to Samuel Tadros, "these include Christians, Nasserites, Socialists, Trotskyites, businessmen, and a portion of the upper middle class." These groups claim a commitment to the protection of rights, freedoms, pluralism, and other democratic values, but they have also historically been quick to abandon these values when they sought to undermine the more powerful Islamists, just as they did in 2013 (see chapter 7) (Samuel Tadros, "Egypt's Muslim Brotherhood after the Revolution," *The Hudson Institute*, October 18, 2011).
2 Barbara Zollner, "Surviving Repression: How Egypt's Muslim Brotherhood Has Carried On," Carnegie Middle East Center, March 11, 2019.
3 While women might not have come to occupy leadership positions in the Muslim Brotherhood organization after the revolution, there were some women who were active in the Freedom and Justice Party that they launched after the revolution. Pakinam El Sharkawy, Morsi's political advisor, was the most notable example.
4 Frantz Fanon, *The Wretched of the Earth*, trans. Constance Farrington (New York, NY: Grove, 1968).
5 The use of English terms like "Mommy" and "Poppy" in Egypt marks an upper-class background.
6 It must be emphasized, however, that this observation about women's leadership is only true of mainstream, male-dominated movements; women have, of course, engineered and led many of their own movements.

7   Jack Goldstone, "Toward of Fourth Generation of Revolutionary Theory," *Annual Reviews of Political Science* 4 (June 2001): 159.
8   Goldstone, "Toward a Fourth Generation," 159.
9   Marnia Lazreg, *The Eloquence of Silence: Algerian Women in Question* (London: Routledge, 1994).
10 Joan B. Landes, *Women and the Public Sphere in the Age of the French Revolution* (Ithaca, NY: Cornell University Press, 1988).
11 Stephanie J. Smith, *Gender and the Mexican Revolution: Yucatan Women and the Realities of Patriarchy* (Chapel Hill, NC: University of North Carolina Press, 2009).
12 Kathleen Sheldon, "Women and Revolution in Mozambique: A Luta Continua," in *Women and Revolution in Africa, Asia, and the New World*, edited by Mary Ann Tetréault, (Columbia, SC: University of South Carolina Press, 1994), 33–61.
13 Tanya Lyons, *Guns and Guerrilla Girls: Women in the Zimbabwean National Liberation Struggle* (Trenton, NJ: Africa World Press, 2004).
14 V.M. Moghadam, *Modernizing Women: Gender and Social Change in the Middle East* (Boulder, CO: Lynne Rienner Publishers, Inc, 2003).
15 Mary Ann Tetréault, "Women and Revolution in Vietnam," in *Women and Revolution in Africa, Asia, and the New World*, edited by Mary Ann Tetréault (Columbia, SC: University of South Carolina Press, 1994), 111–36.
16 Margot Badran, *Feminists, Islam, and Nation: Gender and the Making of Modern Egypt* (Princeton, NJ: Princeton University Press, 1996).
17 Basem would later change his views regarding quotas after witnessing how difficult it was for women to get seats in the first parliamentary elections following Mubarak's ouster. In a follow-up interview I conducted with him in late 2013, he argued for the need to institute parliamentary quotas for women for at least two consecutive terms so that society gets used to the idea of women in political leadership and starts to elect women of its own accord. He believed seeing women in political leadership would also make other women see it as less of a taboo and something they are capable of, which would in turn encourage more female political engagement.
18 Hania Sholkamy, "Women Are Also Part of This Revolution," in *Arab Spring in Egypt: Revolution and Beyond*, edited by Bahgat Korany and Rabab Elmahdi (Cairo: The American University in Cairo Press, 2012), 169.
19 Alan D. Morris and Suzanne Staggenborg, "Leadership in Social Movements," in *The Blackwell Companion to Social Movements*, edited by D. Snow, S. Soule, and H. Kriesi (Malden, MA: Blackwell Publishing, 2004), 174–75.
20 Anthropologist Suad Joseph coined the term "intimate selving" to capture the process of becoming the self through intimate relationships, specifically through familial relationships. The concept is useful in thinking about the ways in which the intimacy between protesters and activists engendered by the revolution shaped their becoming (Suad Joseph, ed., *Intimate Selving in*

Arab Families: Gender, Self, and Identity, Syracuse, NY: Syracuse University Press, 1999).

21 Ibrahim El-Houdaiby, "Focus on Politics, Not Identity," *Ahram Online*, August 14, 2011.
22 The year 1919 was that of Egypt's countrywide revolution against the British.
23 For a discussion of how Egypt acquired this celebrated title, see Amrou Kotb, "The Mother of the World," *Atlantic Council*, February 14, 2014.
24 "Revolution Youth Coalition Refuses to Meet Clinton," *Ahram Online*, March 15, 2011.
25 The youth activists' commitment to Palestine and its central role in the Egyptian revolution was demonstrated during the Gaza attack of November 2012. About 550 youth revolutionaries, including several of my respondents or peers from their respective movements, crossed the Rafah border during the attack to express solidarity with Palestinians from within. It was the first Egyptian convoy to enter the Gaza strip since 1967 ("Egyptian Solidarity Convoy Crosses into Embattled Gaza," *Ahram Online*, November 18, 2012). Footage from this historic visit is available on YouTube (*Hitafat al-shabab al-masri fi Ghazza*, posted on November 19, 2012, https://www.youtube.com/watch?v=6Q0vZDxDE9c). And for a more detailed discussion on how anti-Zionism and solidarity with Palestine played out during the eighteen-day uprising, see Reem Abou-El-Fadl, "The Road to Jerusalem through Tahrir Square: Anti-Zionism and Palestine in the 2011 Egyptian Revolution," *Journal of Palestinian Studies* 41, no. 2 (Winter 2012): 6–26.

Chapter 6

1 Shereen El Feki et al., "Youth Revolt in Egypt, a Country at the Turning Point," *Population Reference Bureau*, 2011.
2 Asef Bayat, "Muslim Youth and the Claim of Youthfulness," in *Being Young and Muslim: New Cultural Politics in the Global South and North*, edited by Asef Bayat and Linda Herrera (Oxford: Oxford University Press, 2010), 30.
3 This is not to diminish the contribution of workers in paving the way to the revolution with their unrelenting labor resistance in the years before 2011, which helped break down the "fear barrier" that prevented regular citizens from protesting against the regime. See Joel Beinin, *Workers and Thieves: Labor Movements and Popular Uprisings in Tunisia and Egypt* (Stanford, CA: Stanford University Press, 2016); Anne Alexander and Mostafa Bassiouny, *Bread, Freedom, and Social Justice: Workers and the Egyptian Revolution* (London: Zed Books, 2014).
4 Juan Cole, "The Arab Millennials Will Be Back," *The Huffington Post*, June 30, 2014. See also Juan Cole, *The New Arabs: How the Millennial Generation is Changing the Middle East* (New York, NY: Simon and Schuster, 2014).
5 One such chant was the following: "*Masr ya umm! Wiladik ahum! Dul alashanik shalu al-hamm! Rahu yifduki bi-l-ruh wa-l-damm!*" (Egypt, our

mother! Your children are here! For you they have borne so much worry! They would sacrifice their souls and blood for you!)

6. That said, it must be emphasized that this is based on my study of the RYC and not the wider revolutionary movement. For example, there were several important movements founded and led by women after the uprising such as No to Military Trials and Operation Anti-SH (Sexual Harassment). But these were issue-based movements, unlike the RYC which was more like a vanguard organization for the larger revolutionary movement.

7. Jo Reger, "Blinded by Gender: The Study of Leadership Dilemmas and U.S. Feminism," *Gender and Society*, May 30, 2017. Robnett's concept of "bridge leaders," which emerged from her study on leadership in the Civil Rights Movement, helps us understand how women who were often excluded from formal leadership still held power and authority within the movement at a local level. However, while scholars appreciate such analyses for clarifying the critical contribution of women in movements and expanding our conception of leadership beyond "formal roles and masculine activities," some caution that equating leadership with active participation and organizing could broaden the definition of leadership to the detriment of the term's analytical capacity; further, this line of analysis risks obscuring the power dynamics in movements (Alan D. Morris and Suzanne Staggenborg, "Leadership in Social Movements," in *The Blackwell Companion to Social Movements*, edited by D. Snow, S. Soule, and H. Kriesi [Malden, MA: Blackwell Publishing, 2004], 177). A discussion of women outside this context fails to address how women excluded from top leadership positions are also deprived of a certain degree of power to influence the orientation and outcomes of movements.

8. Cassie Biggs, "Women Make Their Power Felt in Egyptian Revolution," *The National*, February 14, 2011.

9. Nadia Taher, "'We Are Not Women, We Are Egyptians': Spaces of Protest and Representation," *Open Democracy*, April 6, 2012.

10. Lobna Afifi, Interview, November 30, 2013; Mona Shams, Interview, December 6, 2013.

11. The exception was Zainab Al Ghazali (1917–2005), the only woman in the long history of the Muslim Brotherhood to distinguish herself as one of the organization's major leaders. In terms of contemporary examples, there is the scholar Heba Raouf Ezzat. Although she might not have been a member of the Muslim Brotherhood, Ezzat has long been a powerful voice within the broader and more "moderate" Islamist movement.

12. Mona Farag, "The Muslim Sisters and the January 25th Revolution," *Journal of International Women's Studies* 13 no. 5 (October 2012): 230.

13. Mervat Hatem provides another explanation for why the leaders of women's groups on college campuses were always men: "Women were excluded from the leadership of their own groups on the grounds that male leaders knew more about Islam than women. In other words, despite the visibility of women in the Islamist movement, they were largely represented at the lowest levels. The formation of sexually segregated groups did not necessarily

propel women into leadership positions. Leadership continued to be the sole preserve of men even in women's groups" (Mervat Hatem, "Economic and Political Liberation in Egypt and the Demise of State Feminism," *International Journal of Middle East Studies* 24, no. 2 [May 1992]: 246).

14 In this respect, the absence of Muslim sisters from the RYC leadership is comparable to black women's absence from the top leadership of the Civil Rights Movement in that one of the primary routes to this leadership level was through the black churches, and specifically the office of the pastor, which was dominated by men (Morris and Staggenborg, "Leadership in Movements," 176–77). In both the black church and the Muslim Brotherhood, women were highly active, but often in informal or less visible roles, which shaped their access to leadership in the Civil Rights Movement and Egyptian Revolution, respectively.

15 Maya Mikdashi, "The Gendered Body Public," *Jadaliyya*, January 28, 2013.

16 The photo essay "Young Egyptians Spread Their Message" published by *The New York Times* on February 8, 2011, is the perfect example.

17 In fact, Wael Ghonim was not the sole founder and administrator of the We Are All Khaled Said Facebook page. AbdelRahman Mansour is said to have originated the idea of the page and sought out Wael Ghonim as a partner to build and administer it. Mansour's crucial role on the site has been largely dismissed and overlooked by the media. This might have had something to do with his less privileged background, which is similar to that of the male respondents featured in this study. For more on Mansour, see Linda Herrera, "Meet AbdelRahman Mansour Who Made 25 January a Date to Remember," *Jadaliyya*, January 25, 2013.

18 Asef Bayat, "A New Arab Street in Post-Islamist Times," *Foreign Policy*, January 26, 2011.

19 Morris and Staggenborg, "Leadership in Movements," 174–75.

20 Morris and Staggenborg, "Leadership in Movements," 174–75.

21 Nawara Negm, a journalist, attained much of her celebrity not just from her social media activity but from being the daughter of the famous leftist folk poet Ahmed Fouad Negm.

22 Paolo Gerbaudo, *Tweets and the Streets: Social Media and Contemporary Activism* (London: Pluto Press, 2012), 12–13. Gerbaudo also refers to such activists as "'anti-leaders': leaders who, subscribing to the ideology of horizontalism, do not want to be seen as leaders in the first place but whose scene-setting and scripting work has been decisive in bringing a degree of coherence to people's spontaneous and creative participation in the protest movements" (Gerbaudo, *Tweets and the Streets*, 12–13).

23 Nadje Al-Ali, *Secularism, Gender and the State in the Middle East* (Cambridge: Cambridge University Press, 2000), 124–25.

24 Hazem Kandil, "Soldiers without Generals," *Dissent Magazine*, October 21, 2012.

25 Maha Abdelrahman, *Egypt's Long Revolution: Protest Movements and Uprisings* (New York, NY: Routledge, 2015), 81.

26 Immanuel Wallerstein, "New Revolts against the System," *New Left Review* 18, November–December, 2002.
27 Wallerstein, "New Revolts against the System"; John Chalcraft, "Horizontalism in the Egyptian Revolutionary Process," *Middle East Report* 42 (March 2012): 6–11; Abdelrahman, *Egypt's Long Revolution*, 80–81.
28 Kandil, "Soldiers without Generals."
29 Gramsci spoke about this idea of spontaneity as a method when speaking about the leaders in the Turin Movement that unfolded in Italy in the 1920s: "The leaders themselves spoke of the 'spontaneity' of the movement and rightly so. This assertion was a stimulus, a tonic, an element of unification in depth; above all it denied that the movement was arbitrary, a cooked-up venture, and stressed its historical necessity. It gave the masses a 'theoretical' consciousness of being creators of historical and institutional values, of being founders of a State. This unity between 'spontaneity' and 'conscious leadership' or 'discipline' is precisely the real political action of the subaltern classes, insofar as this is mass politics and not merely an adventure by groups claiming to represent the masses" (Marco Fonseca, *Gramsci's Critique of Civil Society: Towards a New Concept of Hegemony* [New York, NY: Routledge, 2016], 116).
30 Joe Freeman was the first to write and warn about the "tyranny of structurelessness" she experienced in the women's liberation movement. She challenged the feminist rejection of leaders and formal structure in the name of participatory democracy, arguing that it was impossible to have a truly structureless and leaderless movement. What she observed in their place was the emergence of informal structures and unaccountable leaders chosen through friendship networks. She advocated that the movement would be better served by the development of "structural forms that encourage maximum participation but also accountability on the part of activists who are delegated authority and responsibilities" (Morris and Staggenborg, "Leadership in Social Movements," 181).
31 Thannasis Cambanis, *Once Upon a Revolution: An Egyptian Story* (New York, NY: Simon and Schuster, 2015), 252.
32 While Egypt has a long history of labor organizing, it appears to lack a tradition of community organizing similar to the kind we see in the United States. The fact that Egyptians did not have a history of this kind of activism to draw from might explain why they did not turn to this form of organizing after the revolution. That said, the *ligan sha'biya*, or popular committees, that appeared organically during the eighteen-day uprising in neighborhoods across Cairo and Egypt represented an emergent form of community organizing that could have played a key role in sustaining the commitment of the masses to the revolution had the activists connected with them, supported their growth, and imagined how to structure them within the broader, ongoing movement. Understandably, this might have been beyond their capacity, given their limited resources, including time, which was being consumed by the ongoing political battle with the military and Muslim Brotherhood over the direction of the transition. Most of

these committees have since dissolved, but some remain and have made significant gains for their communities through novel forms of organizing. For an excellent example, see Asef Bayat, *Revolution without Revolutionaries: Making Sense of the Arab Spring* (Stanford, CA: Stanford University Press, 2017), 200.

33 Indeed, as Hani Shukrallah points out, they had not even managed to come up with a document such as a "Declaration of Rights" enshrining the values, principles, and overall aims of the revolution expressed during the eighteen-day uprising (Hani Shukrallah, "Egypt's Revolution: As It Might Have Been, as It Could be," *Ahram Online*, January 25, 2013).

34 That Parliament was dissolved six months later, but that is beside the point. The fact that only three revolutionaries were elected into a parliament made possible by the uprising they had unleashed speaks to the ideological and moral dilemmas activists struggled with and will have to resolve if they hope to influence change in the future.

35 Upon its dissolution, the RYC released a final self-audit report entitled "An Account of the Actions of the Coalition of Revolutionary Youth." With this report, their hope was to set an example for other political groups in organizational transparency. "Even though it is not standard operating procedure in Egypt," it read, "we believe it is necessary that every group and/or political entity submit a report that outlines what the organization has done over time, be it good or bad. We contend that it is our duty to publish this account for the Egyptian public, for they placed their trust in the Coalition of Revolutionary Youth, as well as for those who criticized the organization." For the full report, see "In Translation: The Revolutionary Youth Coalition's Final Report," *Jadaliyya*, July 19, 2012.

Chapter 7

1 The word for "civility" in Arabic is *madaniya*. The term is often used to refer to both civilian rule and to the non-religious nature of the state. Here the term is used to connote the former.

2 Transcribed from audio recording of activist Sally Tomah reading the statement on February 11, 2011. For the full embedded recording, see Charles M. Sennot, "The First Day of a New Egypt," *Frontline*, February 11, 2011.

3 "All According to Plan: The Rab'a Massacre and Mass Killings of Protesters in Egypt," Human Rights Watch, August 12, 2014. Estimates of the number of those imprisoned for political reasons are as high as sixty thousand ("Egypt: Torture Epidemic May Be a Crime Against Humanity: Beatings, Electric Shocks, Stress Positions Routinely Used Against Dissidents," Human Rights Watch, September 26, 2017).

4 "Egypt: Torture Epidemic May Be a Crime Against Humanity"; Sarah Carr, "Sexual Assault and the State: A History of Violence," *Mada Masr*, July 7, 2014.

5   "Egypt: Unprecedented Crackdown on NGOs," Amnesty International, March 26, 2016; "Egypt: Execution of Nine Defendants after Unfair Trial Is Retaliation, Not Justice," Cairo Institute for Human Rights Studies, February 16, 2019.

6   Aboulenein, Ahmed. "Egypt Blocks 21 Websites for 'Terrorism' and 'Fake News,'" *Reuters*, May 24, 2017.

7   "Egypt: Security Forces Used Excessive Lethal Force," Human Rights Watch, August 19, 2013; "All According to Plan."

8   As Abdelrahman's testimony suggests and note 25 in chapter 4 alludes to, not all *ligan sha'biya* (popular committees) were necessarily sympathetic to the revolution; in fact, some were outright hostile to it. This was a source of anxiety for activists, particularly during the moments of upheaval when the *ligan* emerged to organize checkpoints, such as during the eighteen-day uprising and 2013 summer events, because it was difficult for them to gauge how the *ligan* would react to them when they stopped them. According to Atef Said, "while the committees claimed and practiced power on the ground" by stepping up during the security vacuum to assume the policing duties of the state, "their participants did not articulate themselves as claiming this power or in any way representing the revolution" (Atef Said, "The Tahrir Effect: History, Space, and Protest in the Egyptian Revolution," unpublished PhD Thesis, University of Michigan, 2014, 213).

9   As noted in chapter 4, many of the youth had considered the Brotherhood's move opportunistic at the time, but they needed the extra numbers and support, so they welcomed the Brotherhood into their ranks.

10   The army is believed to be in control of as much as 40 percent of the Egyptian economy. For an excellent discussion of the army's entrenchment in the economy and what kind of interests were at stake for them in the revolution, see Zeinab Abul-Magd, "The Army and the Economy in Egypt," *Jadaliyya*, December 23, 2011.

11   Jeff Martini and Julie Taylor, "Commanding Democracy in Egypt: The Military's Attempt to Manage the Future," *Foreign Affairs*, September/October, 2011.

12   Nael Shama, *Egyptian Foreign Policy from Mubarak to Morsi: Against the National Interest* (London: Routledge, 2013), 223.

13   One notable example was when SCAF tried to limit the powers of the incoming Parliament in November 2011 through what became known as the Selmi Document. The document would provide SCAF with a veto over Egypt's new constitution and allow them to nominate eighty of the one hundred members of the constituent assembly who would be in charge of drafting it. These stipulations were particularly upsetting to the Brothers, who were expected to sweep the elections, as they saw them as an attempt to curb their power (Matt Bradley, "Islamists Lead Massive Protest in Cairo," *The Wall Street Journal*, November 19, 2011).

14   *Amnesty International Report 2012: The State of the World's Human Rights* (London: Amnesty International, 2012), 136.

15 Ahmed Aboul Enein et al., "Remembering Mohamed Mahmoud: The Good, the Bad, and the Brotherhood," *Daily News Egypt*, November 19, 2012.
16 David Hearst and Abdel-Rahman Hussein, "Egypt's Supreme Court Dissolves Parliament and Outrages Islamists," *The Guardian*, June 14, 2012.
17 Indeed, the disorganization of the secular opposition during the election, particularly the first round, was ruinous for the movement. Underestimating the chances of the old regime candidate, Ahmad Shafik, the Arab nationalist Hamdeen Sabbahi and the moderate Islamist Abd al-Mun'im Abul-Futuh, both of whom were seen as representatives of the revolution, decided to run against each other rather than unite and nominate a single candidate. Together, they won the most votes in the primary race, a combined 39 percent, which would have secured a win for the revolution had the votes not been split. Egyptians took to the polls in record numbers, and a decisive majority demonstrated with their votes their readiness for a leader who supported a secular state and a future free from the corruption and repression of the old regime, but the revolutionaries and their progressive allies failed to deliver (Thannasis Cambanis, *Once Upon a Revolution: An Egyptian Story* [New York, NY: Simon and Schuster, 2015], 184). To borrow the words of the late journalist Bassem Sabry, "a historic opportunity for the movement to lead was squandered" (Bassem Sabry, "The Revolution Will Be Minimized," *Foreign Policy*, June 11, 2012).
18 Ashraf El-Sherif, "The Brotherhood's Downfall (Part 1)," trans. Dina Hussein, *Mada Masr*, August 5, 2013. The claim that the Muslim Brotherhood was determined to advance a well-thought-out plan to Islamize the state is somewhat contentious. There appears to have been a clear sense of the need to pad the ruling establishment with their own people, but that is not quite the same as Islamizing the state. As for the policies they adopted, to what extent they were part of a coherent plan or driven by the imperative to address the demands of the Salafi members in the coalition is a subject of debate.
19 Like Mubarak, Morsi showed little respect for freedom of the press; he tightened control of state media, appointing a Brotherhood member to the post of information minister and replacing the leadership of state newspapers and channels with trusted or controllable figures. He also harassed media figures, subjecting them to charges of "insulting the president" and showing "contempt of religion" (Bassem Sabry, "How Morsi and the Brotherhood Lost Egypt," *Al-Monitor*, July 4, 2013).
20 Sabry, "How Morsi and the Brotherhood Lost Egypt."
21 Morsi failed to appreciate that one of the chief objectives of the revolution that brought him to power was to transform the police establishment that had become so abusive toward its citizens. The incumbent president appeared to have a different concern: how to secure police loyalty so that he could use it to achieve his own ends. His reluctance to introduce police reform beyond a few personnel reshuffles meant the police had the freedom to continue their abuses during his tenure, not the least of which was the lethal use of force

against protesters (Reem Abou-El-Fadl, "Mohamed Morsi Mubarak: The Myth of Egypt's Democratic Transition," *Jadaliyya*, February 11, 2013).

22 Morsi's failure to speak out against police abuse was most glaring in January 2013, when police killed forty protesters in the city of Port Said after courts sentenced twenty-one locals to death for the massacre of football fans at the stadium a year earlier. The verdict angered residents, who believed the police were the real perpetrators of the 2012 massacre. Instead of condemning the police for their unwarranted violence, he praised them in an apparent attempt to win their favor (Patrick Kingsley, "Mass March in Port Said as Anger Grows on Anniversary of Egyptian Revolution," *The Guardian*, February 1, 2013).

23 The constitution produced by this unrepresentative body was lamentable for a number of reasons. For instance, it failed to provide legal protections for minority and disenfranchised groups. Also, in what appeared to be part of a quid pro quo arrangement between the Islamists and the armed forces, the new constitution sanctified the autonomy and special privileges of the military, ignoring the revolution's explicit demand to bring the army under civilian control. These provisions entitled the military to choose its own defense minister, control foreign policy as it related to national security, and continue to try civilians in military courts. Lastly, the constitution defined Egypt as an Islamic state and enshrined sharia law as the basis for legislation, to the chagrin of the champions of a secular state who wanted to institute a code based on universal rights (Mike Giglio, "Morsi and the Military: Egypt President Firm on Constitution Vote," *The Daily Beast*, December 9, 2012; Ginsburg, "The Real Winner in the Egyptian Constitution? The Military," *HuffPost*, December 7, 2012; Abdel-Rahman Hussein, "Egyptian Assembly Passes Draft Constitution Despite Protests," *The Guardian*, November 30, 2012).

24 The infamous measure was a pre-emptive move meant to block the courts from dissolving the Constituent Assembly charged with drafting the constitution. Morsi had legitimate reason to be concerned about the judiciary, since it had proven itself to be at the service of the old regime, ready to go the distance to thwart reform, even targeting elected institutions like when it annulled Parliament. But issuing himself supra-legal powers—even if just temporarily as he intended—was not the solution in the eyes of revolutionaries.

25 As H.A. Hellyer notes, the Muslim Brotherhood's best option for resisting the forces within the deep state that wanted to undermine Egypt's democratic experiment was to partner with the opposition and establish a united political front in the form of a "revolutionary legislative council made up of Egypt's key political forces" (H.A. Hellyer, *A Revolution Undone: Egypt's Road Beyond Revolt* [Oxford: Oxford University Press, 2016], 116).

26 Ola Shahba's testimony on her Facebook page, as translated by the Cairo Institute for Human Rights Studies (*al-Ittihadiya: "Presidential Palace" Clashes*

in Cairo, 5-6 December 2012 [Cairo Institute for Human Rights Studies, December 2012], 20).

27 Ola Shahba's testimony on the talk show *Akher Kalam*, as translated by the Cairo Institute for Human Rights Studies (*al-Ittihadiya*, 20).
28 Egyptian Coptic Christians have long maintained a tradition of tattooing crosses on their wrists to mark their identity as part of the minority community. Sometimes the tattoo is applied in infancy, after baptism.
29 Ola Shahba's testimony on the talk show *Akher Kalam*, as translated by the Cairo Institute for Human Rights Studies (*al-Ittihadiya*, 20).
30 Hellyer, *A Revolution Undone*, 117; Ibrahim El-Houdaiby, "Egypt: Nothing Was Inevitable," *Ahram Online*, September 13, 2013.
31 For an excellent discussion of the role deep-state forces played in precipitating Morsi's and the Muslim Brotherhood's downfall, see Ben Hubbard and David Kirkpatrick, "Sudden Improvements in Egypt Suggest a Campaign to Undermine Morsi," *The New York Times*, July 10, 2013. See also Asma Alsharif and Yasmine Saleh, "Special Report—the Real Force Behind Egypt's 'Revolution of the State,'" *Reuters*, October 10, 2013.
32 Ben Hubbard and Mayy El Sheikh, "New Governor is a Shock to Some Inside Egypt," *The New York Times*, June 16, 2013; El Houdaiby, "Egypt: Nothing Was Inevitable." By this time, military and public confidence in Morsi's ability to manage national security issues was already in fast decline. A scandal had erupted earlier that month, after Morsi met with other political leaders to try to stop a Nile River dam project in Ethiopia, which they considered to be a major threat to Egypt's water security. The meeting was supposed to be closed and off the record, but in fact it was aired live on state television without the knowledge of those at the table. Believing they were speaking in private, the politicians freely debated covert ways for Egypt to thwart the project, their bellicose ideas ranging from arming Ethiopian rebels to destroying the dam.
33 Alaa Bayoumi, "The Challenge for Egypt's Copts," *Al Jazeera*, April 23, 2013. "Egypt: Lynching of Shia Follows Months of Hate Speech: Police Fail to Protect Muslim Minority," Human Rights Watch, June 27, 2013.
34 For a discussion of the power struggle between the Salafi al-Nour Party and the Muslim Brotherhood, see Naglaa Mekkawi, "A Love, Hate Relationship: al-Nour and Egypt's Muslim Brotherhood," *Al Arabiya News*, August 22, 2013"; Khalil Al-Anani, "The Salafi–Brotherhood Feud in Egypt," *Al-Monitor*, February 21, 2013.
35 Sabry, "How Morsi and the Brotherhood Lost Egypt."
36 "Tamarod Petition Has over 22 Million Signatures," *Egypt Independent*, June 29, 2013.
37 Patrick Kingsley, "Tamarod Campaign Gathers Momentum among Egypt's Opposition," *The Guardian*, June 27, 2013.
38 Ruth Alexander, "Counting Crowds: Was Egypt's Uprising Biggest Ever?" *BBC*, July 16, 2013.
39 Alsharif and Saleh, "Special Report."

40 Naguib Sawiris, for example, the billionaire tycoon and secular politician whose businesses were being targeted for billions of dollars in tax evasion, was especially invested in Morsi's downfall. He provided the campaign with ample financial support and rent-free workspaces in the nationwide offices of his Free Egyptians Party. He also provided publicity through his media network (Hubbard and Kirkpatrick, "Sudden Improvements in Egypt"; "Egyptian Tycoon Blames 'Cowardly' Ministry for Tax Dispute," *Ahram Online*, September 30, 2014).

41 See Max Blumenthal, "Egypt's Numbers Game: How Crazy Claims of 33 Million Protesters Were Used to Boost a Coup," *Alternet*, July 19, 2013; Alexander, "Counting Crowds: Was Egypt's Uprising Biggest Ever?"

42 Once again, I use the term "liberal" loosely in this context to refer to the forces who outwardly claim to espouse the democratic values of rights, freedoms, pluralism. See note 1, chapter 5.

43 Hellyer, *A Revolution Undone*, 141.

44 Mohamed Elmasry, "Unpacking Anti-Muslim Brotherhood Discourse," *Jadaliyya*, July 28, 2013.

45 Elmasry, "Unpacking Anti-Muslim Brotherhood Discourse."

46 Hellyer, *A Revolution Undone*, 152.

47 According to sociologist Asef Bayat, what happened in Egypt was more than a coup: "A coup happens when one segment of the ruling elite (such as the military) forcefully takes over power from the other segment without or with minimal involvement of the populace." What happened in Egypt— what he calls "revolutionary coercion"—was more than that; it represents "the paradoxical but inescapable strategy of the revolution that lacked a coercive power to do what the army did on its behalf," namely ousting Morsi. For revolutionaries, "the military's intervention in deposing Morsi served as a catalyst, removing the barriers preventing a stalled revolution moving forward." Bayat contrasts the position of Egypt's revolutionaries here to their twentieth-century counterparts, who had their own coercive resources in the form of militias and revolutionary armies, arguing that if the former had this kind of hard power, "they might have done what they expect[ed] the military to do for them, and that would not have been labeled a 'coup." (Asef Bayat, "Midwife for a Pregnant Egypt," *Jadaliyya*, July 11, 2013). For Bayat, the costs of such a strategy are clear from the outcome: the army that claimed it wanted to save the revolution found the opportunity to terminate it. See also Asef Bayat, *Revolution without Revolutionaries: Making Sense of the Arab Spring* (Stanford, CA: Stanford University Press, 2017).

48 Ironically, Basem condemned the arrest of Brotherhood leaders along with the closure of their media outlets following Morsi's removal, rejecting both as acts of authoritarianism that were no different from the Brotherhood's version, but that did not stop him from supporting the military intervention.

49 Patrick Kingsley, "Killing in Cairo: The Full Story Behind the Republican Guard Shooting," *The Guardian*, July 18, 2013; Elmasry, "Unpacking the

Anti-Muslim Brotherhood Discourse"; Joshua Hersh, "Egypt's Media Counter-Revolution," *The New Yorker*, August 20, 2013.

50 For an excellent discussion of the conduct of liberals at this juncture that puts their decision to side with the military against the Muslim Brotherhood in historical context, see Amr Hamzawy, *Anti-democratic Deceptions: How Egyptian Liberals Endorse Autocracy*, 2015 (YouTube video posted by Stanford Center for Democracy, Development and the Rule of Law). Amr Hamzawy, a prominent figure during the revolution, was among a handful of intellectuals in Egypt who used the term "fascism" to describe the emerging trend among liberal opponents of the Muslim Brotherhood. He spoke out against "the rhetoric of gloating, hatred, retribution, and revenge against the Muslim Brotherhood" and condemned the celebration of the army takeover as "fascism under the false pretense of democracy and liberalism" (David Kirkpatrick, "Egyptian Liberals Embrace the Military, Brooking No Dissent," *The New York Times*, July 15, 2013). It is important to note that liberals were not alone in backing the army takeover. As this article points out, leftists in Egypt also aligned with the military and received similar criticism for their support.

51 The number of weapons the Interior Ministry claimed to have found in Rabaa was in the low double digits, which was relatively small compared to the tens of thousands of protesters in the square. See Ayman Faruq, "Bawwabat al-Ahram tanshur nus kalimat wazir al-dakhiliya fi mu'tamar sahafi ba'd fad i'tisam Rab'a wa Nahda," *Bawwabat al-Ahram*, August 14, 2013; "Egypt: Security Forces Used Excessive Lethal Force," Human Rights Watch, August 19, 2013; and "All According to Plan."

52 "All According to Plan," 32, 82.

53 Even though the Muslim Brotherhood leadership officially denounced violence and called for the protests to stay peaceful, members had engaged in the sectarian incitement against Copts before the coup and were said to have contributed to the widespread attacks against them afterward that took place across Egypt. The attacks were also likely to have been carried out by non-Brotherhood militants who were upset about the turn against Islamists. An al-Qaeda affiliated group called Ansar Bayt al-Maqdis claimed responsibility for several of the post-coup attacks (D. Parvez, "Egypt's Copts Reel from Sectarian Violence," *Al Jazeera*, August 20, 2013; Shadia Nasralla, "Egypt Designates Muslim Brotherhood as Terrorist Group," *Reuters*, December 25, 2013).

54 It is worth underscoring that the phenomenon of revolutionary activists seemingly selling out their movement is not unique to Egypt. As Maha Abdelrahman points out, "the last decades of the twentieth century abound with cases in which New Social Movement activists progressed to become part of a new order, once they had achieved their objective of bringing down at least part of the old regime." She refers to several cases that point to "the sense of betrayal and disillusionment felt by members of these social movements at the hands of their former friends and comrades once the latter

had acceded to state institutions" (Maha Abdelrahman, *Egypt's Long Revolution: Protest Movements and Uprisings* [New York, NY: Routledge, 2015], 81).

55 Disagreements among founders of the Egyptian Current Party over controversial positions some of them took following the July 3 coup and the Rabaa massacre led many to resign. The party had already lost many of its members as a result of its failure to provide a clear program for them to rally behind. Further weakened by divisions that arose from the coup, it merged with the Strong Egypt Party, founded by former presidential candidate and Muslim Brotherhood member Abd al-Mun'im Abul-Futuh. The Strong Egypt Party has been facing dissolution under Sisi's regime since announcing its plans to boycott the 2018 presidential election, and its founder and several other members—including Qassas, who became the party's spokesperson— have been imprisoned and put on a terror list. As of this writing, both Abul-Futuh and Qassas have been held in solitary confinement and denied vital medical treatment for chronic illnesses.

56 Zeinab Abul-Magd, "Egypt's Coming Revolt of the Poor," *Foreign Policy*, March 31, 2017.

57 Amira Howeidy, "Matariyya, Egypt's New Theater of Dissent," *Middle East Report*, June 4, 2015; "Egypt's Sisi Pledges Crackdown on Police Abuses after Shooting," *BBC*, February 19, 2016.

58 Amr Hamzawy, "Egypt's Resilient and Evolving Social Activism," Carnegie Endowment for International Peace, April 5, 2017.

59 Karim Faheem, "Egyptians Denounce President Sisi in Biggest Rally in 2 Years," *The New York Times*, April 6, 2016.

60 "Egypt's Constitutional Amendments Passed by 88.83% in Referendum— National Elections Authority," *Ahram Online*, April 23, 2019. Many activists saw this admission as a good sign, one that probably meant the number of those who disapproved of the amendments was far higher. To them, the fact that the regime felt compelled to report three million "no" votes indicated the opposition to the amendments was so strong that the state could not claim the kind of sweeping support (usually in the high 90th percent) they had claimed in previously rigged elections and referendums.

61 Vivian Yee and Nada Rashwan, "Egypt's Protests Came as a Total Shock. The Man Behind Them Is Just as Surprising," *The New York Times*, September 22, 2019.

62 Sara Khorshid, "Egypt: The Youth Win," *Huffington Post*, May 30, 2014; Hend El-Behary, "Why Is There Low Youth Turnout in the 2018 Presidential Elections?" *Egypt Independent*, March 27, 2018.

63 Both Lenin and Gramsci agreed on the need for a tightly organized vanguard party as the instrument for revolution, but their visions for what that party should look like differed. Gramsci saw that social transformation would not, as Lenin suggested, occur at the hands of a homogenous, elite group of professional revolutionaries interceding on behalf of the proletariat, but would require the effort of the masses. In this respect, he envisioned a much more flexible party structure, an organization that was instructive

and coordinating in its role and devoted to nurturing organic working-class intellectuals to lead. Actively engaged in practical life "as constructor, organizer, 'permanent persuader' and not just a simple orator," these organic intellectuals would orient the intellectual activity of the masses towards a criticism of the status quo and help to stimulate the emergence of a "popular collective will" (Quintin Hoare and Geoffrey Nowell-Smith, *Selections from the Prison Notebooks* [London: Lawrence and Wishart, 1971], 10). While the idea of a revolutionary party per se might not be relevant to Egypt, the question I pose here is what kind of inspiration Egypt's activists might draw from these ideas in future resistance efforts.

64 Bayat, *Revolution without Revolutionaries*, 174.
65 Bayat, *Revolution without Revolutionaries*, 159.
66 Abdelrahman, *Egypt's Long Revolution*, 82.
67 Paolo Gerbaudo, "The Built-In Obsolescence of the Facebook Leader," *Jadaliyya*, September 5, 2014.
68 Gerbaudo, "The Built-In Obsolescence of the Facebook Leader."
69 Cambanis, *Once Upon a Revolution*, 211; Hellyer, *A Revolution Undone*, 140.
70 The Front's adopted structure was intentionally open and loose. In the press release to announce their launch, they stated their goal was to preserve the "horizontal, modular, organic network" that "mirrors the successful products of the revolution," showing little consideration for how this structure proved ineffective for the revolution in the long run. Once again, this speaks to the failure of revolutionaries to think in terms of long-term, organizational sustainability. (This press release was posted on Ahdaf Soueif's Facebook page on September 23, 2013: https://www.facebook.com/ahdafsoueif/posts/396510990478166.)
71 For an account from one of the Tamarod founders of how the military and Interior Ministry co-opted the movement, see Maged Atef and Sheera Frenkel, "How Egypt's Rebel Movement Helped Pave the Way for a Sisi Presidency," *BuzzFeed News*, April 15, 2014.
72 David Kirkpatrick, "Egypt's Crackdown on New Student Protests Arresting Scores," *The New York Times*, October 13, 2014.

Bibliography

Below is a list of references consulted for this study. Not all of them are cited in the text, but each of them has contributed to my understanding of the questions raised in this book.

Abaza, Mona. "Academic Tourists Sight-Seeing the Arab Spring." *Ahram Online*, September 26, 2011.
Abdalla, Ahmed. *The Student Movements and National Politics in Egypt 1923–1973*. London: Al Saqi Books, 1985.
Abdelrahman, Maha. "'With the Islamists? Sometimes. With the State? Never!' Cooperation between the Left and Islamists in Egypt." *British Journal of Middle Eastern Studies* 36, no.1 (April 2009): 37–54.
———. *Egypt's Long Revolution: Protest Movements and Uprisings*. New York, NY: Routledge, 2015.
Abdel Aziz, Sarah Ahmed. "Public Education and Private Tuitions: A System of Inadequacy." *Daily News Egypt*, December 26, 2015.
Abdel Kouddous, Sharif. "What Happened to Egypt's Liberals after the Coup?" *The Nation*, October 1, 2013.
Abou-El-Fadl, Reem. "The Road to Jerusalem through Tahrir Square: Anti-Zionism and Palestine in the 2011 Egyptian Revolution." *Journal of Palestinian Studies* 41, no. 2 (Winter 2012): 6–26.
———. "Mohamed Morsi Mubarak: The Myth of Egypt's Democratic Transition." *Jadaliyya*, February 11, 2013.
Aboulenein, Ahmed. "Egypt Blocks 21 Websites for 'Terrorism' and 'Fake News.'" *Reuters*, May 24, 2017.
Aboul Enein, Ahmed, Basil El-Dabh, Joel Gulhane, and Connor Molloy. "Remembering Mohamed Mahmoud: The Good, the Bad, and the Brotherhood." *Daily News Egypt*, November 19, 2012.
Abul-Magd, Zeinab. "The Army and the Economy in Egypt." *Jadaliyya*, December 23, 2011.
———. "Understanding SCAF." *The Cairo Review of Global Affairs*, Summer 2012.
———. *Militarizing the Nation: The Army, Business, and Revolution in Egypt*. New York, NY: Columbia University Press, 2017.
———. "Egypt's Coming Revolt of the Poor." *Foreign Policy*, March 31, 2017.

Achcar, Gilbert. *The People Want: A Radical Exploration of the Arab Uprisings*. Translated by G.M. Goshgarian. Berekely, CA: University of California Press, 2013.
Albrecht, Holger. *Raging Against the Machine: Political Opposition Under Authoritarianism in Egypt*. Syracuse, NY: Syracuse University Press, 2013.
Alexander, Anne, and Mostafa Bassiouny. *Bread, Freedom, and Social Justice: Workers and the Egyptian Revolution*. London: Zed Books, 2014.
Alexander, Ruth. "Counting Crowds: Was Egypt's Uprising the Biggest Ever?" *BBC*, July 16, 2013.
Ali, Amro. "Saeeds of Revolution: De-Mythologizing Khaled Saeed." *Jadaliyya*, June 4, 2012.
Ali, Fatuma Ahmed, and Macharia, Hannah Muthoni. "Women, Youth, and the Egyptian Arab Spring." *Peace Review: A Journal of Social Justice* 25, no. 3 (August 2013): 359–66.
Al-Ali, Nadje. *Secularism, Gender and the State in the Middle East*. Cambridge: Cambridge University Press, 2000.
———. "Feminist Dilemmas in (Counter-) Revolutionary Egypt." *Nordic Journal of Feminist and Gender Research* 24, no. 4 (2013): 312–16.
Alim, Frida. "The Politics of the Brotherhood Democracy: How the Muslim Brotherhood Burned Their Bridges." *Jadaliyya*, July 19, 2013.
"All According to Plan: The Rabʻa Massacre and Mass Killings of Protesters in Egypt." Human Rights Watch, August 12, 2014. https://www.hrw.org/report/2014/08/12/all-according-plan/raba-massacre-and-mass-killings-protesters-egypt.
Alsharif, Asma, and Yasmine Saleh. "Special Report—the Real Force Behind Egypt's 'Revolution of the State.'" *Reuters*, October 10, 2013.
Amar, Paul. "Egypt after Mubarak." *The Nation*, May 4, 2011.
———. *The Security Archipelago: Human-Security States, Sexuality Politics, and the End of Neoliberalism*. Durham, NC: Duke University Press, 2013.
Aminzade, Ronald R., Elizabeth J. Perry, and Jack A. Goldstone. "Leadership Dynamics and Dynamics of Contention." In *Silence and Voice in the Study of Contentious Politics*, edited by Ronald Aminzade, Jack Goldstone, Doug McAdam, Elizabeth Perry, William Sewell, Sidney Tarrow, and Charles Tilly, 126–54. New York, NY: Cambridge University Press, 2011.
Amnesty International Report 2012: The State of the World's Human Rights. London: Amnesty International, 2012.
Al-Anani, Khalil. "The Salafi–Brotherhood Feud in Egypt." *Al-Monitor*, February 21, 2013.
Anderson, Betty. "The Student Movement of 1968." *Jadaliyya*, March 9, 2011.
Arandel, Christian, and Manal El Batran. "A Shelter of Their Own: Informal Settlement Expansion in Greater Cairo and Government Responses." *Environment and Urbanization* 10, no. 1 (April 1998): 217–32.
"Asma Mahfouz & the YouTube Video That Helped Spark the Egyptian Uprising." *Democracy Now*, February 8, 2011.

Atef, Maged and Sheera Frenkel. "How Egypt's Rebel Movement Helped Pave the Way for a Sisi Presidency." *BuzzFeed News*, April 15, 2014.
Attia, Mona. *Building a House in Heaven: Pious Neoliberalism and Islamic Charity in Egypt*. Minneapolis: University of Minnesota Press, 2013.
Awad, Marwa, and Hugo Dixon. "Special Report: Inside the Egyptian Revolution." *Reuters*, April 13, 2011.
Al-Awadi, Hesham. *In Pursuit of Legitimacy: The Muslim Brothers and Mubarak, 1982–2000*. London: I.B.Tauris, 2004.
———. "Mubarak and the Islamists: Why Did the 'Honeymoon' End?" *Middle East Journal* 59, no. 1 (Winter 2005): 62–80.
Badran, Margot. *Feminists, Islam, and Nation: Gender and the Making of Modern Egypt*. Princeton, NJ: Princeton University Press, 1996.
Bahgat, Mirette. "Coptic Christians in Egypt: Standing at the Crossroads." *Huffington Post*, May 6, 2011.
Baker, Raymond William. *Egypt's Uncertain Revolution under Nasser and Sadat*. Boston, MA: Harvard University Press, 1978.
Bamyeh, Mohammed. "The Egyptian Revolution: First Impressions from the Field." *Jadaliyya*, February 11, 2011.
———. "The June Rebellion in Egypt." *Jadaliyya*, July 11, 2013.
Barker, Colin, Alan Johnson, and Michael Lavalette. "Leadership Matters: An Introduction." In *Leadership in Social Movements*, edited by Colin Barker, Alan Johnson, and Michael Lavalette, 1–23. Manchester: Manchester University Press, 2001.
Bayat, Asef. *Life as Politics: How Ordinary People Change the Middle East*. Stanford: Stanford University Press, 2009.
———. "Muslim Youth and the Claim of Youthfulness." In *Being Young and Muslim: New Cultural Politics in the Global South and North*, edited by Asef Bayat and Linda Herrera, 27–48. Oxford: Oxford University Press, 2010.
———. "A New Arab Street in Post-Islamist Times." *Foreign Policy*, January 26, 2011.
———. "Midwife for a Pregnant Egypt." *Jadaliyya*, July 11, 2013.
———. *Revolution without Revolutionaries: Making Sense of the Arab Spring*. Stanford, CA: Stanford University Press, 2017.
Bayat, Asef, and Linda Herrara. "Introduction: Being Young and Muslim in Neoliberal Times." In *Being Young and Muslim: New Cultural Politics in the Global South and North*, edited by Asef Bayat and Linda Herrera, 3–24. Oxford: Oxford University Press, 2010.
El-Behary, Hend. "Why Is There Low Youth Turnout in the 2018 Presidential Elections?" *Egypt Independent*, March 27, 2018.
Beinin, Joel. *Workers and Thieves: Labor Movements and Popular Uprisings in Tunisia and Egypt*. Stanford, CA: Stanford University Press, 2016.
Beinin, Joel, and Marie Duboc. "A Worker's Social Movement on the Margin of the Global Neoliberal Order, Egypt 2004–2012." In *Social Movements, Mobilization, and Contestation in the Middle East and North Africa*, edited by J. Beinin and F. Vairel, 205–27. Stanford: Stanford University Press, 2011.

Biehl, João, Byron Good, and Arthur Kleinman. "Introduction: Rethinking Subjectivity." In *Subjectivity: Ethnographic Investigations*, edited by João Biehl, Byron Good, and Arthur Kleinman, 1–24. Berkeley: University of California Press, 2007.
Bier, Laura. *Revolutionary Womanhood: Feminisms, Modernity, and the State in Nasser's Egypt*. Stanford, CA: Stanford University Press, 2011.
Biggs, Cassie. "Women Make Their Power Felt in Egyptian Revolution." *The National*, February 14, 2011.
Blaydes, Lisa. *Elections and Distributive Politics in Mubarak's Egypt*. Cambridge: Cambridge University Press, 2010.
Blumenthal, Max. "Egypt's Numbers Game: How Crazy Claims of 33 Million Protesters Were Used to Boost a Coup." *Alternet*, July 19, 2013.
Bradley, Matt. "Islamists Lead Massive Protest in Cairo." *The Wall Street Journal*, November 19, 2011.
Brown, Helen. "Organizing Activity in the Women's Movement: An Example of Distributed Leadership." *International Social Movement Research* 2 (1989): 225–40.
Brown, Nathan J. and Hesham Nasr. "Egypt's Judges Step Forward: The Judicial Election Boycott and Egyptian Reform." Carnegie Endowment for International Peace, Policy Outlook, May 13, 2005. https://carnegieendowment.org/2005/05/25/egypt-s-judges-step-forward-judicial-election-boycott-and-egyptian-reform-pub-16988.
Brownlee, Jason. *Authoritarianism in an Age of Democratization*. New York, NY: Cambridge University Press, 2007.
———. "Democratization in the Arab World: The Decline of Pluralism in Mubarak's Egypt." *Journal of Democracy* 13, no. 4 (October 2002): 6-14.
Buchanan, Ian. *A Dictionary of Critical Thinking*. Oxford: Oxford University Press, 2010.
Burgin, Say. "Understanding Antiwar Activism as a Gendering Activity: A Look at the U.S. Anti-Vietnam War Movement." *Journal of International Women's Studies* 13, no. 6 (December 2012): 18–31.
Burns, William Joseph. *Economic Aid and American Policy toward Egypt, 1955–1981*. Albany: State University of New York Press, 1985.
Bush, Ray. "The Revolution in Permanence." *Jadaliyya*, July 22, 2012.
Camaroff, Jean, and John Camaroff. "Reflections on Youth: From the Past to the Postcolony." In *Frontiers of Capital: Ethnographic Reflections on the New Economy*, edited by Melissa S. Fish and Greg Downey, 267-81. Durham: Duke University Press, 2006.
Cambanis, Thannasis. "The Most Worrying Thing about Egypt's Coup: The Police." *The Atlantic*, July 8, 2013.
———. "What's Missing from Egypt's Latest Revolution? People." *The Atlantic*, July 12, 2013.
———. "Catching Up with the Leaders of the Tahrir Square Uprising." *Spiegal*, April 2, 2015.

———. *Once Upon a Revolution: An Egyptian Story*. New York, NY: Simon and Schuster, 2015.
Carr, Sarah. "Sexual Assault and the State: A History of Violence." *Mada Masr*, July 7, 2014.
Castells, Manuel. *Networks of Outrage and Hope: Social Movements in the Internet Age*. Cambridge: Polity Press, 2012.
Chakravarti, Leila Zaki. "Performing Masculinity: The Football Ultras in Post-revolutionary Egypt." *Open Democracy*, March 8, 2013.
Chalcraft, John. "Horizontalism in the Egyptian Revolutionary Process." *Middle East Report* 42 (March 2012): 6–11.
Cole, Juan. "Democratisation, Religious Extremism, Fragile States, and Insurgencies: Bush's Legacies to Obama and the Challenges Ahead." In *American Democracy Promotion in the Changing Middle East: From Bush to Obama*, edited by Shahram Akbarzadeh, Benjamin MacQueen, James Piscatori, and Amin Saikal, 9–26. London and New York: Routledge, 2013.
———. "The Arab Millennials Will Be Back." *The Huffington Post*, June 30, 2014.
———. *The New Arabs: How the Millennial Generation Is Changing the Middle East*. New York, NY: Simon and Schuster, 2014.
Connell, R.W. *Masculinities*. Berkeley, CA: University of California Press, 2005.
Cook, Steven A. "The Frankenstein of Tahrir Square." *Foreign Policy*, December 19, 2011.
———. *The Struggle for Egypt*. Oxford: Oxford University Press, 2012.
Davis, Nancy J., and Robert V. Robinson. *Claiming Society for God: Religious Movements and Social Welfare*. Bloomington: Indiana University Press, 2012.
de Andrés, Jésus and Rubén Ruiz Ramas. "Charles Tilly's Concept of *Revolution* and the '*Color Revolutions*.'" In *Regarding Tilly: Conflict, Power, and Collective Action*, edited by Maria J. Funes, 135–56. Lanham: University Press of America, 2016.
DeCesare, M. "Toward an Interpretive Approach to Social Movement Leadership." *International Review of Modern Sociology* 39, no. 2 (Fall 2013): 239–57.
Defronzo, James. *Revolutions and Revolutionary Movements*. New York: Routledge, 2018.
Della Porta, Donatella, Hanspeter Kriesi, and Dieter Rucht, eds. *Social Movements in a Globalizing World*. Basingtoke: Palgrave Macmillan, 2009.
De Smet, Brecht. *A Dialectical Pedagogy of Revolt: Gramsci, Vygtosky, and the Egyptian Revolution*. Leiden: Brill, 2014.
Disney, Jennifer Leigh and Joyce Gelb. "Feminist Organizational 'Success': The State of US Women's Movement Organizations in the 1990s." *Women and Politics* 21, no. 4 (October 2008): 39–76.
Dorman, W. J. "Informal Cairo: Between Islamist Insurgency and the Neglectful State?" *Security Dialogue* 40, no. 4/5 (September 2009): 419–41.
Edmunds, June, and Bryan S. Turner. "Global Generations: Social Change in the Twentieth Century." *The British Journal of Sociology* 56, no. 4 (December 2005): 559–77.

"Egypt: Execution of Nine Defendants after Unfair Trial Is Retaliation, Not Justice." Cairo Institute for Human Rights Studies, February 16, 2019.
"Egypt: Lynching of Shia Follows Months of Hate Speech: Police Fail to Protect Muslim Minority." Human Rights Watch, June 27, 2013.
"Egypt: Rab'a Killings Likely Crimes Against Humanity." Human Rights Watch, August 12, 2014.
"Egypt: Security Forces Used Excessive Lethal Force." Human Rights Watch, August 19, 2013.
"Egypt: Torture Epidemic May Be Crime Against Humanity." Human Rights Watch, September 6, 2017.
"Egyptian High School Students Say System Is 'Unfair', Stage Protests." *Ahram Online*, July 1, 2014.
"Egyptian President Mubarak Announces He Will Not Run for Reelection; Reaction From Prince Hassan Bin Talal of Jordan." *CNN*, February 1, 2011.
"Egyptian Solidarity Convoy Crosses into Embattled Gaza." *Ahram Online*, November 18, 2012.
"Egyptian Tycoon Blames 'Cowardly' Ministry for Tax Dispute." *Ahram Online*, September 30, 2014.
"Egypt's Constitutional Amendments Passed by 88.83% in Referendum—National Elections Authority." *Ahram Online*, April 23, 2019.
"Egypt's Sisi Pledges Crackdown on Police Abuses after Shooting." *BBC*, February 19, 2016.
Elmasry, Mohamed. "Unpacking Anti-Muslim Brotherhood Discourse." *Jadaliyya*, July 28, 2013.
Eskandar, Wael. "Brothers and Officers: A History of Pacts." *Jadaliyya*, January 25, 2013.
"Extraordinary Rendition in U.S. Counterterrorism Policy: The Impact on Transatlantic Relations." Joint Hearing before the Subcommittee on International Organizations, Human Rights, and Oversight and the Subcommittee on Europe of the Committee on Foreign Affairs, One Hundred Tenth Congress. First Session, April 17, 2007. Serial No. 110–28.
Faheem, Karim. "Egyptians Denounce President Sisi in Biggest Rally in 2 Years." *The New York Times*, April 6, 2016.
Fahmy, Khaled. "The Long Revolution." *Aeon*, November 3, 2015.
Fanon, Frantz. *The Wretched of the Earth*. Translated by Constance Farrington. New York, NY: Grove, 1968.
Farag, Mona. "The Muslim Sisters and the January 25th Revolution." *Journal of International Women's Studies* 13, no. 5 (October 2012): 228–37.
Farag, Nadine. "Between Piety and Politics: Social Services and the Muslim Brotherhood." *Frontline*, February 22, 2011.
Farah, Nadia Ramsis. *Egypt's Political Economy: Power Relations in Development*. Cairo: The American University in Cairo Press, 2009.
Faruq, Ayman. "Bawwabat al-Ahram tanshur nus kalimat wazir al-dakhiliya fi mu'tamar sahafi ba'd fad i'tisam Rab'a wa Nahda." *Bawwabat al-Ahram*, August 14, 2013.

Fathi, Yasmine. "Torture in Egypt: Never Again?" *Ahram Online*, June 25, 2011.
Fenner, Sofia, and Mohamed Talaat. "Shaabi Cairo after June 30th: The View from Shubra." *Muftah*, November 14, 2013.
FIDH, Nazra for Feminist Studies, New Women Foundation, and the Uprising of Women in the Arab World. *Egypt Keeping Women Out: Sexual Violence Against Women in the Public Spehere*. 2014. https://www.fidh.org/IMG/pdf/egypt_women_final_english.pdf.
Fishman, J. R., and F. Solomon. "Youth and Social Action: An Introduction." *Journal of Social Issues* 20, no. 4 (1964): 1–27.
Flanagan, Constance A. and Amy K. Syversten. "Youth as Social Construct and Social Actor." In *Youth Activism: An International Encyclopedia*, vol. 1, edited by Lonne R. Sherrod, 11–19. Westport, CT: Greenwood Press, 2006.
Fonseca, Marco. *Gramsci's Critique of Civil Society: Towards a New Concept of Hegemony*. New York, NY: Routledge, 2016.
Freeman, Jo. "The Tyranny of Structurelessness." In *Radical Feminism*, edited by Anne Koedt, Ellene Levine, and Anita Rapone, 285–99. New York, NY: Quadrangle, 1972.
Ganz, Marshall. *Why David Sometimes Wins: Leadership, Organization, and Strategy in the California Farm Worker Movement*. Oxford: Oxford University Press, 2010.
Ganz, Marshall and Liz McKenna. "The Practice of Social Movement Leadership." *Mobilizing Ideas*, June 23, 2017.
Gardner, Lloyd C. *The Road to Tahrir Square: Egypt and the United States from the Rise of Nasser to the Fall of Mubarak*. New York, NY: The New Press, 2011.
Gerbaudo, Paolo. *Tweets and the Streets: Social Media and Contemporary Activism*. London: Pluto Press, 2012.
———. "The Built-In Obsolescence of the Facebook Leader." *Jadaliyya*, September 5, 2014.
Gerges, Fawaz A. *Obama and the Middle East: The End of America's Moment?* New York: St. Martin's Press, 2012.
Ghabra, Shafeeq. "The Egyptian Revolution: Causes and Dynamics." In *Routledge Handbook of the Arab Spring*, edited by Larbi Sidki, 199–214. New York, NY: Routledge, 2015.
Ghannam, Farha. *Live and Die Like a Man: Gender Dynamics in Urban Egypt*. Stanford, CA: Stanford University Press, 2013.
El-Ghobashy, Mona. "The Metamorphosis of the Egyptian Muslim Brothers." *International Journal of Middle East Studies* 37, no. 3 (August 2005): 373–95.
———. "The Praxis of the Egyptian Revolution." *Middle East Research and Information Project* 41, no. 258 (2011).
Ghonim, Wael. *Revolution 2.0: The Power of the People is Greater Than the People in Power: A Memoir*. Boston, MA: Houghton Mifflin Harcourt, 2012.
Giglio, Mike. "Morsi and the Military: Egypt President Firm on Constitution Vote." *The Daily Beast*, December 9, 2012.
Ginsburg, Tom. "The Real Winner in the Egyptian Constitution? The Military." *HuffPost*, December 7, 2012.

Gitlin, Todd. *The Whole World Is Watching: Mass Media and the Making and Unmaking of the New Left*. Berkeley, CA: University of California Press, 1980.

Goldstone, Jack. "Toward a Fourth Generation of Revolutionary Theory." *Annual Reviews of Political Science* 4 (June 2001): 139–87.

———. *Revolutions: A Very Short Introduction*. Oxford: Oxford University Press, 2014.

Goodwin, Jeff. *No Other Way Out: States and Revolutionary Movements, 1945–1991*. Cambridge: Cambridge University Press, 2001.

Gudière, Mathieu. *Historical Dictionary of Islamic Fundamentalism*. Lanham, MD: Rowman and Littlefield Publishing Group, Inc., 2012.

Gunning, Jeroen, and Ilan Zvi Baron. *Why Occupy a Square? People, Protests, and Movements in the Egyptian Revolution*. Oxford: Oxford University Press, 2014.

Gustin, Sam. "Social Media Sparked, Accelerated Egypt's Revolutionary Fire." *Wired*, February 11, 2011.

Haddad, Bassam. "English Translation of Interview with Hossam El-Hamalawy on the Role of Labor/Unions in the Egyptian Revolution." *Jadaliyya*, April 30, 2011.

El-Hamalawy, Hossam. "Comrades and Brothers." *Middle East Report* 242 (Spring 2007).

———. "Resistance in Egypt." *MR Online*, August 18, 2008.

———. "Revolt in Mahallah: As Food Prices Rise in Egypt, Class Struggle is Heating Up." *International Socialist Review* no. 59 (May–June 2008).

———. "Egyptian Strikes: More Than Bread and Butter." *Socialist Review* no. 325 (2008).

———. "Egypt's Revolution Has Been 10 Years in the Making." *The Guardian*, March 2, 2011.

Hamilton, Omar. "Everything Was Possible." *Mada Masr*, August 17, 2013.

Hamzawy, Amr. "Egypt after July 3: A Crossroads for Democracy." Atlantic Council, October 24, 2013. https://www.atlanticcouncil.org/blogs/menasource/egypt-after-july-3-a-crossroads-for-democracy/.

———. *Anti-democratic Deceptions: How Egyptian Liberals Endorse Autocracy*. 2015. YouTube video posted by Stanford Center for Demoracy, Development and the Rule of Law. https://www.youtube.com/watch?v=15kz9CVRFHg&t=532s.

———. "Egypt's Resilient and Evolving Social Activism." Carnegie Endowment for International Peace, April 5, 2017. https://carnegieendowment.org/2017/04/05/egypt-s-resilient-and-evolving-social-activism-pub-68578.

Hanafi, Sari. "The Arab Revolutions: The Emergence of a New Political Subjectivity." *Contemporary Arab Affairs* 5, no. 2, (March 2012): 198–213.

Hanieh, A. "Egypt's Orderly Transition: International Aid and the Rush to Structural Adjustment."' In *The Dawn of the Arab Uprisings: End of an Old Order?* Edited by B. Haddad, R. Bsheer, and Z. Abu-Rish, 124–36. London: Pluto Press, 2012.

Hartmann, Sarah. "The Informal Market of Education in Egypt: Private Tutoring and Its Implications." Working Paper No. 88, 2008. Mainz, Germany: Institut für Ethnologie und Afrikastudien, Johannes Gutenberg-Universität.

Harvey, David. *A Brief History of Neoliberalism*. New York, NY: Oxford University Press, 2005.

Hatem, Mervat. "Economic and Political Liberation in Egypt and the Demise of State Feminism." *International Journal of Middle East Studies* 24, no. 2 (May 1992): 231–51.

Hearst, David, and Abdel-Rahman Hussein. "Egypt's Supreme Court Dissolves Parliament and Outrages Islamists." *The Guardian*, June 14, 2012.

Hellyer, H.A. "Lessons from a Lost Revolution: Egypt's Fate Still Hangs in the Balance." *Muftah*, February 1, 2011.

———. "Egypt: Inevitable Consequences of June 30." *Al Arabiya*, November 11, 2013.

———. "Egypt's 'Day After.'" *Al Arabiya*, August 16, 2013.

———. *A Revolution Undone: Egypt's Road Beyond Revolt*. Oxford: Oxford University Press, 2016.

Herda-Rapp, Ann. "The Power of Informal Leadership: Women Leaders in the Civil Rights Movement." *Sociological Focus* 31, no. 4 (November 1998): 341–55.

Herrera, Linda. "'Young Egyptians' Quest for Jobs and Justice: New Cultural Politics in the Global South and North." In *Being Young and Muslim: New Cultural Politics in the Global South and North*, edited by Asef Bayat and Linda Herrera, 27–48. Oxford: Oxford University Press, 2010.

———. "Meet AbdelRahman Mansour Who Made 25 January a Date to Remember." *Jadaliyya*, January 25, 2013.

———. "Youth and Citizenship in a Digital Age: A View from Egypt." *Harvard Educational Review* 82, no. 3 (September 2012): 333–52.

———. *Revolution in the Age of Social Media: The Egyptian Popular Insurrection and the Internet*. Brooklyn, NY: Verso, 2014.

Hersh, Joshua. "Egypt's Media Counter-Revolution." *The New Yorker*, August 20, 2013.

Hickel, Jason. "Neoliberal Egypt: The Hijacked Revolution." *Al Jazeera*, March 29, 2012.

Hill, Evan. "The Youth of Tahrir Square." *Al Jazeera*, February 10, 2011.

Hinnebusch, Raymond A. *Egyptian Politics Under Sadat*. Cambridge: Cambridge University Press, 1985.

———. "The Foreign Policy of Egypt." In *The Foreign Policy of Middle East States*, edited by Raymond A. Hinnebusch and Anoushiravan Ehteshami, 91–115. Boulder, CO: Lynne Rienner Publishers, 2002.

Hitafat al-shabab al masri fi Ghazza. YouTube channel of Ibrahim Saad, November 19, 2012. http://www.youtube.com/watch?v=6Q0vZDxDE9c.

Hoare, Quintin, and Geoffrey Nowell-Smith. *Selections from the Prison Notebooks*. London: Lawrence and Wishart, 1971.

Holmes, Amy Austin. "There Are Weeks When Decades Happen: Structure and Strategy in the Egyptian Revolution." *Mobilization* 17, no. 4 (December 2012): 391–410.

Honwana, Alcinda. *Youth and Revolution in Tunisia*. New York, NY: Zed Books, 2013.

El-Houdaiby, Ibrahim. "Focus on Politics, Not Identity." *Ahram Online*, August 14, 2011.

———. "Egypt: Nothing Was Inevitable." *Ahram Online*, September 13, 2013.

Howeidy, Amira. "A Day at 'Hyde Park.'" *Al-Ahram Weekly*, March 27–April 2, 2003.

———. "Matariya, Egypt's New Theater of Dissent." *Middle East Report Online*, June 4, 2015.

Hubbard, Ben and David Kirkpatrick. "Sudden Improvements in Egypt Suggest a Campaign to Undermine Morsi." *The New York Times*, July 10, 2013.

Hubbard, Ben, and Mayy El Sheikh. "New Governor Is a Shock to Some Inside Egypt." *The New York Times*, June 16, 2013.

Hunt-Hendrix, Leah, and Barbara Ibrahim. "Youth-led Pathways to Social and Political Change: Faith and Service in Contemporary Egypt." *Global Studies of Childhood Studies* 5, no. 2 (June 2015): 158–77.

Hussein, Abdel-Rahman. "Egyptian Assembly Passes Draft Constitution Despite Protests." *The Guardian*, November 30, 2012.

Ibrahim, Ekram. "Muhammad Mahmud Clashes 1 Year On: 'A Battle for Dignity.'" *Ahram Online*, November 19, 2012.

"In Translation: The Revolutionary Youth Coalition's Final Report." *Jadaliyya*, July 19, 2012.

Ille, Sebastian. "Private Tutoring in Egypt: Quality Education in a Deadlock between Low Income, Status, and Motivation." Working Paper No. 178, 2015. The Egyptian Center for Economic Studies.

Iskandar, Adel. "Tamarod: Egypt's Revolution Hones Its Skills." *Jadaliyya*, June 30, 2013.

Ismail, Farrag. "Ex-minister Suspected Behind Church Bombing." *Al Arabiya News*, February 7, 2011.

Ismail, Salwa. *Political Life in Cairo's Popular Quarters: Encountering the Everyday State*. Minneapolis, MN: The University of Minnesota Press, 2006.

———. "A Private Estate Called Egypt." *The Guardian*, February 6, 2011.

———. "Civilities, Subjectivities and Collective Action: Preliminary Reflections in Light of the Egyptian Revolution." *Third World Quarterly* 32, no. 5, (June 2011): 989–95.

———. "The Egyptian Revolution against the Police." *Social Research* 79, no. 2 (Summer 2012): 435–62.

al-Ittihadiya: "Presidential Palace" Clashes in Cairo, 5–6 December 2012. Cairo Institute for Human Rights Studies, December 2012, https://cihrs.org/wp-content/uploads/2012/12/Ittihadiyya.rep_.CIHRS_.Eng_.Dec_.pdf.

Jacinto, Leela. "Enter the 'Baltagiya': Egypt's Repression Spills out of the Torture Chambers." *France24*, February 9, 2011.

Jacobs, Samuel P. "Gene Sharp, the Egyptian Revolt's Prophet of Nonviolence." *The Daily Beast*, February 14, 2011.

Jadaliyya Reports. "Statement of the April 6 Movement Regarding the Demands of the Youth and the Refusal to Negotiate with Any Side." *Jadaliyya*, February 6, 2011.

Jadallah, Dina. "Economic Aid to Egypt: Promoting Progress or Subordination?" *Class, Race and Corporate Power* 3, no. 2 (2015).

Jones, Kathleen B. *Compassionate Authority: Democracy and the Representation of Women*. New York, NY: Routledge, 1993.

Joseph, Suad, ed. *Intimate Selving in Arab Families: Gender, Self, and Identity*. Syracuse, NY: Syracuse University Press, 1999.

Joya, Angela. "The Egyptian Revolution: Crisis of Neoliberalism and the Potential for Democratic Politics." *Review of African Political Economy* 38, no. 129 (September 2011): 367–86.

Kandil, Hazem. *Soldiers, Spies, and Statesmen: Egypt's Road to Revolt*. London: Verso, 2012.

———. "Soldiers without Generals." *Dissent Magazine*, October 21, 2012.

Kassem, Maye. *Egyptian Politics: The Dynamics of Authoritarian Rule*. Boulder, CO: Lynne Rienner Publishers, 2004.

Kaye, Dalia Dassa, Frederic Wehrey, Audra K. Grant, Dale Stahl. *More Freedom, Less Terror: Liberalization and Political Violence in the Middle East*. Pittsburgh, PA: Rand Corporation, 2008.

"Kefaya: The Origins of Mubarak's Downfall." *Egypt Independent*, December 12, 2011.

Ketchley, Neil. *Egypt in a Time of Revolution*. Cambridge: Cambridge University Press, 2017.

"Khaled Saeed: The Face That Launched a Revolution." *Ahram Online*, June 6, 2012.

Khalidi, Rashid. "Preliminary Historical Observations on the Arab Revolutions of 2011." *Jadaliyya*, March 21, 2011.

Khalil, Ashraf. *Liberation Square: Inside the Egyptian Revolution and the Rebirth of a Nation*. New York, NY: St. Martin's Press, 2011.

———. "Tunis Envy." *Arabist*, June 7, 2012.

Khalil, Shaimaa. "Egypt: The Legacy of Muhammad Mahmud Street." *BBC News*, November 19, 2012.

Khorshid, Sara. "Egypt: The Youth Win." *Huffington Post*, May 30, 2014.

Kingsley, Patrick. "Mass March in Port Said as Anger Grows on Anniversary of Egyptian Revolution." *The Guardian*, February 1, 2013.

———. "Tamarod Campaign Gathers Momentum among Egypt's Opposition." *The Guardian*, June 27, 2013.

Kirkpatrick, David. "Wired and Shrewd, Young Egyptians Guide Revolt." *The New York Times*, February 9, 2011.

———. "Egyptian Liberals Embrace the Military, Brooking No Dissent." *The New York Times*, July 15, 2013.

———. "Egypt's Crackdown on New Student Protests Arresting Scores." *The New York Times*, October 13, 2014.

Kirkpatrick, David, and David E. Sanger. "The Tunisia-Egyptian Link That Shook Arab History." *The New York Times*, February 13, 2011.
Kotb, Amrou. "The Mother of the World." Atlantic Council, February 14, 2014.
Landes, Joan B. *Women and the Public Sphere in the Age of the French Revolution.* Ithaca, NY: Cornell University Press, 1988.
Lazreg, Marnia. *The Eloquence of Silence: Algerian Women in Question.* London: Routledge, 1994.
Lenin, Vladimir. *What Is to Be Done?* Translated by S.V. Utechin and Patricia Utechin. Oxford: Oxford University Press, 1963.
Luxemburg, Rosa. "The Political Leader of the German Working Classes." In *Rosa Luxemburg Gesammelte Werke* [Collected Works], vol. 2, edited by Annelies Laschitza and Eckhard Müller. East Berlin: Dietz Verlag, 1970–75.
Lynch, Marc. "Young Brothers in Cyberspace." *Middle East Report* 245 (Winter 2007).
Lyons, Tanya. *Guns and Guerrilla Girls: Women in the Zimbabwean National Liberation Struggle.* Trenton, NJ: Africa World Press, 2004.
MacFarquhar, Neil, and Dina Salah. "Youth Leader in Egypt Straddles the Line of Revolution and Electoral Change." *The New York Times*, November 27, 2011.
El-Mahdi, Rabab. "Does Political Islam Impede Gender-Based Mobilization? The Case of Egypt." *Totalitarian Movement and Political Religions* 11, no. 3–4 (2010): 379–96.
———. "Against Marginalization: Workers, Youth and Class in the 25 January Revolution." In *Marginality and Exclusion in Egypt*, edited by Ray Bush and Habib Ayeb, 133–47. London: Zed Books, 2012.
Mahmoud, Hussein. "MB and NAC's Petition 7 Demands for Change Approaches 1,000,000 Signatures Target." *Ikhwan Web*, October 5, 2010.
Maira, Sunaina and Julie Sze. "Dispatches from Pepper-Spray University: Privatization, Repression, and Revolt." *American Quarterly* 64, no. 2 (2012): 315–30.
Malthaner, Stefan. *Mobilizing the Faithful: Militant Islamist Groups and Their Constituencies.* Frankfurt: Campus Verlag Publishers, 2011.
Mandour, Maged. "The Weakness of the Egyptian Revolutionary Movement." *OpenDemocracy*, August 19, 2013.
Mannheim, Karl. "The Problem of Generations." In *Essays on the Sociology of Knowledge*, edited by P. Kecskemeti, 276–322. London: Routledge and Kegan Paul, 1952 (originally published 1928).
Mansour, Sherif. "Enough Is Not Enough: Achievements and Shortcomings of Kefaya, the Egyptian Movement for Change." In *Civilian Jihad: Nonviolent Struggle, Democratization, and Governance in the Middle East*, edited by Maria J. Stephan, 205–18. New York, NY: Palgrave McMillan, 2009.
Marshall, Shana. "The Egyptian Armed Forces and the Remaking of an Empire." Carnegie Middle East Center, April 2015.
Martini, Jeff and Julie Taylor. "Commanding Democracy in Egypt: The Military's Attempt to Manage the Future." *Foreign Affairs*, September/October, 2011.
Masoud, Tarek. "Egypt." In *The Middle East*, edited by Ellen Lust, 448–77. Los Angeles, CA: Sage CQ Press, 2013.

———. "The Muslim Brotherhood in Egypt." *The Oxford Handbook of Islam and Politics*, edited by John L. Esposito and Emad El-Din Shahin, 475–505. (Oxford: Oxford University Press, 2013).

Mayer, Jane. "Outsourcing Torture." *The New Yorker*, February 6, 2005.

McDermott, Anthony. *Egypt from Nasser to Mubarak: A Flawed Revolution*. New York: Routledge, 1988.

Mclaren, Peter, Gustavo Fischman, Silvia Serra, and Estanislao Antelo. "The Specter of Gramsci: Revolutionary Praxis and the Committed Intellectual." In *Gramsci and Education*, edited by Carmel Borg, Joseph Buttigieg, and Peter Mayo, 147–78. Maryland: Rowman and Littlefield Publishers, Inc., 2002.

Mekkawi, Naglaa. "A Love, Hate Relationship: Al-Nour and Egypt's Muslim Brotherhood." *Al Arabiya News*, August 22, 2013.

El Meshad, Mohamed. "Sisi Sours on the Media." Carnegie Endowment for International Peace, April 29, 2016. https://carnegieendowment.org/sada/63493.

Mikdashi, Maya. "The Gendered Body Public." *Jadaliyya*, January 28, 2013.

Moghadam, V.M. *Modernizing Women: Gender and Social Change in the Middle East*. Boulder, CO: Lynne Rienner Publishers, Inc., 2003.

Morris, Alan D., and Suzanne Staggenborg. "Leadership in Social Movements." In *The Blackwell Companion to Social Movements*, edited by D. Snow, S. Soule, and H. Kriesi, 171–98. Malden, MA: Blackwell Publishing, 2004.

Moruzzi, Norma Claire. "Gender and Revolutions: Critique Interrupted." *Middle East Report* 268 (Fall 2013).

Naber, Nadine. "Imperial Feminism, Islamophobia, and the Egyptian Revolution." *Jadaliyya*, February 11, 2011.

———. *Arab America: Gender, Cultural Politics, and Activism*. New York, NY: New York University Press, 2012.

Nasralla, Shadia. "Egypt Designates Muslim Brotherhood as Terrorist Group." *Reuters*, December 25, 2013.

Nawara, Wael. "Egypt's Crowd Democracy." *Al-Monitor*, July 26, 2013.

———. "Egypt's Ultras: Revolutionaries to Villains?" *Al-Monitor*, November 18, 2013.

———. "Sisi Loses Turnout Battle in Egypt's Election." *Al-Monitor*, May 27, 2014.

Nepstad, Sharon Erickson, and Clifford Bob. "When Do Leaders Matter? Hypothesis on Leadership Dynamics in Social Movements." *Mobilization: An International Journal* 11, no. 1 (February 2006): 1–22.

Nessim, Rana. "Cairo: A History of People's Right to the City." *Open Democracy*, July 19, 2014.

Osman, Tarek. *Egypt on the Brink: From the Rise of Nasser to the Fall of Mubarak*. New Haven, CT: Yale University Press, 2011.

Ortner, Sherry B. *Anthropology and Social Theory: Culture, Power, and the Acting Subject*. Durham, NC: Duke University Press, 2006.

Parvez, D. "Egypt's Copts Reel from Sectarian Violence." *Al Jazeera*, August 20, 2013.

Peteet, Julia. "Male Gender and Rituals of Resistance in the Palestinian *Intifada*: A Cultural Politics of Violence." *American Ethnologist* 21, no. 1 (February 1994): 31–49.

Peterson, M.A. *Connected in Cairo: Growing Up Cosmopolitan in the Modern Middle East*. Bloomington, IL: Indiana University Press, 2011.

Piferro, Elena. "Beyond Rules and Regulations: The Growth of Informal Cairo." In *Cairo's Informal Areas Between Urban Challenges and Hidden Potentials: Fact. Voices. Visions*, 21–27. Cairo: German Technical Cooperation (GTZ), 2009.

Polletta, Francesca. *Freedom Is an Endless Meeting: Democracy in American Social Movements*. Chicago, IL: University of Chicago Press, 2002.

Prokhorov, A.M., ed. *The Great Soviet Encyclopedia*. (Vols. 1–31). New York, NY: Macmillan, 1974–83, 1979.

"Protesters Flood Egypt Streets." *Al Jazeera*, February 11, 2011.

"Protesters Torch Egypt Police Post." *Al Jazeera*, January 27, 2011.

Reger, Jo. "Blinded by Gender: The Study of Leadership Dilemmas and U.S. Feminism." *Gender and Society*, May 30, 2017.

Reid, Donald Malcolm. *Cairo University and the Making of Modern Egypt*. Cambridge: Cambridge University Press, 1990.

Rennick, Sarah Anne. *Politics and Revolution in Egypt: Rise and Fall of Youth Activists*. New York, NY: Routledge, 2018.

"Revolution Youth Coalition Refuses to Meet Clinton." *Ahram Online*, March 15, 2011.

Robnett, Belinda. *How Long? How Long? African-American Women in the Struggle for Civil Rights*. New York, NY: Oxford University Press, 1997.

Rocco, Roberto. "David Harvey in Tahrir Square: The Dispossessed, the Discontented and the Egyptian Revolution." *Third World Quarterly* 34, no. 3 (May 2013): 423–40.

Rutherford, Bruce. *Egypt after Mubarak: Liberalism, Islam, and Democracy in the Arab World*. Princeton, NJ: Princeton University Press, 2008.

Ryder, N. B. "The Cohort as a Concept in the Study of Social Change." *American Sociological Review* 30, no. 6 (December 1965): 843–61.

Sabry, Bassem. "The Revolution Will Be Minimized." *Foreign Policy*, June 11, 2012.

———. "How Morsi and the Brotherhood Lost Egypt." *Al-Monitor*, July 4, 2013.

Safieddin, Hichame. "Revolutions in Tunisia and Egypt: How 'Spontaneous' Are They?" *The Bullet*, February 1, 2011.

Said, Atef. "The Egyptian Revolution: Ethnographic Notes from Tahrir." *Footnotes* 39, no. 6 (July–August 2011): 4, 8.

———. "The Paradox of Transition to 'Democracy' under Military Rule." *Social Research* 79, no. 2 (Summer 2012): 397–434.

———. "The Tahrir Effect: History, Space, and Protest in the Egyptian Revolution." Unpublished PhD Thesis, University of Michigan, 2014.

Salem, Mahmoud. "The Way of the Revolution Front: A Critique." *Daily News Egypt*, October 8, 2013.

Sallam, Hesham. "Reflections on Egypt after March 19." *Jadaliyya*, May 31, 2011.

———. "Elections in the Midst of Revolution." *Jadaliyya*, November 28, 2011.

———. "Letting Go of Revolutionary Purity." *Jadaliyya*, January 25, 2014.
Schielke, Samuli. *Egypt in the Future Tense: Hope, Frustration, and Ambivalence before and after 2011*. Bloomington, IN: Indiana University Press, 2015.
Séjourné, Marion. "The History of Informal Settlements." In *Cairo's Informal Areas Between Urban Challenges and Hidden Potentials: Fact. Voices. Visions*, 17–20. Cairo: German Technical Cooperation (GTZ), 2009.
Selbin, Eric. "Revolution in the Real World: Bringing Agency Back In." In *Theorizing Revolutions*, edited by John Foran, 118–32. London: Routledge, 2005.
Sennot, Charles M. "Cairo: The First Day of a New Egypt." *Frontline*, February 11, 2011.
El-Shakry, Omnia. "Egypt's Three Revolutions: The Force of History behind This Popular Uprising." *Jadaliyya*, February 6, 2011.
Shama, Nael. *Egyptian Foreign Policy from Mubarak to Morsi: Against the National Interest*. London: Routledge, 2013.
Shehata, Dina. *Islamists and Secularists in Egypt: Opposition, Conflict, and Cooperation*. New York, NY: Routledge, 2009.
———. "al-Harakat al ihtijajiya fi Misr." In *'Awdat al-siyasa: al-harakat al ihtijajiya al-jadida fi Misr*, edited by Dina Shehata, 11–20. Cairo: Al-Ahram Center for Political and Strategic Studies, 2010.
———. "al-Harakat al-shababiya wa thawrat 25 yanayir." *Strategy Paper Series* 218. Cairo: Al-Ahram Center for Political and Strategic Studies, 2011.
———. "Youth Movements and the 25 January Revolution." In *Arab Spring in Egypt: Revolution and Beyond*, edited by Bahgat Korany and Rabab El-Mahdi, 105–24. Cairo: The American University in Cairo Press, 2012.
Sheldon, Kathleen. "Women and Revolution in Mozambique: A Luta Continua." In *Women and Revolution in Africa, Asia, and the New World*, edited by Mary Ann Tetréault, 33–61. Columbia, SC: University of South Carolina Press, 1994.
Shenker, Jack. "And the Rich Got Richer." *The Guardian*, November 8, 2009.
———. *The Egyptians: A Radical History of Egypt's Unfinished Revolution*. New York, NY: The New Press, 2017.
El-Sherif, Ashraf. "The Ultras' Politics of Fun Confront Tyranny." *Jadaliyya*, February 5, 2012.
———. "The Brotherhood's Downfall (Part 1)." Translated by Dina Hussein. *Mada Masr*, August 5, 2013.
Sherwood, Harriet. "Egypt Cancels Israeli Gas Contract." *The Guardian*, April 23, 2012.
Sholkamy, Hania. "Women Are Also Part of This Revolution." In *Arab Spring in Egypt: Revolution and Beyond*, edited by Bahgat Korany and Rabab El-Mahdi, 153–74. Cairo: The American University in Cairo Press, 2012.
Shukrallah, Hani. "Egypt's Revolution: As It Might Have Been, as It Could Be." *Ahram Online*, January 25, 2013.
Sims, David. *Understanding Cairo: The Logic of a City out of Control*. Cairo: The American University in Cairo Press, 2010.
———. "The Arab Housing Paradox." *The Cairo Review of Global Affairs*, November 24, 2013.

Singerman, Diane. *Cairo Contested: Governance, Urban Space, and Global Modernity.* Cairo: The American University in Cairo Press, 2009.

———. "The Negotiation of Waithood: The Political Economy of Delayed Marriage in Egypt." In *Arab Youth: Social Mobilization in Times of Risk*, edited by S. Khalaf and R. Khalaf, 67–78. London: Saqi Books, 2011.

———. "Youth, Gender, and Dignity in the Egyptian Uprising." *Journal of Middle East Women's Studies* 9, no. 3 (Fall 2013): 1–27.

Singerman, Diane, and Paul Amar. *Cairo Cosmopolitan: Politics, Culture, and Urban Space in the Globalized Middle East.* Cairo: The American University in Cairo Press, 2006.

Singh, Amrit. *Globalizing Torture: CIA Secret Detention and Extraordinary Rendition.* New York: Open Society Foundations, 2013.

Skocpal, Theda. *States and Social Revolutions.* Cambridge: Cambridge University Press, 1979.

Smith, Catharine. "Egypt's Facebook Revolution: Wael Ghonim Thanks the Social Network." *Huffington Post*, February 11, 2011.

Smith, Stephanie J. *Gender and the Mexican Revolution: Yucatan Women and the Realities of Patriarchy.* Chapel Hill, NC: University of North Carolina Press, 2009.

Sonbol, Amira el-Azhary. *The New Mamlukes: Egyptian Society and Modern Feudalism.* New York, NY: Syracuse University Press, 2000.

Sorbera, Lucia. "Challenges of Thinking Feminism and Revolution in Egypt Between 2011 and 2014." *Postcolonial Studies* 17, no. 1 (June 2014): 63–75.

Soueif, Ahdaf. *Cairo: Memoir of a City Transformed.* New York, NY: Pantheon Books, 2012.

Sowers, Jeannie and Chris Toensing, eds. *The Journey to Tahrir: Revolution, Protest, and Social Change in Egypt.* London, UK: Verso, 2012.

Springborg, Robert. *Mubarak's Egypt: Fragmentation of the Political Order.* New York: Routledge, 2018.

Stensrud, Astrid B. "'You Cannot Contradict the Engineer': Disencounters of Modern Technology, Climate Change, and Power in the Peruvian Andes." *Critique of Anthropology* 39, no. 4 (2019): 420–38.

Swedenburg, Ted. "Imagined Youths." *Middle East Research and Information Project* 245 (Winter 2007).

Tadros, Samuel. "Egypt's Muslim Brotherhood after the Revolution." *The Hudson Institute*, October 18, 2011.

Taher, Nadia. "'We Are Not Women, We are Egyptians': Spaces of Protest and Representation." *Open Democracy*, April 6, 2012.

"Tahrir Square Under Attack: 32 Egyptians Killed, 1,750 Injured in Protests Against Military Rule." *Democracy Now*, November 21, 2011.

"Tamarod Petition Has over 22 Million Signatures." *Egypt Independent*, June 29, 2013.

Tarrow, Sydney G. *Power in Movement: Social Movements and Contentious Politics.* New York, NY: Cambridge University Press, 2011.

Tetréault, Mary Ann. "Women and Revolution in Vietnam." In *Women and Revolution in Africa, Asia, and the New World*, edited by Mary Ann Tetréault, 111–36. Columbia, SC: University of South Carolina Press, 1994.
"The Protest Squares of Cairo." *BBC*, August 15, 2013.
Tilly, Charles. *From Mobilization to Revolution*. Reading, MA: Addison-Wesley, 1978.
Tilly, Charles, and Sidney Tarrow. *Contentious Politics*. New York, NY: Oxford University Press, 2015.
Trew, Bel. "The Third Man: Egyptian Fears of the Foreign Plot." *Ahram Online*, February 24, 2012.
United Nations Development Programme (UNDP). *Human Development Report 2007/2008. Fighting Climate Change: Human Solidarity in a Divided World*. New York, NY: Palgrave Macmillan, 2007. http://hdr.undp.org/sites/default/files/reports/268/hdr_20072008_en_complete.pdf.
Vargas, Jose A. "Spring Awakening: How an Egyptian Revolution Began on Facebook." *The New York Times*, February 17, 2012.
"Al-Wafd Party." *Jadaliyya*, November 18, 2011.
Wallerstein, Immanuel. "New Revolts against the System." *New Left Review* 18, November-December, 2002.
Waterbury, John. *The Egypt of Nasser and Sadat: The Political Economy of Two Regimes*. Princeton, NJ: Princeton University Press, 1983.
Weber, Max. "The Types of Authority and Imperative Coordination." In *The Theory of Social and Economic Organization*, edited by T. Parsons, 324–423. New York, NY: Free Press, 1964.
Western, Simon. "Autonomist Leadership in Leaderless Movements: Anarchists Leading the Way." *Ephemera* 14, no. 4 (November 2014): 673–98.
White, Aaronette. "All the Men Are Fighting for Freedom, All the Women Are Mourning Their Men, but Some of Us Carried Guns: A Raced-Gendered Analysis of Fanon's Psychological Perspectives on War." *Signs* 32, no. 4 (Summer 2007): 857–84.
Winegar, Egypt. "Egypt: A Multi-Generational Revolt." *Jadaliyya*, February 21, 2011.
Wolff, Kurt H, ed. *From Karl Mannheim*. New Brunswick, NJ: Transaction Publishers, 1993.
Woltering, Robert. "Unusual Suspects: 'Ultras' as Political Actors in the Egyptian Revolution." *Arab Studies Quarterly* 35, no. 3 (2013): 290–304.
Wyn, Johanna, and Rob White. *Rethinking Youth*. London: Sage Publications, 1997.
"Young Egyptians Spread Their Message." *The New York Times*, February 8, 2011.
Yee, Vivian, and Nada Rashwan. "Egypt's Protests Came as a Total Shock. The Man Behind Them Is Just as Surprising." *The New York Times*, September 22, 2019.
Zahid, Mohammed. *The Muslim Brotherhood and Egypt's Succession Crisis: The Politics of Liberalization and Reform in the Middle East*. London: I.B.Tauris, 2010.
Zollner, Barbara. "Surviving Repression: How Egypt's Muslim Brotherhood Has Carried On." Carnegie Middle East Center, March 11, 2019. https://carnegie-mec.org/2019/03/11/surviving-repression-how-egypt-s-muslim-brotherhood-has-carried-on-pub-78552.

Index

Page numbers in *italics* refer to maps and figures.

Abaza, Mona 30
Abbas, Mohammed 71, 77, 78, *212*, 238, 249–50, 255–6; activism 94, 100, 103, 104, 112–13, 115, 124, 125, 128–9, 131; Egyptian Current Party 71, 171, 174–5, 179; exile 247–8; gender attitude, changes in 162, 163; Muslim Brotherhood 71, 171–2, 174–5, 192, 227; subjectivity 163, 171–2, 174–5, 179, 184, 198
Abdel-Hamid, Nasser *212*
Abdelrahman, Maha 252, 295n54
Abul-Futuh, Abd al-Munʿim 227, 291n17, 296n55
activists 4, 64–73, *211*, *212*; becoming revolutionaries 6–7, 63–4, 107–8, 128, 198–201; class background 72–3, 156, 167, 193–7; consciousness, formative experiences and 14, 15, 63–4, 107–108; consciousness, family and 50, 83–7; consciousness, neighborhoods/poverty and 73–9, 194–5; consciousness, police/state corruption and 79–82; consciousness, labor struggle 57–8, 99–101; and counterrevolution 203, 217–57; cross-ideological collaboration 52, 56, 61, 91, 95, 103; diversity of 5, 39, 72–3, 103, 107, 199–200, 206, 211–12; education and 72–3, 167, 196; eighteen-day uprising 109–10, 110–52 *passim*; exile 247–8, 255; Islam and 73, 169, 170–1, 197; and January 25 Revolution, memory and meaning 34, 35, 259; and July 3 coup d'état 218, 238, 239–41; and June 30 protests 234–9, 240; localism/myth of Western influence 63–4, 106–108; and Muslim Brotherhood, before revolution 69, 70, 71, 72, 84–6, 87–8, 155–6, 171–4, 198, 199; and Muslim Brotherhood in office 227–32; networked activism 15, 61, 95, 100, 103, 111–12, 113, 142, 188, 202, 297n70; online activism 105; and parliamentary elections (2011) 158–9, 177, 210, 211, 289n34; planning Police Day protests 61, 110–21; resistance movements before revolution 51, 56, 57, 58, 94–103, 110–11, 187, 199;

resistance in university 65, 88–94, 95, 198–9, 256; revolutionary hope, persistence of 248–50, 257, 259; revolutionary leadership and legacy 9, 187–9, 257–8; revolutionary organizing, future of 250–7, 296n63; splits between former RYC members 222, 240, 241–7, 295n54; subjectivities of revolutionaries 5, 14, 15–16, 153, 184–5, 200, 243; subjectivity, anti-imperialism 182–4, 185; subjectivity, class 26, 156, 168–9; subjectivity, gender 16, 156, 159–60, 161–7; subjectivity, sense of self 156–61; subjectivity, imagining democracy 176–9, 185; subjectivity, imagining Egypt's future 179–82, 185, 209; subjectivity, religion and politics 16, 169–76, 185, 197–8, 199–200; *see also* RYC; youth

al-Adli, Habib 113, 216

ahawi (open-air coffee shops) 28

Alexandria Church bombing 103, 111

Algerian War of Independence 162, 191

al-Ali, Nadje 200

anti-systemic movements 6, 202

April 6 Youth Movement 27, 38–9, 57, 58, 233; activism 57, 58, 65–6, 99, 100, 101, 102; and Otpor 106; Facebook 39, 104, 105; ideology and membership/structure 154, 202–203, 206, 212; internal split/April 6 Youth Democratic Front 65, 211, 275n4; planning Police Day protests 111, 116–17; RYC 38, 142; women in 154

Arab Nationalism 45, 84, 180, 181; pan-Arabism 185

army *see* the military; SCAF

ashwa'iyat see informal settlements

Al-Askar Kazeboon (The Army Generals are Liars) 253, 254

authoritarianism 7, 14, 43; Mubarak, Hosni 47–8, 49, 50, 52, 79, 167, 201, 202; Muslim Brotherhood 173, 228, 230; al-Sisi, Abdel Fattah 216, 248; survival of the authoritarian state 5–6, 7, 203, 216, 248

Awsim 66, 87, 115, 118, 139

baltaga (thuggery): *baltagiya* (thugs) 54, 140, 247; popular quarters 78, 79; sexual harassment and assault 54, 96

Bamyeh, Mohammed 128–9

al-Banna, Hassan 48, 174

Battle of the Camel 136–7, 139–40, 141, 144, 160

Battle of Qasr al-Nil Bridge 132, 160

Bayat, Asef 189, 194, 240, 251, 266n10, 288n32, 294n47

Ben Ali, Zine El Abidine 113–14

Birth Certificate of a New Egypt 215–16; *see also* RYC

Black Bloc (al-Kutla al-Sawda) 253

blogger's movement 59, 104

Bouazizi, Mohamed 113

Bread Riots (1977) 46, 86, 89

British Colonial Occupation 43, 97, 133

Bulaq al-Dakrur 118

Cabinet clashes 37, 38

Cairo: eighteen-day uprising 116–17, 127, 129, 133, 135; Greater Cairo *xviii*; housing policies 73–7, 274n11; inequality 47; research in revolutionary Cairo 20, 21–38

Cairo Anti-war Conference 52, 95

Cambanis, Thannassis 207–208
Camp David Accords 45, 89
Central Security Forces (CSF/*amn markazy*; riot police) 54–5, 57, 84, 94, 172–3; eighteen-day uprising 123–4, 126, 127, 131–2, 281n24, 281n26; Mubarak regime 50, 272n31; Muhammad Mahmud clashes 1–2, 210, 225; Port Said massacre 291n22; Rabaa massacre 218, 244, 245; *see also* police; State Security
chants: against the army, *felool*, and Brotherhood 239; against Field Marshal Tantawi 2; against Mubarak 91; against the system 125; asserting peacefulness 129; Egypt as mother 120, 280n12, 285n5; fraternizing the army 133; mobilizing bystanders 117, 121; police's June 30 protest chant 234–5; socioeconomic chants 117; Tunisian chant 125; unifying/nationalistic chants 22, 119–20, 121, 133, 280n12, 285n5
Civil Rights Movement (US) 191, 205, 286n7, 287n14
civil society 9, 36, 47, 58, 90–1, 201, 249; *see also* NGOs
class 26; *baladi* (of the country) 24; *bi'a* (ghetto) 24; class divide under Mubarak 47, 77, 82; education and 11, 27, 68, 82, 195–6; gender/class intersection 11, 196–7; hijab and 24–5, 26–7, 67; leadership and 5, 10–11, 16, 156, 167–8, 191, 193–7; RYC leaders, class positions and attitudes 26, 167–9, 193–7; *see also* middle class; popular quarters; upper class; workers

Clinton, Hillary 182–3
Color Revolutions (Eastern Europe) 106
communism 69, 86
consciousness 8, 110; collective consciousness 3, 64, 103, 107, 128–9; defined 279n1; fresh contact and youth political consciousness 13, 14, 63–4; revolutionary consciousness and leadership 3, 110, 128, 208, 251, 256, 279n4, 288n29; *see also* activists; spontaneity
constitution 224; constitution drafting under Morsi 229, 292nn23–4; Mubarak's constitutional amendments 48; SCAF/Brotherhood's constitutional amendments 224; al-Sisi's constitutional amendments 249
Copts/Christians 169, 175, 267n22, 280n23; Alexandria Church bombing 103, 111; Maspero massacre 34–5; as RYC leaders 40, 143, 162, 165–6, 170; sectarian violence against 61, 103, 111, 231, 233, 244, 295n53; in youth movements 154, 155; *see also* Tomah, Sally
corruption 3, 43, 78–81, 91, 92, 219, 220–1; justice system 81–2, 216; Mubarak, Gamal 53, 58; Mubarak, Hosni 47, 60; police 60, 79–80, 111; al-Sisi, Abdel Fattah 249; state 3, 43, 60, 79, 91, 92
Council of Wise Men 142
counterrevolution 6, 21, 35–6, 136, 203, 211, 225, 228, 234, 252, 254, 255; SCAF and 21, 151; sexual harassment and assault 35, 193, 230; *see also* activists

coup d'état: Morsi 6, 16, 218, 238, 239–41; Mubarak 150, 152, 201; revolutionary coercion 240, 294n47

Daniel, Mina 34
Dar al-Salam 66, *195*
democracy 3, 52, 55, 179, 232, 258; ballotocracy (*sanduqratiyya*) 177; Kefaya 52, 54; Mubarak's democratic reforms 47–8, 55, 60; youth activism/imagination and 56, 176–9, 181, 185, 209; *see also* participatory democracy
Democratic Front Party (Hizb al-Gabha al-Wataniya) 39, 142
Democratic Movement for National Freedom (HADITU/ al-Haraka al Dimuqratiya li Tahrrur al-Watan) 86
The Dignity Party (Hizb al-Karama) 39, 142

economy *see al-infitah*; neoliberalism/ neoliberal order; the military
education: class and 11, 27, 68, 82, 195–6; leadership and 11, 72–3, 167, 194, 195–6; Mubarak's regime 46–7, 82; Nasser's reforms 73, 82, 194, 199, 275n3; private education 82; protests for educational reform 256; Sadat's regime 82; tutoring 67, 276n5; underfunded and overcrowded schools 82; *see also* universities
Effat, Emad, Shaykh 37–8, *37*
Egypt: anti-imperial struggle and 182–4; democracy/democratic reforms 52, 55, 179; demographics 189; foreign policy 3, 44–5, 184, 271n10; inflation 46; liberal experiment 180–1; persistent crisis 249–50; reimagining modern Egypt 179–82, 185, 209; religion in 170, 197; as *Umm al-Dunya* (Mother of the World) 181
Egyptian Current Party (Hizb al-Tayyar al-Masri) 70, 71, 72, 171, 174–5, 179, 198, 247, 296n55
Egyptian Social Democratic Party (al-Hizb al-Masri al-Dimuqrati al-Igtima'i) 69, 225, 234
Eid, Ahmed *212*
The eighteen-day uprising (January 25–February 11) 3, 7, 15, 151–2, 252–3, 257; activists 109–10, 111–52 *passim*; actors 9, 151–2, 153; Battle of the Camel 136–7, 139–40, 141, 144, 160; Battle of Qasr al-Nil Bridge 132, 160; Cairo/national mobilization 116–17, 127; chants 119–20, 121, 124, 125, 129, 133, 280n12, 285n5; Central Security Forces 123–4, 126, 127, 131–2, 281n24, 281n26; communications blackout 129–30; Council of Wise Men 142; demands of protesters 113, 115–16, 133, 134, *134*, 136, 141, 145, *147*, 282n42; fraternizing strategy 133, 134, 281n26, 281n28; Nahya march 121–5, *122*; planning Police Day protests 110–21, *122*; January 28, Friday of Rage, 126, 129–33; leaderlessness in revolutionary process 4, 110, 130–1, 136, 141–2, 144, 149–51, 187–8, 202–203, 204,

207–208, 288n29; the military 54, 60, 132, 133, 134, 135, 137, 150–1, 152, 215, 222, 281n26, 281n28; Muslim Brotherhood 112–13, 116, 125, 130, 139, 143, 146, 152; popular committees (*ligan sha'biya*) 133, 288n32, 290n8; popular quarters, youth from 117, 139, 167–8; revolution's emergence 4, 6, 8, 9, 113–16, 123–4, 125–31, 151, 188, 266n10; RYC 4, 9, 15, 38, 142–50, *143*, 151–2, 204, 205, 207, 215, 282n39; secret strategizing 117–18, 19, 121, 129; sit-in 133–4, 136–7, 140, 144–5; social media, mobilizing on 116, 120, 129; Suez protests, turning point 127–9; Tahrir Square 4, 109, 119, 124–6, 129, 130–1, 132, 133–4, *134*, 135, 136–41, *143*, 144–5, *146*, *147*, 215; Ultras 116, 139, 279n10; violence and death 126–8, 129–30, 131–2, 136–7, 140; women 116, 120–1, 129, 132, 137–8, 145, 163; *see also* January 25 Revolution; Tahrir Square
ElBaradei, Mohamed 58, 101–102, 129, 155, 240; *see also* ElBaradei Campaign; NAC
ElBaradei Campaign (Popular Campaign Supporting ElBaradei/al-Hamla al-Sha'biya li Da'm al-Barad'i) 39, 58–9, 100, 211; ideology and membership/structure 155, 202–203, 206, 212; planning Police Day protests 111, 117; RYC 39, 142; seven demands for change 58, 102, 274n57
elections: *baltaga* (thuggery) 78, 79; election laws 48, 54, 224; low turnout 60; parliamentary elections (2005) 55, 86; parliamentary elections (2010) 60, 103, 111; parliamentary elections (2011) 69, 158–9, *158*, 177, 203, 209, 210, 225, 226, 289n34; parliamentary elections (2014) 246; presidential election (2005) 54–5, 99, 280n20; presidential election (2012) 203, 226–7, 250; presidential election (2014) 246, 250; rigged elections 55, 60, 103, 111, 280n20; voter intimidation 60, 78, 79, 140; *see also* referenda
Eleleimy, Zyad 69, 72–3, 86–7, 89, *212*; activism 94–5, 100, 101, 102, 103, 121, 124, 129, 141, 143, 149, 204; parliamentary elections (2011) 69, 210, 226; subjectivity 170, 176–7, 182
Elsayed, Khaled *212*
Emergency Law 48, 60, 113, 115, 224
ethnography *see Tahrir's Youth* (ethnographic study)
exile 247–8, 255
Ezz, Amr 64–5, 72, 77, 82–5, 91–2, *212*, 221, 275nn3–4; activism 94, 95–9, 104, 106, 118, 121, 124, 126, 127, 129, 131, 132, 136, 138, 172; al-Gama'a al-Islamiya 65, 83–4; Muslim Brotherhood 87–8, 171, 172; parliamentary elections (2011) 158–9, *158*, 210; subjectivity 156, 158–9, 167–8, 171, 172, 179–80

Facebook 57–8, 217–18, 242, 243, *253*, 263, 287n17; Facebook Revolution 63; January 25 Revolution 4, 15, 17, 104,

Index 321

106, 111; Mahalla strike 57; women and 196
Faris, Abdelrahman 71–2, 196, *212*, 259; activism 95, 96, 97, 98–9, 99–100, 104, 115–16, 123; Egyptian Current Party 72; exile 248; June 30 protests and aftermath 217, 218–20, 222, 231, 238, 240, 241–3, 247, 259; Muslim Brotherhood 72, 85–6, 95, 171, 196, 227, 231; Rabaa Square speech 241–2; Rabaa Square massacre 218–20, 247; subjectivity 171
fascism 242, 256, 295n50
Fayoum 71, 86, 95, 98, 100, 196, 220, 247
fear 215; *agendawi* (someone with an agenda) 36; broken fear barrier 3, 51, 114, 118, 125, 127, 130, 132, 258, 285n3; distrust of foreigners 35–6; of the state (*haybat al-dawla*) 51, 79, 80
felool 87, 234, 235, 238, 239, 243
feminism 162, 166–7, 206; Million Women March 166; state feminism 167; *see also* gender; women
Free Officers 86, 133
Freedom and Justice Party 174, 225, 236, 283n3; *see also* Muslim Brotherhood
Freeman, Joe 206, 288n30
fresh contact 13–14, 64

al-Gama'a al-Islamiya 48, 50, 65, 83–4; social welfare services 84; Temple of Hatshepsut attack (Luxor) 48–9, 232
gender 26; femininity/masculinity during the eighteen days 114, 120–1, 138–40; gender-based violence 35, 166, 230; gender/class intersection 191, 196–7; gendering effect of movements 12, 159–160; inter-gender activism 137–8; inter-gender social/conservative dynamics 25, 28, 162–3, 286n13; gendered leadership in movements 10, 129, 166, 190–1, 286n7; RYC leaders, gender positions and attitudes 16, 161–7; *welad sis* (sissies) 139; youth as gender-neutral category 191–2; *see also* men; patriarchy; women
Gerbaudo, Paolo 196, 253, 287n22
Ghad Party (Hizb al-Ghad/Tomorrow Party) 97–9, 112
Ghannam, Farha 140
Ghonim, Wael 104, 113, 194, 282n39, 287n17
Giza 64, 67, 119, 273n2
Global North/Global South 29, 269n9
Goldstone, Jack 8
Gramsci, Antonio 4, 67, 104, 204, 250–1, 278n32, 288n29, 296n63

habitus (youth habitus) 189; *see also* youth
El-Hamalawy, Hossam 50, *134*, *143*, *146*, *147*
Hamzawy, Amr 295n50
Harb, Shady ElGhazaly *212*
El Hawary, Yasser *212*
al-Hayyis Bakery 121
Hellyer, H.A. 239, 292n25
hijab (veil) 18, 20, 24–7, 65, 121, 145, 258; class and 24–5, 26–7, 67; Tahrir Square 24–6, 145, 258; *see also* gender; women
Honwana, Alcinda, 114
human rights 55, 56, 243, 245; human rights abuses 52, 59, 102, 244, 248, 256; human rights

organizations 216, 266n14
Human Rights Watch 218, 244

IAEA (International Atomic Energy Agency) 39
Ibrahim, Samira: "virginity tests" 230
Al-Ikhwan Kazeboon (The Brothers are Liars) 253, 254
Imbaba 64, 66, 71, 74, 77–8, 84, 103, 118, 126, 129, 131, 139, 158
IMF (International Monetary Fund) 46
imperialism 258; US 3, 45, 51, 95; youth and anti-imperial struggle 182–4, 185, 199, 285n25
imprisonment: activists, dissidents, protesters 50, 55, 86–7, 94–5, 157, 216, 296n55; Islamists 83, 84, 86, 95, 296n55; Morsi, Muhammad 216; Nour, Ayman 55, 98; under al-Sisi's regime 216; *see also* repression; torture
al-infitah (economic liberalization): housing policies and 77, 276n11; neoliberalism 194; poverty 46, 276n6; privatization 46; Sadat, Anwar 44, 46, 77, 194; social disparities 46
informal settlements (*ashwa'iyat*) 74–7, 79–80, 83–4, 276n11; activists from 74, 154, 195; *see also* popular quarters
intellectuals 279n4; organic intellectuals 104, 278n32, 296n63
Interior Ministry 132, 221, 228, 234, 245, 281n24, 295n51
International Monetary Fund *see* IMF
International Women's Day protest (March 8, 2011) 166
Internet 103–106; January 25 Revolution 4, 63, 105–106, 193, 194; Kefaya 56; *see also* Facebook, Twitter, social media
Iraq: US invasion of (2003) 51, 58, 94, 199; anti-war protests 51, 94, 95
Islam: activists and 73, 169, 170–1, 175, 197; Islamic law/sharia 163–4, 175, 185, 223, 292n23; *marga'iya islamiyya* 65, 170, 175
Islamism: Islamic state 84, 181, 291n18; Islamist revival 67; Islamist/secularist divide 11, 52, 103, 169, 175, 197–8, 231, 283n1; Mubarak's battle against Islamists 48–51, 84, 90, 174; sexual harassment and assault by Islamists 193, 229–31; women 162–3, 286n11; *see also* al-Gama'a al-Islamiya; Muslim Brotherhood; al-Nour Party; Salafism
Ismael, Salwa 79, 139
Israel 184; Egyptian natural gas and 99, 277n26; Mubarak, Hosni and 45, 51, 52–3, 271n10; October 6 War (1973) 44, 127, 180; Sadat, Anwar and 45, 46; Six Day War (1967 war) 44, 45, 88–9, 180, 199; Tripartite Aggression 127; US/Israel relations 45
Ittihadiyya Palace clashes 229–31

January 25 Revolution 3, 7; absent of radical, revolutionary undertakings 6–7; actors 9, 151–2, 153; as democratic revolutionary movement 176; Egyptian/popular ownership 63, 141, 144–5, 204; explanations for 3–4, 6, 8, 43–4, 73, 107–108; failure/defeat 7, 8, 34, 201, 207–210, 212–3, 216–17, 248; hope and optimism 3, 5–6, 248–50; importance and achievements

8, 257–9; international support 3, 109, 134–5; leadership vs. leaderlessness 3, 4-5, 150–1, 187, 204; the military and 7, 215, 222; Mubarak, Hosni 44, 45, 47, 48, 49, 60–1, 190; organizing 6–7, 205; poverty and 3, 19, 47, 112, 117; as revolutionary movement 7–8, 31–32, 109–10, 115, 125, 127–8, 131, 188; RYC, significance 9, 39; social media 4, 21, 63, 104, 187; spontaneity of 4–5, 15, 63, 107, 110, 125, 151, 153, 187–8, 204, 205; ten years in the making 3, 15, 43–61, 116, 187–8, 285n3; youth leadership 3, 4–5, 6, 14, 60, 61, 73, 109–10, 112, 116–27, 129, 130–1, 133–4, 141–4, 148–50, 151, 152, 187–90, 196, 204, 207–8, 253, 287n22; *see also* eighteen-day uprising; RYC

Al Jazeera 135, 247–8

Jika (Gaber Salah) 228, 245

judges' movement 54, 55, 96

June 30 protests 217, 221, 233–9, 240; chants 234–5, 239; the military 233, 234–5, 236, 238–9; police 234–5; al-Sisi, Abdel Fattah 16, 239–40; Tamarod 233–4

Kamel, Basem 40–1, 68–9, 85, 72, *212*; activism 101–102, 112, 114–15, 150, 208, 252–3; June 30 protests and aftermath 234, 236–7, 238, 240–1, 242, 243–6, 247, 294n48; on Muslim Brotherhood in parliament 225–6; subjectivity 165, 176, 284n1; parliamentary elections (2011) 69, 209, 210, 225;

Kamel, Nagy *212*

Kandil, Hazem 201, 203

Kefaya (Enough!) 52–3, 57, 95–6, 99, 101, 233; 2005 elections 54, 99, 280n20; cross-partisan cooperation 52, 56; democratic reforms 52, 54; Internet 56; protest tactics 56, 95–6; repressed by Mubarak 55–6, 99; shortcomings 56; structure 56, 202–203

Ketchley, Neil 133, 281n26

El-Khouly, Tarek 65, 72, 77–8, 221, *212*, 227; activism 87–8, 91, 92, 94, 95, 99, 112, 115, 116, 119, 124, 126–7, 127–8, 138, 145; corruption, experience of 79–82, 220–1; gender attitude, changes in 164, 168–9, 171; June 30 protests and aftermath 220–2, 236–8, 240–1, 242, 243, 245, 246; on Muslim Brotherhood in office 228–9, 231–2; parliamentary elections (2011) 158; parliamentary elections (2014) 246; subjectivity 156, 158, 159, 161, 164, 168–9, 171, 180–1, 183

labor *see* workers

leadership: anonymity 2–3, 204, 282n42; anti-leaders 287n22; bridge leaders 191, 286n7; charismatic leadership 4, 141, 202; choreography of assembly 196; class and 5, 10–11, 16, 156, 167–8, 191, 193–7; decentralized/diffuse/distributed leadership 6, 202; education and 11, 72–3, 167, 194, 195–6, 287n17; field leadership 144, 191; gender and 10, 16, 40, 129, 132, 142, 161–2, 164–5, 190–3, 196–7, 283n6, 286nn6–7, 286n11, 286n13, 287n14; great man leaders 202; leader, defined 10; leader, functions 10; leaderfulness 137, 145; leaderlessness in Egypt's revolutionary process 3, 4, 6, 32, 110, 130–1, 136, 141–2, 144, 149–51, 187–8, 202–203, 204, 207–208, 251, 255, 288n29; leadership team 144; of organic vs. traditional intellectuals, Marxist theory 104, 110, 202, 251, 278n32, 279n4, 288n29, 296n63; people-oriented and task-oriented leaders 10, 266n16; religion and 11, 16, 169–71, 185, 197–8, 199–200, 267n22; *al-sha'b* (the people) as leaders 130–1, 144, 151, 204, 238; in social movements 10–12; strategic leadership 191; visionary leadership 144, 161, 191, 238; youth as agents/leaders of revolution 12–14, 187–90; youth leadership, January 25 Revolution 3, 4–5, 6, 14, 60, 61, 73, 109–10, 112, 116–27, 129, 130–1, 133–4, 141–4, 148–50, 151, 152, 187–90, 196, 204, 207–8, 253, 287n22; *see also* organizing; revolution, RYC; vanguardism

leftists 67, 68, 69, 86–7, 99, 100, 101, 103, 150, 210, 238; attitude toward women's rights and participation 162; and fascism 295n50; religion and politics 170–1, 197; student movements 89, 91, 199; *see also* Revolutionary Socialists; Tadamun; Trotskyists; Twitterati; Youth for Freedom and Justice Movement

Lenin, Vladimir 4, 110, 188, 202, 204, 205, 250–1, 279n4, 296n63

liberals 65, 97, 178, 142, 154, 155, 200, 283n1, 294n42; attitude toward women's rights and participation 162, 171; Egypt's liberal experiment 180–1; and fascism 295n50; June 30 protests 221, 234, 235, 242, 295n50; NSF 254

ligan sha'biya see popular committees

Luxemburg, Rosa 110, 131, 251

Mahalla strikes 39, 56–7, 99, 274n48, 274n53; *see also* workers

El-Mahdi, Rabab 59

Mahfouz, Asmaa 120–1, 138, 196, 282n34

Mamdouh, Hamza 281n27

manatiq raqiya see upscale quarters

manatiq sha'biya see popular quarters

Mannheim, Karl 13–14, 64

Mansour, AbdelRahman 113, 287n17

Marxism 170–1, 210; Marxist theory of revolutionary leadership/vanguardism 4, 104, 110, 188, 202, 204, 205, 250–1, 278n32, 279n2, 279n4, 288n29, 296n63; *see also* leftists

massacres: Maspero 34–5; Port Said 292n22; Rabaa Square 218–20, 221, 243–4, 246, 247, 248, 295n51; Republican Guard Headquarters 241–2; Tiananmen Square 218

media 5, 21, 168, 246, 263; blackout of revolutionaries 247; Muslim Brotherhood and 237, 239, 242, 248, 291n19, 294n48; RYC and 144, 145, 146, 208,

255; state censorship 140; state media 6, 228, 242, 246, 249, 255, 291n19; Western media 5, 181, 193–4; *see also* social media

men: *gadʿana/gidʿan* (decency) 140; great man leaders 202; male leadership 10, 129, 142, 161, 286n13, 287n14; *raagil* (real man) 114, 120, 132, 139, 159; *rugula* (manhood) 120, 138, 140, 180; *welad sis* (sissies) 139; *see also* gender

middle class 10–11, 25, 101; Egypt's middle and lower-middle class 46–7, 77, 194–5; *hizb al-kanaba* (the sofa party) 234; middle-class poor 194; Said, Khaled and 59; vs. popular class, youth leaders 168, 191, 193–4, 196; *see also* class; popular quarters

Mikdashi, Maya 193

the military: changing attitudes and support for 221, 236–7, 240–1, 242, 243, 245–6, 248, 251, 294n48; counterrevolution 35; economic empire 53, 222–3, 273n39, 290n10; eighteen-day uprising 54, 60, 132, 133, 134, 135, 137, 150–1, 152, 215, 222, 281n26, 281n28; January 25 Revolution 7, 215, 222; June 30 protests 233, 234–5, 236, 238–9; July 3 coup d'état 6, 16, 218, 238, 239–41, 242, 253, 294n47; Mubarak, Gamal and 53–4, 152; Mubarak, Hosni and 53–4, 272n31; Nasser, Gamal Abdel and 43, 53, 273n39; political dominance 7, 15, 53–4, 60, 201, 223, 272n31, 292n23; US military alliance 45, 53–4;

violence by 1–2, 34, 241–2, 35; virginity tests 230; *see also* coup d'état; SCAF

military trials: civilians in 48, 90–1, 224, 226, 286n6; Emergency Law and 48; Muslim Brotherhood 90–1

milyuniya (march of millions) 135

Moanes, Hossam *212*

Mohandiseen 67, 118, 136, 243

Morsi, Muhammad 152, 169, 201; constitutional declaration 229, 292n24; coup d'état 239–40; imprisonment and death 216, 239; new constitution 229, 292n23; in office 227–33, 291n18, 291n21, 292nn22–4, 292n32; opposition to 217, 221–2, 228–9, 231–5, 236–8, 253, 254; presidential election (2012) 227; support for 217, 218, 241, 242; *see also* Nahda Square; Rabaa Square; Tamarod

Mubarak, Gamal: 47, 53, 54, 58, 60, 101, 152; the military and 53, 54

Mubarak, Hosni 15, 180; authoritarianism 47–8, 50, 52, 167, 201, 202; class divide under 47, 77, 82; corruption 47, 60; cultural decay 78, 92, 180; democratic reforms 47–8, 52, 54, 60; education under 46–7, 82; housing policies 77; Israel and 45, 51, 271n10; Islamists, battle against 48–51, 84, 90, 174; January 25 Revolution 44, 45, 47, 48, 49, 60–1, 190; *khitab atifee* (sentimental speech) 135–6, 140; the military and 53–4, 272n31; Muslim Brotherhood and 49–50, 55, 84, 89–90, 174;

neoliberalism 45–6, 47, 50, 61, 77, 194, 202; poverty under 46–7, 56, 61, 77; presidential election (2005) 54–5; prison release 216; regime's repression 3, 48, 49, 50, 55–6, 57, 79, 83–4, 86, 89–90, 94, 99, 111; resignation/military coup 1, 3, 7, 54, 109, 150–1, 152, 201, 212, 215, 240; strengthening the police state 48, 49, 50, 89, 272n31; structural adjustment reforms 46–7, 77; son's succession 53, 54; torture under 49, 50, 55, 59, 91, 135; trial of 212; US and 45, 46, 51, 52–3, 54, 55, 183, 281n29

Mubarak, Suzanne 167

Muhammad Mahmud Street clashes 1–2, 37, 225, 228

Muslim Brotherhood (al-Ikhwan al-Muslimin) 48, 58, 102, 274n5, 89–90; activists' family histories and 69, 71, 72, 84–6, 196, 199; authoritarianism of 173, 228, 294n48; eighteen-day uprising 112–3, 116, 125, 130, 137, 139, 143, 146, 152; Guidance Bureau 112, 125, 146, 173; ideology/Islamism 39, 49, 155, 198, 208, 223, 291n18; legitimacy 49, 50; media and 237, 242, 248; membership 155–6; military trials 90–1; Mubarak, Hosni and 49–50, 55, 84, 89–90, 174; Nasser, Gamal Abdel and 84, 85; in office 227–33, 253, 291n19, 291n21, 292nn22–5; as officially outlawed 49, 84, 155, 244; organizing 7, 39, 49–50, 213; parliamentary elections (2005) 55, 86; parliamentary elections (2010) 60; parliamentary elections (2011) 203, 210, 225; patriarchy 173, 192, 230, 286n13; political dominance 15, 49–50, 88, 155, 223, 225, 231–2; post-coup crackdown on 220, 239; presidential election (2012) 203, 226–7; Sadat, Anwar and 84, 85, 89; SCAF and 222, 223–6, 228, 229, 245; sectarianism 231, 232–3, 244, 295n53; social services network 49–50, 87, 155, 192; transitional period 155, 169, 208, 212, 213, 222, 223–6, 228, 245, 253, 290n13; US and 55; violence against 50, 218–20, 241–2, 247; violence by 229–31, 244, 295n53; women's participation/engagement in 155–6, 162, 192; *see also* Freedom and Justice Party; Morsi, Muhammad; Muslim Brotherhood youth; Muslim Sisters; Rabaa Square

Muslim Brotherhood youth 39, 70, 71: activism 39, 70, 71, 88, 89–91, 95, 96, 100, 103, 104, 199–200; differences with senior leaders 70, 71, 87, 104, 112–13, 198; Egyptian Current Party 70, 71, 171, 174–5, 179, 198, 247, 296n55; excommunication from Brotherhood 70, 71, 174, 211; gender dynamics among 162–3, 192–3, 287n14; and Police Day protests 112–13, 116, 125; revolutionary leadership initiative 198; RYC 39, 142–3, 146, 192, 198, 287n14

Muslim Sisters 116, 137, 155–6, 162–3; and leadership 155, 192–3, 283n3, 286n11, 286n13, 287n14
Mustafa Mahmud Square 118, 123–4

NAC (National Association for Change) 58, 282n42; *see also* ElBaradei, Mohamed
Nahda Square 217, 218, 240, 241; *see also* Muslim Brotherhood; Rabaa Square
Nahya Street 118, 121, 123, 125, 137
Nasser, Gamal Abdel 43, 48, 49, 73; Arab Nationalism 45, 84, 180; educational reform 73, 82, 194, 199, 275n3; industrialization program 77; the military and 53; Muslim Brotherhood and 49, 84, 85, 86; populist socioeconomic policies 44, 46, 194; state-guided development project 44, 273n39; university repression 88, 89
National Association for Change *see* NAC
National Democratic Party *see* NDP
nationalism 119–20, 218, 242; Arab Nationalism 45, 84, 180, 181; pan-Arabism 185
National Salvation Front *see* NSF
NDP (National Democratic Party) 55, 90, 92, 132, 234, 270n5; constitutional amendments in favor of 48, 54; parliamentary elections (2010) 60; youth faction 96, 97
Negm, Nawara 196, 287n21
neoliberalism/neoliberal order 7, 43, 50, 73, 99, 100, 185, 202; authoritarian repression and 50, 59, 79; de-radicalizing effect of 251; inequality and 47; *al-infitah* 194; Mubarak, Gamal 53; Mubarak, Hosni 45–7, 50, 56, 61, 77, 194, 202; power and 251–2; privatization 46, 47, 53; structural adjustment 46–7, 77
network: networked activism 15, 61, 95, 100, 103, 111–12, 113, 142, 188, 202, 297n70; power as network 239, 252
NGOs (non-governmental organizations) 47, 50, 216
Nour, Ayman 55, 97–8
al-Nour Party 233
NSF (National Salvation Front) 254
NSMs (New Social Movements) 6, 202, 250, 295n54

Occupy Movement 37, 257, 269n9
October 6 War (1973) 44, 127, 180
organic intellectuals *see* intellectuals
organizing: community organizing 133, 288n32; decentralized organizing 6, 57, 188, 202–203, 206, 208, 252; horizontal, informal organizing 6, 52, 57, 144, 145, 148, 149, 152, 202–203, 205, 206, 212, 250, 252, 287n22, 297n70; January 25 Revolution 6–7, 205; Muslim Brotherhood 7, 39, 49, 60, 213, 223; popular self-governance 144–5; popular self-organizing defense 133, 136–41; revolutionaries' disorganization 203, 236, 291n17; revolutionary organizing, challenges 6, 204–207, 251; revolutionary organizing, future of 250–7, 296n63; RYC 9, 143–4, 148, 149, 150, 206, 207–208, 212, 252, 255; 288n32 *see also* leadership; participatory democracy;

Ortner, Sherry 11–12
Otpor (Serbia) 106

Palestine: activists and 94, 95, 199; Camp David Peace Accords and 45, 89; Egyptian solidarity with 45, 51, 94, 95, 183–4, 199, 271n10; Second Intifada 51, 94, 183, 199; youth anti-imperialism 183–4, 185, 199, 285n25
Parallel Parliament initiative 103, 111–12, 150
participatory democracy 205–207, 250, 288n30; invisible relational structures 206, 288n30; in Republic of Tahrir 145; RYC 9, 144, 148, 149–50, 205–207
patriarchy 79, 121, 138, 161, 164; Muslim Brotherhood 173, 192, 230, 286n13; women's experience of 142, 160, 164, 166–7, 191, 192, 193; youth experience of 112, 142, 164, 189–90
police: corruption 60, 79–80, 111; fear of 79, 80, 118; lower/middle classes and 59; Morsi's regime and 228, 232, 291n21, 292n22; police brutality 3, 57, 59–60, 61, 64, 80, 96, 101 103, 105, 111, 127, 129, 131–2, 136–7, 218, 243, 244, 245, 249, 292n22; police state 43, 49, 50, 59, 79–80, 104, 111, 118, 124, 132, 139, 220, 246, 248–9, 272n31; popular quarters and 59, 79–80, 118, 139; power of 201, 272n31; surveillance by 50, 79, 92; Tamarod/June 30 protests 233, 234–5, 236; universities and 89, 90, 92–4; *see also* Central Security Forces; sexual harassment and assault; State Security
popular committees (*ligan sha'biya*)
Polletta, Francesca 205–207
Popular Campaign Supporting ElBaradei (al-Hamla al-Sha'biya li Da'm al-Barad'i) *see* ElBaradei Campaign
popular committees (*ligan sha'biya*) 133, 219, 288n32, 290n8
Popular Committees Supporting the Intifada 52; *see also* Palestine
popular quarters (*manatiq sha'biya*) 74–5, 77, 195; activists from 5, 72_4, 77–9, 117, 154, 155, 156, 168; *baltaga* (thuggery) 78, 79; cultural decay 78; Police Day protests/eighteen-day uprising 116, 117–19, 121–3, 139, 140; police state and 79–80, 83–4, 118, 139; popular class and hijab 24, 26–7; popular class and youth leaders 5, 26–7, 156, 164, 167–8, 191, 194–5, 195, 196; poverty 47, 77, 78, 79, 194–5; protests in 99–100, 103; *see also* informal settlements
poverty 79; *al-infitah* 46, 276n6; January 25 Revolution 3, 64, 112, 117; Mubarak's regime 46–7, 56, 61, 77; popular quarters 47, 77, 78, 79, 194–5
power 201, 255; capture of 6, 151, 202, 203, 213, 251–2; dual power 203; intergenerational power struggle 111, 149, 150, 204–205; neoliberalism and 251–2; as network 239, 252; people power 3, 5, 10, 13, 51, 61, 114, 130, 237, 257; police power 48, 80, 201, 237, 272n31; state power struc-

ture 6, 60, 178, 201, 213, 251–2; tripartite ruling power bloc 201
Presidential Palace *see* Ittihadiyya Palace clashes
privatization: *al-infitah* 46; Mubarak's regime 46, 47, 53
protest 51, 99–100; anti-war protests (US invasion of Iraq) 51, 94, 95; flash protests 96, 99, 117; issues and demands 99, 102, 113, *147*; Police Day protests 110–21; popular quarters 96, 99–100, 103, 117–8, 121; protest against police brutality 103; protests against SCAF 1, 21, 224–5, 253; women and 54–5, 120–1, 132, 258; *see also* eighteen day-uprising; June 30 protests; street politics; strikes
protest laws (2013) 216, 246

Al-Qassas, Mohammed 41, 70, 71, 72, 165, *212*; activism 89–91, 95, 96, 98, 100, 103, 104, 112–13, 115, 125, 149, 296n55; Egyptian Current Party 70, 171, 174–5, 296n55; on Internet activism 105–106; Muslim Brotherhood 70, 87–8, 89–90, 171–2, 174–5, 192; subjectivity 162–4, 165, 171–2, 174–5, 176, 183–4, 198
al-Qaeda: September 11 attacks (2001) 52, 295n53
quarters/districts *see* popular quarters; upscale quarters

Rabaa Square: massacre 218–20, 221, 243–4, 246, 247, 248; sit-in 217, 218, 240, 241–2, 243, 295n51; *see also* Muslim Brotherhood; Nahda Square
radicalism: in revolutions, twentieth-century 6, 251; de-radicalizing effect of neoliberalism 25
Ramses Square 218, 277n13
raqi see upscale quarters
Rassd News Network 113, 116
referenda 54, 224, 229, 249, 296n60
religion 20, 25, 26; interfaith community 17, 103, 258; religious tolerance 169; revolutionary leadership 11, 169–71, 197–8; RYC leaders 11, 16, 73, 143, 162, 165–6, 169–76, 185, 197–8, 199–200; *see also* Copts/Christians; al-Gama'a al-Islamiya; Islam; Islamism; Muslim Brotherhood; Salafism; Wahhabism
repression: Mubarak's regime 3, 48–9, 50, 55–6, 57, 79, 83–4, 86, 89–90, 94, 99, 111; neoliberalism and authoritarian repression 50, 202; political repression 3, 64, 79, 99, 195, 199, 201–202, 246, 247, 256; al-Sisi, Abdel Fattah 7, 216, 246, 247, 249, 256; state repression on university campuses 50, 88–94, 198–9, 256; SCAF 224; US complicity in 281n29; *see also* imprisonment; torture
Republic of Tahrir 144–5, *146*, 182
Republican Guard Headquarters 241–2
revolution, Egyptian (1952) 14, 43
revolution 3, 7; defined 7; dual power 203; from activists to revolutionaries 6–7, 63–4, 107–8, 128, 198–201; great revolutions 7, 265n9; as human creation 8; January 25 Revolution's emergence 4, 6, 8, 9, 113–16, 123–4, 125–31,

330   Index

151, 188, 266n10; January 25 Revolution as revolutionary movement 7–8, 31–32, 109–10, 115, 125, 127–8, 131, 176, 188; refolution 266n10; revolution as change 8; revolution as process 4, 8, 109–10, 256, 266n10; revolutionary coercion 240, 294n47; revolutionary consciousness 3, 110, 128, 195, 208, 251, 256, 279n4, 288n29; revolutionary situation/outcome 7–8, 265n9, 266n10; *shabab al-thawra* (revolutionary youth) 64, 157, 158, 190; social revolution 7; sustainable organizational structures 251, 288n30, 296n63; *thawrat giya'* (revolution of the hungry) 250; *al-thawra mustamirra* (the revolution continues) 260; *thawrat shabab/thawrat sha'b* (youth revolution/people's revolution) 149; *thuwwar* (revolutionaries) 128; as war 203; women in 161–2, 191, 283n6; youth as agents of 12–14, 188, 189; *see also* organizing, vanguardism

Revolutionary Salvation Front (Gabhat Inqadh al-Thawra) 149–50, 283n46

Revolutionary Socialists 40, 67, 99, 119, 144, 170, 174

Revolutionary Youth Coalition *see* RYC

Revolutionary Youth Union (Ittihad Shabab al-Thawra) 148

Robnett, Belinda 191, 286n7

Russia 44

RYC (Revolutionary Youth Coalition/ I'tilaf shabab al thawra): anonymity 141, 145, 204, 282n42; beginnings 15, 113, 142, *143*; Birth Certificate of a New Egypt 215–16; challenges faced by 204–208, 211; Christians/Copts as leaders in 40, 143, 162, 165–6, 170; closed-off membership 148–9, 206, 283n45; competing groups and 148–9, 211, 283n45; conventional politics, distaste for 210; criticisms and shortcomings 206–213, 252–3, 289n33; cross-ideological makeup 142–3, 145, 204, 206–207, 211–12; dissolution 152, *211*, 212, *212*, 228, 289n35; eighteen-day uprising 4, 9, 15, 38, 142–50, *143*, 151–2, 204, 205, 207, 215, 282n39; informal alliance consolidation 111–12, 113, 142; intergenerational power struggle 150, 204–205; internal splits 211–12, 227; January 25 Revolution, significance to 9, 39; as a vanguard 9, 100, 110, 148, 187–9, 252, 288n32; legitimacy 9, 145, 204, 206, 283n45; logo *158*; media and 144, 145, 146, 208; member organizations 38–9, 142–3, 165, 206, 282n39; and Muslim Brotherhood 142–3, 146, 174, 198, 208, 211, 222, 224–7; organizational model 9, 143–4, 148, 149, 150, 164, 204, 205–208, 212–13, 252, 255; participatory democracy 9, 144, 149–50, 205–207; SCAF and 208, 283n45; transitional period 148–9, 152, 161, 192, 208–212, 224–7, 288n32; women in 40,

143, 162, 164–6, 190–3, 287n14; *see also* activists; youth

Sabbahi, Hamdeen 227, 291n17
Sadat, Anwar 44, 47, 48, 73, 176, 180; assassination 44, 46; Camp David Accords 46, 89; democratic reforms 47–8, 270n5; education under 82; housing policies 77, 276n11; *al-infitah* 44, 46, 77, 194, 276n6; Israel and 44, 45, 46; Muslim Brotherhood and 84, 85; student movements/leftists 86, 89; US and 44–5
Said, Atef 282n42, 290n8
Said, Khaled 59–60, 102, 103, 111; middle class and 59; *see also* We Are All Khaled Said
Salafism 65, 139, 155, 175, 229, 234; al-Nour Party 233
Salah, Amr *212*
Samy, Mahmoud 66, 72; activism 87, 99, 100–101, 104, 105, 115, 117–19, 121; Internet and social media 104, 105; Muslim Brotherhood 87, 171, 172–4; subjectivity 171, 172–4; working-class struggle 100–101, 117–18
Sayyida Zaynab 66
SCAF (Security Council of Armed Forces): counterrevolution and 21, 34–5, 151, 222–7; Muslim Brotherhood and 222, 223–6, 228, 229, 232, 233, 245, 290n13, 292n23; protests/resistance against 1–2, 21, 117, 184, 224–5, 253, 254; revolutionaries and 34–5, 161, 184, 192, 208, 209, 210, 215, 224, 225, 288n32; RYC and 208, 210, 215, 224, 283n45; transitional period 192, 201, 208, 212, 223–4, 226, 240–1, 245, 290n13; *see also* the military
Seattle World Trade Organization protests 106
sectarianism: anti-Shia violence 233; Copts/Christians, sectarian violence against 61, 103, 111, 231, 233, 244, 295n53; Muslim Brotherhood 231–3, 244, 295n53; protests against 103
secularism 254, 292n23; Islamist/secularist divide 11, 52, 103, 169, 175, 197–8, 231, 283n1; leadership, religiosity, and secular ideology 169, 197–8; *see also* liberalism
Security Council of Armed Forces *see* SCAF
Selbin, Eric 8
September 11 attacks (2001) 18, 52
sexual harassment and assault 61; counterrevolution 35, 193; by Islamists, Ittihadiyya Palace clashes 193, 229–31; January 25 Revolution 54, 193; judges'/Kefaya demonstrations 54–5, 96; Million Women March 166; police/hired-thug assault against women during protests 35, 54–55, 96; state security 59; *see also* violence
al-sha'b (the people) 117, 142, 238, 266n10; as leaders 130–1, 144, 151, 204, 238
shabab al-thawra (revolutionary youth) 64, 157, 158, 190
sha'by see popular quarters
Shafik, Ahmed 227, 289n17
Shahba, Ola 26, 40, 67–8, 72–3, 105, 162, 227, 250, 256; activism 94, 95, 99, 100, 113, 115, 124, 125, 131, 132, 137–8, 164;

attacks on reputation 166, 193; Battle of the Camel 137–8, 160, 164; Battle of Qasr al-Nil Bridge 132, 160, 164; corruption, experience of 81–2; on feminism 166–7; June 30 protests and aftermath 238–9, 240, 241, 242–3; sexual assault, Ittihadiyya Palace clashes 193, 229–31; subjectivity 156, 159–60, 164, 165–7, 170, 177–9
Shalaby, Islam Lotfy 212
Sharabiya 65, 77, 78, 80, 112, 220
Sha'rawi, Huda 162
Sharp, Gene: *From Dictatorship to Democracy* 106–107
Shawky, Mostafa 66–7, 72, 106–10, 212; activism 91, 92–4, 95, 99, 100, 103, 115, 123, 128, 129, 131, 132, 139, 142, 144; subjectivity 156–8, 159, 165, 168, 170–1, 177, 178–9, 181–2, 184, 185
Shaykh Imam (Imam Muhammad Ahmad Eissa) 106, 278n33
Shehab, Mofeed 90
Shenker, Jack 121
Shubra 65, 75, 76, 99, 100, 119, 139
Sinai 44, 45, 89, 180
al-Sisi, Abdel Fattah: authoritarianism 7, 216, 248; July 3 coup d'état 16, 239–40; presidential election (2014) 246; mandate (*tafwid*) to fight "terrorism" 242, 247; public discontent 249–50; repression under 7, 216, 246, 249; youth apathy 250
Six Day War (1967) 44, 45, 88–9, 180, 199
Skocpal, Theda 7
slums *see* informal settlements
social contract 43, 52, 53, 61, 79, 179; eroded/broken 14–15, 46, 50, 51, 59, 79, 107; Mubarak, Hosni 15, 43, 45–6, 50, 53, 79
social justice 46, 61, 117, 145, 177, 178–9, 209, 226, 258
social media 103–106, 263; activists' dependence on/perishing effect 253–4; blogging 59, 104; eighteen-day uprising 116, 120, 129; January 25 Revolution 4, 21, 63, 104, 106, 187; youth movements 57–8; *see also* Internet; Facebook; Twitter
socialism 87, 167, 171, 174, 199–200, 279n4; *see also* leftists, Marxism; Revolutionary Socialists; Socialist Popular Alliance; Socialist Renewal Current
Socialist Popular Alliance (al-Tahaluf al-Sha'bi al-Ishtiraki) 67, 247
Socialist Renewal Current (Tayyar al-Tagdid al-Ishitraki) 67, 68, 100
Sphinx Square 243
spontaneity: defined 279n1; leadership and 4, 110, 204, 205, 287n22, 288n29; January 25 Revolution 4–5, 15, 33, 63, 107, 110, 125, 133, 151, 153, 187–8, 204, 205; NSM 202
state: capture of the state 6, 151, 202, 203, 213, 251, 251–2; civilian state (*madaniyya*) 154, 289n1; deep state 60, 233, 239, 292n25, 293n3; fear of the state (*haybat al-dawla*) 51, 79, 80, 118; Islamic state 84, 181, 291n18, 292n23; neglect by 3, 43, 49, 78, 79, 82, 83, 99, 194–5, 228; police state 43, 49, 50, 59, 79–80, 104, 111, 118, 124, 132, 139, 220, 246, 248–9, 272n31; state

Index   333

feminism 167; state media 6, 228, 242, 246, 249, 255, 291n19; state power structure 6, 60, 178, 201, 213, 251–2; welfare state 15, 43, 44, 46, 49–50, 79, 80, 107, 194; *see also* authoritarianism; corruption; neoliberalism/neoliberal order; violence

State Security (*amn al-dawla*): repression by 48, 50, 83, 86, 126, 157, 247; surveillance 50, 57, 92, 104, 203, 256; torture 49, 59; universities 92–4; *see also* Central Security Forces; Interior Ministry; police; sexual harassment and assault

The Street is Ours (al Shari' lina/Women for Democracy Movement) 55, 273n43

street politics 50, 51; flash protests 96, 99, 117; street activism 88, 95, 96, 99, 105, 117, 152, 190, 208, 253; street dissent 50, 51, 57; *see also* protests

strikes 57, 144; February 9, 2011, nationwide strike 152; Mahalla strikes 39, 56–7, 99, 274n48, 274n53; repression of 50, 57; skepticism of 100; women and 274n48; *see also* workers

student movements 52, 88–9

Students for Change 93, 94; *see also* Kefaya; Youth for change

subjectivity 11–12; defined 11; intimate selving 284n20; January 25 Revolution 153; *see also* activists; class; gender; religion

Suez: 127–9, 51, 44

Suleiman, Omar 109, 135, 142, 143

surveillance 50, 79, 92, 104, 256

syndicates 47, 49, 152

Syria 232

Tadamun (Solidarity) 57, 99, 100

Tagammu' Party *see* Unionist Party

Tahrir Square 20, 21–2, 119; anti-war protests (US invasion of Iraq) 94, 280n20; Battle of the Camel 136–41; eighteen-day uprising 4, 109, 119, 124–6, 129, 130–1, 132, 133–4, *134*, 135, 136–41, *143*, 144–5, *146*, *147*, 215; Republic of Tahrir 145, *146*, 182; Rules of the Square (banner) 2–3; July 2011 sit-in 21–3, 24; November 2011 sit-in 1–2; *see also* eighteen-day uprising

Tahrir's Youth (ethnographic study) 17, 258–9; activist representation 4, 5, 19–20, 21, 34, 38–41, 263, 267n22, 268n2, 270n11–12; focus, leadership in the Egyptian revolution 10–11; focus, revolutionary process 4, 8–9, 14; focus, youth leadership 4, 6, 9, 13, 14, 20; interviews 19–20, 28–9, 32–3, 34–5, 38, 41, 217, 263; language and culture, researcher's position 27–31, 36; methodology 5, 14, 19–20, 38, 263, 268n1; participant observation 33–4, 38; researcher's background 17–19, 22–3; researcher's Egyptianness 20, 25, 30–1, 36; researcher's positionality 20, 22–7, 29, 30, 36–8, 269n4; researcher's subjectivity 23, 37–8, 258–9; researching in revolutionary Cairo 21–3, 29, 31–38; RYC and 4, 5, 9, 38–40

Tallima, Khaled 139, *212*

Tamarod 233–4, 246, 254, 255

Tantawi, Mohamed Hussein (Field

Marshal) 2, 239
terrorism 232, 243; September 11 attacks (2001) 52; al-Sisi's mandate (*tafwid*) to fight "terrorism" 242, 247; war on terror 242, 245, 259
thuggery *see baltaga*
Tilly, Charles 7, 265n9
Tomah, Sally 34, 40, 143, 165, 166, *211, 212,* 270n11
torture 226; Mubarak's regime 49, 50, 55, 59, 91, 135; al-Sisi's regime 216; *see also* imprisonment; repression
trade union 50, 101, 189, 279n4; *see also* workers
transitional period 209, 217; democratic transition 210; identity politics 169, 197–8; Muslim Brotherhood 155, 169, 208, 212, 213, 222, 223–6, 228, 245, 253, 290n13; RYC 148–9, 152, 161, 192, 208–212, 224–7, 288n32; *sanduqratiyya* (ballotocracy) 177; *see also* SCAF
Tripartite Aggression 127
Trotskyists 67, 99, 170, 256
Tunisia 116, 125, 151, 257; 2011 Tunisian revolution 61, 113–14, 115
Twitter 57–8, 105, 217–18, 253, 263; January 25 Revolution 4, 15, 17, 21, 106, 111; women and 196; *see also* Facebook; Internet; social media
Twitterati 5, 24

Ultras: 9, 116, 139, 144, 168, 279n10;
unemployment 46–7; youth unemployment 61, 99, 189
Unionist Party (Hizb al-Tagammu') 39, 98, 130, 282n39
United States 18–19, 26, 29, 179, 272n29; invasion of Iraq 51, 58, 94, 199; eighteen-day uprising 135, 281n29; Egyptian foreign policy and 3, 44–5, 271n10; imperialism 3, 45, 51, 95; Israel/US relations 45, 271n10; Mubarak, Hosni and 45, 46, 51, 52–3, 54, 55, 183, 281n29; Muslim Brotherhood and 55; Sadat, Anwar and 44–5; *see also* Clinton, Hillary
universities: activism in 65, 88–94, 95, 198–9, 256; Ain Shams University 66, 68; Alexandria University 65; American University in Cairo 20, 30, 69, 194; al-Azhar University 70, 72, 155, 233; Cairo University 65, 69, 70, 71, 72, 89, 91, 95, 103; Helwan University 67, 92–3; Mubarak's regime 50, 89, 90–1; Muslim Brotherhood and 87–8; Nasser's university security reforms 88; state repression on campuses and 50, 88–94, 198–9, 256; Student Law (1979) 89
University of California, Davis (UC Davis) 17, 37, 269n9
upper class 10–11, 25, 26, 168, 195; *hizb al-kanaba* (the sofa party) 234; upscale class 195; youth leadership 5, 24, 156, 193–4, 196–7; *see also* class
upscale quarters (*manatiq raqiya*) 72, 75, 195, 276n11; gated communities 77, 155
USAID (US Agency for International Development) 45

V for Vendetta 106
vanguardism (revolutionary) 4, 6; constructing a vanguard organization 148–50,

201–208, 250–2, 283n46;
Marxist theory of 110, 202,
251, 278n32, 279n4, 296n63;
RYC as vanguard 9, 100, 110,
148, 187–9, 252, 288n32;
youth as agents/vanguard of
revolution 12–14, 188–90
violence: anti-Shia violence 233; Battle
of the Camel, 136–7; Battle
of Qasr al-Nil bridge 132;
Copts/Christians, sectarian
violence against 61, 103, 111,
233, 244, 295n53; gender-
based violence 35, 166, 230;
eighteen-day uprising 126,
127–30, 131–2, 136–7, 140,
281n24; from the military
1–2, 34–5; Muslim Brotherhood, state violence against
50, 218–20, 241–2, 247;
Muslim Brotherhood,
violence by 229–31, 244,
295n53; police brutality 3,
57, 59–60, 61, 64, 80, 96, 101
103, 105, 111, 127, 129,
131–2, 136–7, 218, 243, 244,
245, 249, 292n22; SCAF rule,
transitional period 1–2, 34–5,
225; al-Sisi's regime 216; *see
also* massacres; repression;
sexual harassment and assault
virginity tests 230; *see also* sexual
harassment and assault

Waali, Yusuf 86
Wafd Party 97–8, 162
Wahhabism 155
wasta (connections) 81; *see also*
corruption
Way of the Revolution Front 254–5,
297n70
We Are All Khaled Said (Facebook
page) 40, 60, 102, 104, 113,
116, 194, 253, 282n39,
287n17; *see also* Said, Khaled
the West 185, 258; January 25
Revolution and 29–30, 63;
myth of Western influence
63, 106–107; scholars and
journalists from 29–30;
Western media 181, 193–4
women: activists' reputation, attacks on
166, 193; as bridge leaders
10, 191, 286n7; Copts/
Christians in revolution 143,
165–6; Facebook and 196;
gad'ana/gid'an (decency) 140;
January 25/eighteen-day
uprising 40, 116, 120–1, 129,
132, 137–8, 145, 163; January
25 legacy 258; Islamist
women and activism/protests
116, 163, 137, 145, 258;
liberal/conservative women
24, 26; in Muslim Brotherhood, engagement 155–6,
162, 192; in revolutionary
movements, as leaders in
161–2, 191, 283n6; as RYC
leaders 40, 143, 162, 164–6,
190–3, 196, 286n6, 287n14;
upper vs. lower class, as
leaders 191, 196–7; worker's
strike, leadership in 274n48;
in youth movements 154–5,
191; *see also* feminism;
gender; hijab; Muslim
Sisters; sexual harassment
and assault
Women for Democracy Movement 55
workers: eighteen-day uprising 145,
152; movement before
January 25 Revolution 56–7,
274n48, 274n53, 285n3;
movement and youth 57–8,
66, 87, 99–100; working class,
youth leaders 11, 156, 167–8,
194–5; women 274n48;
working-class struggle 56–7,
100–101, 117, 195, 166,

279n4; *see also* class; popular quarters; strikes; trade union
World Bank 46

youth: as agents/vanguard of revolution 12–14, 187–90; apathy 19, 250, 258; defined 12, 41; demographics 189; as gender-neutral category 191–2; habitus 189; the January 25 Youth 190; January 25 legacy 256–7; January 25 Revolution, youth leadership 3, 4–5, 6, 14, 60, 61, 73, 109–10, 112, 116–27, 129, 130–1, 133–4, 141–4, 148–50, 151, 152, 187–90, 196, 204, 207–8, 253, 287n22; patriarchy and 189–90; as political generation 13, 64, 189–90; unemployment 61, 99, 189; *see also* activists; RYC
Youth for Change 56, 95, 202–203
Youth for Freedom and Justice Movement (Harakat Shabab min agl al-Adala wa-l-Hurriya) 27, 39, 57, 67, 100, 103, 202–203; ideology and membership/structure 154, 202–203, 206, 212; planning Police Day protests 111; RYC 39, 142
youth movements 39, 57–8; Copts/Christians 154, 155, 267n22; ideology and membership/structure 154–6, 202–203; organizational model 57, 202–203, 206, 212; and labor/socioeconomic struggle (2006–2009) 57–8, 99–101; and social revolution (2010–2011) 101–103; women in 154–5 191

Zaghloul, Saad 97
Zeinhom morgue 219

www.ingramcontent.com/pod-product-compliance
Lightning Source LLC
LaVergne TN
LVHW021017250326
834688LV00021B/186/J